Greg Growden is a well-known Australian sportswriter and author. Apart from writing on rugby union for *The Sydney Morning Herald*, he has written six books including *A Wayward Genius: The Fleetwood-Smith Story*, *With the Wallabies*, *Gold Mud 'n Guts: The Incredible Tom Richards – Footballer, War Hero, Olympian* and *Rugby Union for Dummies*. He lives in Sydney.

The
Snowy Baker
Story

GREG GROWDEN

RANDOM HOUSE AUSTRALIA

Random House Australia Pty Ltd
20 Alfred Street, Milsons Point, NSW 2061
http://www.randomhouse.com.au

Sydney   New York   Toronto
London   Auckland   Johannesburg

First published by Random House Australia 2003

National Library of Australia
Cataloguing-in-Publication Entry

Growden, Greg
The Snowy Baker story.

ISBN 1 74051 236 7.

1. Baker, Snowy, (Reginald Leslie), 1884–1953.
2. Athletes – Australia – Biography. I. Title.

796.092

Cover and internal design by Darian Causby/Highway 51
Typeset by the Typéfi Publishing System
Printed and bound by Griffin Press, Netley, South Australia

10 9 8 7 6 5 4 3 2

Extracts from Norman Lindsay's *My Mask* © H.A. & C. Glad.

Every effort has been made to identify copyright holders of extracts in this
book. The publishers would be pleased to hear from any copyright holders
who have not been acknowledged.

*To Elizabeth,
Anna and Angus*

Contents

Acknowledgements

Many thanks to Simon Drake at Screensound for helping to unearth rare Snowy Baker material, as did Andy Carr and Warwick Hirst at the State Library of New South Wales. Other great allies to the cause were Alexandra Long, Mark Moylan, Peter Fenton, Bob Marchmant, the Nolan family in Holbrook, Peter Crittle, Graham Shirley, Ray Swanwick, Tom Symonds and Joe Seddon. Thanks also to the staff at the Petherick Room at the National Library of Australia, who know how to make a frazzled researcher feel at home. Most importantly, this book would not have come to fruition without the support and high level of professionalism shown by Meredith Curnow and Lydia Papandrea at Random House.

Introduction

SNOWY BAKER LIVES ON. DECADES AFTER HIS DEATH, HIS FEATS STILL inspire. Clubs are being named after him, even if the links are tenuous.

When a dozen Sydney University sporting scholarship holders first met in 2001 to discuss forming a sporting alumni group that would provide vocational guidance and 'invaluable networking opportunities', Snowy Baker's name was quickly brought up. His feats, impact, extraordinary versatility and stature as the most remarkable of Australian sporting pioneers exemplified everything that is right with the pursuit of an academic and sporting life. They couldn't go past the man often claimed to be Australia's greatest sportsman. A revered figure, Snowy was the ideal icon to act as a figurehead for a club that aims to cater to and care for University sporting scholars. Thus the Snowy Baker Club was formed.

According to the much-told tale, Snowy Baker did everything – most while a humble student wandering the corridors of the University. Numerous sources claimed he had attended Sydney University. It was a line Snowy never stood in the way of during his eventful life. He never sought a retraction. He let the lie live.

The founding members of the Snowy Baker Club were drawn to these popular sources and went with them, explaining in their first newsletter that by representing Australia in the 1908 London Olympic Games he became 'one of Sydney University's first two Olympians . . . At Sydney University, where he studied engineering, he was awarded Blues for Athletics, Boat, Cricket and Football.'

The founding members overlooked some other sources, including W.F. Mandle's entry on Snowy in the *Australian Dictionary of Biography*, and Harry Gordon in his comprehensive book *Australia and the Olympic Games*. Both stated the Sydney University link was wrong. Mandle wrote that Snowy 'did not, as was later claimed, study engineering at the University of Sydney or win several "blues"'. Gordon said in his study of Snowy's Olympic career that the legend 'has been embroidered over the years; he did not, for instance, win four Blues at Sydney University, as has often been claimed, or even attend that institution'.

The presage about Snowy's life came in the final paragraph of the club newsletter: 'Inevitably the legend of Snowy Baker has been embellished over the years. However, he is widely recognised as the greatest all-round athlete that Australia (let alone Sydney University!) has ever produced.'

They went with their instincts, believing the doubts surrounding Snowy Baker's background even enhanced the value of the club, giving it intrigue. Or in the words of one club member – 'mystique'.

Mystique. No better word can describe Snowy.

Yes, Snowy Baker was an Olympian. He did compete in three different sports at the 1908 Olympics in London, and won the silver medal in boxing, losing to the future English cricket captain, Johnny 'Won't Hit Today' Douglas.

But despite the endless claims that he attended Sydney University, no official University records have yet been found to back it up. Several telephone calls and a day searching through the relevant University enrolment records of the time found nothing. No R.L. Baker was discovered among the University's documents. Nor did the researchers in the Sydney University Archives department find any actual proof that Snowy was ever sighted walking through their gates.

Then again, everything involving Reginald 'Snowy' Baker has its unexpected twists and turns, with the occasional touch of blarney. He was one enormous contradiction.

He has been rightfully described as Australia's finest all-round sportsman, excelling in 26 different sports. He represented Australia at international level in boxing, swimming, diving, rugby union, fencing, water polo and polo. He was also a crack horseman.

He tops a list of versatile Australian athletes which includes Dick Thornett, Victor Richardson, Dr Reg Bettington, Herb Narvo and Frank Hagney, who were all outstanding at representative level at a number of sports. But none could boast 26.

And there was the tall, angular, imposing R.J.A. Massie, who apart from playing Sheffield Shield cricket and interstate football for New South Wales, could actually boast four Sydney University Blues. The Sydney University Sports Union records confirm that in 1912–1913

Massie won Blues in cricket, athletics, Boat and football. The Sports
Union has no record of anyone called R.L. Baker winning any such
Blues.

For Baker you could virtually read Massie, especially as Massie was
also a NSW amateur boxing champion before being badly wounded at
Gallipoli in 1915. That's where the confusion probably started. Someone
somewhere has mixed up Baker with Massie, misread something and
the error has snowballed over the decades. It probably all comes down
to one article in the long-defunct *Sporting Life* magazine. The article,
written in 1947, mentions both Baker and Massie as among Australia's
most versatile sportsmen, in particular describing Massie's University
record. Later, some scribe could have mixed it all up – read about Massie
and thought it was referring to Baker and then added it into a later
Snowy story. Everyone else followed.

Nonetheless Snowy was on another level. Whenever this country's
sporting ideals and achievements need to be explained, Snowy Baker's
name is there somewhere with his impressive, short but stocky, physique
and endless feats so perfectly enhancing the image of the successful
self-made sun-bronzed Australian. He tried everything, and invariably
succeeded at everything, proving the virtues of a busy lifestyle.

In 1946, the Australian magazine *Sports Novels* asked its readers to
rate the top 10 Australian sportsmen and sportswomen of all time.
Snowy finished third behind Les Darcy and Don Bradman, and ahead
of Walter Lindrum, Victor Trumper, Hubert Opperman, Jack Crawford,
Vic Patrick, 'Young' Griffo and Bobby Pearce.

Eleven years later, the same magazine conducted its second poll to
find Australia's greatest sportsmen and sportswomen. Snowy polled well
again, finishing fourth – Don Bradman had taken over at number one
ahead of Darcy and John Landy.

But Snowy was also despised. Revered and admired for his exceptional
athleticism, he was to the same degree lampooned for being a spiv. He
was a flash Harry, both on the various playing fields and in his later life as
a street-wise, sometimes sneaky boxing promoter and businessman. He
would drive around Sydney in a flashy bright yellow automobile, which
had a brass snake coiling along each mudguard. When boxer Jack Carroll
saw the near canary coloured car outside titlefighter Dave Smith's house
in Mosman, he uttered: 'You never saw anything so lairy.'

Snowy was a master showman, a clever manipulator of the Sydney press, a man so full of himself that he endeavoured to know everyone, and also knew how to look after himself. He hung around, and ingratiated himself, with the high-life, while also keeping in touch with the low-life and the many grubs who wriggled in between. He knew how to get money out of all of them.

He also knew who in power to keep on side to ensure that the publicity machine was always working on his side. He was known around Sydney as 'The Great I Am'. It was not a term of endearment.

The Sydney University blarney was rewritten with zeal, but never checked by numerous fawning scribes, and so was repeated, even enhanced over the years, until it was treated as plain fact.

Nonetheless Baker, still alive at the time, never stopped this fabrication realising that the aura of a University degree and an array of sporting Blues would perfectly round off the image of the polished worldly man.

Baker's blatant self-promotion really came to the fore when his active sporting life began to peter out. He became Australia's prime boxing promoter, running the Sydney Stadium, which he unashamedly renamed the Baker Stadium.

During his reign as the chief puppeteer in Sydney's premier 'House of Stoush', Australia became the world's boxing mecca, offering the best prize money, and luring the key names from overseas, who because of the power of the local currency were prepared to spend weeks travelling by ship to Sydney only to get beaten at Baker's den in Rushcutters Bay. Boxing is now frowned upon, but then was the lust of a nation, a lifesaver for many, a life blow to others. It attracted and tantalised the hordes.

Baker became renowned as a world boxing figure and a ruthless operator, especially during the period where he was intimately involved in the development and eventual demise of the most tragic of Australian sporting figures, Les Darcy. In the rise and fall of Australia's most romanticised sporting figure, Baker is among the main actors.

Darcy was Baker's most important meal ticket, through endless sell-out Stadium dates, that made the promoter, and his allies Hugh D. McIntosh and John Wren, filthy rich.

Baker was propped up by powerful men, and when favours had to be repaid, the consequences were dire. Darcy, wanting several more fights to set up his family before enlisting for World War I service, fled to the United States, and Baker, who fervently supported the Australian war effort, was forever blamed for being the unforgiving man who forced him out. The anti-Baker emotions among the huge contingent of Darcy followers became so intense that when he ventured to the boxer's funeral in Maitland, he was told to immediately get back on the Sydney train because of the serious threat that he would be lynched.

This hatred has continued for decades, especially among those many members of the Darcy revivalist movement, who still regard Snowy as public enemy number one. Even now, Snowy is widely considered the man who dudded Darcy.

Not even an inquiry in Darcy's home town of Maitland, where Snowy explained his side of the story, successfully bobbing and weaving his way around the many loaded questions, could sway the Darcy clan that Baker was anything but a dubious character.

Baker was brash. He kept bouncing back. Boxing turned sour near the end of the war, crowd figures at the Stadium plummeted and Baker looked elsewhere for money-making ventures.

The most obvious alternative for someone who loved seeing his name in headlines, adorned above boxing rings, in the social pages, and whose favourite assets were a hand mirror and comb was somehow getting himself onto the big screen.

The moving picture industry was starting to gain legs in Australia, and Baker saw that with precise business acumen he could reap the financial benefits of a new phenomenon that was tantalising the public.

Although neglected behind the more popular figures of Raymond Longford, Charles Chauvel and Ken Hall, Baker was one of the true pioneers of the Australian film industry, being its first real matinee idol – a local version of the swashbuckling Tom Mix, performing the most extraordinary stunts before rescuing the damsel in distress.

Even now, more than 80 years later, his movies hold up well. His acting was wooden, story lines fragmented and one dimensional, but the series of movies he was involved in are still innocently endearing.

His best known movie *The Man from Kangaroo* is on the same level as several far more famous Australian pioneer movies, including Longford's acclaimed *The Sentimental Bloke*.

The cinematography in Snowy's movies, plus clever use of the Australian landscape was exceptional. They hold a certain charm.

Surprisingly, he downplayed this part of his career, but unlike other contentious parts of his life, his movie making was something he should have been proud of. He was a legitimate and important trailblazer of the Australian film industry, and deserves greater credit.

He had the courage to be the first to lure top-quality film talent from the United States to Australia to improve the standard and marketability of the local product. He had the original vision to turn the Australian movie industry into an international product. Hundreds . . . thousands have followed his path.

Being involved in all processes of the local industry, it wasn't surprising that he was eventually lured to movie mecca, California, in the hope that he could make it big on the world screen. There he made an impact with his ever-trusty horse 'Boomerang', becoming one of the first Australians to appear in United States movies. He was soon part of the Hollywood hierarchy. It was on the fringes that he most made his mark and became close to the likes of Charlie Chaplin, Harold Lloyd, Spencer Tracy, Douglas Fairbanks, Elizabeth Taylor, Pauline Frederick, Will Rogers, Walt Disney, Olivia de Havilland, Greta Garbo, Gary Cooper, Rudolph Valentino, Shirley Temple, and anyone else of note in tinsel town.

He made a small pocket of Southern California richly Australian, right down to the carefully planted gum trees around his home, with the oh-so-cooeeish name of 'Gunyah'.

As director of the exclusive Riviera Country Club in Santa Monica – a playground for the rich and famous, wayward and wicked, but all soaked in money – he was the friend, ally, teacher, double, ingratiator of the stars, becoming the Australian everyone of note had to know in the Hollywood backblocks. He taught Valentino how to kiss, Taylor how to ride for *National Velvet*, Fairbanks how to properly use a sword, even affecting the production of *Casablanca* when involved in a polo accident with its director Michael Curtiz. He doubled as a stuntman for many of the Hollywood bywords.

He was among Australia's first considerable human exports. A fair effort for someone with so many ifs and buts about his life – especially his early background – Sydney University Blue or no Sydney University Blue.

Chapter 1

Head First

HE HATED THE FACT THAT THEY KEPT CALLING HIM 'SNOWY'. IT RILED him. But he had no say in the matter. When you're in the back streets of Darlinghurst and Surry Hills, running around with a rough mob, you had to cop the good with the bad.

Most of the time it was bad. And considering that all these street urchins were far bigger, far tougher than him, he had to put up with everything that he was called, or suffer a smack to the back of the head or a kick to the guts when he was down.

Really, they had no alternative but to call him 'Snowy'.

His blond, almost snowy locks, stood out. Right from when he could walk, Reginald Leslie Baker was a short, stout figure, with a healthy, almost unkempt crop of light locks that rose up, parted in the middle. and cascaded down either side. He was Snowy from day one. And from day one, it was obvious that he was something different.

There were no airs or graces about his arrival. He was born at home on February 8, 1884, in a small dwelling on the busy thoroughfare of Bourke Street in the rough and tough inner Sydney suburb of Surry Hills. The old stone cottage stood in what was known as 'the Cow Paddock'. He was the third son to George Baker and Elizabeth Jane Robertson – the product of an Irish/Scottish mix who like so many thousands of others had travelled to Australia as part of the gold rush get-rich scheme.

There is some confusion over where the Bakers actually came from, one part of the family arguing that there were Dutch–Germanic links and that the paternal side hailed from the Palatinate region – two small and constantly changing territorial clusters, which included land on both sides of the Rhine River. These were originally the lands of a Count

Palatine – a title held by a leading secular prince of the Holy Roman Empire – which from the 12th century became a great territorial power. However by the late 17th and early 18th centuries it was an area suffering great hardship. First the French monarch Louis XIV ravaged the Rhenish Palatinate causing countless Germans to emigrate. Then the heavily taxed Palatines, who relied on the vines of the Rhineland for their survival, suffered several excruciating winters, which killed most of the crop. At the same time, the Palatines, most of whom were Lutheran or Reformed, suffered religious persecution, forcing a mass emigration as a basic act of survival.

En masse, Palatines, including the Baker descendants, then believed to be named Becker or Backer, boarded small boats and headed down the Rhine. By October 1709, more than 10,000 Palatinians had completed the Rhine journey, the first leg of a courageous trek that would take them to either the United States, England or Ireland.

Queen Anne assigned the Duke of Marlborough to transport the immigrants to England, believing that this Protestant band would help fuel the already strong anti-Roman feelings in her country. From there more than 3,000 Palatines were sent to Ireland with the similar wish to reinforce the Protestant faith. In that group were the Becker, Backer or Bakers, who settled near Limerick, where they gradually changed to the Methodist faith.

A younger brother of Snowy's, Frank Baker, claimed that the family background may have been even more devilish, citing that a key family descendent was a Dutch shipmaster, merchant and eventual pirate, Jan Van Baher. Known as 'Black Baher' because of his dark complexion, long black hair and heavy dark beard, this swarthy sea-going 'hippie' fought against the Spaniards in retaliation to their military governor seizing his estate. He declared a private war on the Spanish forces, attacking supply vessels off the Dutch coast. The Spanish immediately slapped a price on Baher's head, declaring him an outlaw and a pirate.

In 1588, Baher volunteered his services to the England force to ward off the Spanish Armada, and during one battle, under the command of Lord Howard, was severely wounded. On the defeat of the Armada, 'Black Baher' was awarded British citizenship. He died three weeks later. His son, Gart, entered the British service, and within a year was sent to Ireland to act as Constable of a Royal estate in Limerick. Frank Baker argued that Baher became Baker on account of a naval clerk, listing the

British ships, captains and their home ports, evidently mistaking the 'Jan' for the English abbreviation of Jonathan and the Dutch 'H' in Baher for a 'K'. Thus Jan Baher turned into Jonathan Baker.

In Ireland, the Bakers managed to gain control of a considerable amount of Royal lands they administered, which over the decades gradually diminished. Frank Baker claimed that in later years a number of Palatine Huguenots settled on land adjoining the Baker territory of Ballingrane and Curraheen. There they were placed under the patronage of a grandson of Gart, Adam Baker, who had become governor and chief magistrate of the surrounding districts.

Most were relaxed with their lot in the new land, but centuries on, George Baker, a tall, angular child, wanted more. The chance came when according to family lore, George, at the age of six in 1850, was allowed to travel with a tutor on a trip around the world.

It may sound far-fetched, but the Baker family repeatedly stated that George arrived at Sydney Cove as a child and just three days after the news had been broadcast of the first serious discovery of gold in Australia.

As Frank Baker wrote: 'The sturdy East-Indiaman on which my father was a passenger had no sooner tied up than her crew began to desert the ship; and following the example of the majority of Sydney Town's citizens, headed for the new-found diggings beyond the rampart of the Blue Mountains.

'Next went the officers of the salt-rimmed square rigger, followed shortly by the Captain, miscellaneous passengers, and my father's scholarly tutor. But I'm willing to wager that the van of those seagoing gold seekers had not reached Bridge Street before the youthful George Baker was hard on their heels.

'I may add that my paternal parent failed to resume the return voyage to his green native land of Erin.'

George spent some time on the goldfields, but was eventually lured back to Sydney. His family chronicled little about his early years, or who exactly looked after him during these formative years. It remains a mystery. But what was discovered was that athletic pursuits played an enormous role in his life.

George Baker was always an avid horseman, riding horses in Ireland almost as soon as he could walk. Now a teenager in Sydney, he realised the area to settle was near the vast open fields around Darlinghurst and

Paddington. For several years, desperate to find a spot where he could have stables, Baker flitted between addresses in the Bourke Street–Forbes Street area in Surry Hills and Darlinghurst, before settling near Kings Cross in Womerah Avenue.

His dream of owning stables was achieved by holding down a position as a Sydney Municipal Council clerk, rising up the ranks from 'nuisance inspector' to become a local health inspector. With the elevation came the added status symbol of having the finance to boast his own stables, which apart from several saddle hacks and jumpers soon became a haven for every stray animal in the area.

By the time Snowy arrived, the Baker stables were also home to chickens, ducks, 10 to 12 dogs, two monkeys and a koala. Where the monkeys came from was anyone's guess – most probably a bribe from someone who had been intimidated by the sight of a nosy health inspector at their door.

George Baker was obsessed with the importance of keeping oneself fit. Each day before heading into the city to work, he would ride his horses towards where Randwick racecourse and Centennial Park now stand and still have time for a five mile walk before breakfast. Dawn always found him plunging a horse down some sandhill near the sea, or galloping him across the plain fields back towards the outskirts of the slowly spreading city. And after work, he would keep the body in tune with a spar in the boxing ring, often with the legendary Larry Foley – the larrikin who was renowned for being the 'Father of Australian Boxing'.

Foley, a feisty member of an Irish Catholic family from near Bathurst, was feared in Sydney for being a punchy, unpredictable thug, and a notorious leader of a group of hooligans who terrorised sailors in the Rocks area.

Foley was the leader of a Push gang, whom to overcome boredom and to satisfy their high testosterone levels sought out sailors and drunks along Sydney's waterfront and Protestant gangs for an old fashioned 'boots and all punch up'. Their motto was 'darncin', drinkin' and kickin' the tripe out of a mug'.

These were nasty times, with victims sometimes being kicked beyond submission and the occasional death occurring during the gang warfare. And all for honour and side bets of several pence. There were always plenty in the area wanting to fight, fuelled by the low-grade grog on offer at the hotels through the Rocks area, and wanting to get rid of the frustrations associated with lack of money and low living. Sydney wasn't exactly a haven for saints; with the latest boatload from the Old Country often bringing in the dregs. They were naturally lured to those areas closest to where they first sighted their new home – around the Quay.

Baker got to know Foley through his travels around the inner suburbs of Sydney as the ever diligent health inspector. Baker soon realised he had to get onside with this wild character, because he commanded so much power in the seedier areas that Baker had to patrol. It was a basic matter of survival.

Baker needed Foley as an ally to ensure that he could be safe in the dangerous back alleys around the city, especially as he needed access to those out-of-the-way parts of the city few people would have the courage to venture into. He had to front rough and tumble terraces, sleazy inns, out of the way food dens, attempting to demand some sort of standard amidst the squalor. The secret password had to be learnt. They were soon on nodding terms as Foley was impressed with Baker's presence – being 6 foot 1 inch tall, and built like an Irish heavyweight, a Gentleman Jim Corbett in another guise, helped.

Boasting about 20 avid hangers-on, Foley would travel far and wide in search of a fight in his bid for the Foley Mob to take control of inner Sydney ahead of the Rocks Push, under the command of the quarrelsome Sandy Ross, the Gibbs Street Mob and the Glebe Island Boys. The Foley Mob even ventured as far as Paddington, soon becoming overlords of that suburb's streets after belting the hide out of the Rennie Street Mob.

Foley's gangsters then wanted to take on the best – the Rocks Push. However Foley asked for restraint. Realising that his gang would probably suffer mass annihilation in fighting Ross's men on their home turf, with the inevitable problem of locals being able to immediately call in reinforcements, Foley instead decided to take on Ross in a one-on-one bare knuckle battle in the prize ring.

Foley and Ross eventually agreed to fight on a Saturday afternoon in March 1871 near the George's River. Within minutes of the fight being declared, every dodgy character in Sydney was aware of it, prompting thousands to trek to the outer reaches to watch the brutal spectacle. They were 'The Fancy', a group of desperate characters, ranging from the clergy, to the aristocracy and the lowly spiv, who all had one thing in common – an obsession with the prize ring. George Baker knew about the fight, and was keen to cheer on his ally, but decided to stay away knowing it may not be right for a council inspector to be sighted amongst what was bound to be an unruly gathering.

For two hours and 40 minutes, the pair belted away at each other, until in the 71st round, a police raid brought the bout to an abrupt end. As neither fighter had been knocked down, the fight was declared a draw. However Foley had a moral victory – Ross was in a terrible mess whereas he had only suffered a cut lip.

A few days later, Ross conceded victory to Foley, agreeing to call a truce and join forces. Ross became Foley's second lieutenant as the larrikin chief took over control of the Rocks. The following year, it was all settled beyond doubt when Foley knocked out Ross in four rounds.

Foley then decided his days of a street-brawler were over and wanted to be respectable.

A deeply religious figure, Foley took the boxing game seriously, winning 22 bareknuckle fights between 1876 and 1889, during which time he became Australia's first heavyweight champion.

Renowned English fighter Jem Mace went as far as to describe him as the finest boxer in the world after a gold championship belt, valued at least 1,000 pounds, was presented to Foley when he beat the fiery fast-talking Englishman, Abe Hicken, on the banks of the Murray River near Echuca in 1879.

Foley's most vivid memory of the day was a tall, bearded man pushing his way through the crowd to issue his congratulations.

'My name's Ned Kelly,' he uttered, before disappearing into the departing horde.

The fights continued, but Foley decided he could make money an easier way by opening a boxing academy where he could pass on all his knowledge, at the right price, to those irrational, irritable Sydney thugs who wanted to be real, aesthetic pugilists.

He bought the White Horse Hotel in George Street, where in the front bar, Foley, a mine host whom everyone wanted to be on the right side of, could lure the drinkers and admirers into parting their money his way.

Out the back in its large cement-floored cellar, he opened up a boxing academy. It immediately became Sydney's boxing haven, with everyone who wanted to throw their fists around eager to be seen in the company of the best. Demand outweighed size. Soon the cellar became too small, crammed with sober, and not so sober, fighters, who were working the suspended bags or prancing around the ring. Foley had no alternative but to think big and build a ramshackle barn out the back. Always the most convincing of standover men, Foley persuaded the boxers to build the barn for him arguing that all the exercise would be beneficial to their fitness levels. When it was completed the barn could accommodate 2,000 spectators and soon became known all over Sydney as Foley's Iron Pot.

For the next two decades, the Iron Pot lured the best including the 'Black Prince', West Indian boxer Peter Jackson, who arrived in Sydney at age 19 and made Australia his home. In 1886 he became the country's heavyweight title holder. Another Iron Pot regular was Young Griffo, who after beating all and sundry in Australia left for the United States where he ended up drinking himself to oblivion in the New York saloons.

Also at the Iron Pot, tussling with them all, was George Baker. Never of the standard to actually step into the ring for money at stake, Baker was still convinced that if on his daily rounds he was to be able to keep his head up high, and have the respect of the less respectable, he had to know how to properly defend himself. He couldn't let any mug kick sand over him because on his beat the word would soon be out and he wouldn't be able to show his face again.

Whenever possible he would head to the Iron Pot, calling on Foley to provide him with the rudimentaries of the boxing game. Foley, eyeing off another Irishman of a different religious persuasion, would regularly spar with him, as would Jackson, when he was in Sydney. It was a brutal school, with Baker regularly beaten around, but after a few lessons he proved to be a more than able sparring partner to two of Australia's most reputable pugilists. Jackson especially enjoyed Baker's refusal to give in, prompting spirited sparring bouts.

An imposing figure, he also had no problems luring the womenfolk, in particular a striking 21-year-old Sydney-born girl, Elizabeth Jane Robertson. He was 14 years her senior, but this did not stop them from becoming an inseparable couple, who were fast-tracked towards marriage.

In March 1879, after only knowing each other for a few months, they married in their home suburb of Surry Hills. They immediately worked on building the Baker dynasty, having four children in as many years. Joy was mixed with tragedy, as only two survived – Ernest and Fred – with a son and daughter not lasting the early weeks of life.

Snowy was the fifth, born February 8, 1884, and immediately became a daddy's boy. Two more brothers, Harold and Frank, and a sister, Jean, followed a few years later.

'My father was the greatest influence in my athletic life,' Snowy explained many years later. 'He convinced me about the importance of being versatile. Not to show off, but for health and pleasure. I always remember him saying: "My boy, activity is the law of life; idleness is decay." We were our mother's responsibility until we were eight. Father always said a child had no muscular co-ordination until then. From eight onwards he taught us all to ride, swim, box and how to keep ourselves fit.

'He used to take us riding every morning, and he taught us to swim and dive at Farmer's Woolloomooloo baths. We took our first boxing lessons in the backyard.'

Well before turning eight, Snowy was following his father to the stables, demanding to be put on the back of one of the horses and pleading to be part of the early morning rides out past the Sydney Cricket Ground towards Coogee. His father told him to be patient.

Snowy always wanted to be involved in everything and desperate to get out of doors. He was a wanderer as a kid, attracted to the nearby open spaces and groups of kids playing various ball sports and activities, usually not returning home until after dusk, always detouring to clean out the stables before it got dark.

By the time he had reached third grade at the nearby Crown Street Public School, Snowy was a competent horseman, with George occasionally having the nerve to allow his pesky, persuasive son on the largest stallion in the stable. The imp handled it with aplomb, soon learning how to open the stable gates and charge out into the open plains on the most cantankerous stable steed. Falls and tears were occasional.

However, Snowy was never quite satisfied. He always wanted to learn something new, eager to try something different. From his early days at school, he was desperate to attempt every sporting experience known to man, dabbling at cricket, handball, rugby and hockey. He was living in the ideal part of Sydney to learn new skills. Surrounded by open space, the Surry Hills area was invaded with kids similarly driven to get outdoors and challenge each other to whatever was going on. Sport was their excuse to get out in the sun and away from mundane household chores.

But the lure of the sea, surf and the Harbour was the most persistent. Noticing this waterlust, his father was forced to provide the most brutal of lessons. As Snowy recalled: 'My dad just threw me in the water, and calmly told me to get out. I paddled out the best way I could and from that day on I was on my way as far as aquatics were concerned.'

Snowy immediately took to the sea, especially when he discovered several swimming baths situated along the Harbour.

As part of their early morning horse ride, father and son would either head towards the sea – Coogee, Bronte, Bondi or Maroubra – or travel towards the inner city and the Harbour near the Domain and Woolloomooloo, and out towards South Head. Another popular haunt was the Harbour beach at Rose Bay, a favourite spot for Sydney racehorse trainers, where the gallopers were exercised with a dawn swim and a sprint along the beach. If the number of riders was short, Snowy would gladly hop from one racehorse to another to help out.

If Snowy wasn't dragged into the Harbour by his horse, he would strip off and sprint in, thrashing out towards the Manly ferries before returning home. Thankfully for Snowy, he soon surrounded himself with those who were far more fascinated by the actual science of swimming.

For almost half a century, the Woolloomooloo Bay area of Sydney had been the main haven for the city's adventurous swimmers, with races being held at the Robinson's Baths near the Domain since 1846. The swimming enclosure, known as 'The Figtree' or 'Centipede Rock', was formed by mooring a vessel more than 50 yards out in the bay, and then connecting it to the shore with wooden paling fences. For the honour of dipping in the water, hardy souls paid one shilling.

At the time the popular swimming stroke was a bit of a hodgepodge. Some were using an Aboriginal side-stroke. A few used a rudimentary butterfly stroke. Most preferred the easy and relaxing breaststroke, or the basic but effective dog paddle.

Snowy did whatever came easy. During the spring and summer months, Snowy could always be found at one of the numerous baths along the Harbour foreshore, paddling, diving, sun-baking, practising various strokes with a variety of other swimming pioneers. His favourite spot was Farmer's Baths, which was only a 15 minute horse ride, or 20 minute stroll, from the family home. It was the ultimate release.

He was quickly plucked by those in the know as something special, and was coerced into stopping recklessly bombing other people with wild dives and actually learning how to swim properly. With Australian swimming going through its most radical period of evolution, Snowy picked the right time to be dragged along.

The illustrious Cavill family grabbed him, and along with such other enthusiastic sea urchins as Freddie Lane, Cecil Healy, Alick Wickham, Fanny Durack and Annette Kellerman, Snowy helped to push swimming to another level through the development of a new stroke – the Australian crawl.

Frederick Cavill, working on the fact that he had failed by just 200 metres to swim the English Channel, was the self-proclaimed 'Professor' of swimming at that time, and it didn't take long for the impressionable and eager-to-learn Snowy to be under his spell.

Shortly after the Professor arrived in Sydney from England in 1879, he erected swimming baths at Lavender Bay where he promised that he could teach anyone to be a competent swimmer, all for the price of a guinea.

Realising that teaching swimming to city dwellers surrounded by surf, sea and harbour was a money spinner, the Professor branched out, opening a state-of-the-art natatorium in Farm Cove, near the Botanical Gardens, where the open-slatted baths were supported by buoyancy tanks. It became a Sydney landmark, impressing all, especially the journals of the time, with its 'elegant' features.

Snowy became close friends with one of the Professor's sons, Dick, otherwise known as Splash. It was impossible not to be attracted by such an extroverted family, as apart from the publicity-hungry father, his sons were all larger than life characters.

There was Charles Cavill, who became the first man to swim the entrance of San Francisco Harbour, before being killed by poisonous gases in California while performing an underwater endurance trick.

Another brother, Percy, became the five mile swimming champion of the world. He then disappeared for almost two decades. He was eventually found in the Bahamas, living as a beachcomber.

Arthur 'Tums' Cavill was also an adventurer, swimming across the Oregon Bay with his hands and feet tied. Once he was lowered in a bag from a bridge into a river in Pittsburgh. The stunt backfired, when Tums bashed into one of the bridge pylons on the way down. Dazed, he then accidentally stabbed himself with a knife that was to be used to cut himself out of the bag. He somehow survived that, but was not so lucky when he decided on a three-mile swim across Seattle Harbour in the middle of winter. He basically froze, and had to be dragged out of the water. He died in hospital a few hours later. Syd Cavill, another to head to the United States, was the originator of the butterfly stroke.

The youngest, Splash Cavill, was a little more restrained but was as outgoing and eager to push the limits. He and Snowy were soon inseparable, egging each other on to try something new. Around them were several others just as willing to test the boundaries.

Their lives now revolved around the Harbour, with Snowy hurtling towards the Domain for another afternoon of swimming and sunning himself as soon as he finished school. Through endless hours in the sun and sea, his hair was beyond platinum blond and was now virtually white, so that he could only be called Snowy.

He wasn't exactly enamoured with the nickname, believing it was demeaning, even effeminate. He instead demanded that everyone call him Reg. He was simply ignored, especially when the talented gang of aquatic thrillseekers quickly grew in strength and numbers.

Freddie Lane, Australia's first Olympic swimming gold medallist, was the leader of the pack. Four years older than Snowy, he was the young gun Australian swimmer of the late 19th century. At his first swimming carnival, Lane won the inaugural 100 yard race. He was just eight years old. By age 12, he was the Riverview College champion. However, it was a trip to England two years later to collect a family inheritance worth over 170,000 pounds that pushed the tiny, wiry, near elf-like Lane, who left a lasting impression on anyone who met him because he had the most piercing eyes, well ahead of the rest.

While in England, Lane saw the trudgen stroke for the first time. With some resemblance to the butterfly stroke, the trudgen involved a frog-like kick. The arms were alternatively raised over the head and brought down and back parallel to the body. The head always remained out of the water. Lane modified it, swimming on his left side and using a powerful scissors motion rather than the frog kick.

It looked strange, but it worked for Lane who won almost every race he'd entered since his return to Australia. However, it was a very demanding stroke. Lane was a disciple, but it knocked him around enormously. Bleeding profusely from his nostrils, he would often have to be assisted from the water.

Transferring to Sydney Grammar School, Lane, even though usually delirious, won all swimming events in one season, including taking out the All-Schools 100 yard championship and the 100 yard and 200 yard handicap events in 1896. At most of these events, Snowy was at poolside, taking a close note of the midget thrashing away in the water and always winning. He was soon pestering Freddie for advice.

By 18 Freddie boasted the NSW 220 yard title, and shortly after became the Australasian 100 yard champion.

Also on his return to Australia, Lane joined the East Sydney Swimming Club, where he became near inseparable mates with all the Cavill boys and Snowy.

Snowy's restless attitude, which saw him try everything available at the club, including the boxing gloves and scaling the diving board, helped Lane as he prepared for the 1900 Paris Olympics.

While hanging around the Domain Baths, and working out at its small gymnasium, Lane developed the required upper body to make it in the international arena.

'I used to spar at the baths with Snowy Baker. Young Griffo taught me to box. There was a whole team of us, we called ourselves "the Blossom Club", and we would sit around in the sun and swim, box and sling mud,' Lane recalled many years later.

'Every week we each put threepence in the kitty and at the end of the year had a smack-up dinner and a night at the Tivoli. Those were the days!

'We were always trying for more and still more speed. We wore gloves with webbing, but found that the fingers closed with the pressure. Then we tried wooden flippers. We all had our own ideas.'

Tagging along was another impressionable Darlinghurst product, Cecil Healy, who also joined the East Sydney Swimming Club.

Making the mix more cosmopolitan was the arrival of Alick Wickham from the Solomon Islands, who totally changed the line of thinking of all those slinging mud at each other down at the Domain.

The son of an English copra plantation manager and a Melanesian woman from Munda, Alick, when seven, travelled to Sydney with his father in his schooner *Saucy Lass* for schooling.

Alick headed straight for the Sydney beaches, where he showed off a totally new swimming stroke – the forerunner to today's freestyle stroke.

At his first local school swimming carnival held at Australia's oldest rock pool at Bronte, Wickham did what came naturally to him during a 66 yard under-10 years handicap race – an easy, rhythmic stroke, where he swam with head held high, but turning it quickly from side to side, breathing with each complete stroke.

With a short, fast arm action, Alick glided across the water. Standing nearby was one of Sydney's best known coaches – George Farmer – who was astounded by what he had just seen. He turned to another coach, shook his head, and uttered: 'Look at that black boy crawling over the water.' And so the expression 'Australian crawl' was born.

Within weeks Snowy and the rest knew about the new stroke.

'I was down at the Farmer's Baths, one sunny morning. We'd had our dip and were just lying yarning in the sun,' Snowy said 50 years later. 'There were four of us – Cecil Healy, Fred Lane, Dick Cavill and myself. When a young lad with an obvious race of coloured blood in his make-up strolled down and prepared to dive in.

'We didn't take much notice of him until he hit the water. Then we really sat up and rubbed our eyes. We raced over to him and started the cross examination. In a few minutes, we were all trying the new stroke. The lad was Alick Wickham. He explained to us that he had been taught to swim that way by his father, who had learned it from Pacific Island natives.'

Dick Cavill was the most attentive and took it to the next step, finetuning the stroke, until he became the master, so much so that opponents were soon complaining that during races he was crawling all over them. As there were no swimming lanes at that time, Dick who had his head down and arms always moving was guilty of ploughing into nearby opponents.

Dick was also the first to use the stroke in serious competition when he won the 100 yard state championship in 1899.

Several others in the Cavill clan picked up the stroke, with Syd later writing he was 'the man who discovered the crawl' in Apia, Samoa, and that Tums was the first to use it in Australia and Dick was 'the man who perfected it'.

As the debate raged on about who was actually the father of the 'crawl', Snowy didn't need much convincing that the South Seas approach was the most natural way to glide across the water, and he also became an avid exponent, immediately picking up the pace.

This innovative swimming think tank was not totally an all male domain. Also hanging around with the Cavills, Bakers and Lanes were several frisky females, the most forward being an ultra-confident Annette Kellerman.

She had been lured from Marrickville to Cavill's Baths as a means to strengthen her legs, which had been weakened substantially by a bout of polio and left her wearing iron braces on her legs.

That did not deter Kellerman who was taught the trudgen stroke by Lane, while Snowy, another of her coaching teachers, had her up on the diving board within days teaching her the rudiments. The most boisterous of females was soon being egged along by the most adventurous of males hanging around the Domain. They were the perfect pairing, always trying to out do each other. Soon the ever-confident Kellerman was racing Snowy up the high tower to show off her latest daredevil dive.

The leg irons were soon discarded.

Surrounded by so many notables who were totally obsessed with the athletic pursuit and wanting to prove it on the international stage, Snowy didn't take much convincing about what path he wanted to take. The only problem was trying to fit in all of his sporting fascinations.

Chapter 2

Shillings and Seagulls

Snowy's photograph first hit the newsprint on May 26, 1900, in *The Town and Country Journal*. In the top left-hand corner of the page, next to 'Poultry Gossip' by Cockspur, 'The Kennel' by Sir Belvidere and an article on 'Shipbuilding on the Nambucca River', an assured 16 year old is thrusting out his shoulders and looking directly at the camera. He looks proud, and supremely confident. The usually wild, blond locks that stuck up and went in all directions had been slicked down for the important moment.

The caption explained: 'R. Baker . . . winner of the 100 yd and 200 yd swimming championship of NSW Public Schools.' From the grim determination on his face, you could already see that this kid was going places, or at least wanted to.

Snowy was a good, fastidious student and eager to learn. His examination results were above average, his attentiveness noted and his times in detention, or outside the headmaster's office, minimal. Teachers would later explain that Snowy was one of Crown Street's better students. But that had as much to do with what he was doing outside lesson hours.

At Crown Street Public, students were actively encouraged to mix scholastic endeavours with sporting pursuits, especially at a time when former pupils were making such a formidable mark on the international arena. Crown Street prided itself on the sportsmen it nurtured.

As Snowy moved into his teens, Crown Street could boast its involvement in the development of two of the world's best cricketers, who at the time were just down the road breaking a stream of records at the Sydney Cricket Ground.

Montague Alfred Noble, better known as Monty Noble, finished his schooling at Crown Street and a few years later became Australia's 12th Test cricket captain. Modifying his skills in the Crown Street playground, Noble went on to become Australia's first celebrated all-rounder, and a captain described by England stalward Sir Pelham Warner as the best Australia had produced.

As Noble left Crown Street in 1891, an even more formidable cricketer arrived – the masterful Victor Trumper, the most graceful and fluent batsman of the game's 'Golden Age', when Australia was able to establish an international identity through its cricketing success. As his biographer Jack Fingleton explained, the Crown Street playground was instrumental in turning Trumper, Australia's best batsman until the arrival of Donald Bradman some decades later, into a special cricketing commodity.

'It was not until Trumper went to Crown Street Superior Public School – "Public School", in this instance, differing from the Public Schools of England – that he began to shoot ahead at the game,' Fingleton wrote in *The Immortal Victor Trumper.*

'Noble, five years older than Trumper, was in his final year when Trumper came and interest in cricket was already high. Each summer the boys would eat their lunch hurriedly and then it was cricket, and in double quick time.

'Whoever caught the batsman or bowled him out was next in, and Trumper once batted for six weeks. His father would occasionally ask him how he was getting on, and Trumper would reply: "I am still in."'

Crown Street's close proximity to the Sydney Cricket Ground ensured that whenever a visiting interstate or international team were in town, and they were short of net bowlers for a practice session, a call would go out to the school asking for volunteers. As soon as the final lesson bell rang, a horde would charge from Crown Street to the ground.

The lure was not just the chance to bowl at the best, there were also monetary rewards. When Andrew Stoddart's 1894 England team was in Sydney, they invited Crown Street's best to bowl against them. To encourage them, two shillings were placed on top of the bails. If the schoolkids hit the stumps, and the two shillings fell, it was theirs. Not surprisingly Trumper, in a bid to make easy money, was quickly making the short trek and in his path followed Snowy.

As the Crown Street teachers were repeatedly boasting about our Monty and our Victor, anyone who walked into the schoolyards with a cricket bat under his arm was encouraged. Snowy soon sussed that out and was immediately among the throng in the playground trying to be the 'next one in'.

Snowy, a competent enough bat and bowl, commanded respect in the playground and had enough courage to wander across to the Sydney Cricket Ground, and occasionally bowl his left-arm medium pacers at our Monty and our Victor. Compared to the English tourists though, they were more frugal with their money, only occasionally offering twopenny pieces if they were bowled, and the Snowy visits to the nets became more intermittent. His interest in cricket eventually began to wane.

Many years later, Snowy explained: 'After being at school with Victor Trumper and M.A. Noble, I always had an inferiority complex about cricket.'

One writer for *People* magazine, in a glowing piece on Snowy in the 1940s, tried to hoodwink the public into believing that he was 'one of the greatest left-hand bowlers Australia had produced'. It sounded impressive, but it was another example of Baker blarney. Then again it may be another case of a writer mistaking Snowy for someone else who actually was an outstanding left-arm bowler, R.J.A. Massie.

Other sporting pursuits beckoned, to the extent that Snowy was near unbeatable at school athletics carnivals where he mixed up short distance sprint victories with triumphs on the high jump mats and over the hurdling bars. One year Snowy won every race from 100 yards to a mile at the public schools athletics championship.

But the most compelling magnet was the swimming pool. Having already joined the East Sydney Swimming Club, and at the age of 14 having started competing in the members events, he discovered he was almost unbeatable against those his own age. Spending so much time with the true innovators of swimming had pushed him so far ahead of anyone else in the Sydney Public School system.

He began competing at swimming carnivals for Crown Street in 1897, but it was in the two years that followed that he really made his mark. In both 1898 and 1899 he won the overall Public Schools championship, while also securing five eastern district schools championships, four

100 yard and one 200 yard all-schools (NSW) championships, plus 18 other prizes in diving, novelty water events and team racing.

Snowy even had time to compete at school invitational races, including one held as part of the Sydney Government Printing Office gala carnival. A reporter from the Sydney sporting newspaper, *The Referee*, was at poolside and was so impressed with Snowy's maturity that he queried whether he had been dabbling with his birth certificate. 'Judging by appearances, it's about time Baker "chucked" school, unless he's going to stay there all his life. The writer has seen many men with much younger looking chivvies keeping families.'

Hanging around with important people ensured that Snowy was constantly being mentioned in *The Referee* – the best read, the most authoritative and intelligent sporting newspaper to have been published in Australia. Through the pages of this weekly, it was possible to become intimate with Australia's leading athletes. A typical *Referee* item read: 'Monday morning saw Fred Lane and George Read undergoing the process of being oiled from neck to heel for their swim, with clever boxer and fast swimmer Snowy Baker.

'The pelts of all were tanned – almost black in some instances, but a bright copper tint in most – through constant exposure to the sun's rays. Veritable amphibians they are, as much so as the seal . . .'

These seals were also making an enormous impact in the water, especially at the turn of the century when Snowy was a regular competitor in the senior club races, which basically involved the best in the world.

By late 1899, the East Sydney Swimming Club now had well over 100 members, its finances were flourishing and its key members instrumental in making Australia a swimming mecca. Invariably its annual carnival was highlighted with world records being broken.

Club captain Freddie Lane was breaking records both here and in England, while Snowy, aged just 15, had the honour of finishing equal second with him overall in the club handicap competitions. As well, Snowy was doubling up in the club's water polo team, where he was a formidable mid-fielder alongside Cecil Healy. Snowy's first important races for senior New South Wales titles involved competing against many Australian champions including Dick Cavill. Still Lane remained the gun, having just returned from the 1900 Paris Olympics a national hero.

Lane's pursuit of gold also involved some stranger moments. After winning the 200 metre freestyle, held in the murky waters of the Seine near Asnieres, by finishing ahead of Hungarian Zoltan Von Halmay, Lane planned to compete in the 1,000 metre freestyle, but missed the start after a French interpreter gave him wrong directions and the wrong time for the event. Lane, who had finished the 200 metre event in a 'stupor', then opted for the 200 metre obstacle race where the competitors had to weave around rowing boats and under floating punts. They also had to climb into boats and dive from them. He was at a distinct advantage as he had spent so much time with Snowy and the likes swimming out to the middle of Sydney Harbour to check out the most fashionable boats, and so he knew it was smarter to clamour over boats at the stern, rather than fight your way over the sides. He naturally sped across the course.

A few months later, Lane was back in Sydney and at the swimming club showing off the enormous trophies he had won in Paris as Australia's original swimming Olympic champion – a bronze sculpture of a horse, modelled on a Louvre masterpiece, and another bronze monolith of Jean François Millet's 'The Gleaner', which both weighed over 25 kilograms.

Lane was a modest man, but the stories surrounding his Parisian triumphs, overseas adventures, and the trophies that went with it, tantalised the impressionable Snowy convincing him that he wanted to follow a similar course. Snowy began to realise that sporting conquests could help him see the world.

The first step in believing that he was up to international standard was to somehow beat Freddie. The closest Snowy came was at the 1901 East Sydney Club carnival, held at George Farmer's 'spick and span' baths at Woolloomooloo.

For some time, Snowy had been mixing his races, even attempting the long-distance events which saw him finish third to George Read and Dick Cavill in the New South Wales one mile championship. Read finished the 39 laps in the world record time of 24 minutes 46 seconds, with Baker completing the course four minutes later. Once he was even convinced to try out in the three mile championship. But now it was time to return to his favoured sprint events.

Farmer's Baths was an impressive sight on Saturday, December 7, 1901, the crowd milling around the competitors on the wooden frames that surrounded the sea pool. Adding to the carnival atmosphere was the arrival of a Bavarian band that jostled its way into a corner and blasted out good old fashioned drinking tunes between events.

The Referee was enthused with the day, explaining that 'the weather was excellent, the tide just the thing, and the crowd a good profit bringing gathering'. It was not so excited by the organisation, because of too many 'waits' between events – the Bavarian band was obviously getting on the scribe's nerves. But the crowd didn't mind and loved being so close to the action, especially as they had the perfect view of the start, with many standing right next to the competitors as they hurled themselves into the Harbour.

Annette Kellerman had already had the crowd gasping when, after winning the ladies race, she 'evidenced the possession of nerve of no common order by plunging from the top of a structure fully 30 feet above the water'. Snowy had taught the mischievous Annette well.

The key event was the 100 yard championship, where Snowy, in a five-man field, was up against Lane and Healy. Snowy felt relatively confident, especially as the previous year he had finished second behind Dick Cavill in the state half-mile championship held at Helling's Baths in the Domain. This effort prompted *The Referee* to remark that 'Snowy is to be complimented on his splendid showing, which, seeing that he was only swimming as a schoolboy less than six months ago, was very creditable indeed, and gives every indication that something a deal better may be expected of him as the season grows older'.

The *Daily Telegraph* wrote: 'Snowy Baker, who was swimming as a schoolboy less than six months ago, made a fine effort right through. Moving along in good style, and exhibiting stamina and grit of no ordinary degree, he was only beaten by 40 yards, and that in exceptionally fast time (12 minutes 42 3⅕ seconds), less than 3 seconds outside the Australasian record.'

However for one journalist the real highlight of the meet was that 'ladies predominated among the spectators', and during the fancy dress event, one competitor arrived as a snake charmer, with an actual 10-foot long tiger snake coiled around his body.

While a competent long-distance swimmer, Snowy still thought the sprint was his forte. Oiled down and again looking like a seal, Snowy started well and threatened Lane early, who surprisingly began slowly, but Lane eventually pushed himself away from the rest. Snowy finished the event exhausted, partly due to the fact that an hour before the event he had swum in the 1,000 yard championship, finishing second behind George Read who broke the world record.

While Snowy searched for shade, Lane headed straight back to the pool because he wasn't satisfied with his first effort. This time he broke the Australian record.

If Snowy couldn't beat Lane, he thought the next best thing was to join forces. As East Sydney boasted so many impressive swimmers, they knew if they got themselves into some sort of formidable combination, the 500 yards Flying Squadron team race, which had been competed for since 1895 and involved a 100 yard relay and five different swimmers, would be their baby.

Lane was immediately delegated team leader and he soon convinced his closest colleagues and best opponents to join the team. Within days he had an unbeatable unit that included himself, George Read, Cecil Healy and Snowy, and was soon joined by Snowy's younger brother Harold, Alick Wickham and Theo Tartakover.

It was no surprise that for the next four years they were unsurpassed as an assortment of teams from the inner city clubs and from as far as Newcastle struggled not to suffer the embarrassment of being repeatedly lapped.

In 1901, East Sydney won the title in 5 minutes 46.4 seconds. By 1904, the team of Lane, Wickham, Healy, Harold and Snowy Baker had chopped their Australasian swimming record time down by 40 seconds.

The team used their resources to perfection. To immediately intimidate their opponents, Wickham would start off the relay ensuring that by the first change East Sydney held a considerable lead. This had the desired effect of demoralising the other teams, enabling Healy, Harold and then Snowy to consolidate that lead during the second, third and fourth legs. And then Freddie Lane would power home in the final leg, each time guaranteeing another posed photograph, with another large trophy plumped in front of them.

The only time East Sydney was truly troubled was in the 1903 final when Dick Cavill, swimming for Pyrmont, took the 'battle right up to them'. Cavill's aim was to out manoeuvre Wickham, and by imitating his opponent's crawl stroke succeeded. However the combined swims of Healy and Snowy turned the race around, with Baker's 'beautiful plunge, that carried him perhaps 40 feet' instrumental in ensuring East Sydney remained unbeaten.

As the team congratulated each other, the crowd swamped them, with several of the more excited spectators getting too close to the edge and accidentally bumped into the pool. Soon the East Sydney stars were back in the water, rescuing those who were being dragged down to the bottom because of the weight of their weekend best. More cheers as they helped the innocent public back to safety.

Snowy simply loved the adulation and played to the crowd. He now boasted an impressive physique and knew how to show it off. Right from an early age Snowy craved attention. When he became part of the East Sydney clan he realised that as he was surrounded by so many notable athletes, if he was going to get ahead he had to push himself and be noticed.

He strutted. He performed. He flexed the muscles. He knew how to play to the ladies, whenever possible revealing the torso, finetuned by endless hours involved in various sporting pursuits. He was the ultimate exhibitionist. Not surprisingly when several of his mates approached him about being part of a diving troupe, he instantly agreed. This was the chance he had been waiting for – to at last exhibit the showman side of his character.

As with his swimming, Baker relied heavily on Dick Cavill to improve his diving skills. 'The advance I made in swimming,' Snowy explained many years later, 'is due to my association with Fred Lane, Cecil Healy and Dick Cavill.

'In those days we commenced with breaststroke, then improved speed with the single over-arm. I swam right arm out, which was not as common as bringing the left arm out of the water. Then we went to trudgen and finally to the crawl, thanks to little Alick Wickham and Dick Cavill.

'Apart from his great ability as a speed swimmer, Dick Cavill was a great diver and we worked together on diving, with the result that I subsequently gained top honours in this sport.'

At the 1902 East Sydney carnival, the Blossoms diving team made its first appearance. It was an immediate crowd favourite, with the performers getting dressed up in all sorts of odd costumes, including one as a Chinaman, while another wore a Scottish kilt. Snowy was usually, in the words of *The Referee*, either 'John Bull or a toffy deadbeat . . . The wrestling on the spring board was good, as also Snowy's high dives in full costume. By the way, Snowy must have a hard nut to stand that dipper in the dives. The dipper was flattened out a couple of times.' Their 'comical tobogganing on a long slide' was as big a hit.

Soon the high diving team were making appearances at swimming carnivals all around the city. Snowy was the star, performing all sorts of death defying twists, turns, loops and head slams in his diving repertoire. Then he decided to be even more elaborate, more vaudevillian. The new aquatic entertainment troupe, called 'Snowy Baker's Seagulls', soon became renowned for their bizarre tricks which bordered on the burlesque.

The highlight of their show was a re-enactment of *The Count of Monte Cristo*, which included having one of the performers sewn into a large sack. This was usually an old chaff-bag, which was tossed into deep water from the diving tower. The diver would have to perform a Harry Houdini, get out of the sack and reach the surface, even though his hands and feet were still tied. When they performed at a charity function at Balmain, it was Snowy's turn to be the victim.

Everything went to plan, except that when the bag hit the water, the penknife which was sneakily concealed between his two tied hands had been dropped. The knife fell between the bricks that were at the bottom of the bag to ensure that it immediately went to the bottom.

With no way of getting out of the bag, Snowy sank to the bottom and waited, and waited, and waited. Thankfully his swimming and diving pursuits had taught him how to keep his breath for a marathon period. But even he began to worry when after about a minute no-one had come to his rescue.

In the end a spectator sensed something was wrong, dived in and with a penknife, saved Snowy. Snowy, ever the showman, hit the surface, with arms raised, as if to indicate the return of the messiah. After that, the Seagulls modified the trick, tying the knife onto the inside of the performer's wrists to ensure it was never jolted again.

More publicity, more kudos, more ego pampering. Snowy was in his element. Then came another sporting distraction.

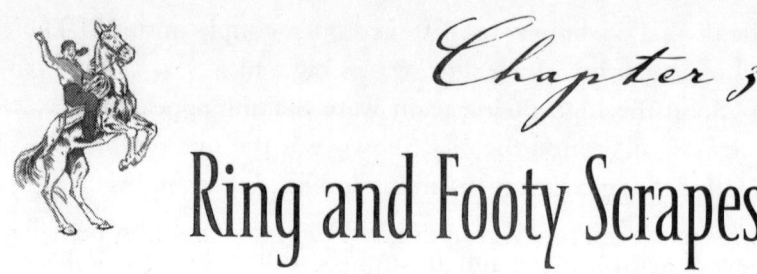

Chapter 3
Ring and Footy Scrapes

For several years, Snowy's summer months had been intense. Apart from swimming training and competitions, there was an abundance of diving exhibitions, with every other minute involved in the indulgence of sunning himself and keeping the body beautiful.

The rest of the year soon became as vigorous. First boxing and then rugby football became his other overwhelming obsessions.

For anyone who boasted a Darlinghurst home address, knowing how to defend yourself was a necessity. The laws of the back lane and gang warfare dominated. The inner city suburbs of Sydney attracted an eclectic mix, but most had that touch of the desperate.

Snowy knew that if he was to have any authority in the area, he had to be able to stand up to anyone. He didn't have to be swayed, especially with Baker Senior explaining how he got on when he first arrived from Ireland. It wasn't just intelligence, money or breeding that made the difference. Sydney, so his father told him, relied on bare-knuckle justice. Whatever his father said, Snowy took as gospel.

Snowy idolised his father, who stressed upon him the importance of a rounded life. While pleased that Snowy was a good, honest student, being especially proficient in English and mathematics, father Baker saw that he had the sporting attributes to be something special. His father would repeatedly tell him the importance of a basic education, and was particularly impressed with his writing capabilities which had seen him win several school essay competitions, but that he should never forget his sporting pursuits because it gave him an edge on everyone else. His father could see sport as a vehicle for Snowy to get ahead of the rest and make a name for himself. Snowy needed little prompting.

At the age of 17, Snowy left school with a respectable mark that enabled him to get a job as an office junior at the Colonial Sugar Refining Company (CSR), which brought in enough money for him to pay his board at home. But Snowy didn't need much money to keep going; he basically had no social life because of the many sporting pursuits which took up all of his spare time. The most pressing when he was ending his teen years was boxing.

Making the art of self-defence an even greater priority was that most his age were considerably larger than him. He was a bit of a runt and was naturally concerned that he could be seen as an easy target. He was around 5 foot 8 inches tall, and while not tiny, he was still self-conscious that so many his age and beyond towered over him. It forced him to develop elsewhere, especially in his upper body.

In the end, he could boast as good a physique as anyone causing trouble in Sydney, and was as fast on his feet. And just as importantly he was fearless. He had to be. 'As a lad,' Snowy recalled, 'I used to go around the back lanes in Darlinghurst and join in the bouts of the many youngsters, who every evening would make a "human ring" and spar with each other under the gaslight glitter of a handy lamp-post of those days.'

It was rudimentary stuff, but it gave everyone the chance, with a few well chosen lefts and rights, to get rid of all that pent-up aggression. It didn't take long for Snowy to revert from observer to participant, immediately enjoying the thrill of 'nosing around and toughening up by getting smacked around'. He got off on the pain.

Down at the Domain Baths, he met the 'grand old man of fisticuffs', Peter Jackson. Some years previously, Snowy's father had duelled Jackson at Foley's George Street gymnasium. Now it was the son's turn to learn the necessary tricks from a boxer who had enjoyed the highs and lows of this brutal venture.

The West Indian-born fighter had travelled to Australia as a teenager and, coached by Foley, won the Australian heavyweight title in 1886. Lucrative boxing deals then lured Jackson to the United States and England where the 'Black Prince' was involved in several notable bouts, including a marathon four-hour, 61-round no contest with 'Gentleman' Jim Corbett in San Francisco.

After many gruelling years on the road, Jackson returned to Australia in a bid to regain his health. He became a publican and shortly after an alcoholic. But he tried to stop himself from falling right away, knowing that he could still keep himself fed and watered by boxing at circus exhibitions.

Fast living had knocked him around, but Jackson persisted with his fitness regime, which included going down to the Domain Baths every weekday morning.

'He always did his early morning training at the baths,' Snowy said. 'Part of his routine was to swim one lap of 45 yards under water.

'My long blond hair appealed to Peter and he allowed me to spar two rounds with him.'

For Snowy, the bare-knuckle days were over, with Jackson demanding that Snowy don boxing gloves for the first time.

'After sparring with Peter, all kids my age I thought were duck soup for me.'

Snowy's time with Jackson was brief, as shortly after he died of tuberculosis, but crucial as it gave him the urge to stop being a scrapper and instead treat boxing as a meticulous, precise science. Jackson taught him the rudiments – the soft-shoe shuffle, how to defend, attack and be unpredictable.

Snowy enjoyed the mix of ballet and brutality, and the fact that it was pure exhibitionism. Adding to the attraction was that in the laneways near the family home there were an abundance of boxing dens and gymnasiums where trainers and pugs would hang out. The lure was just outside his front gate.

Soon Snowy, with leather gloves slung around his neck, was going up old, dark staircases and entering musty halls where overwhelmingly sour body odour, sweat and liniment irritated the nostrils. Jackson had taught him the basics; he now had to work on the subtleties.

However, the smartest move Snowy had made was to bring his father down to the Baths one morning to see him waltz with Jackson. George Baker saw enough that morning to know his son had something. The next day Baker brought along his old sparring partner, Larry Foley, and he gave the quiet nod of approval. Foley explained to Baker that he required proper tuition, not the rough-house grounding that had turned Foley into a gang-leader. Foley suggested two names.

Within a week, George Baker had arranged for his son to have six months' tuition with two of the best teachers in Sydney – George Seale and his partner Arthur Scott.

Seale and Scott provided Snowy with the finetuning he required, and by the end of the six months were so impressed with their new student that they recommended he don't waste the lessons learnt. He was fast enough, courageous enough and resourceful enough not just to defend himself adequately, but to actually join the competitive ranks.

They told him what he wanted to hear, and with his father gladly providing the one pound entry fee, the following day, when just 18, Snowy lodged an application to make his competitive boxing debut at the 1902 NSW amateur championships.

Once again, Snowy showed that he would not do anything in half measures. There was never any thought of him starting his boxing career in a dingy, second-rate den against some nobody. Why not strive for the best straight away? Seale and Scott were cautious and suggested that something as lofty as the NSW amateur titles may be too much, too early for an inexperienced teenager, but Snowy was already convinced and could not be swayed.

Adding to the attraction was that the NSW amateur titles were to be staged at a new, state-of-the-art venue, the Australian National Sporting Club, which had just opened in the middle of the Sydney business district in Castlereagh Street.

In the words of *The Referee*, the club aimed to be the equivalent of the National Sporting Club of London, the Knickerbocker Club of New York and the 'fashionable' Olympic Club of San Francisco.

With such facilities as a gymnasium, a 2,000 seater athletic hall, reading rooms, punching ball platforms, hot and cold baths plus a billiard hall, and 'electric light installed throughout', the club immediately attracted the Sydney blue bloods. Boxing was their prime passion in an era where fighting was the meal ticket for so many, and at a time when no-one questioned the brutality and risk of such a pursuit. Boxing was then a noble sport. It had its detractors, with the 'wowser' element increasing in force. But they didn't have the numbers or the influence to venture anywhere near the National Sporting Club to try to sway the unconverted about the barbaric nature of boxing. The size of the crowd was simply too intimidating, as was the political influence of those who were boxing's main backers. Invariably at ringside were Sydney's makers and breakers.

Understandably those involved at the National Sporting Club were keen to impress the not so easily impressed. That required the inclusion of fixtures and fittings that matched the best stoush houses in the world. The club soon earnt a reputation as an ideal venue for the boxing spectator. Built on three tiers, the athletic hall enabled the spectator to basically sit on top of the boxers, with those on the top level looking down on the competitors. For the boxers, there was nowhere to hide, as every person in the crowd was only metres away, and could be easily identified. Intimate, but daunting. Every word uttered by the crowd could be heard by the fighters, while the audience, judging by the high level of barracking, were obviously not turned off by the large sign near the ring which said 'Betting Prohibited'.

So impressive were the facilities that the organisers of the State amateur titles, the NSW Sports Club, had held back their competition more than a month so that they could be part of the grand opening.

They had even beckoned in Lieutenant-Colonel Murray, 'an old Oxford heavyweight amateur champion, a well-known swordsman and barrister of this state', to add more class to the competition by being referee over four nights.

Also in the front row was the Sydney Lord Mayor, Thomas Hughes, to hand over the gold medals, containing 'not less than five carats', to all the division winners. A lucrative award, but the competitors were warned that this could not be used as part of a get-rich-quick scheme. The competition programme booklet demanded that if an entrant wanted to retain his amateur status, he could not 'pawn, sell, barter or turn into cash any prize won'.

Baker was entered into the lightweight division and cruised through the first three nights, winning several lopsided bouts before coming up against Lou D'Alpuget in the final. It was the most anticipated of division finals, described by *The Town and Country Journal* as pitting a well-known swimmer up against a well-known footballer. D'Alpuget was a first-grader with the Eastern Suburbs Rugby Club.

During the tournament, Baker had suffered from several nervous moments, sometimes trying to get ahead of himself with his youthful exuberance and committing himself to the knockout blow far too early. He was also relying far too much on his right hand, prompting Arthur Scott, who was at ringside in an honorary capacity for the organisers, to quietly take Snowy aside and tell him to be more patient and better balanced in his stance.

This had the desired effect, the final ending up a short, sharp affair. The *Daily Telegraph* reported: 'Such a sorry time did D'Alpuget get in the second round that towards the end he very wisely capitulated, and Baker won. Vanquished and victor were loudly cheered.'

The Referee elaborated: 'Snowy, the well known swimmer, and D'Alpuget, the last two left in the lightweight division, made matters very warm. Baker stood well up. D'Alpuget crouched. The pair fought determinedly and cleverly, with Baker, who made a very fine showing, always in the lead, sending left and right home constantly and effectively, till late in the second round, when D'Alpuget, finding he had no hope, cried enough, amid cheers as loud and long for the loser as the winner.'

Overall, *The Referee* correspondent was impressed with Snowy, but did recommend some refinement. 'Snowy has pluck enough and physique enough, as he is very clever, but he must drop that habit of leading with the right: It leaves him too open, and opposed to a man who could counter, well, would prove disastrous.

'Then again, on the first night he was at too high a tension in mind and muscle — screwed up to snapping point almost — a very exacting condition that needs exceptional bodily attunements to back it up, but, fortunately, Baker's state was equal to the occasion.

'However, I was glad to notice that he relaxed considerably in his later showings, and consequently fought freer and more effectively.'

Mission accomplished. And with it another distraction.

At ringside that night, apart from his father, trainers and swimming colleagues, were a small but noisy group of footballers, who were as convinced he could make it in yet another sport — theirs. After all, just a few weeks earlier they had all been together in a finals campaign, with Snowy their chief on-field organiser.

In between his boxing training, swimming and diving adventures, Snowy had often ridden one of his father's horses to Centennial Park where he had noticed a lot of his schoolmates running around a field, chasing a knocked-up old football.

He didn't take much convincing to tie up the horse to the boundary fence and join in. As simple as convincing him that he should be the team's half-back.

Snowy would later say that rugby union was his strongest sporting love. The first tingle occurred in the Crown Street school playground, and it developed in Centennial Park, especially as those he had originally watched were from the formidable Warrigals club, one of the original powers in the Sydney City and Suburban competition.

Formed in 1899, the Warrigals, whose players primarily hailed from the suburb of Woollahra, had made Centennial Park their home and were immediately a strength in the sub-district competition. Boasting the navy blue and yellow colours, the Warrigals were runners-up in 1901 and 1903, and finalists in 1902, the year Snowy played.

Also in the side was another formidable name, Herbert Henry 'Dally' Messenger, who would later earn international renown as Australian rugby league's greatest player, after prompting headlines by being the first star rugby union performer to move to the professional code.

Snowy was immediately at home with the Warrigals, with his speed, endurance and incredible strength, cultivated by endless hours of training for his other sporting pursuits, making him a near unstoppable midfield force. Like all good half-backs, he was cheeky, cocky and oh, so confident.

Right from day one, Snowy had strutted with a certain air of superiority. He knew he was special and was prepared to stand up to anyone – in particular those who hovered over him. He would always draw himself up to his full height and refused to take any nonsense from anyone. As you'd expect from someone who had grown up in the rough and tumble inner Sydney suburbs, he also had the gift of the gab, the smart quip, the tough guy line to unsettle intruders. He was perfectly suited to the most devious position on the rugby field – the scrum-half spot. To be a good half-back, you not only had to be a proficient footballer, but also a bit of a con man, a sweet-talker around referees, insolent when required and know how to make the most of any opportunity.

And if there was a scrap, often the case in the unruly world of sub-district football, Snowy was naturally right in the middle of it. He might have been among the tiniest on the field, but opposition teams soon discovered not to mess with him. His right jab was devastating. Opponents generally did not come back for a second dig.

Like Dally Messenger, it didn't take long for Snowy to be lured to one of Sydney's more reputable clubs, which had formed to be part of the new district grade competition.

The Eastern Suburbs Rugby Club boasted impressive connections in the sporting, political and social fields from the start. It was the haven for the more notable names of Eastern Suburbs society, who wanted to be part of Sydney's most flourishing winter sporting code. When the club was formed at the Paddington Town Hall in March 1900, the audience was dominated by politicians, aldermen, influential administrators and journalists, including E.S. Marks and J.C. Davis.

Davis was one of Australia's most notable sports writers, using the nom de plume 'Not Out' for his cricket writing, and 'The Cynic' for the latest football news in *The Referee*. He was prolific, everywhere and had impeccable sources. He was smart enough to know that you had a better chance of getting a scoop story if you were inside the meeting rather than waiting outside with the rest of the hacks. Being a club delegate to the NSW rugby and cricket associations also helped him get the big stories.

Marks had his hands in so many sports following a fruitful athletic career and his involvement in the formation of many sporting bodies including swimming, boxing, wrestling, surfing, billiards, coursing and athletics. He later became a touring manager at the Olympic and Empire Games and travelled with the first Wallaby rugby union team, which toured Great Britain in 1908.

Both were nest hens, hoarding away everything that came their way, to the extent that their vast sporting collections, donated to the State Library of New South Wales on their deaths, would easily fill a museum. In both collections are some of the most valuable Australian sporting memorabilia items, plus numerous vital works, books, articles, photographs, scrapbooks and oddments.

Davis actively supported the motion for the formation of an Eastern Suburbs club, and Marks was appointed to the general committee to ensure the new organisation had solid footing. Their involvement ensured a bevy of politicians in the president and vice-presidential ranks, and the Governor of New South Wales, Sir Frederick Darley, the inaugural club patron.

For anyone who wanted to be anyone in Sydney this was the football club to join. They had power, influence and money, demonstrated by being the first club to complete all payments to be eligible for the opening round of matches in the 1900 season. But it wasn't entirely gold carpet treatment. For their first match at Rushcutters Bay Oval, Easts players had to chase seagulls off the field before they could kick off against Newtown.

Easts' off-field might was matched by the calibre of their on-field talent, interspersed with some extraordinary characters. In their inaugural line-up against Glebe, played at the Sydney Cricket Ground, were many identities who were all intimate with Snowy's sporting skills, especially his boxing prowess. In the first-grade team was forward Frank Underwood, who doubled as the NSW Boxing Association Secretary. He also ran the NSW Sports Club, which organised the state boxing titles. And in reserve grade that day was Lou D'Alpuget, Snowy's opponent in the state boxing final.

Another notable figure appearing in the Easts colours was Harry 'Jersey' Flegg, who later became a crucial figure in the formation of the breakaway NSW Rugby League. Stan Rowley, the 1900 Olympic athlete who only had to amble around the track to win a gold medal, was another lured to the club, adding glamour to the Easts back line.

With so many movers and shakers in the club, they soon became the most active recruiters in the competition enticing players from everywhere — from other teams, from the country, from the suburbs and even New Zealand.

In 1902 the whisper had gone around the Easts Club to get to Centennial Park and watch Snowy. Snowy was known intimately to a good many Easts members, primarily because of his swimming and boxing feats, but few were aware of his vast footballing skills.

One game was enough to have Easts officials making numerous visits to the Baker Darlinghurst household in a bid to persuade him to lift his sights and play grade football. Snowy loved the attention, played hard to get for a short period, but eventually agreed to join Easts for the start of the 1903 season.

Easts went in hard to get Snowy, because apart from knowing that he had the capabilities of becoming a representative player, the first-grade team was struggling appreciably at the time. The 1902 season had been miserable, primarily because they'd lost so many players through injury. At half-back they tried a bevy of sub-standard performers, including one with the apt surname of Hogflesh. Easts were deeply embarrassed and the recruiting net for 1903 went far, luring through the strong club network Queensland Test forward Paddy Carew, who was enticed to Sydney with the promise of a first-grade cricket and football spot, and Baker's swimming mate Cecil Healy, while on the club membership list H.H. 'Dally' Messenger's name was added.

For Snowy, even though the club boasted an assortment of stars, he was immediately graded into first-grade, joining up with his old boxing rival D'Alpuget as the Easts half combination. But it was Snowy who received all the attention, with several newspapers making note of Baker, 'better known in athletic circles and an amateur swimmer and boxer', having moved from the Warrigals to Easts.

After his opening grade match against Glebe at University Oval, *The Referee* commented: 'Baker, one of the new backs, shaped well at half, but lost his side much ground through hanging on, and putting the ball into the scrum carelessly.'

Just a few rounds later, *The Referee* wrote that during the win over Western Suburbs, 'the new Eastern Suburbs half-back, R. Baker, quite apart from his "snowy" head, was one of the most prominent men on the field.

'Defensively he was great, always in the thick of the struggle. His quickness in tackling was one of the features of back play of the match. In attack he is energetic and resolute, but must guard against plunging back into the pack with the ball.

'It is all right when men have broken up, but while the scrummage is still formed it is punishable by a free kick to carry the ball back into the scrum. Baker is a very dangerous customer near the line.'

As in his suburban days, he was prepared to mix it and show off his pug side if life on the field became testy. Rugby union may have been the domain of the aristocratic amateur, with its history steeped in the English Public School system, but in the rough and tumble outpost of Sydney, the club competition soon developed a reputation for wild outbursts of aggression.

Sydney's most important football competition was not the place for shirkers. Wild play and unruly spectators were so common at the grade games that the Inspector General of Police agreed to provide plain-clothes constables at most grounds.

One player was attacked by a spectator swinging a two-metre paling. On the field, many players were knocked out cold in back play, often with a gutless king hit. A referee, who had been heckled by players and spectators all through the game, suddenly produced a pistol out of the pockets of his shorts, waved it above his head and threatened to use it if he suffered any more abuse. Forwards would fill their pockets with pepper and fling it in the eyes of their opponents as soon as a scrum was set. It was as fierce on the other side of the field markings, with club officials keeping the rabble on the sideline from intruding onto the field by hitting them with small pieces of sapling that doubled as an effective cane.

Judiciary hearings were also frightening affairs, with police escorts often required to get the rugby counsellors safely through the angered hordes who had been waiting for hours outside the meeting room to hear the verdict.

In his autobiography *Viewless Winds*, the first Wallaby captain Paddy Moran said the grade competition was 'always a form of local warfare'.

'When you sank on the ball to stop a dribbling rush, half-a-dozen feet rattled on you like heavy knocks at a door which would not open. Sometimes in a distant suburb when you fell out of bounds the local partisans affectionately trod on you. Both sides, indeed, were accorded the status of belligerents,' Moran wrote.

Moran recalled how front-row forwards would grow beards before games and 'thus armed at all points would rub their faces against the newly shaven cheeks of their opposite numbers ... Sometimes they added onions to their luncheon diet, so what with the sour smell of unwashed jerseys, that had been lying all the week in a locker, and the heavy odour of men's sweaty bodies, the atmosphere of the scrums was pungent'.

There were also lighter moments. One first-grade match was stopped when the referee had to order the captain off for rough play. The captain refused to leave the field, threatening the referee that if he pushed the issue he would punch him on the nose.

Suddenly a woman pushed her way through the crowd and confronted the referee. 'Don't you mind him, sir,' she cried. 'He's only a trifle bad tempered, and he'll be sorry for it later. Watch me settle him.' And turning to the captain, she added, peremptorily, 'Jack, tha're a' fool, an' tha knows it. Come off t' field at once, or I won't marry thee.' Without another word Jack followed his girl to the ropes, and the game was resumed amid the ironical laughter of the delighted spectators.

Snowy stayed out of the way of referees and demanding women, but was soon getting bashed around, often being dragged into rucks and getting an uncivilised shoeing from opposition forwards. But he was more often too evasive to get caught and by mid-season found himself getting the attention of not just the Eastern Suburbs followers.

Gradually as Easts pushed their way to the top of the competition ladder, several new faces began arriving at their games – impressive looking gentlemen, who doubled as the NSW team selectors. They were looking for players to appear in the Waratah colours for an end-of-season four-match tour of Queensland, and their prime targets were those who could add some cheek and drive to their sometimes erratic attack.

New South Wales had been tussling with Queensland since 1882, but the interstate fixtures had suddenly increased in importance with Australia finding itself opposition on a regular scale at the international level.

After Australia played its first rugby Test in 1899 against a touring British side, there had been a four-year break before another national team ran onto the field. That came when New Zealand made its first official appearance in Australia in 1903 for the inaugural Trans Tasman Test held at the Sydney Cricket Ground in August.

Anticipation was high. According to J.C. Davis in *The Referee*, rugby had 'jumped into the hearts of the people; its intercolonial contests are far greater events than those of the southern states and its internationals are something that can never be realised by the Victorian game'.

Snowy was at the Sydney Cricket Ground that day, wanting to be part of a historic crowd witnessing the rise of a new international power. Instead it was a rude awakening as Snowy soon realised that while New South Wales and Queensland rugby may have rated itself the toughest of cauldrons, the Australian brand was still a long way behind the rest of the world, mainly because it was all adrenaline and no science. New Zealand humiliated them, winning 22–3.

After the game it was all gloom. In its report on the Test, the *Sydney Mail* said: 'Will we ever be able to put a genuine Australian team in the field, whether Rugby, Australian or soccer? I am sure never at Rugby . . .'

The Australian half-back that day was Queenslander Austin 'Grally' Gralton, who had now suffered successive international defeats behind the home pack. The Australian selection panel, then dominated by New South Welshmen, knew they had to start looking for alternatives.

The New South Wales side were also eager to experiment, using four different halves in a succession of matches against Queensland and New Zealand in Sydney, matches that drew crowds of between 10 and

30 thousand spectators. Even midweek New South Wales matches were drawing large crowds, not surprising when the Queensland opposition included such drawcards as full-back Bertie St John who only had one arm.

This impediment did not stop St John from marking anything that came his way, while being fearless in defence. It also didn't stop him from becoming a Queensland tennis champion and representing Brisbane in cricket.

As the club season was drawing to a close, the New South Wales selectors were attracted to Easts fixtures, especially as they needed to win the final few matches to be premiers ahead of Glebe. On the sideline, they couldn't help notice a head-strong young half-back who wanted to be involved in everything. His name was marked down and highlighted shortly after when the selectors were told that two back line players were unavailable for the Brisbane trip. There was now an opening to select the untried Snowy.

One day Snowy, with the rest of the Easts players, received a medal at a banquet held at Schneiders Cafe in George Street for his involvement in a premiership winning team after losing just two of their 13 matches. The next day he received a letter from the NSW Rugby Union inviting him to join the state team for its Queensland tour.

There was no hesitation in accepting.

Snowy was so excited that on the day of the train trip to Brisbane, he walked, with football kit over his shoulder, from home to Central Station. There he was greeted by a select group of footballers, headed by Stan Wickham, who had led Australia against New Zealand a few weeks before, and clubmates J.W. Maund, P.V.J. Macnamara and E.L. Buchanan, who had also been picked.

Intermingled with the players was a huge group of hangers-on, all dressed in official New South Wales blazers. Suddenly Snowy discovered the other side of rugby. The large gravy train. As J.W. Maund explained about the Brisbane jaunt: 'There seemed to be as many officials as players on the trip. The officials ate oysters and drank whisky on the train but the players didn't get any.' And there wasn't much time in Brisbane for frivolity, as four games had been scheduled against Queensland, Brisbane and Toowoomba in the space of just nine days. Adding to the tension was that the New South Wales team soon found themselves surrounded by controversy.

Snowy kept his head down and his state debut was exemplary, with his fine service from the scrum and change of options helping New South Wales to an opening 11–3 win over Queensland. He was involved in all of New South Wales' three tries, either providing the pass or directing play to the required area of the field.

Despite his inexperience, Snowy took no time to show his authority, keeping the referee on edge with his constant barking and shouting orders to his forwards. The smallest was also the loudest – as was expected from any self-respecting half-back.

The Sunday Times said that Snowy 'worked the scrum well and used his foot with judgment, but was penalised several times for illegally picking the ball out'.

That was a relatively staid game, but the tension intensified midweek when their match against Brisbane turned into a fiery affair. In the New South Wales pack was the talented but feisty Newtown backrower Harold Judd, who had already tested out the New Zealanders with some several well-aimed punches, one of which saw opposition forward Rupert Cooke sent off after he retaliated. Judd always stood his ground.

But not so impressive was how Judd took offence at his Brisbane opponent, Mickey Dore, and according to one report 'pummelled' into him. Although referee Bill Beattie warned Judd, he opted against sending him from the field.

After the game, Beattie, who was designated to officiate the second New South Wales–Queensland match three days later, made it known that if Judd played, he would not be the match referee.

Beattie wrote to the New South Wales management that he wanted to bring to their notice Judd's 'disgraceful conduct'. Beattie explained that in his capacity as a member of the Queensland Rugby Union Executive, he was in the position of being a host to the New South Wales team, which 'restrained' him from sending Judd off. As New South Wales had asked him to be the referee for the Queensland return match, he would only accept on one proviso – that Judd did not play.

The New South Wales management promised Beattie that Judd would not be picked. But that changed overnight when officials discovered they would have a player revolt on their hands if Judd was not in the starting list. They were told if Judd didn't play, neither would most of his team-mates.

The New South Wales management backed down and picked Judd. Beattie refused to have anything to do with the game and in desperation, Queensland called on its illustrious player Poley Evans to be referee.

Not surprisingly Queensland came out full of bluff and bluster, and for a time upset their opponents. But gradually Queensland deflated and New South Wales gained control in midfield, where Wickham excelled. By the end of the game, Wickham boasted all of New South Wales' points, through either tries or penalties, in a 12–5 triumph. Snowy again received special mention for providing the required service from around the forward base. *The Sunday Times* said Baker 'passed and tackled well'.

A jaunt to Toowoomba for a 16–9 victory against the local team and the unbeaten New South Wales team were then on their way home to Sydney, their officials most delighted that they had at last found a half-back of note. So enthused were they with Snowy that he was even offered a few oysters on the train trip home.

Chapter 4

The Real Test

THE DOWNSIDE TO SNOWY'S ELEVATION TO THE NEW SOUTH WALES RUGBY team was that he was unable to defend his state boxing title that year. The 1903 NSW amateur titles coincided with the rugby team's trip to Brisbane, forcing Snowy to be a late withdrawal. Through his heavy schedule, something had to give and reluctantly it was boxing this time around.

Snowy was accustomed to sacrifices, his busy sporting life prompting him to have a limited social life as he was usually in bed by 8 pm. Unlike most 19 year olds, who boasted a string of girlfriends, Snowy didn't have time, or the energy, to flirt. He didn't seem too bothered about it as he was obsessed with what he thought were bigger prizes, and he was getting enough emotional satisfaction from the competitors and organisers he fraternised with in the various sports he was involved in.

Instead he was driven by the sheer joy of competition. This was instilled in him at an early age from his father and emphasised when he and his brothers, Fred and Harold, also began making a name for themselves in various athletic pursuits. Fred, Snowy and Harold encouraged each other and, as with most families, wanted to outdo each other. Fred was a handy swimmer and fighter and he pushed Snowy along, while their younger brother Harold kept them all honest, especially Snowy who started showing off from an early age that he was outstanding in the water. All wanted to prove themselves to their mentor, their father. The tussle to be the favoured son saw them attack their sporting pursuits with relish.

But for Snowy, there were even higher motives and more obsessive drives. He looked upon his sporting prowess as a way of getting ahead in the world and making a name for himself. Of all the sons, Snowy was easily the most ego driven. He was also the most focused.

Even though only involving himself in amateur sporting pursuits at that time, where allegedly it was difficult to make any money out of your abilities, Snowy soon realised that these events attracted the movers and shakers of Sydney and that invaluable contacts could be made. It wasn't long before he knew most of the established names of Sydney society, who said that they would finance him and help him achieve his aim of international success. This would come in the way of private sponsorship if he wanted to head overseas and prove himself as a boxer, while also being actively involved in public subscriptions, which would give him the added funds required to take on the world.

Snowy was very smart, focusing on those sports and organisations that were the private fancy of those who made an impact in Sydney. He was obsessed with proving himself overseas and this was the way to do it. Becoming pals with those in the money who could get him there was imperative. He wasn't pushy, instead using gentle persuasion, dropping into conversation every now and again how he wanted to go that next step but was worried that a lack of funds may curtail his dream. He tugged at the emotions of those who loved nothing else than being seen with, or fraternising with, a promising sporting star.

In between his swimming, diving, boxing and football ventures, Snowy found time to join the Royal NSW Lancers. The pomp, ceremony and flash of this military regiment, which began in 1885 as the Voluntary Cavalry Corps, appealed to Snowy, especially as it was only part-time and it gave him the opportunity to hone his skills on 'fine horseflesh'. Just as importantly, it also brought him into contact with the right people. Adding to the allure was that their headquarters were just around the corner from the Baker household at the Moore Park Rifle Range in Paddington.

The Lancers, with their impressive steeds and showy dress uniforms, were always in the public eye, either participating in tournaments, displays, highland gatherings, or escorting Lord Hopetoun to various ceremonies, including his own swearing-in ceremony as Governor-General in Centennial Park. The Lancers attracted the upwardly mobile elite Sydney gentleman and Snowy, ever eager to network with the right people, realised the advantages of being part of an admired, high-profile organisation. He could be seen to be doing his bit for the country's defence and at the same time take advantage of all the benefits it brought.

While a well-disciplined, highly-organised military organisation, it also ensured its members were entertained through endless sporting activities. Its military tournaments involved sword duels, bayonet fights, wrestling on horseback, tent-pegging, rescue races, rifle shooting and boxing. Here was a chance for Snowy to improve on so many athletic facets. He may not have enjoyed all the endless drills, but he was soon putting his name down for every sporting endeavour the Lancers ventured into. The sporting side, rather than the military side of the Lancers appealed to Snowy.

As usual, Snowy decided not to focus on one event. He wanted to win everything, and usually did. He soon became renowned in the Lancer ranks for his horse skills, excelling at tent-pegging, mounted tug-of-war and wrestling on horseback, while his exhibitionism came to the fore when winning special medals for dashing at top speed and slicing a lemon with a glittering sabre.

Back on firm ground, Snowy was as formidable. Although he was rising up the representative rugby ladder, he didn't want to neglect his boxing. Because of the call-up to the interstate rugby ranks, he was unable to train for the NSW boxing titles. He instead focused on the NSW Lancer boxing titles.

Realising that he had some sort of advantage over most other Lancer pugs, he decided to intensify the pressure by nominating himself in the most difficult weight division. Although a lightweight, he opted for the heavyweight class, duelling fighters far older and several stone heavier than him. The weight advantage may have been against him, but a succession of victories saw him crowned the 1903 NSW Lancers Heavyweight Champion.

Another successful summer frolic at the pool, with a triumphant defence of the NSW Flying Squadron title alongside Alick Wickham, Cecil Healy, Freddie Lane and his brother Harold, before he was back on the football field getting ready for the most anticipated of international guests. New Zealand was Australia's closest international rugby foe. But in the eyes of the Australian rugby public they were not regarded as the most important. Australia's stifling links with the Mother Country saw anyone who came from the British homeland treated with overwhelming reverence.

The 1903 All Black tour was invigorating, reminding Australia they were still off the international rugby pace, but everyone knew the real test would be in 1904 when the best of British would be here for a three-Test duel.

For that reason, the Sydney and Brisbane grade games were more intensely followed, crowds increased and state and national selectors were given strict edicts from their respective bodies to find the right talent to ensure that they would at least be competitive against the masters. Adding to the tension was that the officials knew they were about to encounter the first fully representative Great Britain team to tour Australia, with more than half the squad fully-fledged internationals from England, Wales, Scotland and Ireland.

As the tourists had selected all of the Welsh wizards including renowned fly half Percy Bush, described by J.C. Davis in *The Referee* as 'a human tom tit, his opponents never knowing which way he could turn', the dark fear was that Australia was about to be humiliated.

This feeling was hardly eased when Great Britain encountered New South Wales in the opening match of the tour. The visitors, headed by the dim, dour Scot David Bedell-Sivright who had the nickname 'Darkie', not for his complexion but for his underhand playing methods, were not just resourceful, but prepared to be openly antagonistic. After all, Darkie was Scotland's heavyweight boxing champion.

They loved a brawl and proclaimed or decreed or declared on the long boat trip across that they would not be intimidated by any underhand act of trickery from the 'Colonials'. 'Colonial' was usually expressed with the nose firmly stuck up in the air.

This was a mighty but mean touring team who were to show no mercy to their hosts. One of their key forwards was Blair Swannell, who was described by Paddy Moran as being 'extremely ugly', and whose 'conception of Rugby was one of trained violence'. Swannell's personal hygiene also left a lot to be desired. An incessant bore, who continually boasted about his military conquests such as fighting among the insurrectionists in the Republic of Uruguay, Swannell would always arrive at a game in a filthy once-white sweater, bearing the badges and dates of all the countries he had represented on it. His prized possession was an also once-white pair of football breeches, which he refused to wash and wore in every match.

The team arrived in Adelaide and even though the South Australian capital had not taken to the rugby code, the players were still accorded a hero's welcome. They received the same reception in Melbourne, where just as in South Australia, the Chief Magistrate met and entertained them.

In Sydney, Central Station was crammed with well-wishers who followed the team down George Street, as they were transported to the Town Hall and a NSW Rugby Union reception, where Bedell-Sivright put a dampener on proceedings by refusing to crack a smile, stressing: 'We have come here to play football, not skittles, so we have to keep ourselves fit.'

The message was straight. Don't try to bluff us with your hospitality. We are not being distracted. The team left shortly after Bedell-Sivright's moan. Another function was organised on match eve at the National Sporting Club, which attracted everyone who was anyone in Sydney. That did not stop Bedell-Sivright ending proceedings at 10 o'clock by demanding that his players leave with him for their hotel to ensure proper rest before the next match. They left the room to the accompaniment of 'great cheering'.

The New South Wales selectors remained at the function, drinking away into the early hours after picking a team which they thought could irritate the tourists for at least a short period of time. There was only one option at half-back – Snowy was still far and away the best scrum-half in Sydney and the poise shown during his New South Wales trip to Brisbane had enthused the selectors. What was required against the Brits was some snap and cheek and Snowy definitely had both of those in abundance.

Mindful that the Brits loved a fight and loved to intimidate, the selectors realised that it was imperative New South Wales had at least one player who could defend himself, even if he was the tiniest person on the field.

Pressure had also come from the Australian selectors to persevere with Snowy. An opening at Test level emerged after the incumbent Australian half-back, Austin Gralton, informed the Queensland Rugby Union that after a decade of representative football he was about to retire.

Snowy was cocky, and when told by New South Wales officials that if he 'kept his nose clean' he would be the next Australian half-back, he replied with a confident: 'No problems.' But behind the facade, Snowy was a nervous wreck. Arriving at the Sydney Cricket Ground and seeing it crammed with 35,000 spectators didn't help.

NSW Rugby Union officials knew their team didn't have much hope, but were ecstatic all the same. After all, they had just come to an agreement with the Sydney Cricket Ground Trustees where the NSW Rugby Union was to receive 85% of the gate receipts. All they had to pay was the 'gateman's wages'. As the players weren't paid, the British tour was a financial windfall, especially as they had struck an agreement with their Queensland counterparts that they finance the overall visit. To have the team in Brisbane later in the tour, Queensland had to agree to give New South Wales '50% of the profits or 300 pounds in cash'.

No wonder the New South Wales heavies were handing out cigars in the Member's Reserve shortly before kick-off in the tour opener.

Downstairs in the dressing rooms the players weren't so animated. Snowy was sitting by himself in a quiet corner, trying to get himself in some sort of condition for his biggest sporting moment. This was not exactly a friendly frolic down at the Domain pool, or a three-round ding-dong with a mate in the boxing ring. He was about to face supposedly the best footballers in the world.

Snowy was overawed, as was the *Sydney Mail* correspondent. He wrote: 'The scene, viewed from the centre of the playing area, was magnificent. The rich colours of the fair sex, occupying pavilions and grandstand, presented a charming picture, long to be remembered, and one that came as an eye-opener to our visitors from the British Isles, whose praise is sufficiently expressed in the words of Mr Bedell-Sivright, the British captain: "It was a most brilliant spectacle, it is a magnificent ground", and referring to the match "The game was a particularly pleasant one".'

Understandably so, considering that Britain totally humiliated the hosts 27–nil, scoring five tries. *The Referee* noted gloomily: 'Their display proves beyond any shadow of doubt that as far as Australia is concerned theirs will be a march to the music of victory. They are too clever and brilliant, and too ably organised for our teams. "What do you think of them?" said an old footballer to an old comrade. "The best I have ever seen," was the reply.'

The *Sunday Sun* glumly started its report with: 'NSW rugby players have still a lot to learn.'

New South Wales tried again a week later and at least this time, in front of 30,000 spectators, scored. Snowy was far more prominent, mixing up his game with several excellent clearing kicks in the first half, and passes which enabled the team to finish with two tries. Unfortunately Britain scored seven, for a 29–6 triumph.

The *Sunday Sun* analysed Snowy's game in its report, and while believing he was a certainty for Test selection, were concerned about some glaring frailties including that he failed miserably in attack. 'Baker is unable to get his three-quarters moving. Whenever he secured the ball from the scrum he stood still when passing it back. Consequently the man to whom the ball was being sent was also stationary, and in almost every instance he was downed before he had an opportunity of even getting in a kick.

'On almost every occasion the three-quarters were started so slowly that they found an almost hopeless task ahead of them. Not only were they called upon to beat the opposing three-quarter, but the forwards also had time to swarm down upon them, with the inevitable result that the enemy was too strong.

'But Baker's defence is so good that his services, at any rate against the Englishmen, are invaluable. For that reason he will be persevered with.'

Before the two-match series, New South Wales were hopeful of dominating the Test team, but their collapse in front of the tourists forced the selectors to bring in seven Queenslanders in the hope of avoiding another humiliation.

But Snowy, although chastened by the *Sunday Sun* barb, was safe, being picked at scrum-half for his first official national sporting representative appearance. With him in the Australian team, which played in the light blue jerseys of New South Wales with an impressively large waratah on the left breast, were several peripatetic footballers. Centre Charlie Redwood hailed from Toowoomba, while forward Bill Richards was beckoned from the flourishing far north Queensland gold town of Charters Towers. Pat Walsh meanwhile sought leave from the Newcastle railway station, where he worked as a porter, so he could make the trip to Sydney.

In charge was Queenslander Frank Villeneuve Nicholson and underneath him were an eclectic mix, which included medical students, wharf labourers, clerks, beach inspectors and gold prospectors.

Also in the team were Dinny Lutge and Alex Burdon, who would be instrumental in the breakaway movement to rugby league.

The Australian team was rated no chance. As the *Sydney Mail* wrote: 'It is almost a national calamity that Australia at rugby is represented simply by New South Wales and Queensland. Our opponents are drawn from four countries, England, Scotland, Ireland and Wales. Our resources are decidedly limited. Just think what would be the effect if we could draw upon all the States of the Commonwealth. We are a long way behind Great Britain, and I might just as well say — for it is probably in the mind of the reader — New Zealand. The climactic conditions of both countries are more favourable to a strong winter game than are those of Australia, especially Queensland.'

Nonetheless the Australian players were relatively relaxed before kick-off as they sat in the rooms waiting for the Vice-Regal Military Band, under the baton of Mr L. de Green, to finish their repertoire of marching tunes. Not much was expected of the Australians, so they knew if they did anything of note it would cause wild excitement. As everyone was anticipating a lopsided Test, they could be daring. They apparently had nothing to win, or lose.

In front of 34,000 people, including the Governor, Sir Harry Rawson, and the Archbishop of Sydney, Australia surprised everyone early by containing Britain, to the extent that at half-time the score was deadlocked at nil-all. And if Australia had properly used their chances, they could even have been ahead, as several times they came close to the opposition try-line. The crowd was astounded by Australia's unexpected pluck and courage, with Snowy, according to the *Sydney Morning Herald* 'earning loud applause for breaking through the scrum'.

Taking note of the *Sunday Sun*'s criticisms, Snowy attempted to show off his attacking prowess and give his backs something to use.

But Australia's over-excitement and inability to finish off a move, including one where Snowy in open space made the break putting Burdon away, proved crucial.

In the end the Baker move was fatal for Australia. After Snowy's pass went through four Australian hands just on half-time, winger Charlie White was away, but collapsed when he tried to fend off his opposite Willie Llewellyn. Llewellyn was dazed, but White had to be helped from the pitch with a broken rib. At that time replacements were forbidden, forcing Australia to play with one man less.

As the teams left for the break, the crowd ecstatically cheered the Australian side for not ridiculing themselves. Some were even muttering about whether they were about to witness one of the great upsets.

As 'The Cynic' wrote in *The Referee*: 'The first half of the Test match was as fine a display of rugby football as anything we have seen in Sydney for some years.'

But when the Australian team returned for the second half there was confusion within the crowd. The *Sydney Morning Herald* had a reporter on the Hill at the Sydney Cricket Ground who explained that a chorus of 'a couple of hundred voices' enquired of Baker: 'What's the matter with White, Snowy?'

'"Snowy" rubbed his ribs, and the crowd gathered that the player had sustained damage to that portion of his anatomy,' the *Herald* explained.

'It was a shivery day for the hill dwellers,' the *Herald* added. 'The smoke haze from many pipes did not dwell so persistently before the game of those in the shilling reserve as in previous matches. A derrick, with a pile of stones, used for the reconstruction of the wall that had tumbled into the Royal Agricultural Society's ground, formed a point of vantage from which many could see, while they buttoned up against the wind that came off the snow.'

As White sat dazed in the dressing room, getting attention, Snowy was also soon groggy and disorientated. Snowy had burrowed his head into the bottom of the ruck one too many times and had been kicked blatantly in the face by a British forward. He reeled out of the ruck holding the side of his head, which had just been used as a football.

A few minutes earlier on the Hill, the call went out as Snowy dived at the bottom of the feet of three marauding British forwards: 'Snowy'll get his head kicked off.' 'No,' yelled another lair, 'no fear they don't kick in the head, them blokes.'

The British forwards, as expected, showed no mercy, particularly when they saw the familiar face of a pesky opponent just sitting there waiting to be booted. As usual, Swannell was there first and did an elaborate tap-dance on Snowy, followed by several other toey British forwards.

Snowy was suffering from double vision and had the most hideous of headaches, but had no alternative except to continue on. Australia were in enough trouble with just 14 men against Britain's 15. Losing another would be suicidal for the home team. Adding to the pressure was that Britain had the benefit of a strong breeze in the second half.

It didn't take long for the numbers, breeze and overall conditioning of the British team to win out. Australia began to tire, with the British backs enjoying the extra space out wide, particularly on the wing where the home team had no-one in counter defence. Through careful passing, overlaps were inevitable.

Three second-half tries followed and Australia left the ground, not exactly humiliated, but still suffering from a one-way 17–nil loss.

The press was kind, with *The Referee* remarking: 'The Australians made an infinitely better showing than is indicated by the scores.'

Snowy was the only Australian player to be singled out by 'The Cynic' in *The Referee*. 'Baker, who worked the scrummage, was the strongest defender among the Australian backs. He has made the most of his chances to perform in big football, and is improving every match, especially in his power to combine in attack with the other backs, once the ball gets into the open.'

The *Sunday Sun* correspondent, an early critic of Snowy, also praised him. 'Of the backs, Baker played the game for which he is now famed. On innumerable occasions he fearlessly dropped on the ball, but it is doubtful, by the way, if he would be allowed to do this if the rules were strictly interpreted. As a matter of fact, falling on the ball should be followed by a free kick.'

But Snowy had no time to relax, sit back and gloat about the positive press reports. He had to head straight back to the gym, because just five days after his first Test appearance Snowy had an appointment at the National Sporting Club in the city where he was entered in the middleweight division of the NSW Amateur Boxing Championships.

Even in the lead up to the Test, Snowy would sneak off after every Australian team training, back to Woolloomooloo and the home gym where he spent the night hours finetuning his boxing manoeuvres in front of his loyal teachers Arthur Scott and George Seale.

After the Test, he was really in no condition to continue bashing his head around. The success of the British forwards in almost kicking his head from his body saw him suffering with blurred vision and an uncontrollable migraine for several days. Just putting on his boxing gloves made him wince.

But he said nothing to either Scott or Seale, as they would have immediately withdrawn him from the state titles because of the obvious dangers to his health. Snowy didn't want to be regarded as a wimp and mindful of the publicity he would receive if he could double up in another prestigious sporting event in less than a week after representing Australia, decided to tell no-one and fought a solo pain battle.

He was still seeing double on the first day of competition, but it didn't stop him from being relentless in the ring. Moving up into the middleweight class, Snowy, described in *The Referee* as the 'well-known footballer and ex-champion swimmer', made short work of his first two opponents. First Snowy 'made a punching bag' out of W. Edgar, before accounting easily for his next opponent, A. Carter.

The Referee also noted the major improvement in Baker's repertoire. It even suggested that it was time for Snowy to contemplate getting serious about boxing and join the flourishing professional ranks. *The Referee* said Baker 'shaped' more like a professional than an amateur and would make a name for himself in the near future if he 'decides to go after coins instead of medals'.

Snowy was not the only Baker to hit the headlines at the titles. His elder brother Fred was successful in winning the NSW Lightweight Championship, prompting *The Referee* to remark that he was a boxer built like the famous fighter Bob Fitzsimmons.

For some time, Baker had been toying with the idea of turning professional. And *The Referee* remark had him pondering again. Although the boxing circuit was not flourishing at the time, as it would do a decade later, it was still a thriving business, with a host of venues in Sydney, which could lure capacity crowds week in, week out and offer substantial prize money. Boxing was establishing itself in Sydney as the sport of the real people, and numerous pugs succeeded, for a short period at least, to live the high life through the high-stake money.

However Snowy, now 20, knew that if he went professional, so many other sporting outlets, including rugby football, would be placed well out of reach. If he was 'tainted' by making money from boxing, he would have been deemed a professional sportsman and unable to continue playing many sports, in particular rugby, which were strictly amateur. Rugby officials rammed down the throats of those involved in the sport that anyone found taking money to play the game would be treated the same as a criminal, with dire effects. They would be ostracised, ridiculed and cast aside. Rugby was *the* amateur game.

As Snowy was eager to achieve so much in as many fields as possible, in the end there was simply no question. He had to remain an amateur, because it opened up so many fields.

Through the strong contacts made in the rugby, swimming and boxing worlds, Snowy was able to secure a promotion to the reasonably well-paid position of engineering draughtsman with the Colonial Suger Refining Company (CSR) in Ultimo. The money was good, he was still living at home so his expenses were minimal and the company was also flexible enough to allow him to disappear now and again to represent whoever, whenever. Just as long as he kept mentioning CSR if approached by any pesky sports writers.

He was soon at his supervisor's door, asking for a few days off so he could continue representing Australia in rugby in the Second Test in Brisbane. The company agreed, especially as the Australia–Great Britain series was now headline news after the tourists headed to Newcastle and into controversy when they became the first team of note to walk off during a game.

Britain were well in control of their match against Northern Districts when early in the second half the referee, Hugh Dolan, ordered the visiting front-rower, Denys Douglas Dobson, from the field claiming he had used abusive language when questioning one of his decisions. A seething and ever combative Bedell-Sivright reacted immediately, signalling to his men and leading them all from the field.

Adding to the team's ire was that as they left the field, a group of small boys followed them pelting the players with mud and stones as they sprinted towards their dressing shed.

After a half-hour delay and numerous meetings between the British team management and the referee, with the tourists demanding that Dobson be allowed to continue playing, the game was resumed without Dobson. Britain won 17–3.

Bedell-Sivright was roundly castigated for his actions. But he laughed it all off, repeatedly arguing his innocence, claiming that Dobson had not used an offensive expression. In the NSW Rugby Union Board minutes it was later alleged that Dobson had said to the referee: 'What the devil was that for?'

all were having a grand time Reg

A young Reg 'Snowy' Baker *(centre row, fourth from left)* with friends at a picnic at Bondi Beach.

(Photo: Author's collection)

The famous East Sydney Flying Squadron swimming team. *Back row:* Harold Baker and Freddie Lane. *Front row:* Cecil Healy, Alick Wickham and Snowy.

Snowy showing off one of his dives at a Harbour pool. (Photo: Author's collection)

The 1904 Australian Test team with Snowy *(front row, first on left)*. (Photo: Author's collection)

Snowy Baker as he appeared at the 1908 Olympic boxing competition.

(Photo: Author's collection)

Snowy *(third from left)* with the diving team which travelled through Europe in 1908.

(Photo: Author's collection)

Hugh D. McIntosh or Huge Deal
as he was affectionately, and sometimes
not so affectionately, known.
(Photo: Author's collection)

Snowy introduced to the
crowd at the Sydney Stadium.
(Photo: Author's collection)

INTRODUCING "SNOWY" BAKER.

The Norman Lindsay poster of the Burns–Johnson fight. (Photo: Author's collection)

Snowy Baker Stadium, 1913. Dave Smith and Jerry Jerome are about to start battle. Snowy is standing in the right aisle. (Photo: Courtesy Arnold Thomas)

An advertisement in *Snowy Baker's Magazine*. (Author's collection)

Les Darcy and Snowy
meet on the steps of
Baker Stadium.
(Photo: Author's collection)

A group of boxers at Frenchs Forest building homes for Australian soldiers wounded in
the First World War. Solar Plexus (Will Lawless), Les Darcy and Snowy are in the front
row. (Photo: Author's collection)

Rugby Union Football : The "All Blacks" Victorious

Harold Baker *(third from right)* backing up for Australia against the All Blacks in 1914.
(Photo: Author's collection)

Harold Baker.
(Photo: Author's collection)

Snowy with his father, George. Standing between them is
renowned boxer Eddie McGoorty. (Photo: Author's collection)

Bedell–Sivright took the high ground, arguing that the referee's actions threw a 'reflection on the personal character of the team'. For a Colonial to do that to a group of esteemed gentlemen from the Mother Country was simply not on!

The referee was so angered that after an inquiry the NSW Rugby Union had decided against taking any action against Dobson, that 'he disqualified himself from holding any position under the Union'.

But he was not the only Australian to be disgusted by the Brits.

The drama continued a few days later when the British team arrived in Brisbane to play Queensland before the Second Test. Their reckless forward, Blair Swannell, was at it again, kicking away at any opponent who got in his way. Queensland forward, Alex McKinnon, even had to leave the field with a badly lacerated head after being relentlessly stomped on by Swannell.

Swannell was roundly jeered by the crowd, earning their wrath even more the following week when he wrote a lengthy letter to *The Referee* defending his 'dirty play'. This volatile correspondence did nothing to endear Swannell or his British team-mates to the Queensland public. When the British side ran out for the Second Test at the Exhibition Ground, a section of the crowd booed Swannell when he came into sight.

A series of special upcountry trains from Ipswich, Toowoomba and towns further north had pushed the crowd past the 16,000 mark, enthused that the Australian selectors had stuck true to the local players by picking seven locals, including in the centres their esteemed sprinter from the western districts, Doug McLean.

Luckily the selectors had chosen plenty of Queensland home blood, because due to a mess-up in the team travel arrangements the rest of the team were in disarray on match day. Stan Wickham, who had taken over the captaincy, was smart and left for Brisbane from Sydney a week before the game. However, the rest of the New South Wales contingent followed like lost cows. The next group, which included Snowy, arrived three days before the Test, but full-back, Jack Verge, and five-eighth, Jack Manning, both struggled to get away from their day jobs and didn't arrive in Brisbane until 9.20 pm on match eve.

Adding to all the confusion were the strange scenes on the Brisbane platform when Snowy's contingent arrived. New South Wales front-rower, Alex Burdon, boasted the nickname 'The Baron', and according to *The Town and Country Journal*, 'a wire was dispatched to the northern capital giving information that a Baron was coming with the NSW players.

'Great excitement was caused, and many prominent persons attended at the station to do honour to "The distinguished visitor." There was much rushing about on the arrival of the train, but no Baron could be found. Eventually it dawned on the player that he was the person concerned. Explanation, it is said, followed, and with a single exception, all laughed in a hearty manner over the little joke.'

But the *Sydney Mail* correspondent didn't find any of the haphazard travelling schedule funny: 'Did we use our best endeavours to put the Australian team into the field under such conditions as made for victory, or, in other words, did we not ride for a fall? There is nothing like combination; nothing like training together.'

This Australian team couldn't have a training session because they didn't have a full team until match day.

'How could we get combinations under such circumstances?' the *Sydney Mail* queried. 'Hence all the more reason for arranging for a week's hard work together prior to such important fixtures as Test matches.'

As the team, which included six new caps, were still introducing themselves to each other on the way to the ground, they again had no chance. Australian rugby was still very, very amateur, badly disorganised and somehow progressing in spite of itself.

Then, the surprise to beat all surprises. Australia were the first to score when after an exchange of kicks, and a fumble by the supposedly faultless Percy Bush, Glebe waterside worker and sometimes barber, Burdon, scored, prompting the crowd to become 'quite excited'.

Burdon charged after the kick which had been directed towards the British tryline. A swarm of British players failed to regather it, prompting Burdon to dash into an opening and fall on the ball, which had bounced over the try-line.

Buoyed by their unexpected success, Australia held firm until half-time, keeping their three point lead. However everything again went into disarray in the second half, with Britain, noticing that Australia were tiring appreciably, nonchalantly scoring three tries for a conclusive 17–3 triumph.

The Brisbane *Courier* newspaper said: 'The British had the better of the play, but some faulty taking of the ball spoiled more than one chance.'

Yet again Swannell had been up to his old tricks, in the final minutes flattening Australian back-rower Pat Walsh and full-back Jack Verge. Snowy was among the first to retaliate, throwing several well-aimed lefts at Swannell, before the Australian pack gleefully came to his aid. Swannell was soon back-pedalling, until he was protected by the referee Bill Beattie, who issued him with a caution.

The *Courier* took a swipe at the most unpopular of rugby players: 'There were little bits of rough play every now and then, Swannell being the worst offender, but till the last two minutes the game was played in quite the proper spirit.'

Snowy also received special mention, being singled out by both the *Courier* and *The Referee* for his excellent defence and being a 'great rush-stopper'. As in the ring, Snowy was totally fearless on the football field, belying his small frame.

But this was not enough to save Snowy. When the Australian team was announced for the Third Test the following weekend in Sydney, Snowy's name was missing. In desperation, the Australian selectors threw the names up in the air, eventually deciding upon an extraordinary 13 positional changes. Snowy discovered he had been overlooked for New England grazier Francis 'Pony' Finley, who had joined North Sydney after representing NSW Country.

The *Town and Country Journal* found the fact that the selectors dropped eight players bewildering, while *The Referee*'s J.C. Davis was aghast. He said Snowy's exclusion was 'puzzling, inasmuch as his form in representative matches played in Sydney has been excellent, and he is reported to have shaped soundly at Brisbane'.

'In view of the superiority of the British combination, the experiment of playing two very strong defenders as halfbacks would have been justified.'

'The Cynic' countered that Snowy should have been picked alongside Finley, or the Eastern Suburbs mid-field combination of Snowy and D'Alpuget would have been far more acceptable.

'It is difficult to believe that this team will improve in any way on the form shown by Australia in either of the other two matches, or that the selectors themselves anticipate its doing so,' 'The Cynic' warned. 'Finley is one of those players who rise to the occasion, and in this instance he will need to do so to display better form than Baker has shown against the Britishers in Sydney.'

The old mates act definitely helped Finley. Apart from being an integral player in the North Sydney first XV, he also doubled as the club's honorary treasurer. All of Australia's three Sydney-based selectors, MacManamey, Henderson and Lowe, had deep North Sydney links and were strong allies of Finley's. Henderson doubled as the Australian team manager, which also helped Finley. Then again, Snowy couldn't complain about someone using the system to his own advantage, as he had always been careful to join the right clubs to meet the right people.

As expected, the new-look Australian team made no impact at all, losing 16–nil in another fiery international where the referee struggled to keep several 'ardent belligerents' in control. Finley made little impact in his one and only Test appearance.

While Britain ventured off for a short trip to New Zealand, where English forward D.H. Traill, discovered a country that was 'awfully fond of blowing their own trumpet . . . but they can play football', Snowy discovered that he was still wanted by representative selectors.

New South Wales were about to embark on their annual end–of–season tour of Queensland and the selectors compromised by picking Finley and Snowy as their half combination. Their team manager, James McMahon, was so impressed with the standard of the spirits and oysters on the train trip up that when the team arrived in Brisbane he boasted that he was in charge of the strongest rugby team ever to leave New South Wales.

It was again a strenuous schedule, with three games in one week, and the high demands eventually told on Snowy.

In the first match against Queensland, won by New South Wales 10–6 at the Gabba, Snowy showed off his first-rate kicking skills, often putting the one-armed opposing full-back, Bertie St John, under pressure with high balls, tackled himself to exhaustion and had to be revived during the second half after being knocked out by a marauding Queensland forward.

Snowy backed up mid-week against the Queensland second XV, before being an early casualty in the return game against Queensland, hobbling off the field with a damaged ankle.

Battered, bruised and unable to walk because of several months of outright battle on the football field against the Brits and Queenslanders, Snowy was starting to wonder whether boxing was a safer sporting pursuit.

Chapter 5

Further Fields

WHILE DELIGHTED THAT HE NOW BOASTED AUSTRALIAN REPRESENTATIVE status, Snowy's rugby adventures forced him to be sidelined for one of the few times in his early sporting life. Snowy's ankle injury was so debilitating that his dream to become the Australasian middleweight boxing champion had to wait a year.

Shortly after returning from Sydney, the selectors of the Australian amateur boxing team, which was about to leave for New Zealand, were at Snowy's door, enquiring whether he was fit for the voyage across the Tasman. He had to cry off. He couldn't walk, let alone get into a boxing ring.

The best way to rehabilitate was to hobble back into the swimming pool. By the end of the year, his body was back in sync, enabling Snowy to enjoy another East Sydney 500 yard Flying Squadron championship triumph with Alick Wickham, Freddie Lane, Cecil Healy and his brother Harold, knocking five and a half seconds off their own Australasian, make that world, record.

While recuperating, Snowy had time to think and to work out his priorities. Stunned that he had been overlooked for Australian selection for the Third Test, he pondered whether representative football should be his chief sporting pursuit. The injuries and batterings he had suffered had begun to take their toll and he was astounded at the great divide between the athletes – unpaid and often neglected – and the officials – so many of whom used the game to get on the gravy train and enhance their own standing. Financially, the players received nothing, and had to stick strictly to their amateur status. The officials took advantage of this, often forcing the players to pay for everything, sometimes even their own playing jerseys, while those off the field enjoyed all the perks, using the game to improve their own business interests. The money went in one direction – straight into the administrators' pockets. Naturally they hid behind the fact that they were part of an all-important national or state rugby body. But large amounts of money often went missing and it never went the way of the players. The players were instead convinced into believing that they were fortunate just to get the opportunity to play. Snowy was one of the luckier ones, latching onto a flourishing club, Eastern Suburbs, which did everything it could to keep the player costs down, supplying them with most of their required equipment. Australian rugby was starting to get itself into a strong financial position.

While besotted with rugby, and loving the camaraderie that went with being in a successful team at both club and state level, the two thrashings Snowy suffered in the Australian colours had been demoralising. To then be dropped from the Test team had hit deeply at the core of the most vain of athletes. Pride is often intermixed with paranoia and Snowy suddenly realised that he would struggle to hold onto his half-back spot at New South Wales and Australian level. He was good, constantly being praised for being 'a rare tackler ... and as hard a player for his weight as has been seen in the game'. Melbourne *Punch* magazine was particularly effusive, explaining that: 'In the opinion of those who know, there has never been a greater defensive player in the game in Australia. He was ... the idol of the crowds for his gameness and boldness.'

Touching words, but Snowy was quickly discovering that the competition for his representative spot was intense, not just from Queensland, but also among the eight Sydney clubs, as well as the vast NSW Country area. Longevity was not guaranteed.

In the boxing ring though, he reigned supreme and was fawned upon. To miss the Australasian boxing titles because of a football injury irritated him as he knew all he had to do was turn up for the boat trip to New Zealand and the title would have been his.

By the end of 1904, he decided that he would continue playing rugby at club level, but devote his representative pursuits to boxing. He told the NSW rugby selectors a few months later, when just 21, he would be unavailable for the state.

Although finetuning his responsibilities, it was still an intensely busy period for Snowy. He had become more intrigued with rowing, joining the Mercantile Club, where in his opening year he was among the winning crews in the Maiden Fours, Junior Fours, Maiden Eights and Junior–Senior Fours.

Snowy found rowing ideal for his boxing, helping to build up his upper torso, while improving his stamina. Water polo remained part of his schedule, being part of the East Sydney team, which won four successive Sydney competition premierships.

He was also on the move in the football field. Despite boasting so many representative footballers, the 1904 season was a disaster for Eastern Suburbs, dropping to fifth on the competition ladder.

Adding to Easts' despair, at the end of the year the NSW Rugby Union agreed to the introduction of a new first-grade club called Sydney whose boundaries cut deeply into what was traditionally Eastern Suburbs territory.

Consequently Easts lost eight prominent first-graders, including Test representatives Ted Mandible and Snowy, because he was living close to Kings Cross at the time. At 21, Snowy decided to move away from the family home, but only a few hundred metres down the road in a terrace house, which he shared with two of his brothers. The rent was cheap and as he wasn't wasting his spare cash on wine, women or song, he was still able to put away some savings in readiness for that big trip overseas to prove himself. Snowy lived on virtually nothing, understandable considering that his social life remained minimal. He had no interest in liquor, not only because he was obsessed with the body beautiful and had convinced himself that booze had to be avoided, but more importantly because he hated the smell and taste of the stuff. One gulp of warm beer was enough for him. He wasn't a wowser. It was simply that grog didn't appeal to him.

Besides, he just didn't have time. There were more training sessions to attend, especially as the new football club he had joined was keen to make an immediate impact. Buoyed by the highly efficient administrator E.S. Marks taking the role of Sydney Club Secretary, Snowy agreed to be an inaugural member of the club committee. The team was based around a core of Easts players and some unexpected newcomers, including the scourge of the British team, Blair Swannell, who had decided to live in Australia following the British tour.

While Easts collapsed in 1905, falling to the bottom of the table, Sydney soon established itself as a formidable middle-of-the-ladder power. Now not chasing representative honours, Snowy was allowed to show off his versatility, agreeing to fill whatever hole there was in the Sydney back line, including at full-back. Wearing the all black colours of the Old Pirates, Snowy relished the freedom.

Sydney also had no qualms about Snowy missing the occasional football training session while he focused on retaining his NSW middleweight boxing title. The sweetener was that Snowy promised a collection of Sydney players and officials good seats for the finals. It did help that the peripatetic administrator, Mr Marks, held a lot of sway at the NSW Sports Club, which were again running the state titles. Marks's many titles included being the chairman of the Sports Club.

Again it was standing room only at the National Sporting Club, with no riffraff allowed among the 2,000 plus crowd. The minimum dress code was suit, tie, cap, dress hat or bowler hat. Most patrons kept their hats on, which was no problem to the person sitting behind as the seating, on several levels, was tiered sharply.

The highlight of the opening night was the duel between George Graham, who had won the middleweight title two years earlier, and Snowy. However, just before the first round, Snowy's seconds asked that Graham's weight be checked. A set of scales were found and Graham was disqualified because he was 2½ lbs over the limit.

One serious competitor was out of the way and another soon followed when Snowy completely outclassed a certain J. Dixon, sending him 'to the boards' in the second round. The semi-finals were as lopsided with Snowy, now weighing 11 st 1¾ lbs, immediately thrashing away at E. Forest. *The Referee* reported: 'Baker sent his left straight to the face twice, and then crossed the right to the jaw, and down went Forest for seven seconds. He was no sooner up than a right again dropped him, and the referee stopped it and awarded the palm to Baker.'

The final was even easier. Snowy was up against G.F. Cox. But when his opponent came into the ring, it was discovered he had a badly-injured right hand and couldn't fight. Still there was little doubt Snowy would have won the final if Cox had been fit. He had already shown that he was far and away the classiest boxer competing in the championships.

The Referee commented: 'Snowy Baker was head and shoulders over all others in point of skill, and his boxing gives the impression that he might do particularly well as a professional. Snowy would in all probability have secured heavy-weight supremacy, as though Peter King (the winner of that division) is a strong, gritty hard-punching boxer, he lacks the quickness and the science of Baker.'

Snowy was also reminded that his endeavour, while slurred by certain sections of the general public who considered boxing barbaric, was loved by those who inhabited the right end of the city. In other words, those who had an actual say in day-to-day proceedings in Sydney.

When presenting the gold medal to Snowy, Sir Francis Suttor MLC, explained that: 'Boxing does not make the brute. The brute was there before wherever it existed, and would be here whether the man was taught to box or not.'

Sir Francis said that when he was the NSW Minister for Public Instruction, he attempted to get boxing taught on a compulsory basis in the schools, because he thought 'every boy in the country should learn the art'. But he was overruled in Parliament by the 'Wowsers'.

Snowy felt cleansed once again.

The following week Snowy was on his way to Brisbane for the Australasian championships, where the Australian team were up against five different boxers from New Zealand. In the end, Snowy fought another Australian boxer, Scanlon from Brisbane, for the middleweight title. It must have been some final, with the Brisbane *Courier* newspaper explaining that the bout was 'loudly applauded by an enthusiastic audience, who were generally of the opinion that they had seen the best display of boxing ever given in Brisbane'.

In winning the title, Snowy, according to *The Referee*, 'did the neatest head and foot movements, struck the cleanest and straightest, broke away the most promptly and gracefully, and gave admirable lessons in style, temper and endurance'.

The most lavish report was in the Christchurch newspaper, *The Canterbury Times*. Their correspondent was a sycophantic Snowyphile, writing: 'In the final, Baker (called Snowy by reason of his tow-coloured hair) completely outclassed Scanlon, who was badly punished. He tried all that a game man could do to make an impression on a wonderful two-handed fighter; but strong, active, determined and willing as he was, he was hit away with a coolness, a certainty, and a confidence that makes "Snowy" Baker the greatest boxer I have seen in the ring.

'After seeing the Sydney man perform, I should rate the man who could beat him as a marvel. And what a fine fellow he is outside his peerless position in the amateur Boxing ranks! I could tell you hundreds of stories of his kindness, his consideration, his thoughtfulness, his high character, his manliness. He is a man!'

The following year, Snowy became even more obsessed with his boxing, so much so that he even cut back his swimming pursuits with East Sydney, opting against being part of their unbeatable Flying Squadron combination.

This time Snowy, now 22, decided to enter the heavyweight division in the NSW titles and was soon boasting the 1906 belt. Snowy had now bulked up to 11 st 11¾ lbs, and was again well above the quality of the rest as shown in the final, which ended prematurely. *The Referee* reported: 'Snowy gave a fine exhibition of skilful boxing, he jabbed and staggered and landed right and left hand body blows, placing them accurately as a rule, whilst his opponent, F. Walsh, stood the gaff like a Trojan, biding his time, which came now and again, when one or more blows made impact with Snowy's face as if to remind him that there were two in it. Brave and all though Walsh shaped, the white haired chap carried much too many guns for him, and referee Harry Beckett mercifully interfered at the end of the second round.'

Baker was a first choice selection yet again in the Australian contingent in the Australasian championships, this time held at his favourite National Sporting Club arena in Sydney.

At ringside was Lionel Lindsay, the brother of artist Norman Lindsay, ecstatic that he was able to beat the mob and get a seat so he could draw a series of illustrations for *The Town and Country Journal*.

Not so lucky were many ordinary punters who couldn't find a seat, let alone get into the building for the most eagerly anticipated boxing event of the year. Hundreds had to be turned away each night, while those lucky enough to get in struggled to breathe they were so crammed into the confined space. Not helping the situation were overzealous officials, who were pushing spectators in all directions in a bid to get more into the room.

Adding to the mayhem was the announcement by the referee, Harry Beckett, that in between bouts he would fight an exhibition bout with one of the Members of Parliament in the audience, Colonel Ryrie MLA. Despite not having boxed for 18 years, the Colonel was coaxed into the ring and started bashing away at the referee. Beckett, an ex-middle and heavyweight champion of New South Wales, didn't know what hit him.

He thought it would be a lighthearted bout to calm the crowd down, but the Colonel had other ideas, knocking him to the canvas.

In the third round, the Colonel knocked out the referee. As the groggy referee was being helped to the dressing rooms, the Colonel used the moment for a bit of political grandstanding, taking the megaphone to explain that he had fought for a specific reason. Realising that a section of the public decried boxing, he wanted to show there was at least 'one representative of the people who did not hold the noble art as a degrading form of sport, but a fine, mainly elevating one'.

At that moment, the referee, vomiting all over his seconds, had other ideas. Still Beckett was revived quickly enough to return to the ring shortly after to officiate the middleweight final between Snowy and New Zealand's A.L. Nash.

The referee, still seeing double, was delighted that Snowy didn't muck around. 'Snowy was loudly cheered as he entered the ring,' *The Town and Country Journal* wrote, 'and made the pace so hot that one bout left him the victor.

'He had the "all-black" beaten from the jump, and a swiftly planned upper-cut floored the New Zealander, who failed to rise to time, and was counted out.'

The Referee reported that not even having 'the heart of a Trojan' helped Nash, especially when Snowy hit him directly on the chin. 'No-one appeared surprised when poor Nash went to the boards, and remained deaf to the count. Snowy is a fine boxer, beyond doubt. The man from across the Tasman was unlucky in being asked to beat such a brilliant exponent of the game.'

The streak of brilliance did not end there. Snowy wanted to achieve even more. Within days of his Australasian defence, he was told of an interstate duel involving New South Wales and Victoria to be held in Melbourne.

The lure was strong. The NSW titles were again up for grabs, but Snowy was also given the chance of trying out for two different divisional titles on the one night. With the coaxing of the NSW officials, in particular the team manager and old Easts rugby colleague Frank Underwood, Snowy was persuaded to enter both the middleweight and heavyweight divisions.

To help his cause, the organisers agreed to rejig the scheduling of the boxing and wrestling tournament, staging the middleweight section, comprising three rounds of three minutes each, first on the program and having the heavyweight title last on the night. This would at least give Snowy a 45 minute break in between the two events.

Snowy agreed and in late November 1906, headed for Melbourne. Many decades later, in an article in *The Sporting Globe* newspaper, one of the tournament organisers, Storky Adams, recalled the night and Snowy's impact in Victoria. 'We had heard a great deal about the prowess of "Snowy" Baker, and it was principally on his account, as a drawing card, that we felt the show would be a success,' Adams wrote. 'When the competition got under way we soon learned that Snowy was all that he was cracked up to be. He scored a double victory by defeating Scott, our very clever middleweight, and our genial heavyweight, "Block" Wardle, of the Fire Brigade.'

Snowy knocked Scott out in the second round, and then in the heavyweight bout went the distance against Wardle, although the Victorian was at a distinct disadvantage from the first round when he started to bleed heavily from the nose. Snowy won on points.

'It was a great night for Baker,' Adams went on. 'He was a whole show and a brass band. I still had my troubles that night, as the fans in their eagerness to get good seats crashed into a glass panel of the entrance doors, and Peter MacGregor, the Scottish professional wrestler, was so vociferous in his rooting for the Sydney wrestlers that I had to try and calm him down.

'Peter threatened to put a strangle hold on my boiled shirt. When I let him know that I would have him dumped bodily out of the hall by a bunch of wrestling friends in adjacent seats, he restrained his "burr" and all was well. In those days we conducted the competitions with considerable decorum.'

Snowy was the star of the tournament and revelled in the celebrations that followed where he could boast the rare achievement of winning two titles, in different weight divisions, on the same night. Few other boxers, even in the international professional ranks, could boast anything that came anywhere near that feat.

It also convinced him to go one step higher. His Australasian title triumph, and then his domination of the interstate titles, prompted interest from off-shore and the unexpected invitation for him to compete in the 1907 England Amateur Boxing Association Championships.

When the invitation for Snowy to be the Australian representative in London arrived at his home, he needed no convincing. Within days, he had alerted his superiors at CSR that he was chucking in his engineering draughtsman job and at the same time informed the Sydney rugby officials and East Sydney swimming heavies that they would have to do without him for awhile.

He was at last off to achieve his prime goal – international stardom. For so many years lazing around the East Sydney pool, he had been envious of the stories told by Freddie Lane and the Cavill brothers of their international adventures, conquests, places seen, people met, women wooed.

Snowy had followed their escapades through reports in the Sydney newspapers, which always treated their overseas triumphs in gushing terms. The tone of the reports indicated that you weren't really anyone until you had proven yourself overseas.

Australia was gradually establishing an international identity through the bush, the goldfields and the increasing cosmopolitan lure of Sydney and Melbourne. But sporting endeavours were still the prime vehicle in reminding the rest of the world, in particular the revered Mother Country, of Australia's existence. It was one of the few areas where Australia could prove they were the best in the world.

As Snowy discovered when he left Sydney for England in the final days of 1906, those with the daring to head overseas chasing sporting dreams were treated as part of a special breed – national heroes.

A fund was organised to finance Snowy's trip, with well over 150 pounds collected within the first week, including substantial donations from sporting associations, team-mates, officials and politicians. The NSW Lancers, at the request of Snowy's squadron leader, Lieutenant Phillips, pitched in with more than 28 pounds for their long-time trooper. An amount of 150 pounds was officially announced in the press, which adequately covered the travel costs to Europe, but the real amount Snowy took away with him was considerably more.

Snowy's intense networking over the last several years had been successful, with many businessmen and associates privately approaching him in the final days before he left and handing him bulky brown envelopes, which ensured that his pockets were full with English pounds.

When Snowy eventually got himself away, he discovered he had around 600 to 700 pounds in his pockets. The large pile of bills was quickly hidden away among his luggage. He could now relax, knowing that as he was mainly going to restrict his costs by staying with family and friends while away, he would be able to comfortably feed himself for a reasonable amount of time.

The night before he left on the RMS *Oroya*, the fund-raising committee held a dinner for Snowy at the NSW Sports Club, where he was described by a host of speakers as 'one of the best all-round athletes Australia has produced'. In the audience were many influential sporting identities, including Captain James McMahon, an officer in the NSW Lancers who became a highly influential rugby administrator, managing the first Wallaby tour to Great Britain two years later, and W.W. Hill, a future NSW Rugby Union President and long-time Secretary.

The following morning, several thousand people headed to Circular Quay to see Snowy off, including representatives of every branch of local amateur athletics, plus his old Easts comrade, Frank Underwood, W.W. Hill, Nat McDonald from the NSW Rowing Association and W.H. Howe, the Secretary of the NSW Metropolitan Rugby Union. Among the Baker clan on the wharf were Snowy's swimming mates Alick Wickham and Cecil Healy, plus several old Australian rugby team-mates.

From the ship's side hung a banner, which showed a life-size photograph of Snowy stripped to his shorts and showing off his impressive, muscular upper torso. With chest thrust out, hair flicked back, and the most stoic of Snowy poses, he had the look of a Greek god.

Written across the banner was: 'Our country. To her we drink, for her we pray, for her we'll fight, come what may. The Sunny South for ever.' The bottom of the banner simply said 'Au revoir'.

The Referee was there, explaining that 'great enthusiasm prevailed, and hearty indeed were the handshakes the departing champion had to submit to, and sincere the good wishes expressed by all.

'Cheers, loud and long, rent the air, while handkerchief were shaken and hats whirled round their owners' heads as the boat swung from her moorings. Then the whole company joined in "For He's a Jolly Good Fellow". It was an inspiring scene indeed, and one that the principal figure in it is not likely to soon forget.'

The *Sydney Morning Herald* described the scene as 'the finest send-off accorded to an athlete for many years'.

Adding to the excitement were 20 attractive young ladies in a small rowboat who pursued Snowy's ship until it passed through the Heads.

Similar scenes occurred when the ship picked up passengers in Melbourne, Adelaide and Perth. The banner was unfurled, and 'For He's a Jolly Good Fellow' given another airing. Snowy attempted to look bashful. It proved impossible. He was instead overwhelmed with pride, soon convincing himself that he was already a national identity.

For the next month Snowy kept himself busy on the ship, sparring with the captain, Commander Parker, and jogging relentlessly around the ship's perimeter.

In February 1907, Snowy arrived at Tilbury, but not before making a devastating mistake during the cruise. The ship had stopped at Port Said where Snowy disembarked with several passengers who headed straight to a local bar. His comrades insisted that Snowy join in on a round of whisky. But as he was a teetotaller, Snowy instead opted for two glasses of water.

For the rest of the trip, Snowy felt off colour, but tried to fight off the lethargy when he left the boat in England. He had been summonsed to London, where he was guest of honour at a National Sporting Club dinner, which preceded several bouts of amateur boxing.

After being made an honorary member of the club, Snowy was surrounded by inquisitive Fleet Street journalists who wanted to know a few facts about this supposed Australian superstar. He was, as ever, willing to play the game.

The *London Sporting Life* explained that Snowy had a two-fold object in mind – one to win the English boxing title and two to prolong his visit 'to a couple of years in order that he may improve his engineering knowledge'.

'With his bronzed complexion and gentlemanly bearing, he strikes one as being an ideal athlete,' the impressed *Sporting Life* correspondent wrote.

'Naturally I have come over to England,' Snowy said, 'with the intention of winning your middleweight championship, but I guess the quality of the boxers I shall meet will be better than those in the Colonies.'

Snowy then stuck out his chest, and began to beat it, telling *Sporting Life*: 'I have not come over expressly for the boxing, for I intend taking part in the Royal Military Tournament at Olympia, and also in some of your swimming championships. You understand, I do not stick to one sport, and I think I am just as good at swords and bayonet exercises and swimming as at boxing.'

Snowy explained that through the NSW Lancers, he had won 'many prizes at military events in Sydney, and I hope the same success awaits me at Olympia'.

'Diving I consider myself very good at, and I think I shall take part in your next championship at Highgate Ponds.'

And his tip for sporting excellence. 'I am a teetotaller and non-smoker, who likes to get to bed early at night, as one feels better the next morning.'

Accompanying Snowy to the Sporting Club was the London *Sportsman* correspondent, who 'noticing him give a shiver just before the boxing commenced, suggested we should remove to a warmer part of the theatre.

'He readily agreed, and after the show went to Waterloo. Here he had to wait some time on the platform, and while doing so complained of the cold.'

The following day at Snowy's apartment in Putney, with the new arrival deliriously ill, a doctor was called. Snowy was diagnosed with enteric fever. The two glasses of water in Port Said had been his downfall.

Chapter 6

An Olympian

Snowy's hopes of competing in the English boxing titles and showing off his many and varied skills at the Royal Military Tournament were dashed. He spent the next two months recuperating in hospital, where for the first few weeks he was on the 'gravely ill' list.

Hardly helping him was the confusion among some hospital staff over what exactly constituted an Australian. One nurse objected to her superiors when told that she had to care for an Australian called Baker, complaining that she did not believe in 'nursing a blackfellow'.

When at last well enough to write, he sent a letter to *The Referee*, which printed it in full under the headline: 'From Snowy Baker. His Condition and Prospects.'

'To travel over 13,000 miles and then to meet defeat without having a chance of putting one's hands up is pretty hard luck, to say the least of it. However, it's the old story over again: "Man proposes and God disposes",' Snowy wrote.

'One should be satisfied to accept the good with the bad or the bad with the good. Don't know that there's too much good with my little lot so far. However I feel happy in knowing that the undertaker has been defeated for a time, and that health and strength are gradually becoming my glorious possessions again, although for at least three months I will not be able to attempt any exercise of a vigorous nature, so the doctors have informed me. They have ordered me three months complete rest away from London.'

Snowy wrote that 'after being stretchered out in hospital for the first, and I hope, the last time of my life', his recollection of his first few weeks there were 'very dim'.

'After that the temperature began to drop, and so things began to brighten.'

When well enough, Snowy headed for Ireland, with the express wish to meet his family's relatives in Limerick. The trip proved the elixir, helping him back to full health. But again there was confusion whenever he mentioned he was from Australia. It remained the unknown land, far away, far forgotten.

He was often asked if Australia was dark at the same time as it was 'at Home', while a prominent medico expressed his sympathy for Australia being in the unfortunate position of having no rivers to prevent the terrible bushfires. He repeatedly had to tell people that Australia was not entirely a dry, barren desert. It actually had towns, and white people. That staggered the Irish.

In another letter to *The Referee* in July 1907, Snowy wrote: 'I've been living for the past month with relations in the old homes of my forefathers.

'This is the most beautiful part of the Emerald Isle, both from a picturesque point of view and a health resort. I'm now weighing in the vicinity of 13 stone, and feeling better than ever, although of course training or hard work of any description is out of the question yet awhile, owing to the stomach still being weak after the fever.

'However, my uncle has arranged a fine gymnasium for my use here, so I hope, when strong enough, with the aid of a few young fellows in this district who are anxiously awaiting to give me a thumping, to get back in the best of good condition.'

Snowy may have been weak and not at his best when mucking around in the gymnasium, but he soon had an avid following of local Irishmen who cheered his every move. 'The average Irishman only has to learn that you are interested in boxing, and he'll immediately take you to his heart,' Snowy later recalled. 'Whenever I think of the Irishman's desire for participation in anything to do with the "noble art", it always brings to my mind the excitable, wild type of Irishman seated in a ringside seat at the Stadium while an exciting bout was being fought. He kept jumping to his feet, and edging towards the ringside, where an usher grabbed him, and tried to put him back to his seat. The Irishman was wildly excited, and wanted to hit somebody, and asked the usher: "Was it a private fight, or could anybody join in?"'

After missing the British boxing titles, the call for Snowy to return home to Australia, as it was the only place to recuperate, especially if money was running short, began. Snowy mulled over the idea, before deciding to stay exactly where he was. 'Although having every wish to be back in sunny NSW (have not seen its equal yet) again, I cannot see the way clear for such a course until I, at least, make some attempt for victory in the athletic world. Needless to remark, remaining on this side of the line till the boxing championships come round again, which probably means next March, would be at my own expense entirely.'

Despite disappearing from public view, he was not forgotten by the local media. The *Apollo* magazine, London, mourning the fact that Snowy would miss the English boxing titles, wrote: 'He probably is one of those whom Spenser had in mind when he wrote:

In wrestling nimble, and in running swift.
In shooting steady, and in swimming strong;
Well made to strike, to leap, to throw, to lift,
And all the sports that shepherds are among.'

Opportunities eventually appeared. Invitations arrived enquiring as to whether Snowy wanted to compete in an international swimming gala in London, which involved Belgium, French, German and Swedish competitors. He was also asked if he wanted to be part of a Royal Lifesaving Society team that was to compete in Holland, Germany, Finland, Sweden and Denmark. The invitation had come from the founder of the Royal Lifesaving Society, W. Henry, so Snowy was suitably chuffed. He agreed and started devising ways of getting back in the water for some much-needed training.

'About ten minutes walk from here is a fine big lake, where I am arranging a springboard and a hundred yards swimming stretch, so I intend, if health will allow, to begin light training in a couple of weeks' time.'

By month's end, the locals were wondering who the lunatic was powering up and down their lake, and in between doing the most death-defying dives from a makeshift plank of wood into the freezing water. Snowy was getting plenty of odd looks, but it worked, enabling him to get to London in time for the carnival.

Helping his recovery was that he now had a travelling mate from Sydney. Theo Tartakover, an old East Sydney swimming club companion of Snowy's, had also decided to try out on the international circuit and joined up with him at the London tournament. Theo had immediate success, just getting beaten in the final, while Snowy, still obviously affected by his typhoid bout, finished near the back of the field.

With several months still to go before heading off for Europe with the Royal Lifesaving team, Snowy and Tartakover opted for a trip around Scotland where they'd been invited to appear at numerous swimming carnivals. Snowy was the showman – the star of special high-board diving exhibitions and 'fancy' swimming – while Tartakover was the main attraction in the swimming events through Glasgow, Edinburgh and in the far north of Scotland. Due to an English amateur rule, Snowy couldn't compete in the swimming events, because any person 'having his or her expenses paid shall not take part in any race where a prize is offered'.

After several months of hell, the trip north revitalised Snowy, especially as the local Scottish swimming authorities treated the pair like royalty, billeting them in the best lodgings throughout the country, while the local womenfolk, it appears, did everything they could to accommodate two lonely visitors.

Both were an enormous hit with the Scottish lassies, as hinted in a letter home from Snowy. After the Glasgow carnival, where Snowy performed off a 4-foot and 14-foot board, 'a ball and supper was held at a city hall. We both put in an appearance, just as they were ready to be seated for supper in kilts. Can we ever forget how those bonnie lassies spanked our legs? Why I actually blushed – Tartakover is beyond that. Although it being a farewell, we did not leave till two days later.

'The following evening at Paisley was our final carnival. Yet another victory for Tartakover – not to mention anything of his many victories with the ladies. At the completion of the race he gently – oh, how gently – was lifted from the water by five ladies. You will probably observe an undercurrent of jealously in these words; but who could help it?'

They also endeared themselves to the toughest of male Scots during a tour of the country, which saw Snowy give diving and water polo shows in Glasgow, Edinburgh, Aberdeen, Dumferline and Greenock. 'Our next place of visit was Peterhead, the most north-easterly point of Scotland, and I believe the home of the Scotch fishing industry. Before leaving for this town we were advised to be very gentle with the Peterhead people, the fisherman particularly, or to putting it word for word, "Be careful.

Those Peterhead people will either love or hate you, and should it be the latter, look out for stones."

'I began to think of the old Rocks and Woolloomooloo days. However, if their opinions were ill, nothing was uttered, for we had a ripping night, and although only a 15 yard bath, our efforts met with kindly reception. In a polo match, Swimmers v Fisherman, I was asked to take part; this time as a fisherman. The "fisher" blokes won by five goals to three. I had the good fortune of putting four between the posts.'

Snowy became the hero of the fisherman, who took him out for a long night of revelling. It was then time to leave Scotland, after receiving 'a very hearty and flattering "send-off" from the station by many swimmers of both sexes.

'Scotland, a beautiful country, with brawny, big-hearted men and bonnie, sweet lassies, will live through our lives as one of the happiest recollections.'

Numerous broken hearts were left behind.

Onto Europe and boundless success throughout the Continent with the Royal Lifesaving Society team, which included winning 50 metre and 500 metre international scratch races in Finland, victory in the Denmark 100 metre international scratch race and a Ribbon of Honour from the King of Sweden after winning a 500 metre international race. Snowy was also a member of a victorious 'England' water polo team which defeated Denmark, Finland and Rotterdam.

In between Snowy conducted diving exhibitions in Rotterdam, Amsterdam, Berlin, Hamburg and across France. Throughout Europe crowds flocked to watch this tiny foreigner clamber up the most rickety of diving towers, before performing flips, dives and leaps into specially constructed pools, or the ocean. To keep them entertained, Snowy also mixed in a bit of vaudevillian wrestling, boxing and gymnastics.

Ribbons were pinned on him, awards bestowed upon him, endless functions were organised to celebrate the feats of the petite man from Australie. Eventually all the adulation lured him to the drink.

At a Finnish reception for the victorious British aquatic team, with Snowy special guest of honour, his team-mates, like his ship companions in Port Said, kept pestering him about ending his teetotaller stance.

'Look what happened in Port Said!' was his retort.

'They offered me whisky, but I refused,' Snowy said.

'Then somebody said, "Have some of this, it's teetotal!" I tried a glass and liked it very much. So I had another and another and promptly fell off my chair.'

Snowy had been drinking lethal Finnish fruit punch, which had been laced with schnapps and several different spirits.

'They sat me up again, but I felt skittish, and in need of exercise. A local bigwig, all got up in uniform and wearing a sword, was speaking nearby. So I grabbed his sword and made a few fencing passes at him,' Snowy later recalled.

'It was all in fun, but my eye wasn't as good or my hand as steady as when I went through my sword drill with the NSW Lancers. Anyway, I stuck the sword an inch or so into his round stomach.

'I'll never forget the start it gave me when I saw the blood spurt out over his uniform. They put us both in hospital for four days, in the same room. The bigwig shook hands with me when he left so all was forgiven, if not forgotten.'

Following a few more weeks avoiding European sporting functions, and running away from anything that resembled fruit punch, Snowy returned to Ireland where as part of his buildup for the 1908 English boxing titles he agreed to fight against one of Belfast's leading fighters, Tom Majury. Before the fight, Snowy admitted to feeling 'off-colour' and after an uneventful three-round spar 'was sweating pretty freely, foolishly dressed and went out into a bitterly cold frosty night'.

The next day while having lunch with a friend, Snowy collapsed. 'Two days later,' Snowy wrote home, 'the temperature had reached 105, and pneumonia diagnosed. The same evening I found myself stowed away in an ambulance, and shortly after stretched out in a private ward at the Royal Victoria Hospital.'

Another month in hospital and another English boxing championship missed.

Theo Tartakover wrote home that Snowy, after his second serious bout of illness, was now at his wit's end and in exasperation had given up any hope of achieving overseas stardom. He was virtually resigned to returning home without having achieved anything, a humiliating failure.

'Poor old Snowy Baker had a bad time of it with that attack of pneumonia; his temperature went up to 107,' Tartakover wrote. 'The doctor said Snowy must not do any training for three months, and has advised him to go back to Australia, advice which he intends following. Consequently you may expect to any morning hear of his departure homeward.'

Snowy, often in the depths of depression, tried to keep his dwindling spirits up in hospital, at least pleased that he was receiving some old-fashioned Irish compassion.

In a bizarre letter to the *Belfast Journal*, Snowy thanked the hospital staff for attempting to keep him buoyed up and sent out a signal that a desperate soul was searching for some Irish love.

'There is a deep debt of gratitude to the nurses – noble ladies and staff, whose kindly treatment made sickness not a pain or misfortune but a pleasure. During the past year I have travelled most countries this side of the Line, and also had the good fortune of meeting people of the various nations, and I can say without doubt that the Irish, for brave kind-heartedness and true hospitality lead the van.

'It is during these moments I feel most proud of my Irish parentage. So much have I been impressed with your people of the Emerald Isle that I have decided to take upon myself an Irish wife. As a rule I'm not very successful with the fair sex, so mention this in hopes of it being a little help to my happy despatch.'

Snowy was eventually well enough to return to London – without an Irish wife, again unlucky in love – to pack up his belongings and organise a passage home. But yet again an invitation arrived at just the right time.

A letter came from the NSW Swimming Association, which said that as it was noted that Snowy and Tartakover were expected to remain in England for some time, both their names had been entered for the swimming events at the upcoming 1908 Olympic Games to be held in London. With it was a letter of verification from Richard Coombes, the head of the Australasian Amateur Athletic Union.

Snowy knew he was really in no condition for Olympic competition, and that time would be against him, but ego won out. The opportunity to represent Australia at serious international competition was too hard to resist. He immediately called off his trip home.

In the next return mail to Australia, Snowy and Tartakover wrote to the NSW Swimming Association and to Coombes to gush that they would be delighted to be their representatives at the fourth modern Olympic Games.

Snowy explained to the officials that: 'Although rather a poor representative, I intend training to do my very best.'

Little did he know that he had also been entered in the Olympic diving events and that the Australian boxing authorities had placed his name on the list for a third competition – the middleweight division.

Suddenly Snowy was facing the most demanding programme offered to any modern Olympic competitor – somehow having to cope with three gruelling, totally different events.

Thankfully for Snowy his competitions were staggered, with the Summer Games events, including swimming and diving, being held from July, while the Autumn Games events, which included boxing, were held back until October.

Unlike recent Olympic Games, where Australian teams are organised to the minute degree and involved in military-like manoeuvres to ensure excellence in performance, in 1908 it was very much look after yourself and get there by yourself.

As the Australian Olympic officials couldn't finance a team to travel to Europe, they relied upon amateur athletes who were prepared to attend the Games at their own expense. Consequently, reputable sportsmen, such as Snowy and Tartakover, who were already living in London, were ideal targets.

There were no selection trials. The team instead revolved around those who could get there at the required time, prompting an urgent meeting of all the Australasian representatives at the Polytechnic Institute in London just before the Games started, so that a headcount could be made. It was also then that they determined who exactly would appear in what event.

Fourteen athletes appeared, including several from New Zealand, who were told that their countries were stringently behind them and were praying that they could bring pride to their far-off lands. After all, this was the first time Australasia had competed as a supposedly organised team at an Olympics.

But in the next breath, these pioneers were told they had to pay their own way, even the bus and train fares required to get them to and from the competition.

One consolation was that the management, which had originally forgotten to discuss the subject of a national uniform, had at least persuaded the Federal Government to provide some funds to enable the team to march at the opening ceremony in official garb, with 'the coat of arms to be worn on the breast' behind a 'handsome banner'.

What was promised and what actually arrived in London in time for the Games opening were totally different, prompting newspaper reports to describe the small band who marched behind the Australasian banner as looking 'impoverished and out of place'.

With the track and field athletes wearing small green caps, dark T-shirts and white shorts, which had green-and-gold bands sewn on to them, and the five-man swimming team, including Snowy, appearing in their swimming gear, forcing them to march barefoot, they looked a rag-tag mob. An official photograph taken of the team after the march emphasises the point, with the men looking more like they were about to go to a scout jamboree, rather than preparing themselves for the world's premier athletic event. Snowy is sitting cross-legged in the photograph, obviously proud to be wearing whatever Australia had provided for him, but made to look ridiculous by wearing an all-too-small cap. He looked like a kid on a big adventure.

With Australasia written across their singlets they paled into insignificance against the tailored teams from Europe and the spit and polish of the Americans. But not much more could be expected from a hastily organised team that had received only token government or public support.

Nonetheless, they were not the only odd sight at the opening ceremony, with the Americans disgusted to discover not one Stars and Stripes flag among those at the White City stadium. The distressed Americans showed their dismay by opting against dipping the flag when passing King Edward VII during the parade. Finland meanwhile marched flagless, as they refused to march behind the Russian flag, in objection to the Russian occupation of their country. Irish athletes were also angry that they had to compete for Great Britain and marched some distance away from the rest of the team.

The animosity between the Americans and the British continued unabated during the Olympics, especially when host officials unashamedly coached their athletes while judging events. The Americans thought the British snobbish and arrogant, walking out of the tug-of-war event and refusing to compete in a 400 metres rerun. The Brits turned their noses up at the Yankees, describing them in the London press as being 'full of themselves'.

The Americans weren't too impressed with the Olympic movement either, with one of its leading officials describing the founder of the modern Olympic Games, Baron de Coubertin, as a 'well-meaning, fussy and incompetent little Frenchman'.

In an Olympic Games described by one historian as 'a tragicomedy', Australians also discovered themselves bit-players in several bewildering events, in particular the marathon. The finale to that event is still classified as one of the most extraordinary moments in modern Olympic history.

Three Australian runners, George Blake, Victor Aitken and Joseph Lynch, began the marathon on the lawns of Windsor Castle, with the Princess of Wales in charge of the starting gun. Aitken hung around with the leaders, while the other two were early withdrawals — not surprising as they were new to the event.

Blake's withdrawal after just six miles was not entirely his own fault. He was being followed by an attendant riding a bike, who while handing him a cup of beef tea accidentally hit him with the handlebars. The bike then struck Blake's leg and according to Snowy 'the next thing he knew there was a tangled mass of humanity and bike on the ground'.

Then Aitken collapsed, followed by the South African, Charles Heffernon, who suffered extreme stomach cramps after accepting a glass of champagne from a spectator, enabling a delirious Italian runner Dorando Pietri to meander into the main stadium by himself.

The crowd gasped because Pietri was obviously in another world. First he started heading in the wrong direction, before falling onto the track still some way from the finish line. Officials stayed away, realising that any physical help to the runner would see him disqualified. Eventually they had no alternative and helped him get to the finish line, because as the official Olympic report later stated: 'It was impossible to leave him there, for it looked as though he might die in the very presence of the Queen.'

Pietri collapsed five more times before eventually breaking the tape. As the *New York Times* reported: 'He staggered along the cinder path like a man in a dream, his gait being neither a walk nor a run, but simply a flounder, with arms shaking and legs tottering.'

The Italian flag was immediately run up the flag pole to indicate his victory, even though the second placed runner, American John Hayes, was just about to cross the line. The Americans immediately protested and Pietri's five seconds of fame was over. As he was being carried away on a stretcher, Pietri was disqualified and Hayes, who worked at Bloomingdales department store in New York where a special cinder track had been made for him on the roof, was named the victor. All this did was intensify the animosity of the British towards the Americans, with the general view being that they were merciless in declaring victory over an athlete who was stretchered away close to death.

Snowy was at the Olympic Stadium that day, and wrote in a letter to his brother, Harold, which was published in full by the *Sunday Sun* newspaper, that during the marathon the capacity crowd was kept informed of the progress of the runners via megaphone.

'"The runners are in sight," loudly yelled the megaphone man,' Snowy wrote. 'A few seconds after the slim and tottering little figure of Dorando came stumbling through the gates. I was in the arena, alongside the track, as he entered and the only possible way I can describe the appearance of this brave little Italian, as he blindly struggled on, is to liken him to that of an animated corpse.

'It is certainly a morbid comparison, but those were the thoughts that rushed to my mind as I beheld the drawn and wasted looking features of Dorando. Oh but what a cheer greeted him! All distinctions of nationality were forgotten, and the huge crowd stood on their feet as one, and cheered to the echo this brave and heroic runner.

'He reached the track with a shambling stride, which resembled a child at its initial attempt to walk, and, to the utter dismay and sorrow of the cheering and excited thousands, he fell in a huddled mess, as though in complete collapse. But, no, a great heart within had conquered, and Dorando was on his feet again.

'Struggling blindly on another 50 yards to the frenzied shouts of everyone; but no, it could not be, and down he went again. But this time many officials had gathered around, and plainly saw that he could not regain his feet in time to win the race without aid. Just then the second competitor entered the Stadium.

'They lifted Dorando up, and on he tottered a few more yards, and down he went again. Placed once again to the perpendicular he feebly assayed to run, which in reality, was hardly as fast as a child could totter.

'Dorando! Dorando! Come on! Come on! the vast audience yelled. He had about 15 yards to go, when the American (Hayes) was struggling for victory 50 yards to the rear. He's got you! He's got you! screeched the people in sympathy of Dorando, and with a superhuman effort, he sprinted – one might call it a sprint compared to the pace he'd done the last hundred yards – and the tape was broken, as he fell forward in an unconscious condition into arms ready to receive him.'

Compared to the high drama of the marathon, the swimming events were relatively mundane. But it still had its moments, especially with the swimming pool out in the open in the middle of the Olympic stadium.

The 100 metre long pool, twice the normal length of an Olympic pool, had been dug into the athletic area, with no filtration or chlorination, turning the water into thick pea-soup. Competitors couldn't see anything six inches ahead of them. For most of the meeting, the competitors worried that they would come down with some mysterious disease from what was obviously the most unhygienic of pools.

The crowd in the grandstands couldn't see much either because of hordes of officials and hangers-on standing around the pool blocking their view. Also the events were so haphazardly organised, no competitor really knew when their next event was about to start. This prompted everyone to hover around the area and wait for hours on end because of the fear that if they moved out of earshot they may miss their event.

Snowy had been beckoned into the Australian swimming 4 x 200 metres freestyle relay team, to accompany Tartakover, Frank Springfield, who had also been working in London, and a young, shy 17-year-old Melbournite, Frank Beaurepaire, rated the best up and coming swimmer in Australia.

A few months earlier, Beaurepaire had set sail for England in a dingy steerage berth, and with only 16 pounds in his pocket, discovered London inhospitable and frightening. To save money Beaurepaire stayed with a variety of relatives, to ensure he'd have enough funds to remain the required four months to compete in the Olympics. Upset that no swimming official had met him on arrival in England, he didn't tell anyone that he was in London for well over a month.

Opting against using the new Australian crawl stroke, Beaurepaire continued working on his own version of the trudgen stroke that prompted success at the Australian titles in Perth and saw officials sound him out about possible Olympic selection. Yet again, it depended not just on raw ability but on whether he could muster up the money to get to England in time. Travelling in steerage was the only way, and as he was the lowest class of passenger, he was forbidden from using the swimming pool whilst on board the ship.

Swimming in England on arrival was also restricted as Beaurepaire didn't have the money to pay the full entrance fee at the public baths, forcing him to train in freezing conditions at Highgate Ponds. It was free, but the downside was that the water, even in the middle of summer, never rose above 14°C, no-one really knew what the distance of the swimming area was and there were no designated lanes.

By this stage, Australian Olympics officials were wondering where Beaurepaire was. Beaurepaire was also wondering where he was when he emerged from nowhere and, bulked up on a strict diet of bread, cheese and copious ginger beer, decided to make his first public appearance with a training swim in the Thames. He immediately developed a cramp and sank below the surface, having to be saved by one of Australia's marathon runners, Vic Aitken, who had accompanied him down to the river. A few weeks later, Beaurepaire made his first official start in a 15-mile swim in the Thames, only to collapse at the six-mile mark. Again he had to be rescued.

Undeterred, Beaurepaire entered the five mile championship of England, but dropped out early. Eventually his fortunes changed, travelling to Bradford in Yorkshire to win the English half-mile championship in a freezing pool which saw him so numb at the end, he couldn't stand.

At his next appearance at Nottingham for the English 220 yard championship, Beaurepaire complained to the pool attendant that he found the local conditions too cold. The attendant was so obliging that he turned the pool temperature up to 28°C. Great for Beaurepaire, who won the event comfortably, but not so enlightening for the spectators who couldn't see anything because of the thick steam.

By this time, Beaurepaire was ready for anything, including the Olympic pea-soup pool and a poorly organised programme, which he said was conducted under 'Rafferty's rules'.

Beaurepaire was the star of the Australasian swimming team boasting a silver medal in the 400 metres freestyle and a bronze in the 1500 metres freestyle by the time of the team events.

In the first round of the team race against Denmark, it was agreed that Beaurepaire would start off. It proved the right move, with Beaurepaire giving Australasia a 40-yard lead when Springfield hit the water.

Springfield increased the lead to 60 yards, when Snowy started the third leg. The Olympic official report said that: 'Though slower than Beaurepaire and Springfield, the third Antipodian was still fast enough to draw farther ahead, Dam (the Danish swimmer) losing another 20 yards on the two lengths.'

Tartakover brought the team home, with the winning distance being 90 yards, in a time of 11 minutes 35 seconds. Snowy's time for the 200 metres was 2 minutes 59.8 seconds, third fastest of the Australasians.

Australasia changed the order for the final, where they were up against the United Kingdom, Hungary and the United States. This time Beaurepaire swam the last leg. But by the time Beaurepaire hit the water, Australasia were way out of medal contention, drifting well behind the other three teams.

Snowy wrote home that the team assumed that they would at least finish with a bronze medal. 'The struggle for premier place between Great Britain and Hungary was a stirring one. Von Halmay was last to swim for the Hungarian squad. He took the water some yards ahead of Henry Taylor, England's distance swimmer, and a man whom people hardly considered for a sprint like 200 metres.

'Taylor, who is possessed with an extraordinary amount of dogged determination, raced after the speedy Hungarian as though to do or die. Half-way back on the second lap it looked odds on Halmay, but a few yards more and it was plainly seen that he had shot his bolt, and was swimming an erratic course; 25 yards from home he crossed over diagonally, and struck the side of the basin. Taylor, who seemed to notice his plight, put in a 'dozen' and passed him as though he were left standing.

'Beaurepaire, last man off for our team, swam an excellent race, and pulled up a lot of ground that Daniels had gained on me, but only sufficient to place Australia fourth, four or five yards from America.'

The United Kingdom, through Taylor's mighty swim, won the gold, ahead of Hungary and the United States. Australasia, for finishing fourth, won a 'Diploma of Merit'. Halmay, who lost consciousness immediately after finishing, had to be hauled from the pool before he drowned.

Also to be hauled from the pool was the high diving apparatus for the next event on the aquatic programme. To the amusement of the crowd, the diving tower was lowered beneath the surface of the water when not required, and according to the official Olympic Games report 'raised again in a few minutes according to the necessities of the programme'.

The crowd also discovered it was worth sticking around for the diving events. In the platform diving section, Great Britain's George Cane lost control while attempting a double somersault, landed awkwardly and was knocked out. The unconscious form eventually floated to the surface, face down, and it was only the quick work of opposing competitor, Hjalmar Johanssen, who fished Cane out of the water, that saved him from drowning. Johanssen, who had become a close friend of Snowy's as he had also been part of the Royal Lifesaving team which toured Europe, went on to win the event.

The springboard diving section, in which Snowy was entered, was also a relatively tricky event involving a succession of dives that were marked according to their difficulty. Snowy was not exactly confident that he would go anywhere in this event as even though he'd been involved in many diving exhibitions throughout Europe, they had involved various trick dives, where he'd been allowed to be loose. He hadn't been working on the strict dives that would gain him maximum points.

As expected, Snowy's involvement in the Olympic diving section was short and sweet. To compensate for a large field of 23 competitors from throughout Europe, Great Britain, the United States and Canada, five heats were conducted. Snowy was placed in heat four, where he finished sixth and last, with a tally of 61.3 points. Germany's Albert Zurner won with a tally of 85.5 points.

With the first part of the Olympic Games now over, the crowds and the Australasian team dispersed. But Snowy had to hang around. He now had to prepare himself for his main Olympic venture – the middleweight boxing title. Unlike the diving section, where he was ill prepared, this time Snowy couldn't complain about lack of time to get ready. The boxing titles were still three months away.

Chapter 7
International Stardom

AUSTRALIA LEFT THE BEST UNTIL LAST. WHILE SNOWY HID HIMSELF AWAY, staying with Australia's world champion sculler, George Towns, in London and conducting an intense daily training regime in readiness for his quest for an Olympic boxing title, many of his old footballing mates had also arrived in Britain, trailblazing in a different pursuit.

Following Snowy's short foray as a national rugby representative, Australia had slowly improved its standing on the international scene, even succeeding in drawing with the mighty New Zealand All Blacks in 1907.

Buoyed by such unexpected success, Australian rugby officials found the courage to organise the big adventure – 29 players to be selected for a 31-match tour, across Great Britain, culminating in internationals against England and Wales.

Many of those chosen were known to Snowy, including several who had been club opponents four and five years previously. As soon as they arrived in Britain, Snowy was in contact, visiting the team when they began their tour against Devon. The links became even closer when it was decided that the tourists would be Australia's representatives in the rugby section of the Olympic Games.

Rugby had been introduced to the Olympic Games in Paris in 1900, but it wasn't exactly the most popular event. Only three teams competed – France, England and Germany – and rugby didn't make an appearance at the 1904 Games in St Louis.

The 1908 event also just got off the ground, despite being held in supposedly strong rugby territory. The organisers struggled to get a quorum for an Olympic final and had to scramble to find even the minimum of two teams – Australia and Cornwall, who were chosen by the English Rugby Union to represent the United Kingdom.

In the end, the Olympic rugby final was a sham – a lopsided non-event played alongside a swimming pool. But it did see Australia win its one and only Olympic gold medal for rugby.

Snowy was among a small group of Australian supporters who travelled to the Olympic stadium for the final, which was played on the other side of the pool where he had doubled up in the swimming and diving events.

The water had been drained out of the pool and huge mattresses spread along the rim to prevent injury to any player who was pushed over the sideline and accidentally fell into the pool. To add to the bizarre scene, men with long poles and small nets successfully fished for the ball when it went over the top of the netting, into touch and into the swimming pool.

Thankfully, no Wallaby crashed into the pool and damage was relatively limited as Australia cruised to a 32–3 victory over a second-rate opposition. Snowy joined the revellers in the Australian dressing room, where he was asked if he had any interest in joining up with the Wallabies for the latter stages of the tour as a guest backup half-back.

He gratefully declined, arguing that his football days were long over and that he now regarded boxing as a safer sport. The Wallabies looked at him aghast.

As he would later explain: 'Boxing has no equal. Teaches perfect control of body, limbs and temper. Some people say boxing is dangerous. I have boxed in over 100 contests, and have never carried more than a couple of scrapes, and those only for a day or two. In football I have had my fingers broken, ankle broken, and a hundred and one other hurts. Which looks the softer game?'

However Snowy couldn't dwell too long with his old footballing colleagues, as the next day the Olympic boxing titles were being staged at the Northampton Institute in Clerkenwell, London.

He was followed by the Wallabies, who agreed to be his vocal core of supporters in the bleachers as Snowy attempted to continue the Australian Olympic glory streak.

It was much-needed support because Snowy faced the most onerous of tasks. The boxing event had been set down for just the one day, starting at 11.25 am and finishing with the finals less than 11 hours later.

In that short period, Snowy had to survive three preliminary bouts if he wanted to make the final. His chief opponent for the middleweight title – the highly-renowned British boxer, J.W.H.T. Douglas – had the advantage of an easier draw, which included a bye midway during the programme. A bye that enabled Douglas to rest for several hours in the middle of the day.

Snowy was first up against the 1897 English middleweight and heavyweight champion W.J. Dees, who surprisingly failed to make any impact. After Snowy, dressed in white shorts and a T-shirt, which had the word Australasia and the Australian coat of arms emblazoned across it, out-defended him in the first round, Dees was knocked out in the second. The London *Daily Mail* noted glumly: 'Dees was not up to his top form.'

The second round bout against the current British middleweight champion W. Childs was just as one-sided. As the Olympic official report explained: 'The Australian made the pace very fast, and scored on the body and neck. In the second round Childs went for his man very hard, but Baker got home a heavy uppercut, and soon afterwards Childs fell through the ropes from a rushing attack cleverly avoided by Baker. The Australian was clearly the superior in the last meeting.'

Snowy won on points.

His energy levels now affected, Snowy realised that if he was to hold on for the final, the semi-final encounter against a third British fighter, W. Philo, had to be short and sharp.

He couldn't mess around and prolong the fight for three rounds, because he would basically have nothing left for the medal-determining final.

Snowy rushed out at the start of the first round and unleashed a mad flurry of punches, most connecting with the fast retreating Philo. A hook to the chin, a right to the body, a left flush to the face, followed by a right cross, and the contest was over. The *Daily Mail* said Snowy 'landed his right square on Philo's jaw, and he was left dreaming'.

In less than a minute, Philo had been knocked out, prompting the Wallabies to rise to their feet as one, wildly cheering their compatriot as he was announced the winner.

By this stage Snowy was exhausted and the effects of his illness was starting to hit. He tried to find somewhere to hide for an hour before the final against Douglas, who was appreciably fresher having enjoyed two quick bouts – one which was over in a minute and the other finishing early in the second round – plus a bye in between.

Also to Douglas's advantage was the intense hometown support, which went as far as his father, J.H. Douglas, being at ringside, but more importantly being heavily involved in the running of the tournament in his role as President of the Amateur Boxing Association.

Douglas was well known and widely admired throughout Britain being, like Snowy, the most versatile of athletes and apart from the small pocket of Australian fans in the crowd, mostly the touring Wallabies, the rest were in Douglas's corner, wanting to see one of Britain's best-known sportsmen finish with gold. Snowy was not exactly the ogre, especially with the London *Daily Telegraph* that week stating that Australia had 'never sent to England a sportsman who has been more popular than Mr Baker'. But Snowy still knew that the crowd and environment would work against him.

While a formidable boxer, Douglas was an even better known cricketer, skippering the Essex county team for many years and later advancing to the England Test skipper ranks.

Unlike Snowy, he was no exhilarating entertainer, as demonstrated during a tour of Australia when those who invade the Sydney Cricket Ground Hill gave him the less than endearing nickname of Johnny 'Won't Hit Today' Douglas, for his boring, defence-orientated batting. He was a dim, dour character, not exactly renowned for revelry, but perfectly suited to the boxing ring, and the most grim of England–Australia cricketing battles. On the cricket field he was often unforgiving and merciless towards fellow team-mates, and renowned for insensitive comments and heartless acts. A strong but sometimes erratic disciplinarian, he hated shirkers or those who showed any form of weakness.

Douglas told one county team-mate at the end of the day's play that if he had missed a certain difficult catch a few hours earlier he would have broken his neck. Douglas delighted in telling a young Percy Fender, when he first joined the England Test team, that 'there is no man in England whose bowling I would rather bat against than yours; and there is no batsman in England I would rather bowl against either'.

It was no surprise that one critic wrote that Douglas's captaincy at Essex was 'not only bad but brutal, almost incredible in his ruthlessness'.

One player became a mental wreck after being bullied by Douglas for several years. As the English would say, he was a horrid man. A rotter.

The London *Times* said that Douglas's prime fault 'is a lack of imagination'. In the ring, Douglas was as unremitting. It came from his father, a dominant figure who loved to bully others. They were especially close. Douglas Senior was heavily involved in the destiny of his own son, going as far as putting pressure on the Essex club committee to make his son captain, by reminding them that he held the mortgage on their ground and that if someone else was made skipper, he would foreclose. The next day, J. W. H. T. Douglas was announced as Essex captain.

Throughout Douglas's sporting career, his father stood right by his side, providing the funds to allow his son to travel the world first class and enjoy a luxurious lifestyle, but he still remained the most blue-blooded of amateurs. Thanks to his many benefactors, Snowy still had plenty of money in his pockets by the time of the Olympic final, but nothing compared to Douglas.

In the boxing ring, unlike the cricket field, Douglas was anything but a stonewaller. He was a ferocious, aggressive fighter, who wanted to take the initiative and dominate the centre of the ring. Rarely would Douglas seek refuge on the ropes.

British sportswriter Denzil Batchelor said Douglas had 'a classic style, the courage of a Spartan, and enough character to refuse to be withered by one glance of a blue, Napoleonic eye'.

As part of his preparation for the Olympic final, several weeks earlier he had even agreed to spar with the first and only Canadian world heavyweight professional champion, Tommy Burns, who was in London for a series of fights.

Growing up in abject poverty in western Ontario, Burns, born Noah Brusso, the 12th of 13 children born to a German–Canadian cabinet-maker, was a deeply troubled youth, affected by the early death of his father, and subjected to beatings from his alcoholic stepfather.

Once when sleeping in, his stepfather charged into Noah's bedroom and smashed him over the head with a baseball bat, before punching and kicking him. He was forever reminded of the incident as it left a scar on the bridge of his nose.

To relieve his frustrations and keep a lid on his aggression, he mixed boxing with lacrosse, where in a wild and generally rule-free game, Noah became renowned as a skilful, aggressive attacking player. Even on the lacrosse field, he was someone not to mess around with. In one match, when a goalkeeper and Noah were trying to retrieve a ball which was behind the net, the goalkeeper kept tapping Noah on the arm.

Angered that someone had invaded his private space, Noah dropped his stick and belted the goalkeeper in the face, knocking him out. Yet again, Noah found himself suspended.

Another time he was arrested, after knocking out Ben 'Gorilla' O'Grady in Detroit. Brusso had just succeeded in enjoying his 20th knockout win, when it was discovered that O'Grady was close to death on the canvas. O'Grady spent four days in a coma.

At ringside, police were called. They handcuffed Noah, charged him with assault causing bodily harm and led him away. As he was thrown into the lockup, Noah was told the charge would be upgraded to manslaughter if O'Grady died. Eventually the charges were dropped when one of Noah's lacrosse colleagues smuggled O'Grady out of Detroit.

While depressed that his punch had turned O'Grady into a raving lunatic, Noah had also distanced himself from his mother, who was shocked that he was involved in a brutal sport which was outlawed in many states. To avoid her scorn, he changed his name as a way of hiding his occupation from her. He was first interested in Ed Burns, before deciding on Tommy Burns, the same name as a popular Canadian jockey.

Even though there was some concern that sparring with such a high-profile, professional fighter could affect Douglas's amateur status, his father smoothed that over by giving it the required approval through the Amateur Boxing Association.

Burns was assuming that the spar would be an exhibition and before the bout told his opponent not to be concerned about serious injury as he would be holding back. It was supposed to be all show and few blows. This only antagonised the proud Douglas, who immediately went for the killer punch. Burns was seething.

In Dan McCaffery's biography on Burns, *Tommy Burns: Canada's Unknown World Heavyweight Champion*, he wrote: 'The bout was supposed to be nothing more than a friendly match in which the two men would do a little sparring for the crowd. Everyone understood that no verdict would be rendered at the conclusion.

'Nevertheless, the vainglorious Douglas went after the professional champion, hoping to score a knockout. Taken by surprise, Burns had a difficult time holding his own over the nine minutes of fighting. When the bell rang to end the bout the Canadian was seething with rage.

'For one moment he considered making a scene. But with scores of people looking on, including several reporters, he thought better of it, deciding instead to congratulate the Englishman on his showing.

'"If this is what you call a sparring exhibition," he said in a jovial tone, "what is your honest-to-God fighting like down here?"'

Little wonder Snowy tried to hide away for as long as possible before the final, so that he'd have enough reserve energy to ensure that he'd put in some sort of show against easily the best amateur boxer he had faced in his career.

Douglas, realising weeks before the Olympic final that Snowy was his key rival, had researched him diligently, even to the extent of having scouts watch several of his training sessions. Douglas knew everything about his key opponent – in particular his spate of illnesses.

Douglas knew that the main danger for him would be the first round, as Snowy wouldn't be keen to prolong the bout because of his concern that a lack of stamina would work against him if the fight was extended into the third round.

Douglas was anticipating that he'd have to endure an early barrage of punches from the Australian. But if he could weather that, all it required was for him to try to wear Snowy out over the next three rounds. Douglas knew that Snowy, despite his recent illness, was in great trim. Photographs taken of Snowy that week show a boxer so grimly determined and so well proportioned in the upper body, particularly his arms. He may have been small, but everything required for him to be a formidable boxer was evident. Those clenched fists were obviously devastating weapons, while the legs were finely tuned, but strongly developed.

Tactics were imperative.

As expected in the first round, Snowy led with his favourite body blow which hit Douglas low in the ribs. Douglas retreated, but somehow turned from defender to aggressor by the middle of the round and succeeded in pinning Snowy momentarily into a corner.

However, using the same deft sidestep and swerve that served him so well with NSW and Australian rugby teams, Snowy was soon out of the danger zone and before the end of the round had succeeded in hitting Douglas with several well-timed rights. The first round ended with honours even.

In the second round, Snowy led off again, but Douglas wasn't bothered, reminding himself it was imperative that he move his opponent around the ring so that he would tire himself out. For the first half of the bout, Douglas adopted an uncharacteristic defensive position, retreating wherever possible, until noticing that Baker's stance had slipped. The arms had dropped momentarily. He immediately went on the attack.

Within seconds Snowy was on the canvas. The official Olympic report stated that Douglas 'got home a decisive blow on the jaw which took the Australian off his feet'. However, as Snowy lifted himself, well before the end of the ten count, he pointed to his shoes in a bid to convince the judges that he had actually slipped.

Riled by the embarrassing blow, which he later described as hitting him 'on the side of the head, delivered with the padded portion of the wrist', Snowy chased after Douglas, now knowing that he had to deliver a similar blow to get into the fight. A knockout was now crucial.

It almost worked, as described by the *Sydney Mail*: 'Baker, however, was very far from done with, and the moment he was on his feet he caught the Englishman a couple of beauties, which thoroughly roused Douglas. The cricketer stepped out to slog, and had almost got his man dizzy, when Baker's glove came off, and, assisted by the slight pause, the Australian gamely lasted out time.'

As the fighters headed to their corners, the crowd were on their feet, cheering one of the greatest rounds ever fought in an Olympic boxing competition. First a knockdown, then the most epic of comebacks, which almost saw Douglas also hitting the deck. Douglas had won the round, but not by much, especially after Snowy showed so much pluck to immediately take the ascendancy after his so-called 'slip'.

Douglas then showed his cleverness in the final round. He deliberately slowed the pace, hoping that this would wear Snowy out. But it didn't. Snowy picked up the pace, finding reserves of energy from somewhere and for the next three minutes succeeded in trading blow for blow. Several times Douglas looked at his opponent in wonderment, struggling to comprehend how he was still standing.

Still, Snowy knew he needed a knockout and wherever possible went for the outlandish blow. But Douglas just wouldn't drop.

By the end of the round, Snowy had succeeded in delivering far more blows to the target than his opponent, but he knew that 'slip' in the second round would work against him. At the end, Snowy had just enough energy to slump himself across his opponent as they congratulated each other for a fight described in the Olympic report as a 'beautifully matched bout (which) produced the best boxing of the day'. The official report was glowing in its description of Snowy in the final, describing him as 'one of the best amateur performers ever seen in a ring'.

Understandably, not all in the hall were convinced that Douglas was the winner. And it wasn't just the Australian contingent who believed that Snowy was the better fighter, but also other more independent judges argued that overall the Australian had produced the better display.

This was evident when the official announcement that Douglas was the gold medal winner and Snowy the silver medallist was accompanied by rousing boos. As the London *Sportsman* explained: 'Many in the hall thought the verdict should have gone the other way.

'Baker had proved himself a model of style, a splendid judge of distance, a master of ring craft, and a fairly hard hitter into the bargain, and it was a general opinion that Douglas was running up against his toughest proposition. The heat was worth going a long way to see. Power was with Douglas, and cleverness with the Australian.'

The Referee added: 'Halfway through the second round Douglas had Baker in difficulties, and he never really recovered from the effects. Still, he made an excellent show, and it was not everyone who thought that Douglas had won – there were a few remarks!'

The British *Australasian* wrote: 'This was undoubtedly the event of the whole competition. In the first round Baker piled up points, in the second he received a half-punch and slipped down, and on getting up put in some very fine work. Honours now appeared even, and in the final round he rallied, and looked to have had a winner's margin in points; but his luck was out again, and Douglas was declared the winner.

'The fact of having to fight so often in such a short space of time certainly told on Baker after his severe illness. There was a great amount of hooting when the decision was announced, and had Baker won it would undoubtedly have been a popular victory.'

Then came the conspiracy theories, which continue to this day. The main one was that Snowy never had a chance in the final because Douglas's father was the referee. This has been repeated so many times in newspaper and magazine articles that it is now virtually regarded as fact. The oft-written tale is that one judge gave his vote to Douglas, the other to Snowy. The referee, allegedly J.H. Douglas Senior, was then called in to give his casting vote and not surprisingly it went to his son. A short time later, father presented his son with the gold medal at the official ceremony.

For years Snowy said he had no qualms about the decision, saying on more than one occasion: 'I felt perfectly satisfied that on the day Douglas fully deserved the decision. He was the best conditioned man I have ever seen in any ring, amateur or professional. You might say that I was thoroughly satisfied to be beaten by such a sportsman as Douglas.'

But in 1952 he added to the intrigue when he said in a interview with Sydney journalist Norman Bartlett: 'Some people say I should have won on points. The referee was the winner's father.'

Ever since, Baker's loss has often been credited to the fact that his opponent had the major advantage of the referee being in his corner.

However, there is just as strong evidence that Douglas Senior was not the referee. In his book *Thirty Years a Boxing Referee*, published in 1915, Eugene Corri stated that he was the referee of the Douglas–Baker fight. Corri, the famous professional and amateur referee who officiated at numerous world title fights, reminisced about his career, including his involvement in the 1908 Olympic event. In a chapter 'Amateurs I have Known', Corri eulogises Douglas, before explaining: 'I refereed that bout at Northampton Institute, out Clerkenwell way.

'Before meeting Baker in the final, Douglas beat Rube Warnes, who was amateur middleweight champion no fewer than five times – about a record, I should think. The final bout with Baker was two rounds of three minutes and one round of four minutes.'

Corri said Douglas had the best of the first round, while the second round was 'as nearly level as possible'. Corri describes Douglas's knockdown blow as a 'right punch to the chin'.

'Nothing happened in the third round till near the close, when Baker got home a real good right-hand punch which shook Douglas up considerably. But in the end Douglas had done just enough to win on points, acquiring the high honour that sticks to a man through life, like a "Varsity Blue".

'There can only be one middleweight champion at a time, while there can be a host of Blues. I said I refereed Douglas's championship bout, but, as a matter of fact, there was no need for me to give a decision, as the two umpires agreed, so making my verdict unnecessary. Had the umpires disagreed, I should have given the decision to Douglas.'

So much for the disputed vote and Douglas Senior coming to his son's rescue.

The other furry, and again often-printed story from that period is that Snowy was so riled by the Olympic medal decision that he couldn't resist the opportunity for a return bout when he and Douglas were invited to dine at London's prestigious National Sporting Club.

The story goes: 'In the course of the evening the pair were persuaded to remove their dinner jackets and set to with bare knuckles. This time the contest ended when Baker knocked out Douglas in the second round.'

A marvellous anecdote, but again dubious. Those who wrote it were the same people who claimed that Baker was a University Blue and that he'd been dudded by Douglas's father in the Olympic final.

However, actual evidence that this bare knuckle fight occurred is impossible to find. Comments made by Snowy on his way home to Australia after the fight also don't help. When he arrived in Fremantle, Snowy was asked about the Olympic final and replied that 'It was a hard and a willing go, and I honestly think the best man won.

'Douglas got the verdict on points, but many people thought that if the contest was not awarded to me it should have been declared a draw. I should have liked to have had another go with Douglas, and will when I revisit England, as I hope to do in a few years.'

If he had been involved in a bare knuckle Douglas knockdown, surely it would have been mentioned then, instead of Snowy issuing a wish for a future bout.

This bout, in the end, never eventuated, with Douglas devoting his later sporting life to cricket, before dying tragically in 1930 when he and his father drowned in a shipping accident at sea.

After almost two years away from home, Snowy knew it was now time to return to Sydney. Despite suffering serious illness during his time away, it was still difficult for him to leave London especially when the local newspapers took delight in eulogising him. The day before he left, the London *Sportsman* wrote: 'Reginald Baker will now leave for his far-off home, and he will go back to the Colonies with the best wishes of everyone with whom he has been brought in contact.

'I am quite sure Snowy has not an enemy in England. He has been reported as the most popular athlete in all Australia. This is saying a good deal, but I can add one thing, and that is, that he cannot be better liked even at home than he is here. A gentleman in every sense of the word, Baker combines with his social side all the best qualities of an athlete.'

As he left St Pancras station in London, to join his ship *The Omrah*, the platform was crowded with well-wishers, while he was handed hundreds of telegrams and letters, many calling on him to stay in London. Numerous were written in a female hand.

But this was nothing compared to the scenes that greeted him when he eventually arrived in Sydney Harbour in December 1908.

Chapter 8

Huge Deal

AT DOCKSIDE IN SYDNEY HARBOUR, WAITING FOR SNOWY'S RETURN, WERE virtually the same crew that had waved him away. They led the cheering shortly after the ship was seen peeking its way through the Heads. The reception was as colourful, noisy and exciting as the farewell all those long months ago. As soon as he was off the boat, fighting through the streamers and endless backslaps, Snowy was whisked away to the NSW Sports Club for a celebratory 'welcome home' function.

Sitting next to him at the lunch was a gregarious, larger than life, total ratbag of a character. A man always after the big effect. With a voice laced with brandy, he shouted into Snowy's ear: 'I want to talk to you about something.'

That was the start of a long, bizarre and eventful relationship. Snowy's life was about to change.

The bulky, smothering, bullfrog-like figure with a distinctive pencil-thin moustache leaning heavily onto Snowy's left shoulder was Hugh D. McIntosh — officially entitled entrepreneur and businessman, but as much con man, grifter, total opportunist, and in Sydney at that time, the man of the moment.

Through sheer cheek and guile, McIntosh had organised an historic boxing event that had already wowed the world. In a few weeks time, Sydney would be the venue for the first white versus black professional heavyweight championship title fight. McIntosh wanted Snowy to play a pivotal role in the Tommy Burns–Jack Johnson title fight, by far the most important international sporting event to have been staged in Australia. He demanded that Snowy be the referee. Snowy immediately agreed. He knew there was no other option, because when McIntosh had a nagging thought in his mind, it was impossible to sway his opinion.

McIntosh was one 'Huge Deal', as he was affectionately, and not so affectionately, known to all. And when he was chasing the 'Huge Deal', no-one, not even the street-wise Snowy, could stand in his way.

The Burns–Johnson fight – a duel that was assumed would never happen, especially in such a faraway place as Australia – was just the latest in a series of amazing Huge Deal coups.

Snowy had known about Huge Deal for some time – he was always hanging around the periphery of various sports looking for an opportunity to make a quick quid – and would credit him as the most extraordinary Australian he ever met. They were instantly attracted. Spivs and shonks usually hover in the same circles.

Snowy's life was different, but even he knew that the Huge Deal story was impossible to top. You name it, he did it. He flitted from being the master showman, gambler, restaurateur, pie man, politician, caterer, theatre owner, sporting promoter, newspaper magnate, and even milk bar operator.

Only Huge Deal would have had the nerve to walk up to H.G. Wells, of *The Time Machine* and *War of the Worlds* fame, and open the conversation with: 'I don't like your political views.'

An astounded Wells, who was wondering who this brash, bullying Australian was, replied: 'What books or articles have you read?'

'Not one,' bellowed McIntosh.

They then went off arm in arm for a five-hour extended lunch, where they finished off drinking bottles of burgundy.

Another boisterous figure, NSW Labor Premier Jack Lang, described Huge Deal as the 'Barnum of Australia . . . He called himself an entrepreneur. Other people called him at times many things not half as complimentary.'

Punch magazine described him as an unadulterated hustler. Or as *Smith's Weekly* explained, if given the chance Huge Deal 'would probably have made a fortune selling moustache-cups to ballerinas or promoting an all-in wrestle between Hitler and the Archbishop of Canterbury.'

Norman Lindsay said Huge Deal's eyes were like a predatory cat, with 'that intent, watchful, slightly ruthless look which never wavers, no matter what other emotion the face is expressing. It is the exclusive property of men equipped for instant action in the conflict of affairs, physical, financial or polemical'.

The fighter Jack Johnson explained Huge Deal succinctly: 'That McIntosh, he could give two pecks to a jaybird and beat him to a tick.'

The get-up-and-go gripped Huge Deal from an early age. By his mid-teens, he'd been a travelling salesman, dug for silver in Broken Hill, worked in a Sydney surgeon's office, worked as a milkman, navvy, farm-hand, woodcutter, miner, boundary rider, engine driver, tarboy in a shearing shed and baker's boy. He had even appeared on stage in a 'Dick Whittington' pantomine.

Being an attendant at a Sydney swimming bath did not excite him, nor did working as a waiter at the Sydney Masonic Hall where he had to occasionally drop rowdy eaters down the back stairs with a quick jab to the ribs. So at 16 he 'drifted into a little catering business'. In other words, selling meat pies to the masses. Starting with just one tray, and six dozen pies, Huge Deal trekked the hard yards, selling pies to hungry punters as they left Sydney racecourses, prize-fight venues and brothels. He even had the nerve to venture into some of Sydney's more notorious cathouses offering pies and pasties to the most famished of prostitutes and clients. The tray was usually empty by the time he left the bordello. While there, he often bumped into famous Sydney identities, including several notable Members of Parliament, whom he would later lean on for special favours.

So successful was the business that within months Huge Deal was selling his product throughout Sydney. Within two years, he boasted 138 salesmen and a chain of cafes, aimed at the masses, where the pies were always 'piping hot' and the food and drink cheap.

Huge Deal always knew his market. He also knew how to diversify and keep his name in front of the public. One minute he had decided to become a boxing instructor and was in charge of a physical culture school. The next, he was trying to clean up the professional cycling ranks, realising that there was easy money to be made in sports promotion.

Huge Deal, who had dabbled in competitive riding but went nowhere, couldn't avoid taking notice of a cycling boom at the turn of the century. It was a worldwide craze. Apart from a dramatic rise in the number of people who were using bicycles as their prime mode of transport around Sydney, there was great interest in the competitive cycling ranks, which unbenown to many was totally corrupt, with the chief riders at the beck and call of the bookies and the serious punters.

Leading riders would gang up on each other, play dead, purposely force someone to crash, or give another rider a special run to ensure that the right result was achieved. Collusion between riders was common to guarantee everyone got their proper share of the prize money. It was a nasty, often violent world. But it was a money-spinner, with leading wheel races attracting capacity crowds, lured by the colour, glamour and danger of the events.

Huge Deal decided to push his authority through official channels by becoming the paid Secretary of the NSW League of Wheelmen, and from there the promoter of the Sydney Thousand race, held at a floodlit Sydney Cricket Ground each year. The Sydney Thousand quickly became the richest individual cycle event in the world. Huge Deal knew that if he was going to make money out of the event, he had to spend it. The trick was to get the best riders to Australia. That was easy. Cyclists were total opportunists and hardly brain surgeons. If you offered the fancy prize money they would come.

For the first Sydney Thousand race at the Sydney Cricket Ground in 1903, McIntosh provided a first prize of 759 pounds, which had the desired effect of luring the best American riders to Sydney. His biggest coup was attracting the black world champion, Marshall W. 'Major' Taylor, who became the immediate favourite of the Australian crowds.

Taylor is now near forgotten, but back then was one of the true identities of the international sporting world. He was the second black world champion in any sport, preceded only by bantamweight boxer George Dixon, and the first black athlete to compete regularly in open, integrated competition for an annual American championship.

In Australia, this shy, religious competitor, who for many years refused to compete on Sunday and even preached at the Wesley Church in Sydney during one visit, was a curiosity item as he was one of the first legitimate international sporting stars to visit the country.

Thousands were at Sydney Harbour for his arrival, including a flotilla of boats that greeted the *Ventura* as it headed towards Circular Quay. His training sessions lured capacity crowds, and they naturally flocked to see him compete. Huge Deal rubbed his hands in delight. Taylor was a money-making machine.

In Adelaide, Melbourne and Sydney, crowds of more than 20,000 were common. Taylor outclassed all the local riders, enabling him to earn more than 4,000 pounds for three months' work. This was the equivalent of the average Australian wage earner's income for 12 years.

However for Huge Deal, having Taylor in town was not entirely easy pickings. While Taylor was admired by the crowds, he was hated by the other American riders and was the victim of racist slurs both on and off the track. Opposing riders, who abhorred the fact that they were being humiliated by a 'darkie', ganged up on him during races, tried to block him, pocket him, knock him down, and often threatened him with physical violence.

For Taylor's second visit to Australia in the 1903–04 season, McIntosh also invited two of his greatest enemies, Americans Floyd MacFarland and Iver Lawson, who were both disgusted when beaten by someone whom they regarded as their social inferior.

MacFarland and Lawson had often tussled with Taylor. According to Taylor, MacFarland was 'the ring leader of the gang of riders who had sworn among themselves to bring about my dethronement as champion of America at all costs'.

MacFarland, a gutter-mouth creep from California, never hesitated in calling Taylor a 'nigger'. He even insulted other white riders when they were 'beaten by a nigger'.

After beating MacFarland and Lawson in one American competition race, Taylor had to retreat to the dressing room where MacFarland again physically and verbally threatened him, taunting him with a large plank of wood.

As for Lawson, he was once asked by an Australian journalist of his relationship with Taylor. He replied: 'We never speak, and we pass in the street without noticing one another.'

Huge Deal was aware of this volatile relationship and knew he could build it up to entice even larger attendances. The black–white line was a promoter's dream.

Huge Deal was on Major Taylor's side, describing him as a 'wonderful darkie'. But elsewhere in Australia, the black cyclist encountered racism, which included bad decisions from judges, dodgy races where the rest of the field were allowed to gang up on him and the withholding of prize money.

Before the 1904 Sydney Thousand event, Taylor complained to an Adelaide newspaper that local officials 'entertained a disgusting prejudice against me. They have regarded me merely as a revenue-earning machine, nothing more. I could fill up your papers with incidents of how this bias has been displayed.'

Lawson and MacFarland revelled in this atmosphere, bullying Taylor by working together in races, until Lawson was suspended for a year for a foul in a match race in Melbourne which saw Taylor crash heavily. According to Taylor, Lawson swung to the centre of the track, aiming directly at his black opponent. 'It looked like murder,' Taylor said, 'and although no bones were broken I suffered the worst fall I ever had, and was unable to ride for the next fortnight.'

In Sydney, Huge Deal heard a rumour that another scheme to thwart Taylor had been organised. For the Sydney Thousand final, MacFarland was allegedly trying to fix the event, plotting with several other riders to organise a betting coup by pinning Taylor to the back of the field, which would permit one of the long-priced riders to win the 759 pound winner's prize. Those involved in the fix would share the prize money, plus win a mountain of money on the side through an intermediary backing the winning rider with the unsuspecting bookies.

At first, everything worked to plan. Taylor, who started from scratch, was pinned to the back of the field through clever blocking moves, mainly conducted by MacFarland. In the last lap, Taylor attempted to make his charge and was again checked, eventually finishing fourth, ten lengths behind the winner, Larry Corbett, who had started with a 110 metre handicap.

Huge Deal, who had a notion of what had happened, encouraged the second placegetter, Paddy O'Brien, one of the few honest riders in the event, to lodge a protest against Corbett. After being prodded long enough by Huge Deal, O'Brien claimed that Corbett and third placegetter, New Zealander D.J. Plunkett, had collaborated to stop him winning. As soon as the protest was lodged, a seething MacFarland confronted Huge Deal, screaming: 'I'll kill you, ya fat swindling bastard.'

Huge Deal refused to be stood over, looked MacFarland up and down, and said very slowly: 'Watch what you say son, and keep your fists to yourself. You can't fight any better than you can ride. I'll kill you.'

During his days as Secretary of the League of Wheelmen, Huge Deal had become accustomed to intimidation, especially at judiciary meetings where cyclists would walk in and place their hand guns on the table. That was a sign that they weren't going to be messed around by the official body.

Huge Deal would simply sweep the guns off the table and onto the floor. He was also prepared for them, having a roll of music on his desk. He would tap the roll, which consisted of the song 'Oh! How Wonderful!', on the table to indicate that inside it was a solid bar of iron, which he wouldn't think twice about using if some upstart cyclist tried to get heavy with him. As soon as a cyclist heard that distinctive, ghostly tap, tap, tap, they knew it was time to retreat. Huge Deal always made certain that everyone knew exactly who was boss.

Huge Deal also played tough with those who had rigged the Sydney Thousand. He disqualified seven of the 11 starters for periods of between six months and three years. The ringleader, MacFarland, was outed for three years, Corbett two years and Plunkett 12 months.

The protest was also upheld, with O'Brien receiving the winner's prize and Taylor the runner-up prizemoney of 100 pounds.

Norman Lindsay became a close colleague of Huge Deal during that period. The artist explained how volatile the situation was in his autobiography, *My Mask*.

'My position on that sporting rag, the *Hawklet* gave me free entrance to such events, and it was due to that privilege that I met Mac. The running in that big race had become extremely crook, and Mac was given the Herculean job of disqualifying any rider who disobeyed the regulations for straight riding. On that score there were plenty of riders who did not stop short of murder when it came to putting out of action a rider who looked like winning a race. This was done by a contact with his back wheel, which sent both rider and bicycle skidding across the track with a velocity begotten by the speed they were travelling at.

'Of all the denizens of the sporting world I had to do with in those days, bike riders were the toughest. It is not an overstatement to say that Mac risked being maimed for life when he charged in among them to select subjects for disqualification. In his account of the fights he had with them, prize-ring rules were dispensed with. No street-fighting tactics were barred, from a clout with a lead pipe to a kick in the _____ well, I believe the correct synonym for that section of the male anatomy is the groin.

'But Mac was equipped for such a job. Stockily built but quick on his feet, with powerful shoulders and a knock-out punch in both fists and with pugnacity in every line of his short-nosed, broad-cheeked, square-jawed face, he might have been as potent a figure in the prize-ring as in promoting fights with other bruisers.'

Eventually interest in cycling began to peter out, and the always restless Huge Deal was looking for other fields to conquer. Boxing soon tantalised his business senses.

Even though he had sold his pie carts to Sargents, Huge Deal remained involved in the catering business, investing in numerous hotels and guesthouses, including The Creel near Jindabyne, where he became 'the first man to take china cups to the top of Kosciusko'.

But he assumed larger fortunes could be made closer to home. The imminent visit of the 12,000 strong American Fleet in late 1908 to Sydney, on a triumphant tour of the Pacific, had him seriously thinking. With the Japanese influence in the Pacific intensifying, and a widespread xenophobic fear of a Yellow Peril invasion, Australia was eager to latch itself onto the might of the Americans.

This prompted an official government invitation to Teddy Roosevelt's Great White United States Pacific Fleet, so that Australia could prove to those irritants within Asia to stay away because the power and numbers were with them.

The arrival was treated as a crucial and historic diplomatic occasion, intensifying strategic links between Australia and the United States, as well as a timely opportunity to show themselves off as a vigorous, burgeoning nation.

But for Huge Deal he had only one thought in mind – how could he fleece the visitors. With so many sailors in town, it was ripe for a smart entrepreneur to make a killing, especially if he could come up with the ideal way to entertain them and take their money.

And what better way than a world heavyweight title fight involving one of their own.

When Huge Deal heard the Fleet was on their way, he hired all the amusement parks, halls and sports grounds in Sydney as well as all the motor boats in the Harbour. He sought a week's option on 'every dance hall, restaurant and theatre in the city – so that when the Fleet dropped anchor I should have the entertainment market cornered'.

One of Huge Deal's best scams was to buy up all the flags in the Commonwealth, so that the Australian Government, desperate to provide the ideal welcome, had to buy all the bunting from him, naturally at an exorbitant price.

'It seemed to me that someone ought to make a whole lot of money out of that visit. I saw no reason why it should not be Hugh D. McIntosh. I was told that the Fleet's visit would bring 12,000 sailors into Sydney – and out of the blue it came to me – a fight between their hero Tommy Burns and an Australian. That would pull 'em in by the thousand.

'I grabbed a sheet of paper and a pencil and dived into a sea of calculations. I emerged breathless, but more wildly enthusiastic than ever. "Twelve thousand sailors," I reasoned. "If only half of them want to see the fight – that's six thousand. And six thousand sailors at ten bob a head represents 3,000 pounds."'

Huge Deal cabled his offer to Burns – 4,000 pounds for two fights against local fighters, plus fares and expenses. Not surprisingly, Burns, a Canadian-born scrapper who was perceived by many to be American, immediately accepted the offer for what he assumed would be two easy walkovers.

Even though Huge Deal then conceded that 'people thought I had gone crazy', the general public were making further serious questions about his sanity when they realised he didn't actually boast a boxing arena to stage any of the planned fights.

Out came the Huge Deal rat cunning.

He'd noticed a large open area of market gardens at Rushcutters Bay – the perfect size to erect a large multipurpose stadium. The area was owned by a local ironmonger named Jim Furness. Huge Deal had heard Furness was interested in leasing part of the land for a reasonable price, so he could use the money to renovate his shop in Kings Cross.

One day, Huge Deal decided to confront Furness about the plot of land. Dressing down to look like a tramp, by wearing an old shabby suit, worn out shoes, and patched pants that didn't extend down to an old pair of dirty socks, Huge Deal put his best Hang Dog Harry look on, walked down to Rushcutters Bay from the city and wandered aimlessly around the vacant land.

'Are you the boss?' Huge Deal asked Furness, who was about to shoo the intruder from his property.

'Yes, I am. What do you want?'

'I'm looking for a place to put up a nice two-man boxing show with a view of making a bob or two during the Fleet week, and am wondering if you may be able to rent some of your land for the occasion.'

Furness looked Huge Deal up and down and laughed.

'You wouldn't have the money to pay what I'd want.'

For effect, Huge Deal then scrounged through his pockets, produced a few old, crumpled pound notes, and then let them slip through his fingers onto the ground.

The haggling began. Eventually Furness felt sorry for 'the shabby stranger', agreeing to a deal where two pounds weekly rent would be paid for two years, with the right to a renewal for the same terms at four pounds a week.

Several days later, the owner was shocked to see on his property vast piles of building material, wooden structures and seating, with the man, not so long ago in hand-me-downs now resplendent in a three-piece suit, top hat and smoking a large cigar, supervising a mass of workers.

'What's going on?' a staggered Furness asked the re-made man.

'Oh nothing,' replied McIntosh, thrusting the rental contract into his suit pocket, 'Just getting ready for a world title fight.'

Thus the famous Sydney Stadium was born, and Furness suddenly realised he was the victim of a sting. Huge Deal was now made, even if he was still strapped for cash. This prompted him to borrow the slats of wood, required for the Stadium seating, by promising a timber yard operator he would bring all the timber back at the end of the boxing season.

Getting an opponent for Burns, the same scrapper who several months earlier had been angered that J.W.H.T. Douglas had hammered away at him during an exhibition bout, was easy. Bill 'Cyclone' Squires, the favourite boxer of Melbourne businessman and illegal totalisator operator John Wren, was eager for another go at Burns. Squires, also known as 'Boshter Bill', was a shearer from Narrabri and had fought Burns in San Francisco and Paris without luck or longevity in the ring.

The Burns wins were short and sweet, but Squires, gloomily eating a pie in one of Huge Deal's cafes some months later, said to the matchmaker: 'I reckon I could beat Burns easily under the Australian sun.'

'Right, you're on!'

Huge Deal then headed to Adelaide to greet Burns, who had travelled by sea from Europe for what the Canadian assumed would be a short Australian sojourn. Burns was easy to pick. He was a Napoleonic-like figure, with dark hair brushed across a pale forehead, atop a short, tubby figure. He had the physique of a boxer, but the head of a puffy dictator. After an official lunch in Adelaide, the pair caught the train to Melbourne before heading to Sydney the next day.

On the day of the fight, Huge Deal knew that his hunch was right. The open-air stadium, tacked together with borrowed wood and galvanised iron, boasted 20,000 spectators, while hundreds more jostled outside, trying to find a way to sneak in after the 'house full' signs were put up. Desperate fans even tried to sit atop telegraph poles to get a glimpse.

Huge Deal boasted a British Empire record gate of 13,600 pounds, and a fight which lasted until the 13th round when Burns, struggling with influenza, eventually knocked out the gallant Australian.

Minutes after the knockout, Huge Deal made an unexpected discovery. While musing what a great hunch it had been to plan a huge fight to coincide with the American Fleet's visit to Sydney, he suddenly stared and blinked in astonishment. 'I looked to the right and the left, in front of me and behind – and nowhere could I see the familiar blue of a sailor's uniform. In a sea of straw hats there wasn't a single doughboy.

'No-one else realised how my calculations had misfired. But while everyone was congratulating me on my astuteness I knew that only an amazing stroke of fortune had made my first boxing promotion a success.

'The Fleet upon whom I had depended had given me the cold shoulder – but I had packed the Stadium without them! As a matter of fact there were only two sailors in all that vast crowd – and they were both fighting drunk! They staggered into the ring after the big fight and offered to fight anyone in the Stadium for half a sovereign.

'In spite of this, Australian fight fans had rolled up in their thousands, and so it was that the biggest mistake I ever made brought me a fortune.'

Then again, Huge Deal was given some sort of hint that the locals were gripped in everything boxing when 4,000 people greeted Squires as he arrived at Sydney's Central Station for the fight, and again a few days later when 7,000 people, including several hundred women, milled around the area to greet Burns's train from Melbourne.

Huge Deal now knew what the licence was to print money. Organise world ranked title fights and the Australian crowds would come. You didn't need American Fleets as excuses – the locals were hungry for international quality competition and were far easier to manipulate. And what better fight than a world title fight involving black versus white. Apart from the natural sporting appeal, old-fashioned racism would act as another teaser at the box office. Thousands would come just to see a white man knock out one of those mysterious, dangerous 'darkies'.

In Huge Deal's favour, Burns was already in the country. All he had to do was convince the most formidable, most boisterous, most charismatic, most fearsome, most hated boxer to make his way to Australia and take on Burns for a world title fight.

In the end, luring the gargantuan black American fighter, Jack Johnson, was relatively simple. He just had to offer money. Burns was more difficult, especially as for some time he had been bobbing and weaving around Johnson, avoiding a black–white tussle for the world title.

You can easily understand why anyone would want to keep Jack Johnson at arm's length. Hailing from Galveston, Texas, he was the most brutal of pugilists, having learned his trade in the most frightening of arenas where six Negroes would be 'pitchforked' into a ring, with the last man standing receiving a purse of five dollars. With no referee and no actual rules, the other five would always turn on Johnson because he was the biggest foe. Refusing to be intimidated by such weight of numbers against him, Johnson, who had learnt the basics defending himself on the waterfront, would always somehow turn his opponents back onto each other, with his brilliant body slide and angry tongue either seeing him knock each one out in turn, or distracting them enough for him to win the money.

As his opponents lay squirming on the canvas, Johnson darted around the ring, grabbing as much of the coin shower, before fleeing into the distance, usually chased by the gamblers who had lost out on their bets. Desperate for money, Johnson and the likes would agree to such battles, even to the extent of being blindfolded, or fighting in the nude.

After that regular ordeal, the professional boxing ranks were a breeze, and soon Johnson was knocking out anyone and everyone. However, the opponents were selective. So many formidable white boxers refused to go anywhere near Johnson citing the colour line and the fact that it was demeaning to lower yourself and fight a filthy, dirty nigger.

Eventually running out of opponents, a disgusted Johnson had to leave America in search of fights. In December 1906, Johnson headed to Australia for the first time.

Johnson remains one of the most extraordinary sporting characters ever to visit Sydney. A big, swaggering man, he was so proud of his colour, so proud of his heritage, and so full of himself. He dressed like a dandy, with coat, cane, cap, and female accessory on the right arm.

But he was a mighty competitor. As Huge Deal described him: 'Arrogant and unconquerable, bestriding the world like a black colossus, insolently cocksure that nowhere was there a man to beat him.'

Within days of first sighting Circular Quay, Big Jack was making his mark and striking a victory for black over white, which all came out in a court case some months later.

Johnson loved maiming the white male flesh in the ring, and in the bedroom manipulated white female flesh, especially those from the theatrical trade. For white women, in particular Tivoli showgirls, he soon became a sexual magnet. This included a certain Miss Alma Adelaide Lillian 'Lola' Toy, who was shattered to read in a local paper that Jack had told a Californian journal that he was about to marry her. While enjoying Papa Jack's company in his private room at the Sir Joseph Banks Hotel in Botany, she wasn't exactly delighted that Sydney society, of which she was a serious part, had discovered her sexual longing for the other colour. She feigned innocence and sought libel damages of 2,000 pounds. As one newspaper put it: the wealthy Lola was as 'White as her gold was yellow'.

In a sordid court case, Lola somehow convinced the jury that she was innocent, even though witnesses said that she was seen entering Johnson's hotel room on a regular basis, watched him train, had been seen driving around town with Johnson in a sulky, and that Johnson had given her the nickname: 'Baby'.

The case against Lola was convincing, but the jury, impressed by how she had spectacularly fainted when leaving the witness box, awarded her 500 pounds damages.

Big Jack, who was still being avoided by most opponents even on this side of the world, had time for a few bouts in Australia, winning them quickly and easily. He was just as volatile out of the ring. Suddenly he was at odds with his manager, a certain Mr Maclean. Maclean argued that Johnson owed him 112 pounds, but the boxer refused to give him anything, having spent all his money on certain 'expenses', in other words wining, dining and squiring Sydney showgirls.

Maclean, with a sheriff's officer by his side, fronted Johnson in the main bar of the Commercial Hotel in Castlereagh Street. They went out into the street and the sheriff handed Johnson the writ. Johnson took one look at it and smashed his right fist into Maclean's nose, breaking it in several places. The force of the impact saw Maclean catapulted into a nearby tobacconist's shop.

Johnson was arrested and sent to the lock-up. In the Police Court the following day, evidence was provided that Johnson had been provoked by his manager, who had called him a 'big black . . .'. That didn't convince the magistrate, who obviously thought the same of Johnson, fining him five pounds.

What had prompted Maclean to pursue Johnson for missing funds was that he'd heard the boxer had made a windfall at a Melbourne race meeting. The whisper was that Johnson had made more than 7,000 pounds betting on a horse. Shortly after scuffling with Maclean, Johnson fled Australia for San Francisco in mid-1907, with most of his money intact, but vowing he would 'never return'.

Then again money can make anyone dance. Especially the most cantankerous and conceited like Big Jack.

Chapter 9

Still Got It Son

Huge Deal hovered above Snowy.

'Still got it son,' Huge Deal breathed all over Snowy, who was sitting on his haunches in a ramshackle dressing room at Huge Deal's makeshift Sydney Stadium, trying to recapture his breath.

Huge Deal had not only convinced Snowy he had to be the referee for the Burns–Johnson stoush in December 1908, but that he should also bring in the crowds two weeks before the big event by agreeing to a special exhibition bout with the world champion. Snowy still had some money left from his overseas venture, but needed a steady income flow to pay the rent at the Kings Cross terrace which he again shared with two of his brothers, Fred and Harold. They didn't have to bother too much about food, because Mrs Baker, who lived down the road towards Darlinghurst, regularly arrived with meals and other supplies. But some money was required to keep the landlord away.

Huge Deal came to the party, offering Snowy a lucrative retainer to do some work for him, which included being prepared to be a punching bag for Tommy Burns. Although still allegedly an amateur boxer, Snowy crossed the line, agreeing to be paid for jumping into the ring. They just had to keep it quiet, so he could continue the illusion that he was a pure amateur. He knew it helped his public image.

That week Snowy discovered he was still a revered figure in Sydney, when a capacity crowd flocked to the Domain Baths to be part of a 'welcome home' fete. In response, the showman gave a display of 'the latest Continental diving' from the 60-foot tower and springboard.

A few days later, Snowy was in the new Stadium ring, delighted that he remained a local idol and determined to show he was of a similar standing to the formidable Tommy Burns.

As *The Referee* reported: 'Ten thousand people, among whom was a liberal sprinkling of ladies, had gathered within the huge enclosure at Rushcutters Bay, and thus paid a remarkable compliment to the two famous athletes who were the principal figures in an excellent show.'

Beginning proceedings was Sir Francis Suttor, now the president of the Legislative Council.

'Sir Francis Suttor, directly the roar of applause which greeted Snowy Baker's appearance in the ring had subsided, referred to the young Australian's popularity, his experiences abroad, his ill-luck as far as illness was concerned and his successes.

'Snowy spoke well and from his heart. He was glad to be home again. He had been unfortunate in some respects, but there were compensating happenings. Many true friends had been made, and the past two years would be looked upon by him with a pleasure that could not be explained. (Cheers).

'Regarding his narrow defeat in the final of the Olympic Games middleweight boxing championship, he had nothing further to say than that it was the fortune of war that he had been called upon to box four times in one afternoon. The man (Mr Douglas) who beat him was the best boxer in the whole competition, and the decision was a fair one. (Great applause.)'

Off went the dressing gown, and straight into a tussle with Burns.

Snowy looked strapping, but even more impressive was Burns, who despite several months of the good life, appeared trim and terrific. After agreeing to McIntosh's terms of 6,000 pounds for the Johnson fight, and putting away several local boxers, Burns and his wife Jewel moved into a Sydney harbour mansion; Tommy spent most days going to the races, while Jewel frequented the best clothing and hat boutiques. At night, they were often seen in the front row at the symphony. They also swanned around town in their new Fiat automobile, eyeing off prize real estate.

From there they spent a few weeks in a resort owned by Huge Deal near Mt Kosciusko, before heading for Sheilah, a majestic cottage at Medlow Bath, near the Hydro Majestic Hotel resort in the Blue Mountains. All a vast contrast to what he had come from.

Burns was a major contradiction. In his early days, he was obsessed with violence. But like so many boxers attempting to overcome their guilt, he later became a religious zealot, spouting the word of love. But not even his days spreading the deeds of the gospel would stop him from being arrested for drug possession. His other obsessions were strong booze and strong cigars. This ensured that he always had a fat face above a stately paunch.

He was penny pinching one minute, renowned for being 'as crooked as a dog's hind leg' and relentless in demanding exorbitant purses for his fights, then unbelievably generous the next. He was a ruthless boxer, who convinced himself that he hated his opponents, and then just minutes after smashing them to oblivion would invite them out to dinner.

Modest one second, an impossible showoff and boring braggart the next. Foul-mouthed in the ring, he was so well spoken out of it. During his time in Sydney, he drew capacity crowds at special charity shows, where he would have people weeping as he explained how poor he was as a child. Then an uncontrollable inferiority complex would return that saw him repeatedly exaggerate his own feats when interviewed by boxing writers. One writer W.W. Naughton, *The Referee*'s American correspondent, described Burns as being 'puffed to the bursting point with his own importance'.

It was all bluff, especially as Burns told British referee, Eugene Corri, before sailing for Australia that he would give Johnson 'the fight of his life'. But Burns conceded to Corri that he didn't think he could beat Johnson.

Burns and his wife had been accepted by Sydneyites, who believed he was the man to put 'that ugly, big, black coon' in his place. He was the saviour of supposed clean living, who would prove that the white race remained dominant and supreme. As the *Sydney Illustrated Sporting and Dramatic News* cried: 'Citizens who have never prayed before are supplicating Providence to give the white man a strong right arm with which to belt the coon into oblivion.' 'Coon' was a relatively pleasant term for Johnson, when compared to *Fairplay* magazine which described Tommy's black opponent as a 'huge, primordial ape'.

Interest in the fight was overwhelming, generating pages and pages of copy in newspapers and magazines in the weeks leading up to the bout, with the fighters' every move chronicled in minute detail. It was an engrossing melodrama.

To turn away thousands of people from the Burns–Baker exhibition was yet another example of how much the fight had gripped Sydney.

Huge Deal was even inundated with letters from women who wanted to watch Burns train. They complained that as they were not allowed to attend the fight, they could at least get a sniff of it at the gymnasium. Huge Deal, ever the opportunist, obliged, permitting women to attend Tommy's Wednesday and Saturday sessions, even putting on a pot of tea and a table full of pastries. As *The Bulletin* explained: 'McIntosh has a tender feeling towards the fight-loving female. She is going to make the cinematograph pictures profitable after the war is over.'

Burns also didn't hesitate in agreeing to Huge Deal's request to be the main attraction at a special exhibition bout at the Stadium against Snowy. It lured around 1,500 women who were attracted by Burns's boyish looks and the presence of a string band, which Huge Deal had decided to have playing when Tommy bashed his own rhythm during a ball-punching routine.

Sir Francis Suttor, like all windbag politicians, had to eventually be coaxed out of the Sydney Stadium ring, enabling Snowy and Burns to start tussling in a four round bout.

The Referee correspondent liked what he saw: 'Now and again, some hard blows were landed, mainly through the vigor of the go and its speed. Snowy's fine left was brought well into play a few times, and Tommy rattled them home from both sides.

'They fought out and close with sustained vim right through each round. All the while the greatest good feeling prevailed, and thousands stood up and cheered a splendid display. It was a fine breather for the champion — something akin to that gallop which the racehorse must have before he may be relied upon to do himself justice.

'Burns added considerably to his admirers by the manner in which he acquitted himself, for Baker is undoubtedly very clever. Nothing better, of its nature, has been seen in Sydney for many a day.'

As the standing ovation subsided, Tommy demanded the megaphone. 'When in London, I boxed with Douglas, the English man who recently so narrowly defeated Mr Baker in the Olympic Championships,' Burns told the crowd. 'And this evening I have had a bout with Mr Baker, and can truthfully tell you, ladies and gentlemen, that I could not say either of the pair is better than the other. I can assure you that Mr Baker is one of the best amateur boxers I have met.'

The crowd again got to their feet. Baker bowed his head. He had won them over yet again. But Snowy had made a fatal mistake. He'd got too close to the Burns camp. And if he wanted to remain the third man in the ring for Australia's most exciting sporting event he had to distance himself from the Burns entourage, and quick. Jack Johnson was no dummy and would not be keen to be dictated to by a referee who had been seen openly fraternising with the enemy.

Snowy's first exercise in trying to convince everyone that he was totally neutral, and would be fair to both Burns and Johnson, was to distance himself from quotes attributed to him when he arrived in Fremantle on his way back from London – comments he'd made before he was approached to be the referee.

In the December 8, 1908 issue of *The Referee*, Snowy was quoted as saying: 'Personally, I think Burns will win. I fancy Burns has too much head for Johnson. Burns's self-control is marvellous and Johnson has not got that facility for keeping himself under control that the Canadian has.'

The following issue of *The Referee* contained an extraordinary retraction, under the heading 'Never Tipped Burns'. It said that Snowy was now 'desirous of having it made known that the reports stating he tipped Burns to win the world's championship were pure invention. He never saw Burns fight, and consequently could not venture an opinion of any kind.'

Obviously Snowy was in a corner and, embarrassed by something he'd said, used the common course of so many edgy, devious sportsmen. Blame the press and then use the press for your own devices.

Jack Johnson was still not convinced.

Big Jack had arrived in Australia in October 1908, prompting one newspaper to cry, 'De big coon am a-comin'.

Although the sports press kept saying that the prize purse would be 7,000 pounds, which would see Burns get 60% and Johnson 40%, the reality of the matter was weighted far greater in the Canadian's favour.

But Johnson didn't seem to mind. Despite his bluff and bluster, Johnson knew where he stood in the world.

When luring Johnson back to Australia for the title fight, Huge Deal's agent told Johnson that Burns had already agreed to a 6,000 pound fee. Although Johnson almost 'fell out of his clothes', he was sceptical, especially after fighting for small purses by John Wren the last time he was in Melbourne, and then having to put up with the notorious businessman complaining that he had lost money on the deal. In the end, Johnson struggled to get his money out of Wren.

Even so, Johnson decided to up the ante, demanding 1,000 pounds. He never thought Huge Deal would agree to it – especially as the highest amount he had received to fight was 200 pounds. But Huge Deal immediately said that 1,000 pounds was his, plus an extra 100 pounds for his share of the film rights.

Johnson headed straight for Australia, still uncertain whether he was involved in an elaborate hoax and whether he would see his promised money.

Huge Deal met Johnson when he arrived in Melbourne, after the black boxer had made a whistlestop in Perth, explaining to local scribes that he was going to kill Burns.

'How does Burns want it? Does he want it fast and willing? I'm his man in that case. Does he want it flat footed? Goodness, if he does, why I'm his man again. Anything to suit; but fast or slow, I'm going to win.' Johnson intensified the pressure by calling Burns a 'bluffer'.

On first sighting, Huge Deal and Johnson were immediately at odds with each other. 'I went to welcome the big negro at Melbourne . . . and from the start I disliked him,' Huge Deal said.

'His bounce and swagger, his exaggerated clothes, and his mouth of glittering gold teeth, all jarred on my nerves.'

The ill wind became even more foul during the trip to Sydney when Huge Deal told Johnson that as he had been in trouble with the police on his previous trip to Australia, he wanted him 'to avoid any such unwelcome publicity' while he was under contract with him.

'For a moment Johnson contemplated his doubled fist. Then, looking me straight in the eye, he said levelly: "If any dirty sucker double-crosses me I'll knock him cold."

'I saw red. "You black swine!" I said leaping to my feet. "If ever you lift your hand to me I'll blow your black head off your body. They'll identify you by your clothes."

'That was no idle threat. I had a revolver in my pocket, and if Johnson had made one pass at me I should have pulled it.'

Johnson's manager, Sam Fitzpatrick, tried to heal the rift, telling Huge Deal that Johnson, now sitting in another carriage, wanted to apologise. 'So far as I'm concerned Sam, Johnson can go to the devil. I don't like him and I don't like his manner. And you can tell him so. In future I'll deal with you only.'

Huge Deal eventually did agree to deal with Johnson, which, not surprisingly, prompted further volatile moments, usually over the subject of whether Snowy should be the referee, or the intricate details of his fight contract.

While Burns was either at the opera or up in the mountains, Johnson headed for the inner Sydney suburb of Botany, where he hammed it up better than anyone. He agreed to do anything for publicity, including improving his stamina by having a red kangaroo brought in a crate to his training camp. The kangaroo was let go and then chased upon by Johnson, who eventually crash tackled the exhausted beast to the ground. 'I raced a kangaroo for a bet, and won,' Johnson bellowed. 'The kangaroo must have been old because he dropped dead.'

A razorback pig was next and then the final test – whether Johnson could catch a hare, that had been let go at a nearby oval, within 20 minutes. This stunt naturally attracted a large crowd and a horde of punters and bookies who wagered on whether Big Jack could mow down the frightened hare. Johnson plucked it by the ears with three minutes left on the clock.

Then it was off into town to meet Huge Deal in his offices in Martin Place to work out who was going to referee the bout. Strangely, Huge Deal had given the boxers the authority to decide between themselves who should be the man in the middle.

Knowing that Burns was difficult and Johnson impossible, Huge Deal was prepared for them – especially the 'nigger' he hated.

Artist Norman Lindsay arrived just before the boxers were to meet and observed: 'I happened to notice a roll of music on Mac's table, which investigation discovered to be rolled round a length of lead pipe.

'"What the devil is this for, Hughie?" I asked.

'"It's for that big black bastard if he ever comes any funny business with me," said Mac. As an instance of Mac's sense of humour, the title of the music was "Sing Me to Sleep, Mother".'

Huge Deal had called for Lindsay to produce a fight poster, which in itself was a masterpiece of race relations propaganda. Lindsay's poster depicted Johnson as a large, wild beast, hovering over and trying to maim a short, statuesque white warrior.

With the music roll strategically placed on his table near his right arm, Huge Deal beckoned the boxers in.

'Look, let's get this referee issue over and done with now,' Huge Deal said to the two boxers, sitting well away from each other, and angrily eyeing each other off.

'I want Snowy Baker as the referee. He is respected here. He has just returned from the Olympic sports championship, and knows his stuff. He knows the boxing game better than anyone else here, and will be totally impartial.

'He is the best amateur athlete in Australia, and a celebrated referee. I nominate Snowy Baker.'

Burns, whittling a stick with a pocket knife, nodded his head in agreeance, but Johnson screamed: 'No way. No way.'

'Why do you object to Baker?'

'Waal, big chief. He's a blond, and I don't like blonds. I saw him walking down the Corso, and well Mr Mac, I saw that guy Snowy Baker, and I tell you, Mr Mac, no blond loves a nigger, so there ain't going to be any Snowy Baker referee for this fight.'

'Oh come on. Baker doesn't hate niggers. If you are not satisfied with his verdict, by reason of any supposed dishonesty, lack of knowledge, or anything of that sort on the part of Mr Baker, I will forfeit 1,000 pounds, which I will specially lodge with *The Referee* newspaper office.'

'No. No. No. This is a contest for the championship of the world, and I am entitled to have a black referee as much as Burns is entitled to have a white one. I'm not asking for a black referee, but I know whatever referee I'll get I'll lose three points in every ten on account of the colour of mah skin.'

Burns butted in, without looking up: 'Yes, they don't like niggers, do they?'

Johnson, who had been nursing a young girl, angrily rose to his feet, while calling out to his manager, Fitzpatrick: 'Sam, take this girl outside.'

'What do you call niggers, Tahmy?'

Johnson strode towards Burns: 'Now, you dirty mongrel I'm going to give you just a taste of what you'll get in the ring.'

Burns made a grab at the heavy ink well on Huge Deal's desk and moved as if he was about to hurl it at Johnson. However, Huge Deal grabbed Burns's arm and ran him into a corner. Ink went everywhere, smearing the table and the Canadian's hands.

'Let him loose, Mr Mac,' Johnson sneered. 'He's tame and harmless. There's ink on your hands, Tommy, you won't be so anxious to fight next Saturday.'

Johnson then accused Burns of swearing in front of a child, prompting Burns to break from Huge Deal's grip, pick up a chair and attempt to smash it over Big Jack's head. Just in time, Huge Deal pulled the chair away from Burns.

Huge Deal recalled: 'At that Burns jumped up and clapped a hand to his hip-pocket as though reaching for a gun. As he did so Johnson shrank back, his face distorted with fear.'

'It was the only time I ever saw him afraid. He would face any man in the world, but he was terrified of firearms. I did not know whether Burns was carrying a gun, but his eyes were blazing, and I had visions of my plans for a world-title match ending with a bullet in Johnson's brain, and a murder charge against Tommy.

'I jumped behind him, twisting his arm up his back, but when I felt in his pocket there was no revolver there. Eventually we succeeded in quieting him down.

'"That guy was going to shoot me," said Johnson, refusing to believe that Burns did not carry a gun. "I know he had one," he insisted. "And you saved my life."'

As the pair were about to leave the room, Huge Deal told them once again: 'If you two do not agree on a referee by tomorrow, I will be appointing Snowy Baker.'

To which Johnson responded: 'If you do, there'll be no fight.'

Huge Deal stood his ground: 'There will be a fight, and you will be in it.'

Johnson turned on his heel and left the room in a huff. Burns followed, saying to Huge Deal: 'Good night', and to Johnson: 'Good night, skunk.'

While Johnson kept saying that he didn't like Baker because of his hair colour, underpinning his disdain was another meeting where the boxer and a female companion were sitting in a Sydney cafe and allegedly heard Baker, at a nearby table, mouthing off about the 'nigger'.

Johnson hadn't actually heard it, but his companion (Hattie McLay, whom he called his wife) had, and Baker was suddenly out of the running.

As *The Referee* reported in its fight day coverage: 'He [McIntosh] put up a sturdy shoulder to the nomination of Snowy Baker, whom Johnson would not have at all because of "something" he alleged his wife had overheard at a restaurant, but which something he refused to divulge.'

Johnson hadn't forgotten about Snowy and Burns being photographed arm-in-arm after their exhibition bout. He was also less than impressed with a refereeing decision Baker had made in a local fight a few weeks earlier, when one had thrashed the other, but to the chagrin of the crowd, Snowy adjudicated it a draw.

The other refereeing candidate, Harry Beckett, was no chance after it was discovered he was close colleagues with two big-time Sydney punters, who had backed Johnson heavily.

Peeved that he was suddenly out of the running, Snowy, via Huge Deal, demanded to see Johnson the following morning to sort out the problem. They met in Huge Deal's office.

After being introduced to Johnson, Snowy asked why he objected to him as referee.

'Johnson said to me,' Snowy recalled, '"Mister, no blond likes a coloured man and Mister, if you is referee I won't be in the ring."'

Snowy accepted it in silence.

A few hours later Johnson drove to the Stadium to confront Huge Deal with the most unexpected deal. He wanted Huge Deal to be the referee. Huge Deal was understandably taken aback. He had never refereed before and now, to salvage the world's biggest fight, was asked to be the important third man.

'You're crazy. I've never handled a big fight. And anyway as promoter I couldn't think of it.'

'OK,' Johnson said. 'Then the fight's off.'

Huge Deal argued and threatened, but Johnson kept shaking his head.

'It is all very well of you to say that, but what about Burns?' Huge Deal asked Johnson.

'Ring him up, and find out.'

A few seconds later, Burns was on the phone.

'Tommy . . . Jack Johnson is sitting here with me. He says he wants me to referee. How does that look to you?'

Burns, after a pause, said: 'You will do me, Mac, and tell that nigger, that black skunk, I will knock his head clean off.'

Huge Deal turned to Johnson and said: 'Tommy says he is satisfied for me to act and that he will beat your head off next Saturday.'

Johnson laughed it off.

Huge Deal asked Johnson why he wanted him, especially with all his responsibilities as promoter. Johnson said that McIntosh was the only person he could trust because he couldn't afford to do anything wrong.

'OK then, piss off, I don't want to see either you or Burns till I meet you in the ring.'

Huge Deal immediately contacted Snowy, telling him the bad news that he couldn't convince Johnson he should be the referee, but quickly raising his spirits by saying that he desperately needed his help on fight day. While Huge Deal would be the official referee, he wanted Snowy at ringside where, through an elaborate system of hand signals, he could indicate to him what to do if he found himself in trouble and what decisions he should make to keep the boxers and crowd at ease.

Snowy readily agreed, especially as Huge Deal promised him that if he helped him out, the favours later would be flourishing – including being appointed the Stadium's chief referee. Huge Deal also said he would make certain Snowy received part of the fight profits. Snowy replied that he'd be there when the gates opened.

Luckily Snowy was an early riser, because if he had left his run any later on the day of the fight, he wouldn't have got anywhere near the Stadium. With the fight scheduled to start at 11 am, so it wouldn't clash with the Randwick race meeting, thousands of spectators had decided to camp in the area the night before so they could get the best seats when the gates opened at 7 am.

The fight had tantalised the whole country. Everyone wanted to be there, to the extent that an hour before the first round, the crowd inside the Stadium was well over the 20,000 mark, with another 10,000 milling around it, trying to find a vantage point from any tree or terrace house in the vicinity. Many others were bashing on the Stadium doors complaining that they had tickets, but couldn't get in. It was one wild, chaotic scene.

They had travelled from as far as Melbourne and Brisbane; some even sailing in small crafts down the coastline from the north of Queensland. Some collapsed through liquor even before they got into the Stadium, while those who did get in were served a variety of hot snacks by French, Italian and Greek cooks including, of course, Huge Deal's famous meat pies. Strangely the only casualty among those not in the ring on the day was a policeman, who fell from a tram bound for Rushcutters Bay.

There was also a bit of argy-bargy alongside a platform near the ring, which had been commandeered by the official photographer. When he arrived, the snapper discovered an entrepreneur with a panorama camera had taken over the platform. Police refused to intervene, but eventually the official photographer called in a hefty bouncer who threw the intruder off the platform, and threatened to kick 'the heads off any others who attempted to follow'.

So important was the fight that it had lured boxing writers from around the world, and literary heavyweights such as Jack London, author of *The Sea-Wolf* and *The Call of the Wild*, who had sailed into Sydney on his ketch, *Snark*, to cover the fight for the New York *Herald*, the *Argus* in Melbourne and *The Australian Star*.

So overwhelmed was Huge Deal to have the world's most popular writer in the crowd that he permitted London's wife, Charmian, to be the only official female spectator.

It was a significant moment for women's liberation, because, as the *Argus* put it: 'No lady has ever been admitted to an important fight in Australia before.' In the end, there were two women in the crowd – the other dressed up as a man to get past the gatekeepers.

In the front row, just down from London and his wife, was Snowy and a few seats further along was the infamous One-Eyed Connolly – Australia's most famous gatecrasher. For decades, this devious shonk had somehow conned his way into every important sporting, political, legal and diplomatic affair by talking his way in and out, choosing various guises and names.

This time One-Eyed had actually bought a ticket but maintained that he hadn't lifted his standards, arguing that he was able to pay for the ringside seats through the proceeds of a swindle he and a colleague had conducted on a well-known Sydney shopkeeper.

Attorney-General Billy Hughes was also at ringside and like everyone else, was unaware of the drama which was occurring in the dressing rooms just minutes before the fight.

While Huge Deal was getting changed into his refereeing garb in a little tin shed behind the main tier of seats, Fitzpatrick, Johnson's manager, was banging on the door. Snowy had just left, advising Huge

Deal that he would be perched near Burns's corner and that he should keep looking his way for instructions.

Snowy also advised him: 'Don't take any crap from either boxer. They'll try everything on you. The only way you'll get their respect is to stand up to them. You must always be regarded in their eyes as the Boss.'

It proved handy advice, especially as Fitzpatrick's first words were: 'Say, Mac, I'm sorry to have to tell you that the black coon says he won't get into the ring unless he gets another 3,000 pounds.'

Suddenly Mac produced a pistol from his coat pocket and brandishing it in front of Fitzpatrick yelled: 'Tell him to be in the ring at half past 10, or he will be in the morgue at quarter to 11. Just tell him. If he's not in the ring in the next few minutes, I'll blow his brains all over the floor.'

Fitzpatrick sauntered off, but was back within seconds.

'It's no good. He's not going into the ring.'

Huge Deal, remembering how Johnson quivered when Burns threatened him with an invisible pistol, decided that to stop any more nonsense, he had to confront Johnson face-to-face. He burst into Johnson's dressing room and growled: 'If you're not in the ring in two minutes, I'll blow your brains all over the floor.'

Suddenly Johnson wanted to fight, replying: 'Massa Mac. Ah'm on mah way.'

However, the shenanigans continued when the boxers entered the ring under an overcast sky. Burns had received a wild ovation, Johnson a trickle of applause, washed away by a chorus of boos. Suddenly, Johnson felt as if he was in the Colosseum, surrounded by lions.

Before heading to his corner, Johnson noticed something strange about Burns. There was an unusual swathe of elastic bandages around his elbow.

Huge Deal recalled: 'Just as the timekeeper was about to give the signal to begin hostilities, Johnson suddenly called out to Burns: "Take the bandages off", pointing to his elbows. I went over and examined the bandages and publicly announced through the megaphones that the bandages were all right.'

Johnson immediately replied that there would be no fight. He threw an overcoat over his shoulders, and 'looking like a sulky bear', announced: 'No fight. No fight.' He let his gloves fall to his side, and dropped down on his stool. The great Larry Foley headed towards Johnson's corner, hoping to 'talk some sense with him', but was ignored as the black boxer, according to *The Bulletin* 'sat grinning at the rage of the crowd'.

'For a moment I was stunned. If the fight flopped I stood to lose a fortune. That was the thought that hammered in my brain as I crossed to the negro's corner,' Huge Deal continued.

' "Listen Johnson", I whispered savagely between clenched teeth. "If you don't fight you won't get a shilling from me, and I warn you, you'll live to regret it."

'Deliberately he ignored me. Yawning, he stretched, one hand out to a second. "Say fellar," he said. "get this glove off. I can't waste time around heah."

'In a cold fury, I turned away. "I'll give you just 60 seconds to change your mind." Then leaning over to the timekeeper, I called: "One minute from now – bang that gong."

'I waited with my heart in my mouth while the seconds ticked away. Johnson did not move, and I could hear the crowd, growing impatient at the delay, beginning to murmur. I knew that if there was no fight there would be a riot. I knew that unless something happened in the few seconds that remained I should lose many thousands of pounds.

'Thus I stood, waiting and wondering and silently counting . . . 48 . . . 49 . . . 50. With ten seconds to go, Burns looked across at me and then to the motionless, defiant figure of his challenger. Then with an impulsive gesture, he ripped the bandage from his elbow. Almost as he did so the gong rang, and while the crowd roared white man and black came leaping from their corners. The fight was on!'

Burns had made a fatal error. He should have kept the bandages on. In the end a Johnson disqualification was the only way he was going to win this mismatch. Within seconds, it was obvious that Burns was way out of his league and his world heavyweight title was about to be farewelled.

At the 15 second mark, Johnson, breaking away from a clinch, caught Burns with a right uppercut, knocking the champion flat on his back. The crowd were aghast. The great white hope had only lasted a few seconds. Johnson hovered over Burns, taunting him with, 'All right Tahmy, here I am', showing off his array of gold-filled teeth.

Huge Deal, wearing a garish large golf cap and white garb, looked towards Snowy, who was sitting next to the Stadium doctor, Sir Herbert

Maitland. With Snowy wildly waving his fingers, Huge Deal took this as the sign that he should start counting Burns out.

Huge Deal began the count at 'five', but Burns was up on his feet on 'eight'. Thankfully, Burns had averted a major catastrophe. If the fight had lasted just 25 seconds, the crowd would have rioted, with Huge Deal the main target.

Burns later said that when Johnson first hit him: 'I dropped like a log. The world spun crazily, a huge red blur obscured everything . . .'

Nonetheless the fight was over. Footage of the film shows a grossly distorted, often ridiculous bout. For the next 13 rounds, Johnson taunted Burns, propping up the fat, sprawling figure, who often used Big Jack as a holding rail. Throughout the rounds, Huge Deal scurried around the ring, making out as if he knew what was actually going on but instead appeared totally lost as he watched Big Jack take Burns on a long meandering waltz around the canvas − pushing him this way, knocking him another.

Johnson was running the show while Huge Deal tried to convince himself that wandering aimlessly around the ring, looking stern, was the way to bluff anyone. Johnson knew that he had conned Huge Deal and could do whatever he liked, later revealing that McIntosh had been nervous during the fight, and soon gave up trying to separate the boxers in the clinches.

'Incapable' was how one of Australia's leading boxing experts, Will Lawless, who wrote under the nom de plume 'Solar Plexus', later described Huge Deal's refereeing abilities.

If Burns, who appeared as though he was about to fall flat on his face at any second, connected with a punch, it didn't register. While Johnson kept bashing away at a pathetic opponent, throughout the footage, you can see his constantly babbling pitter-patter, pitter-patter in Burns's ear, 'Good boy, Tahmy. When are you going to have a go, Tahmy? Oh oh oh you get me a good one there. What about your right, Tahmy, where is it? You can't hurt. You can't hurt. Who taught you to hit, you clown? Your mother? Come on you yellow cur. I'm here to fight, not to talk. Come on leedle Tahmy let's fight − if you've got the guts. You're white, dead scared white − white as the flag of surrender. You like to eat leather? Try this. Poor little Tahmy, did someone kid you you were a fighter. Even money, Burns is there at the finish. A hundred to one he don't black my eye.' Pitter-patter. Pitter-patter.

Johnson even had time for conversation with ringside guests, telling them how useless Burns was. During one round, he posed for a ringside photographer, yelling out: 'Did you get that one? Anyway I'll give you a good picture.'

He even goaded Burns when one punch split Johnson's lip, prompting him to spit blood. 'See Tahmy, the same colour as a white man's blood. The same colour as a yellow fella's blood.'

This was no proper fight, it was an embarrassment. Or as Burns put it many years later: 'It was strictly a throwback – a couple of cavemen meeting on some long-forgotten path in an ancient forest, both disputing the right of the other to pass.'

Between rounds, the chief caveman, Johnson, would fill his mouth with water, gargle away, and then spit it all over the nearby press bench. Snowy narrowly avoided one long snake-like slag that hit several members of the Sydney sportswriting entourage, including the man from the *Sydney Morning Herald*.

Meanwhile Burns, who after each round had his hair combed and parted to look his best for the official film, was being rubbed down with champagne. The bubbles were supposed to revitalise the body. In Burns's case, it was a sheer waste of quality alcohol.

By round 11, it appeared as if Burns's jaw was broken. Even Huge Deal was starting to wonder: 'For several rounds Burns boxed with his mouth wide open, almost everybody being of the opinion that his jaw was broken.'

By this stage, Burns was looking shocking. His face was streaked with dribbling blood, his eyes and cheeks puffy.

The champagne bottle was put aside, especially when Johnson's camp kept yelling: 'Take him away! His jaw's broken.'

The police began to move in and then Superintendent Mitchell during the 14th round, when Burns crashed to the floor yet again following another mighty right to his jaw, called out to Huge Deal, 'Enough.' In the background, Snowy was also waving away, trying to get Huge Deal's attention to call the fight off before Burns was badly maimed.

Huge Deal ignored the calls, prompting Police Superintendent Mitchell to try to climb through the ropes, near where Burns had fallen in a heaving state. Eventually Huge Deal noticed the Superintendent, and screamed out as Big Jack went in for the kill, 'Stop, Johnson.'

Huge Deal then waited for silence. 'I declare Johnson winner on points.'

The announcement was met with resounding boos, as much anguish that the white man was not as superior as they once thought, as to the fact that Johnson had got on everyone's nerves by taunting and playing with them for the past hour. The black baboon had been a buffoon. The white supremacy crowd did not take kindly to that, arguing that the 'brown man had received too fair a deal'.

Burns, battered and bloodied, pleaded with Superintendent Mitchell to give him another chance, just another round. The Superintendent just waved the pathetic figure away.

Down below Jack London was churning out the metaphors for hungry newspaper editors around the globe. London was angry. He was an avowed racist. He hated Johnson, and everything that he stood for. Before the fight, London admitted that he wanted Burns to win. 'He is a white man, and so am I. Naturally I wanted to see a white man win.' Now the venom oozed out of his typewriter keys.

'The fight! There was no fight! No Armenian massacre could compare to the hopeless slaughter that took place in the Sydney Stadium. The fight, if fight it could be called, was like that between a pygmy and a colossus. It had all the seeming of a playful Ethiopian at loggerheads with a small white man – of a grown man cuffing a naughty child – of a monologue by Johnson who made a noise with his fist like a lullaby, tucking Burns into a crib – of a funeral, with Burns for the late deceased, Johnson for the undertaker, gravedigger and sexton, all in one.

'So far as damage was concerned, Burns never landed a blow. He never fazed the black man. He was a glutton for punishment as he bored in all the time, but a dewdrop had more chance in hell than with the Giant Ethiopian. Goliath had defeated David, that much was clear.

'Johnson play acted all the time, and he played with Burns from the opening gong to the finish of the fight. Burns was a toy in his hands. For Johnson it was a kindergarten romp.'

London then stressed that a great white hope, namely the number one white boxer, Jim Jeffries, had to be lured out of retirement to put someone in their place. 'But one thing now remains. Jim Jeffries must emerge from his alfalfa farm and remove the golden smile from Jack Johnson's face. Jeff, it's up to you. The White Man must be rescued.'

Australia's leading writer, Henry Lawson, was as disgusted by the triumph of black over white.

'It was not Burns that was beaten – for a nigger has smacked your face. Take heed – I am tired of writing – but O my people take heed, For the time may be near for the mating of the Black and the White to breed.'

The London *Observer's* correspondent was more succinct. For him, the whole day was a 'degrading spectacle'.

When news of Johnson's victory reached the United States, innocent blacks were lynched in several Southern State towns, resulting in at least 14 deaths.

A popular US ballad explained it all:

'The Yankees hold the play,
The White Man pulls the trigger,
But it makes no difference what they say,
The world champion's still a nigger.'

Chapter 10

Blows In
and Out of the Ring

WITHIN 12 MINUTES OF JOHNSON BEING DECLARED CHAMPION OF THE world, the Sydney Stadium was empty. A disenchanted crowd dispersed. As they left, journalists scurried around getting opinions from anyone who was anyone on what they thought of the big fight.

Snowy was sought after and found. He told *The Referee*: 'Jack Johnson was much too good for Burns. It was physical power that triumphed all the way.'

Snowy wasn't giving too much away, especially since Huge Deal had promised him nice pickings after agreeing to be the silent referee at the fight. In the end, the bout was so lopsided Huge Deal didn't have to rely on Snowy too much. Big Jack controlled the fight; not Huge Deal.

But Huge Deal, not Big Jack, made a killing out of the fight. Huge Deal worked out that 250 police, 150 mounted police, 250 pressmen and, more importantly, 20,400 spectators attended the fight, and paid 26,400 pounds for the privilege. More than 40,000 people, including hundreds who had paid their weekly wage of a pound for a ticket but were turned away, milled outside for the fight at the Stadium.

Staging the fight cost 10,700 pounds – with Johnson eventually getting 1,538 pounds and Burns 6,212 pounds – while Huge Deal distributed 1,200 pounds among his 244 employees, giving him a clear profit of 14,500 pounds. On top of that came the net profit from the motion picture sale of the fight worldwide which came to 37,000 pounds – including well over 3,000 pounds for 18 performances in Sydney.

Huge Deal also won a 50 pound bet with Johnson that the takings would exceed the Burns–Squires total (13,400 pounds). In all, Huge Deal made 51,550 pounds, supposedly setting himself up for life. To celebrate the windfall, Huge Deal bought three luxury Pierce-Arrow automobiles, and called on his friend Norman Lindsay to paint his coat of arms on the side. He also bought one of the most plush harbourside houses at Darling Point.

Snowy received his cut of 100 pounds. Still, he was soon calling on Huge Deal for help. He couldn't live on that 100 pounds forever. The first favour came just three days after the fight when Huge Deal called on Snowy to be the referee at the Australian lightweight championship bout between Frank Thorn and Rudolph Unholz over 20 rounds at the Stadium. The added highlight was that Big Jack would be in Unholz's corner.

Such an attraction drew a crowd, but Big Jack soon discovered he was hardly an admired winner. In virtually every media outlet, Johnson was castigated for his behaviour. In an editorial, the *Sydney Morning Herald* said Johnson had 'robbed himself of any acclaim which an Australian public . . . might have accorded him on his victory by the display of what the circle he moves in would understand as "flashness".' The *Sydney Mail* explained that Johnson had 'disgusted the public with his tigerish caperings in the ring. We do not altogether regret the contest at the Stadium, but with it we should say, "Halt" for the sake of the fair repute of our city. In view of our opinion of the contest we refrain from giving more than a bare pictorial record.'

Usually the *Sydney Mail* swamped its readers with a multitude of photographs of important events. For the Burns–Johnson debacle, they only published two pre-match posed shots of the boxers, and the crowd leaving the stadium after the fight. No actual shot of the fight was published. Australia did not like flash niggers.

Johnson knew exactly where he stood the following day when 8,000 people returned to the Stadium to watch Huge Deal's movie of the fight. Throughout the showing of the film, Johnson was endlessly jeered, while whenever Burns did anything of note, and that was only occasionally, a wild cheer would erupt.

At the end of the ninth round, the light was lowered temporarily, the film stopped, and with it a great cheer as Burns stepped into the ring to stand beside the grinning Huge Deal. Hat and caps were waved, and many sang 'For He's a Jolly Good Fellow'.

The screen was lowered, and the ex-champion whipped up the crowd even more by saying: 'I was by no means done up in the 14th round, and had the police not interfered I think I might have won.'

The film then continued, with Johnson's appearance being met with loud groans. Across town Johnson appeared at the Tivoli, walking out on stage to a round of cheers, mingled with some hooting.

Johnson hung around Australia for several months, where he suffered endless racist taunts, which ranged from his automobile being vandalised, to posters around town advertising his next public appearance splattered with graffiti and nasty slogans, such as 'The Big Black Skite'.

Huge Deal was off, heading for London, Paris, Berlin and finally the United States to show off his film. He continued to rake in the money as wherever he went, the Johnson–Burns film was a big hit. Before leaving, Huge Deal visited Snowy, and told him he was now the Stadium's official referee.

Burns remained in Australia far longer. Driven by an insatiable passion to drink and gamble, Burns had to keep the money coming in and agreed to travel to the major cities over a six-week period conducting boxing exhibitions on the Tivoli circuit. With him was Snowy and formidable Australian middleweight fighter, Les O'Donnell, who agreed to be his sparring partners.

For Snowy, it was easy money, and appealed to his theatrical sense. He was also a huge Burns fan. His real views on the Burns–Johnson fight only emerged several years later, when he wrote in *The Evening News*: 'All were disgusted at the big black beating the white, and to add to the agony of it, laughing and joking as he did so. The nigger banter hurt the pride of the whites more than anything else.'

Big Jack was right all along. Snowy, an unabashed racist, would have made it hard for him in the ring.

In the meantime, on various stages throughout Sydney, Brisbane, Melbourne, Adelaide and Perth, Snowy would ham it up against Burns, occasionally agreeing to either be the victim of a classic knockdown, or having the former world champion on the ropes with several well-timed, but just missing, hits to the jaw.

It got testy in Adelaide though, as Snowy recalled: 'It was a pleasant engagement until one night at the Tivoli I left-hooked Tommy on the peeper – probably by accident. It cut his eyebrow and blood flowed.

'I never ran backwards faster and farther in my whole life to prevent Tommy from getting revenge by planting a sleep-producing punch on my chin. I'd never been knocked cold in my life . . . Such is life.'

Eventually Burns grew tired of all this, went back to Sydney, and for the next six months, proceeded to lose most of his money from the Johnson fight to Sydney bookmakers. Backing wayward racehorses was a Burns speciality. He eventually left Sydney without a cent or a whimper.

While travelling around Australia with Burns, Snowy somehow managed to fit in a whirlwind romance. After one of the performances in Melbourne, he met a widow named Ethel Rose Mackay, who was 12 years his senior. The daughter of a squatter and the widow of a Victorian physician, Augustus Daniel Kearney, Ethel was immediately swept up by Snowy's athleticism and charm. Adding to the allure was that Ethel was a noted horsewoman, while her deceased husband had been a Victorian representative tennis player and former doubles partner of Sir Norman Brookes.

Up to now, Snowy had been luckless in the love stakes, not surprising considering his very limited social life, and his sporting obsessions, which meant that night life was an impossibility.

Snowy floundered when he first met Ethel, who was astounded that such a worldly, supposedly confident figure, was so shy, so bumbling, when confronted by an interested woman. It was more the case that Snowy had no experience in this area and was a love-struck buffoon. He was immediately impressed with Ethel being so forward, and so keen to make the first move. He loved being wooed. She asked him out to dinner, and they spent the night talking sport. He was captivated, knowing that she wasn't pursuing him for money, as she had been left a substantial sum from her well-to-do husband.

They soon became inseparable, with Ethel following Snowy to Adelaide and Perth, where their affair intensified. Snowy had found his match; a tough, strong-willed woman, who said what she thought. Like so many egotists, he was attracted by someone who was forthright and tried to be his equal. He was also impressed with her practical nature and an eagerness to be successful in whatever she did.

With Ethel came a ready-made family – with two young daughters, Joan and Margaret, aged two and one. As Snowy proposed to her, Ethel warned that due to complications with the birth of her two children, a

Baker son or daughter may be difficult, but that didn't irk the aspiring groom. He said he was more than happy to be a doting father to two ravishing daughters. He had no great ambition to start a Baker male dynasty. He preferred the softness of being surrounded by females who fussed over him.

Within two months they were married, becoming Mr and Mrs Baker on March 31, 1909 at St Mark's Anglican Church in Darling Point – conveniently placed just down the road from the Stadium. Convenient, because later that day, Snowy had to referee a title bout. The honeymoon would have to wait.

The wedding was a low key affair, ignored by most newspapers, but written up by Snowy's most loyal journal, *The Referee*: 'Popular Reg L. (Snowy) Baker entered the bonds of matrimony on Wednesday last, much to the surprise of the great majority of his friends, and they are legion. Snowy has made a good choice indeed; his wife is a very estimable lady, the widow of the late Dr Kearney, erst Victoria's champion tennis player.'

Now 25, with a wife and instant family, Snowy realised it was time he actually established himself in the professional world. He knew he had to curtail many of his sporting activities and establish himself in business.

The regular refereeing position was his financial base, but occasionally Snowy would be lured into showing the broader side of his sporting skills – including one Friday evening at the Stadium where he was talked into joining the Australian buckjumpers show. It wasn't exactly a success, as he was immediately tossed off by an irritated stallion landing bottom first in the sawdust ring.

Snowy also branched out by utilising his sporting skills and athletic passions to open a state-of-the-art gymnasium in Belmont Chambers in the middle of the city in Castlereagh Street.

During his time in Europe, he had visited countless gymnasiums, including several operated by Eugene Sandow, a noted physical instructor. While training in these gymnasiums, Snowy would jot down the makes and models of the various fitness equipment, even getting in contact with the most important suppliers. By the end of the trip he was convinced that similar gymnasiums would work in a country far more orientated towards fitness. He decided to imitate Sandow in Sydney.

Snowy spent months getting a vast range of fitness machines to ensure that by its opening in late 1909, his gymnasium was the place to be seen stripping down and making the body beautiful. Snowy was the high-profile head instructor, and the man to beckon if someone wanted tuition in a variety of sports. It was now time for him to rake in the dollars from his vast sporting knowledge.

His old MP mate, Sir Francis Suttor, did the honours at the opening, explaining how he was so proud that such a skilful young athlete was about to provide Sydney 'with something this city badly needed'.

Then followed a typical Snowy showy display. First he produced swords and proceeded to flail away in foil and bayonet exercises. Then Snowy showed off his skipping prowess, before finishing off with several rounds in the ring, knocking his younger brother, Harold, to oblivion. Within days, the gymnasium was overflowing with those who wanted to be the next Snowy. And within weeks, Snowy, who described himself as a 'physical culture specialist', was widely advertising the virtues of his gymnasium.

Through a regular advertisement in *The Referee*, Snowy recommended coming to his gymnasium where: 'By the aid of scientific exercise, as taught by me, you can secure and maintain splendid health, develop perfectly every part of your body, and thoroughly enjoy life.' Underneath the headline 'Let me give you health and strength' was a photograph of Snowy, stripped down, showing off what he assumed was the perfect body. Vanity was not going to stand in the way of Snowy getting rich.

He also took advantage of his strong links with so many sporting codes, contacting countless football, swimming, athletics and boxing clubs and offering them special deals if their members trained at his gymnasium. His name was a strong lure, and his gymnasium soon became the place for any established or upcoming sportsman to be seen. Snowy worked the network, and in between special classes, made an effort to make everyone, from the best to the nobody, feel as if he was on his way to athletic stardom.

Snowy also started a correspondence course, where people could write in for special brochures on how to get fit, or get one-on-one tuition from Snowy.

A letter came from a client in northern Queensland who was disgruntled that he was not getting the progress he expected and was struggling to lose weight.

Snowy wrote back: 'Do more walking.'

A week later another letter with a northern Queensland postmark hit Snowy's desk. It said: 'Thanks for the advice, Snowy. But I don't know whether it will work. Actually I'm a policeman on the beat.'

The gymnasium became his daytime haunt. At night, he would trek to the Stadium for a series of high-profile fights. In between he tried to see his wife as much as possible, but Ethel soon discovered that she was not exactly at the top of the pecking order. It was an arrangement she became relaxed with, especially as Snowy provided her and her two daughters with a good standard of living, and intense care and loving when he could be dragged away from his many other pursuits.

As with his marriage, Snowy soon discovered he had to be prepared for anything and everything at the Stadium.

Inspired by the money on offer from the Burns–Johnson fight, pugs from around the world headed for Australia, making Sydney a boxing mecca.

Consequently each week, fights of the highest quality were on show at the Stadium. Not surprisingly, the Stadium was usually full, and Snowy was in charge of the often emotional proceedings.

Snowy also had to somehow keep control of his own emotions, as he immediately found himself at the centre of a variety of bizarre events. One great advantage of watching the pugs at the Stadium was that you were under the stars and so close to the action. Terrific when it was dry; not so when the rain came.

In April, 1910, Snowy looked apprehensively towards the skies just before the start of the Australasian lightweight championship, when he beckoned to both boxers, Johnny Summers and Hughie Mehegan, for the pre-match instructions.

Snowy knew he was in trouble when a wild clap of thunder coincided with him shouting, 'Gentlemen.' By the end of the sentence, the ring was almost under water, as torrential rain hammered Rushcutters Bay. It stopped momentarily, allowing the fight to start and the crowd to take off their coats, which had shaded their heads from the hail.

Soon the fighters were slipping this way and that, but there was never any thought of calling off the title bout. The crowd thought it was hysterical and would have charged the ring if the boxers and referee had taken shelter from the storm. They wanted entertainment, and got it, when Mehegan's feet slipped right from under him and, according to *The Referee*, 'he flopped down on his hams with a bump that must have shaken him up a great deal'. Summers slipped over during the next round, which saw him crash through the ropes and onto the saturated press table.

The downpour intensified in the 15th and 16th rounds, and by the 19th round, the ring looked like 'a shallow, miniature lake'.

The end came in the 19th, when Summers, wiping the water away from his eyes, threw a desperate left jab that connected with an unguarded jaw, and 'down went Hughie like a log, to be counted out, and then carried from the ring, limp as a snake, on the stalwart shoulders of his trainer–manager Tom Boyle'.

But what *The Referee* failed to mention was that Mehegan almost drowned.

After being decked by Summers, the unconscious Mehegan collapsed head-first into a large pool of water. Unaware of Mehegan's plight, Snowy kept counting him out, until alerted by spectators at ringside that the boxer was in deep trouble. Luckily Boyle dragged Mehegan's face out of the water – just in time.

Some months later, Snowy's own pugilistic skills were put to the test when he officiated a fiery bout between the reputable American fighter 'Cyclone' Johnny Thompson and Bondi local Tim Land. Despite having the disability of a withered, crippled left leg, Land was supremely confident before the fight, telling Snowy that he would buy three cows for his dairy farm from the winnings. One of the milkers he would call 'Cyclone', another 'Snowy' and the third 'Stadium'.

It was some bout, with the *Daily Telegraph* headlining its report with 'A Whirlwind Fight. Wild Scene at the Stadium. Men fight like tiger cats'.

An excited *Telegraph* boxing scribe wrote: 'The fight was one never to be forgotten. For 19 rounds, Land and Thompson fought like tiger cats in a rage. How they withstood the punishment meted out was a miracle. Their constitutions must have been cast-iron.'

The crowd were behind the Sydney boy, chanting: 'Land, Land, Land' throughout a fight, where Snowy had to constantly get in between the two boxers who were trying every underhand trick to get the upperhand. Snowy was struggling to keep control, prompting him to repeatedly caution either boxer, or push them away from each other, whenever it became especially heated. Snowy wanted to stay in charge by determining the pace and rhythm of the fight.

In Thompson's corner was another visiting American boxer, Jimmy Clabby, who was in town chasing the Australasian welterweight title. The Connecticut-born Clabby was a constant visitor to Sydney, renowned for his impish sense of humour, love of local women, Australian racehorses, and New South Wales beer, in particular ales. He eventually owned a stable of local racehorses.

From the early rounds, Clabby began screaming instructions to Thompson, prompting a warning from Snowy and an attendant to shut up, or he would be kicked out of the Stadium.

The Thompson camp, in particular Clabby, were fuming as they thought Land had applied arnica to his hair and that the fumes were getting into their boxer's eyes, badly blurring his vision. After Thompson complained twice, Snowy went across to Land, grabbed the offending bottle and smelt it. Snowy said it wasn't arnica and demanded that the fight continue. Clabby jeered him.

In the 15th round, Clabby became extremely agitated. Snowy had just cautioned Thompson for holding with one hand and hitting out with the other. While Snowy gave Thompson a strict talking to, an enraged Clabby yelled out to the referee, 'You're a crook, Baker.'

Snowy ignored the jibe. At the end of the 19th round, Thompson knocked Land down. Standing over Land, Snowy counted the seconds and had just pronounced 'nine' when the gong for the end of the round sounded. Land was immediately rushed into his corner by his seconds, who realised that he had been saved momentarily.

Clabby couldn't believe what had occurred, yelling to all around him that Snowy had deliberately slowed down the ten count to save Land. Clabby then screamed at Snowy. 'Robbery!'

Land was revived just in time for the start of the 20th round, but within seconds was back on the canvas, laid out and counted out.

As the crowd started to disperse, Clabby was seen leaping through the ropes and charging straight at Snowy, who was standing in the middle of the ring. Clabby screamed at Snowy, 'You god-damned cheating Australian c___', to which he replied with a copybook left hook to the jaw. A stunned Clabby was flat on his back, with an angered Snowy standing over him, beckoning to him to get to his feet.

Under the front-page headline of 'Riot at the Stadium . . . Referee and Boxer in Holts', *The Sun* reported: 'For a couple of seconds they wrestled around the enclosure, and several blows were struck. The crowd rushed the ring, and a surging, fighting mob threatened serious trouble. SubInspector Matthews, followed by a couple of policemen, jumped into the ring, and simultaneously Clabby left the enclosure.

'The crowd, however, reeled backwards and forwards, and many blows were struck by partisans of the men. Meanwhile the fighting spirit had spread to the crowd. Ordinarily quiet men were tearing about and inviting fights from anybody who disputed their version of the troubles.

'Many of them lost their hats during the excitement, and had them trampled underfoot. The people in the "bleacher" seats appeared to be in a dangerous mood. They wanted to be in it, and many climbed over the barriers and rushed to the ringside and jumped over the ropes.

'The less venturesome remained in the enclosures in which they had been seated, but they pressed forward in such a manner that the barriers threatened to collapse. The police, however, soon got busy. Half a dozen burly officials hopped over the ropes, and in a few seconds bustled everybody out. There was sufficient excitement in that period to satisfy the greatest glutton.

'There were many split lips and sore heads amongst the spectators, but no arrests were made.'

The usually staid *Sydney Morning Herald* was even excited to be a witness to the brouhaha. 'After the excitement had quietened down the wire barricades were seen to be all twisted, and in places torn down, from the rough handling they had received from the spectators, and it was also ascertained that one of the metal supports which sustain the posts carrying the ropes of the ring had been snapped through like a carrot.'

Both Clabby, who according to *The Referee* was 'uproariously hooted', and Snowy, who was cheered from the ring and all the way to the dressing rooms, were approached by *The Sun* after the fight to give their side of the story. Clabby wanted to continue on with it; Snowy to put his spin on the matter.

'I'm very sorry for what happened,' the chastened American said, 'but I could not avoid it. I thought Land was counted out in the nineteenth round and I didn't hesitate to say so. That is what Mr Baker took exception to. When the fight was over he called to me, and I went towards him. He asked me: "Do you say Land was counted out?" and I answered: "Certainly".

'"You're a lying . . ." Baker said to me, and before I knew anything was happening I got a clout on the jaw just to the left side of my face. Of course I wasn't for standing that, and I hit back.

'We got into holts, but there wasn't much damage done. I don't think I did anything very serious in disputing Mr Baker. If Mr Baker is not satisfied he can be accommodated. He is a boxer, and I am a boxer, and the Stadium management can arrange a match if they desire. I wouldn't mind if they did.'

Snowy had no regrets, but was surprised to hear that Clabby wanted a re-match.

'If I was forced into a similar position I would act in the same way,' Snowy said defiantly.

'It was not a thing that developed in a few seconds. It had been brewing all night. Clabby was troublesome all the time he was in Thompson's corner. He was calling out and shouting, and yelling instructions to me. I spoke to him once, but he did not take any notice.

'He made himself doubly troublesome after the alleged knocking-out of Land in the nineteenth round. He persisted in calling out, and went so far as to accuse me of robbing Thompson of a win. I was helpless. I had plenty to do to control the men in the ring.

'When Land had been counted out, and immediately after I had declared Thompson the winner, Clabby came towards me. Many harsh and ugly expressions were used, and then I hit him. There was a clinch, and several blows were struck. Then we were pulled apart.

'I'm very sorry for what happened, but even now I cannot see that there was any other course open to me. I had to assert my authority. I had to defend my position as referee, and I did it in the most convincing style possible. I hit Clabby first, and I cannot say that I regret it.'

Denying that he swore at Clabby, Snowy continued: 'Clabby says I can be accommodated, does he? Well, that's funny. I am not a professional ring man, and there's no likelihood of me being one. Clabby knows that, and realises that there is no possibility of his being matched with me.'

The following morning, *The Evening News* headed to Snowy's gymnasium for the latest update. After Snowy finished a brisk boxing bout with a pupil, he beckoned the news hack to his office, where his seat was surrounded by large portraits of himself. The reporter thought he was talking to 10 Snowy Bakers, who all wanted to elaborate on what happened the previous night.

'Last night there was continued cries of "robbery" from the American's corner, and then Clabby accused me of counting Land out at the end of the 19th round and letting the fight go on. The public and Press can bear me out that Land was saved by the time check, which was correctly kept.

'Finally when I was called an objectionable name, I felt that I could no longer ignore them, and I struck Clabby. Somebody pulled us asunder snarling like a pair of wild dogs.'

Snowy reiterated that he had not called Clabby as bad a name. 'Although I have mixed with boxers, rowers, swimmers and athletes generally for years, I never make use of bad language in any form, not even the mild "D-A-M-N". I have heard plenty of bad language, but have never acquired the habit of using it.'

As for the arnica accusation, Baker smiled. 'I smelt it. I put my nose close to the bottle, and it was a very nice, refreshing smell indeed. I think it was rose water.'

Not eucalyptus?

'No. It seemed to me to be a mixture of rose water and water, and was very mild indeed.'

Snowy's biggest concern was that he would be chastised by his boss. Huge Deal had returned from his whirlwind world tour, and was soon informed about his punchy number one man.

Huge Deal immediately laughed off the moment.

'Good old Snowy. Have to keep those upstart Yanks in their place.'

Land missed out on his three milkers, but Snowy received a pay rise – the real Huge Deal seal of approval. Huge Deal, forever the businessman, did offer the carrot of a large purse for Snowy to fight Clabby at the Stadium. Snowy refused.

A few days later, journalist W.F. Corbett brought Clabby to Snowy's gymnasium in a bid to heal the rift. Snowy recalled several years later: 'We shook hands, and were the best of pals. He said: "I didn't call you what you thought I did," and I said: "You did." Jimmy still says he didn't, and I still say he did.'

Not surprisingly, with Snowy able to show that he can still acquit himself in the ring, many spectators went to the Stadium as much to see what the referee was up to, as the two protagonists. Snowy usually didn't fail to entertain.

Snowy also came better prepared. A few weeks later, Snowy refereed Clabby in the ring against the highly-rated fighter, Dave Smith. Noticing dark skies over Sydney before he left for the Stadium, Snowy brought a heavy mackintosh and rain cap with him, which he wore from the start of the fight.

The crowd thought it was hilarious, but Snowy's foresight worked in his favour when from the 11th round the Stadium was hit with torrential rain. While the drenched boxers slipped and slid all over the ring, the referee stayed bone dry.

Snowy also gained a reputation for his astuteness in the ring. After drying himself off, Smith found himself up against the world middleweight champion, Billy Papke. Smith was obviously in trouble early on, when in one moment of distress, he tore a plate of false teeth from his mouth and threw it to his men in the corner. However, the plate was dropped and broke in several pieces. Snowy had to stop the fight so they could sweep Smith's many teeth off the canvas.

A few rounds later, Smith was hit with a low blow, which saw him writhing in agony on the boards of the ring. The crowd thought Snowy had got it all wrong when he started counting Smith out. The chorus 'foul, foul, foul' echoed around the Stadium.

But Snowy was completely in control, knowing that he had to do the ten count before awarding Smith the winner because of a foul blow. He milked the crowd, and when he raised the unconscious Smith's arm, the crowd went wild.

Refereeing appealed to Snowy's showmanship, but occasionally it left him bewildered and disorientated. Another time at the Stadium, Snowy was refereeing a fight between American Eddie McGoorty and one of Australia's best Aboriginal boxers, Jerry Jerome.

'It was a 20-round affair, and it went the whole way,' Snowy recalled. 'It was a furious battle all right. I had to watch both men pretty closely, especially Eddie, who got a bit excited and was swinging some foul blows. I saw one foul punch coming up from the American boy on Jerome and stepped into it myself. It landed with terrific force, knocked me against the ropes, and I sat down hard. Eddie was so upset about it he hauled me to my feet, held out his hand to me, which, of course, I shook, and the bout went on. Eddie didn't try another haymaker after that.'

Huge Deal was also on the go, working his international network well to ensure that the best boxers kept coming to his venue. As fighter

Rudolph Unholz told the Chicago *Evening American*: 'We are getting big money here, and the people are crazy about the game. Just so long as it is square and on the up-and-up it gets the highest support, and Hugh D. McIntosh sees to it that it is on the square. He is the biggest promoter in Australia, and when he sleeps the whole of Australia sleeps in regard to sport.'

Realising that Australia was overflowing with boxers in the lighter divisions, Huge Deal kept the crowds enthused by continually importing world quality middleweight and heavyweight fighters from the United States, including two formidable black boxers – Sam Langford, known as the 'Boston Tarbaby', and Sam McVea. They were also known as 'Little Smoke' and 'Big Smoke'. They didn't exactly like each other. When McVea first met Langford, he produced a silver pipe from his pocket. Presenting it to Langford, McVea said: 'My daddy gave me this and told me to keep it until I found an uglier nigger than me.'

Langford chased McVea from the room.

The two Sams stayed in Australia for close to two years, fighting each other on six occasions – Langford successful four times and McVea once, with one draw.

Their first bout on Boxing Day 1911 was special, and rated by Snowy 'as the best contest I've ever refereed or witnessed'.

Underneath a blazing sun, in front of a capacity 20,000 plus crowd, Snowy stood out. The blacks glistened and flashed away at each other, while Snowy remained erect wearing green trousers, felt hat and braces, over a plain white shirt. Photographs from that bout show Snowy constantly getting between the two fighters as they clinched, wrestled and rested on each other as much as they could during a gruelling 20-round event.

Snowy was upstaged by Langford who entered the ring wearing a garish emerald green dressing gown. The vastly taller McVea towered over his opponent as Snowy beckoned the fighters together for instructions.

'Both must break fair,' Snowy told them.

'I'm gonna break dis big nigger right in two,' Langford snapped back. 'You'll 'ave no trouble dat way, boss.'

At the end, the two fighters were still on their feet and Snowy had to make a decision. When Snowy put his hand on the steaming shoulder of McVea and declared him the winner, it was met with widespread booing.

As C.A. Jeffries wrote in *Famous Fights at the Stadium*, 'a considerable section of the audience was surprised, and said so frankly. This section said it was sorry it hadn't brought a dead cat with it. Some regarded it as a draw, and not a few would have given Langford the verdict.'

Snowy had more vivid memories, especially when he had to bob and weave to avoid being hit by missiles. He later recalled: 'I gave what I believed to be a definite points advantage to McVea. Many in the crowded assemblage thought me right – more thought me wrong.

'For more than 10 minutes after I had given my decision I was the main attraction in something that bore a cousinly resemblance to the Donnybrook Fair or a Brooklyn baseball game. That irate bunch of fans hurled bottles with the labels of every brewery and soft drink manufacturer in greater Sydney, loaded and unloaded. And did they keep me sidestepping.'

This decision would shortly cause Snowy problems. But that night he didn't have time to ponder whether he had made the right ruling. He had to rush back to the gymnasium to apply the finishing touches to yet another radical business venture.

Chapter 11

Branching Out

ON JANUARY 6, 1912, A NEW MAGAZINE HIT THE AUSTRALIAN BOOKSHELVES. It looked impressive, important. On the front cover was an athletic Roman gladiator wearing robes and garland, holding a smoking torch and peering over a list of the magazine's contents.

No-one could be under any misapprehension as to who the editor was and what the magazine was about. Emblazoned across the front cover were the words '*Snowy Baker's Magazine*'.

Inside, Snowy welcomed his readers with: 'My object in publishing this monthly magazine is to furnish authoritative, interesting and informative articles on all manly health-giving pastimes.

'Beginners in all sports can learn points from the methods adopted by champions, so that they may endeavour to develop their powers along similar lines. Students of correct methods for improvement of body will be provided with instructive articles on judicious exercise.'

And for well over two years Snowy brought out the big names each month to ensure his readers received the right advice. In the first few months he called on Cecil Healy to provide tips on how to swim distance and sprint races, champion sculler George Towns explained how to 'scull an outrigger', L.S.W. Seaborn expounded 'the joys of Rugby Union football', Annette Kellermann penned pieces on 'physical culture for women', 'how to acquire graceful lines', 'weight reduction for ladies' and 'how to wear a corset', while brother-in-law Andrew Sime told Snowy's readers 'how to train for a marathon' and a cricket nut called 'Bosie' gave tips on 'how to bowl a googlie'.

Snowy also used the magazine to push his own theories, products, correspondence school, training facilities and his latest product – a 'splendid first aid remedy' called Snowy Baker's Embrocation. Snowy stressed to his readers that 'you ought to keep a bottle handy' because the embrocation: 'Overcomes Rheumatism. Banishes Lumbago. Knocks-out Stiffness. Extracts Pain from Bruises.'

'Your Health Is What YOU Make It!!', Snowy stressed in one ad. 'If you neglect Exercise you neglect your health. Because, without Exercise your blood circulation becomes feeble, its quality impoverished, its nourishing qualities banished.'

Then the big sell.

'Walking is a fine exercise, but few can find time for a daily five-mile jaunt. But everyone can spare 15 minutes a day. Devote that time to my judicious HEALTH EXERCISES and you'll be delighted with the results.

'My Health Exercises apply scientific principles to ensure a vigorous blood circulation, a thorough exercising of the vital organs, and complete relaxation. Their benefits are quickly apparent, because they go right to the spot.

'My prospectus gives more detailed information about my tuition.'

In another ad, Snowy argued that 'Every man can increase his business ability by scientific exercise.

'Good rich, pure blood will course through your veins, giving nourishment to the brains, muscles and tissues of your frame.'

Snowy provided all the hints in his magazine, everything from how to avoid stammering, the key trick being to 'read aloud', how to care for your teeth, how to become a master at jujitsu and how to look after a bull terrier to cleaning out the liver, how to avoid being bilious, 'what is beauty', how to hit a tennis ball, the tricks of acrobatic diving, the why of a 'cough', how to wrestle, how to ski, what causes headaches, how to excel at golf, why we get tired, how to overcome constipation (green salads are terrific), safe ways to keep thin, 'what's up with your stomach', how to play water polo, how to fence, the fun of whaler racing, how a girl can 'acquire a graceful figure', 'who loves a fat man', the sweet tooth, 'boxing for the man in the street' and even how to take a bath.

And with it came all the endorsements. From Edmund Burke, the principal basso of the Melbourne Opera Company, to the 1912 Australian cricket team, who were so excited that Snowy had offered them tips on how to use their time constructively on the ship during the long journey to England for the triangular tournament.

John McCormick, the 'celebrated tenor', was an unabashed fan of Snowy's regime. 'Your breathing and abdominal exercises have been simply splendid, and the variety you bring too by introducing medicine ball throwing and ball punching, skipping etc, makes your course an absolute recreation, and it was for that reason that I paid my daily visit to you,' McCormick wrote to *Snowy Baker's Magazine*.

'The results were really astonishing. In fact you will be glad to know I have never sung so well in my whole career, as I have since I first started with you. My only regret is that I cannot continue on just another while with my boxing, as my progress has been so rapid in the "noble art", that I began to look upon myself as a possible "white hope".'

Comedian Leslie Gaze frothed: 'I feel I can't leave Sydney without writing to thank you for all you have done for me. Two months' work in your studio has converted a nervous, tired out dyspeptic into a hale and happy man again.'

Alongside this recommendation was a photograph of Snowy's gym. It showed a series of cubicles, each one furnished with a punching ball, exercise mat, chest weights and a range of fitness equipment. Above the cubicles, which were separated by drawn curtains, was a large framed portrait of Snowy who was looking down at all his disciples.

As Snowy explained in the same advertisement: 'Your instruction will be absolutely private. Your instructor is the only person who sees you exercising, You're isolated in a private cubicle. There's nothing to distract your attention. Your mind is concentrated on your exercises. Improvement quickly makes itself felt.

'If you find the heat troublesome, you'll quickly find relief if you visit my rooms. My exercises tone and build up the system to enable it to repel the summer languidness. You'll do more work with less fatigue.'

Not surprisingly, Snowy ran articles from enthusiasts who had been converted by 'Psychologia Snowy Bakeri'.

A Mr J.H. Toohey wrote: 'I like the culture which "Snowy" calls physical. Visit his rooms when operations are in full swing and you will find yourself amongst laughing youngsters, whistling noises and clattering feet – a pandemonium verily, but with redeeming features; for the whiz of the shower and the odours of ointment seems to cool and refresh the atmosphere, whilst what appear to be untoward and confused general conditions turn out on investigation to be orthodox methods regulated by little brother Fred, toned down by the gentleness of Ray, and presided over by the valiant "Snowy" whose genial smile and words of encouragement are seen and heard, here, there and everywhere, but whose supervision, though persistent, is never embarrassing – Psychologia Snowy Bakeri.'

Snowy's hobbyhorse was how to improve oneself. He was a man seeking the perfect master race. He looked upon himself as the superior human being. In nearly every issue were diagrams of Snowy doing various arm, leg and body exercises, with instructions on how to get rid of the flab. Snowy simply couldn't tolerate physical weakness of any kind.

He repeatedly stressed how important swimming was to one's well-being.'Every man, woman and child in Australia should be able to swim,' Snowy told his readers.'It should be compulsory by law of the land.The knowledge of how to save your own or your fellow creature's life is of the greatest importance, and should occupy an equal place in our school curriculum as arithmetic.'

Snowy was as adamant that an honest man should know how to look after himself with his fists. In another full-page advertisement, with Snowy yet again stripped down, putting on the gloves he asks, 'Must you first get a beating before you learn to box?' It was the Charles Atlas don't be the kid that has sand kicked in his face routine, only this was decades earlier.

'I teach boxing by post. So you've no excuse for remaining crude and inexperienced – a good target for the first "bully" who torments you. Let me make you a cool, determined, scientific boxer, with a substantial punch and effective guard – a manly man, well able to look after himself, and win the respect of others.

'Write today. It may be the means of saving you the ignomy and bitterness of defeat.'

As well, he used the magazine to promote future bouts at the Stadium, discuss his own refereeing prowess, analyse boxers who were about to arrive in Sydney and, wherever possible, publicise himself beyond belief. Then again, he could do what he liked; it was his magazine, he was the editor and what he said went into the magazine.

Snowy used the magazine as his sounding board for whatever was irritating him at the time. One week it was the cheat in rugby football, with Snowy complaining that 'we had to suffer for our sins and watch a match won by foul play, trickery, chicanery and all the hundred and one things that go to make up the Thieves' Code in what is intended to be Rugby Union Football. Of course, I know what I am writing about, because in playing days I used to engage in all these tricks myself, being out to win by fair means or foul every time.'

The next, Snowy would rabbit on about how fumigation was a waste of time in trying to stop diseases. One issue later, he would be condemning women who wore 'extremely high heels' and smoked cigarettes.

Snowy explained that if you 'put a tobacco victim in a hot bath, let him remain there till a free perspiration takes place; then drop a fly into the water the fly will instantly die.'

As for high heels, 'when worn it upsets the whole equilibrium of the internal organism. If persisted in, they will permanently destroy the bone structure of the feet, and upset the delicate balance of the natural functions. It is a later generation that probably suffer most, unfortunately, so severe and exacting is heredity.'

As for the amateur boxer, his diet should be – for breakfast, a chop with a couple of eggs, toast and a glass of milk. The midday meal should consist of fish, stewed or raw fruit, milk puddings and biscuit, finishing off with an evening dinner of roast beef or boiled mutton, green salads, biscuits and cheese.

To finance the magazine, Snowy had gone back to the same benefactors who'd enabled him to get to Europe. Several became minor shareholders and Huge Deal came to the party covering the publishing costs of the first few issues. As the magazine sold well, Snowy soon paid everyone back and found himself making a small, but still satisfying profit from the subscription sales and advertising revenue.

Following on from the success of the magazine, Snowy brought out a 126-page book, *Snowy Baker's General Physical Culture*, and at the same time a small 32-page pamphlet entitled, *Scientific Boxing in your Home*.

Scientific Boxing was basically a hard sell, Snowy promoting himself as Australia's ultimate sportsman and the man to teach anything and everything about fitness – in particular boxing by correspondence.

If you wanted to be a 'manly man', there was only one thing to do – subscribe to Snowy's postal course and over the course of 30 lessons you could become a 'lamb at home, and a lion in the chase'.

'The practice of boxing inculcates coolness and courage in the face of danger. It leads to a general sense and sentiment of fair play and honour.

The man who can defend himself with his fists despises cunning and deceit. With a knowledge of boxing we learn the value of our own strength, and consequently can afford to be lenient, sympathetic, and more patient with our less fortunate creatures.

'There are two things Australians pride themselves on – good judges of horses and knowing how to box. You never know when you may be suddenly and unexpectedly attacked by a rough, and it is certainly of great value to know first how to defend yourself and give the miscreant a sound thrashing.

'Or perhaps you might be called on to resent an insult to your wife, sister or sweetheart, or defend and help a friend out of a difficulty who has not been fortunate enough to have learnt boxing himself. It will be a great feeling of satisfaction to your manhood to feel, if the time does come, you can "deliver the goods", and give the undesirable a thorough licking in a manly way.'

General Physical Culture was a less hysterical volume.

For 'his fellow countrymen and women of Australia; even my good friends', Snowy produced an impressive book, which, almost a century on, holds up well.

It is a comprehensive guide to numerous sports and exercises, with Snowy again calling on his strong stable of friends to provide the right advice, and to push the line that physical fitness was the key to a healthy society.

After all, as Snowy rammed home: 'Poverty, misery, crime and destitution are the products, primarily, of physical unfitness.'

And with it more hints and such gems as: 'strong drink makes weak men'; 'Accustom yourself to going about bareheaded, except in the hottest weather. Baldness and nervous headaches are encouraged by too constant use of the hat'; 'Woollen singlets and pants are too warm, and shrink in the wash, consequently becoming too tight, and making the skin tender and irritable'; 'Cultivate the faculty of observation. A quick-sighted person is never lonely, and misses none of the "good things" in life and nature'; 'Free exercise daily will soon do away with the necessity for "the blue pill and black draught"'; 'If you breathe through your nostrils, "you will not suffer from sore throat, nor are you likely to fall into the habit of snoring in your sleep"'.

And for the ladies: 'Do not be afraid to perspire. It is Nature's own skin bath'; 'Ball punching is a splendid exercise for developing the bust'; a 'languid, anaemic type of maiden' is not attractive to men, and if she manages to 'secure one, she turns out an indifferent wife, and an unsatisfactory mother'; 'Scraggy necks are the bane and nightmare of many women who are otherwise pleasingly rounded. Leave the neck as free as possible.'; 'Many of the maladies from which women suffer have been caused by the "dragging down" from the waist of a number of articles which are worn more as a convention or habit than because they have any real purpose. The use of garters cannot be too strongly condemned'.

Cecil Healy wrote a chapter on 'the crawl stroke', champion rower George Towns provided advice on 'sculling an outrigger', while tennis champion H.A. Parker gave a 'brief sketch' on his favourite sport.

Snowy's younger brother, Harold, also gave his vast views on surf bathing. This was hardly nepotism on Snowy's behalf, considering that Harold had suddenly become a national hero.

William Harold Baker, sometimes called Harald, was three years younger than Snowy and as adept a sportsman. Harold, or Harald, mimicked Snowy's career in many ways, first excelling as a swimmer, where he became a NSW champion over 100, 220, 300 and 440 yards, as well as Australasian champion over 100 and 220 yards, was a team-mate of Snowy's in the famous Flying Squadron relay team and represented Australia at water polo. He was also an outstanding oarsman with the Sydney Rowing Club.

A long, sombre, often morose man, Harold was one of the original members of the Maroubra Surf Club, where he was involved in more than 100 rescues, a competent horseman, winning the Wrestling on Horseback title with the NSW Lancers, and a regular first-grade forward with the Sydney rugby team.

Harold was well known around Sydney, but became famous across Australia due to an extraordinary surf rescue he was involved in at Coogee Beach on January 28, 1911.

At the time, Harold was running the kiosk at Coogee; a lucrative business considering that it was one of the few places along the beachfront where sunbathers could get drinks, ice creams or anything to save their skin from the heat. That day, Harold was the only competent lifesaver on the beach as the Coogee club had travelled enmass to a surf carnival at North Steyne.

Harold was leaning over the front of the kiosk, watching the northern end of the beach where, following a wild week of storms, a stormwater pipe had gouged a large hole into the sea, prompting an enormous backwash, an unpredictable swirl and a treacherous undertow. Thousands of tons of water were being sucked out to sea.

Around midday he was joined by renowned footballer and Wallaby representative, Jimmy Clarken, who had wandered down to the beach to have a 'yarn with Harold'.

Concerned by the churned-up water caused by the stormwater pipe, Harold had earlier in the day thrust a red flag into the sand nearby to indicate to swimmers that it was a dangerous spot and they should stay out of the water.

But the flag had no impact on a group of workers and their girlfriends who immediately plunged north of the pipe, but due to the strong current quickly drifted into the danger zone.

Harold leapt over the front of the kiosk, complaining to Clarken: 'They've taken no notice of the flag. You'd think anyone would know "red for danger". If they get down to that hole it could be murder, I'll go down there and tell them.'

At the same moment, a sandbank collapsed and suddenly 13 swimmers slipped into the sea, straight into the freak deathtrap where they were not only fighting the sea, but each other, as dumper after dumper hit them.

Harold sprinted to the water and, not having time to take his clothes off, plunged into the waves. Clarken followed, grabbing a lifebelt and relieving Harold when he returned to shore with the first patient – a young girl choking and screaming.

However, Harold was lucky to return at all, as when he arrived in the area where the swimmers were trying to stay afloat, three women clutched at his singlet and trousers, dragging him under.

For several seconds, with clawing fingernails ripping into his skin, hands fixed rigidly around his throat, and another grabbing onto his testicles, he had to desperately fight off the trio so he could again get his head above water. He later explained: 'You wouldn't believe what a woman would hold when she's frightened.'

Harold somehow shook two of them off, before bringing the third back to shore. After placing her on the sand, Harold flung off all his clothes and in the nude, rushed back into the water.

Harold, who now had Clarken by his side in the wild sea, returned to the rescue area, where both were attacked by the delirious women who had crowded around the lifesavers.

One grabbed Clarken around the throat and to save both himself from strangulation and her, the Wallaby struck her on the jaw, knocking her out. Three meanwhile had clambered onto Harold, prompting him to take similar measures. Several punches quietened them down, enabling Harold and Clarken to get the four back to shore.

About 10 metres away, another woman was sobbing uncontrollably, muttering: 'Mister, oh, please mister, don't leave me.'

While dragging the three, Harold replied: 'Hang on a minute. Try and keep your head out of the water, and I'll be back. I'm coming back for you. Stay calm.'

On his way to rescuing the women, Harold helped two men to get onto the surf lifebelt still being manned by Clarken and they were carried to shore.

The woman was crying hysterically by the time he returned for the third rescue attempt and Harold had to grab her tightly around the head to get her back without a fight.

Harold had also noticed several other men in the area, but when he swam out a fourth time, couldn't find anyone. Returning to the beach, he discovered the sand was covered with retching bodies, dead bodies and unconscious bodies. It was a horrific scene.

The final tally was 12 rescues, and four missing, all men, including a 12- and nine-year-old child.

Despite their heroic efforts, Harold and Clarken were deeply distressed and couldn't be consoled on the beachfront. Harold, in tears, kept repeating: 'We should have got the lot, Jim! We should have got them.'

'The job was too big for just the two of us!' consoled Clarken.

'Harold,' asked Clarken. 'How'd you get those three girls in at the one time without having them strangle you?'

'Socked 'em.'

Clarken sighed. 'I didn't want to say this before – but I had to sock one, too. She was a looker . . . Hope she never finds out.'

The press were soon on the spot and Harold struggled to keep his emotions in check. 'I really have little to say. I don't want to talk about it much.'

But Harold was eventually convinced by the *Daily Telegraph* to explain why he had opted for a nude rescue.

'It wasn't the time to study appearances, and clothes were in the way, so I just let them drift ashore. This time I got right in among a bunch of girls. I had neither belt nor life-line.

'They got all over me. I went down – so did some of them, and it steadied them a bit. But I had to knock them off, and Clarken hit a girl who was going the best way about drowning herself and him and rendered her senseless.'

An exhausted Clarken praised Baker, stating that 'without him, at least nine or ten people might have been drowned. I don't suppose there's his equal in the surf in this country.'

Clarken also explained his knockout blow.

'Two women and a man grabbed hold of me; they all seemed wild. A girl got me around the throat. She dragged me under twice, so that I had to hit her, just enough to make her let go. She's all right now, barring a stiff neck.'

Adding to the despair was that some grub had rifled the till at the kiosk while Harold was out saving lives. Then a few days later, a wowser wrote to the local newspaper complaining about 'the disgusting sight witnessed at Coogee'. The writer protested that a man had been sighted on the beach 'naked, and without his trousers'.

Thankfully more broad-minded people ensured that Harold and Clarken received the accolades they richly deserved. The tragedy led to the Surf Bathers Association drafting new laws and the institution of Saturday afternoon patrols to ensure beaches always had a healthy number of lifesavers nearby.

The pair received Albert Medals for bravery and were the centre of a major media campaign that saw their pockets eventually lined with gold.

The *Sydney Morning Herald* ran an editorial praising Harold and Clarken's 'swiftness and skill under great odds', explaining that the tragedy disclosed 'a great defect in management of the beach'.

Hugh Ward, a well-known Sydney actor and manager, came forward with the proposal of raising 1,000 pounds as a reward for the Coogee heroes. Within hours, Ward was inundated by people offering donations with money coming from all directions, including Test cricketer Victor Trumper, *The Bulletin* and the Tattersall's Club. That tally was soon reached, especially after Ward contacted Huge Deal and Snowy about staging a special carnival at the Stadium as a show of appreciation.

Everyone responded and a capacity crowd witnessed one of the more unusual of boxing nights where champion scullers Dick Arnst and Harry Pearce fought each other, swimmers Harold Hardwick, Cecil Healy and Alick Wickham were tempted to put on the gloves, and Harold Baker was persuaded to go three rounds with the reputable American pug, Billy Papke.

The highlight of the night, which raised well over 800 pounds, was Snowy up against Hugh Ward. Both play-acted over three rounds, taking turns to crash to the boards and mimicking knockouts.

Ward who spent most weekends frolicking on the harbour on a luxury yacht with actors, actresses, Huge Deal and his inseparable mate, the influential Labor politician William A. Holman, was a close confidant of Snowy's. Huge Deal was so often in Holman's company that the pair were described by one Sydney newspaper as 'Beauty and the Beast'.

At the end of the charity night, Ward had to rush back to the Palace Theatre where he was performing in a play. The play stopped as those in the front rows yelled out wanting to know how the fight went. Moving well away from the script, Ward, shaking his hands above his head in triumph, said: 'And in two rounds!' Then back to the play.

Back at the Stadium, the Artillery Band eventually brought Harold Baker and Clarken onto the stage to the strains of 'The Conquering Hero' and loud cheers.

Harold, unlike his elder brother, was the reluctant hero. 'We did nothing more than anyone would have done in the same circumstances,' Harold told the crowd. 'We did it more out of a sense of duty than anything else. It was merely our duty to our neighbours.'

Clarken added, 'This has brought all I have to say into one lump – it's here,' putting his hand to his throat, and again the crowd burst into frantic cheering.

The pair bowed and left the stage to the sound of the band belting out 'Jolly Good Fellows'.

Having Harold write a chapter for his book, definitely helped sales of Snowy's *General Physical Culture*, as did Cecil Healy's involvement. By the time the book was released, Healy was held in the same regard as Harold.

Healy had just returned from Stockholm where he was at the centre of one of the great acts of Olympic Games sportsmanship. Healy was among the contestants in the 1912 Olympics 100 metres swimming event, winning the first semi-final.

However Healy was distressed that three Americans, including the famous surfer Duke Kahanamoku, had, through a misunderstanding, missed the start of their semi-final and had been disqualified.

With his main opponents out of the way, Healy was the undisputed favourite to win gold. But Healy pleaded to the Australian officials that the Americans deserved a second chance and the trio were eventually allowed to swim in a reconvened semi-final.

Kahanamoku qualified for the final and defeated Healy, who finished second for silver. Sportsmanship had cost Healy gold, but that didn't bother one of Snowy's best mates. Deep in his heart, Healy knew he had done the right thing and the Australian community responded in kind, treating him with great reverence on his return.

Unlike the Harold Baker testimonial, it was not such a jolly night at Snowy's next appearance at the Stadium, when he had designated himself to officiate the second McVea–Langford fight. Snowy was still being lampooned for his decision to award the first fight to McVea, in particular from the Langford camp who believe the Stadium's chief referee was blatantly biased against their boxer. Even *The Referee*, one of Snowy's most avowed supporters, was critical of his refereeing.

The sports writer, who used the nom de plume 'The Amateur', wrote that 'the white haired referee made a mistake, as I said at the time, and have stated on many occasions since, which I could not understand until he explained later that a good deal of Langford's work at close quarters – his uppercuts and right chops – were not allowed because it occurred in "clinches". Never was such an untenable defence of a decision heard before.'

To avoid any further distress, Snowy opted against being the referee, handing over the duties to his deputy, Arthur Scott.

This time Langford won easily and according to Snowy, who was at ringside, 'Sam McVea's face was a total wreck. Langford had closed his two eyes, burst his lips and nose, causing a considerable flow of blood.

'The moment the fight was stopped, Sam McVea's beautiful blonde wife, decked out to beat any fashion show, jumped into the ring, threw her arms around Sam's neck and kissed him with all the effusion of a Hollywood screen lover.

'By the time the ring attendants assisted Sam's stunning blonde through the ropes she was looking like someone in the process of being converted into a Red Indian, she was bloody, but unbowed.'

Snowy also rushed to McVea's rooms, again showing that he had a close affinity with the flashy boxer. This had a lot to do with McVea's style, which included importing two French automobiles during his stay in Australia. Both boasted 120 horsepower racing engines. One was gilded with gold and red silk-lining on the seats, studded with ornaments and had red electric light bulbs. The other was painted violet, with an ornamental snake with green eyes coiled in front on the hood. Snowy, McVea and the blonde wife were often seen in one of the garish automobiles speeding off towards the mountains for the weekend.

Snowy was seething. The fact that the Langford camp didn't want him in the ring, and that they had applied pressure to remove him, hit deeply at Snowy's ego and self-dignity.

The catalyst for action was a small article in *The Referee*, which said that 'the Langford party had made up their minds to have a referee ... other than the gentleman – Snowy Baker – who usually officiates at the Stadium.

'In a city where almost every fight follower considers himself at least as good a judge as the specially employed expert, it should not be difficult to discover a fit and proper person, but when it comes to searching for the man who will have the confidence of the principals and those above them, as well as the public, the task needs some getting over.'

Snowy was furious with the article and, on top of the sledge from 'The Amateur', was driven to write to *The Referee* to state that he had resigned as Stadium referee.

'In view of the prominence given in your columns last week on the appointment of referee for the McVea–Langford contest, and as my position of official referee to the Stadium would have rendered it injudicious for me to make any comment on the various criticisms directed against me in that capacity, I now take the earliest opportunity to place on record my unqualified protests of the participants of the McVea–Langford, or any other contest being permitted to virtually veto the Stadium management's nominee.

'My views on this point are so strong that I am disinclined to further act as referee while such conditions exist.

'I look upon the duties of referee as being purely judicial, and that I was appointed to the position because my knowledge, experience and integrity qualified me to efficiently and honestly carry out the onerous task, and that I possessed the confidence of the public as well as the management.

'It places me in a very humiliating position to be laid aside at the whim of an unsuccessful contestant. I have this day written to Mr McIntosh, managing director of the Stadium, notifying him of my resignation as official referee.'

Huge Deal laughed it all off. He had bigger ideas for Snowy.

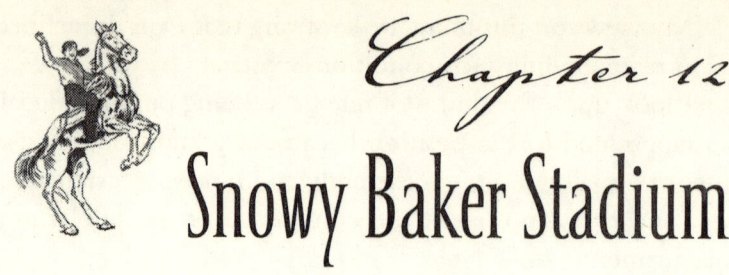

Chapter 12

Snowy Baker Stadium

HUGE DEAL WAS ONCE AGAIN DISTRACTED. THE STADIUM BUSINESS WAS starting to bore him. He'd been around the world, was tantalised by the bright lights and big cities, and wanted to branch out even further.

While in London and Paris showcasing the Burns–Johnson film, Huge Deal had succeeded in promoting fights of a slightly lower scale. The British aristocracy filled his ringside seats at the London Olympia, including titled ladies in evening dress and arms studded with diamonds who commanded the best positions so that they could be splattered with blood. Huge Deal's big fight nights became as popular as a night at the opera, ballet, or a hit play in the West End. During his travels in the United States, he also bought 'the finest car in the world' and then raced it at a Florida beach.

On his return to Australia, besides his work at the Stadium as a boxing organiser and promoter, Huge Deal found home life too staid and he needed a challenge. The challenge was to take over Harry Rickard's Australasia-wide Tivoli theatrical circuit. Huge Deal wanted to stage spectacular musical shows, the best in vaudeville, and bring out the great acts from the United States. He already had his eyes on inviting back a little-known juggler called W.C. Fields, who had first been brought out to Australia by Rickard in 1903.

Rickard, a proud actor who loved getting photographed in Napoleonic garb, had turned the Tivoli circuit into Australia's prime entertainment house by luring the best to Sydney and Melbourne, with Fields joining Harry Houdini, Carter the Great, Chung Ling Soo, Marie Lloyd and Little Tich on the local stages in front of capacity crowds.

This had been Huge Deal's dream. Forget the house of stoush stuff. He wanted to be respectable. Hang around the imaginative, rather than the immobilised. He wanted to be the world's number one theatrical entrepreneur. He wanted to be a bigger, better version of Harry Rickard.

The opening to take over the circuit came in 1911 when Rickard died in England while on a 'talent-buying' trip. But Huge Deal needed money. He needed quick funds so he could complete the first step of leasing the Sydney Tivoli, before he could then take control of the circuit for the substantial sum of 100,000 pounds.

An obvious start was to sell the Sydney Stadium.

Snowy picked the perfect time to make an unexpected call at Huge Deal's office. For some time, Snowy had been mulling over the idea of increasing his role at the Stadium. The gymnasium was going well, two of Snowy's brothers, Frank and Fred, taking care of the day-to-day running along with renowned swimmer Harold Hardwick. *Snowy Baker's Magazine* had a flourishing circulation and the first royalties from his book had given him a solid financial base.

But like Huge Deal, Snowy had grandiose ideas and he believed he could easily become the king of fight promotion in Australia and beyond. He had the nous, was convinced he had better contacts than Huge Deal and knew the fight game far more intimately. He understood the psyche of the boxer, but more importantly their managers. He had been dealing with them for well over a decade and knew when to pander and when to be tough.

But it was no use just being a referee as you weren't involved in any of the fight takings, instead getting a basic fee. Being fight promoter and owner of the Stadium enabled you to take a cut at every stage of the fight, enjoying an accumulated percentage. With Australia now rated the prime boxing venue, running the Stadium was a way of making good money.

In December 1912, Snowy, who was sticking to his ideals of not being Stadium referee until the power of the boxer was diminished, decided it was time to broach the subject with the big man. He knew Huge Deal was edgy about funds, especially after deciding to put a roof on the Stadium.

While the new roof enthused fight patrons, who had tired of getting drenched, the structure had put a huge dent in Huge Deal's bank balance, and, with the Tivoli venture his main passion, he was interested in ways of recouping his money.

Snowy knew that.

'I was about to have lunch at my rooms in the city when Arthur Deery, the well-known solicitor, dropped in. "Say Snowy," he said, "why don't you buy the Stadium business from Hugh McIntosh? He intends going into the theatrical business in a big way."

'Buying the Stadium sounded funny, but interesting, to me at that period. It seemed like buying John Rockefeller out of the Standard Oil Trust. But I decided to look it over.'

Twenty minutes later, Snowy was in Huge Deal's office. Huge Deal was having his lunch, sucking on a mutton chop.

'Have a chop,' said Mac.

As they chewed chop bones together, Mac said: 'Well, what do you want?'

'I've come along to buy you out of the Stadium. What'll it cost?'

'Forty-five thousand quid, walk in and walk out. What are you going to do for money,' he replied.

Five minutes later, still chewing on the bones, they shook hands to seal the deal. Snowy took over the Stadium business on a rental of 75 pounds per week, with an option to purchase outright at 45,000 pounds.

Snowy still needed a lucrative fight early on to get the financial base to buy Huge Deal out. It came in the next McVea–Langford fight at the Stadium, which netted Snowy well over 3,000 pounds.

At the time, Huge Deal and Snowy kept quiet about their business deal, and so it was into Huge Deal's office a distressed McVea barged one afternoon, complaining that one of his fingers had turned white after he'd had a dispute with his car. After Huge Deal had closely inspected McVea's finger, he called for the doctor who arrived with an 'amputating axe in his hand'. McVea almost fainted at the sight of the axe, but was quickly reassured by the doctor that the wound had been healed – soaked by petrol, his finger had basically been bleached white. He was permitted to fight and on Boxing Day 1912, entered the ring to provide Snowy with his financial windfall. McVea did not come out of it as well, flattened by Langford in the 13th round.

Snowy still required a silent partner, and although both Huge Deal and his Melbourne rival, John Wren, agreed to act in that capacity, he opted for his friend, insurance entrepreneur and politician, Sir John Garvan.

The unmarried Sir John had met Snowy through the equestrian world, as the knight was an obsessed polo player being a member of the team which twice won the Countess of Dudley Cup. An avid racehorse owner, he was the brains behind the Mutual Life and Citizens' Assurance Company (MLC).

By early 1913, the money was paid over and according to Snowy: 'Sir John and myself owned Rushcutters Bay Stadium, lock, stock and barrel.'

The Referee exclusively revealed the original change of ownership on December 31, 1912, explaining that the necessary documents had been signed where payment of 30,000 pounds, at the rate of 3,000 pounds per year, had been agreed to. The disparity between the 30,000 pounds mentioned in *The Referee*, and 45,000 pounds mentioned by Snowy several decades later, was obviously to keep the tax man at bay.

While Snowy was publicly saying that Garvan was his partner, there were far more fingers in the Stadium pie. Harold and Fred Baker had also taken a small share of the ownership, while John Wren invested a 'substantial sum' of money to be a considerable partner. And despite what was said publicly, Huge Deal was not entirely left out, still holding onto a minimal ownership share.

Wren and Huge Deal had been opponents for many years – understandable considering that the notorious Melbourne businessman was the undisputed 'King of Australian Boxing' until Huge Deal came along and stole the limelight.

But through the most unexpected of meetings, they had called a truce. The pair, due to lack of accommodation, had to share a sleeper carriage on the overnight train from Melbourne and Sydney. When heading to the top bunk, Huge Deal was impressed that before getting under the covers, Wren had dropped to his knees and quietly said his prayers. Suddenly Huge Deal, the most suspicious of human beings, thought that despite all of Wren's shady dealings, the act of praying indicated he at least must have a heart.

They became secret partners in several business ventures, including working together in arranging visits by key American boxers, in particular heavyweights. They would share the freight, so that the boxer would appear in Huge Deal's stadium in Sydney, and Wren's venues in other states. Another deal was to make sure that Snowy became the public frontman of the Stadium, even if in the background they pulled the strings.

Snowy immediately put the boxing world at ease, explaining that 'strong efforts will be made to attract the best American and English boxers Australiawards. Already overseas wires have been at work to that end.

'Wrestling, jujitsu, physical culture competitions, and all branches of amateur sport are to receive attention in turn.'

Snowy had big ideas, as shown in a front page report in the Saturday *Referee & Arrow*, which headlined: 'Mr Snowy Baker aims to make it an Olympic Club, as well as Mecca of World's Boxers.'

'Have I any features to introduce? Yes. While boxing will remain the main issue, as in the past, I hope to encourage kindred sports. But my arrangements, or negotiations, and ultimate purchase from Mr McIntosh, of this huge institution was hasty. Consequently I have not had an opportunity of going thoroughly into matters.

'But I can say that I have set my mind on encouraging wrestling championships . . . and yes, we are to teach swimming at the Stadium. But will it be managed without the water? Why, of course, the swimming pool will be on the premises, if the permission by the authorities be granted, for after securing permission I intend to straight away erect a basin. Just imagine the effect of a dip in the briny after undergoing an electric light bath. I intend to make the Stadium the athletes rendezvous, and at that as attractive as possible to men who delight in exercise as well as those who look on.'

Snowy also wanted to stage jujitsu and fencing contests at the Stadium.

Nearby *The Referee* made certain they ran overseas endorsements of Snowy's rise to ownership. The London *Sportsman* was effuse in its praise, describing Snowy as 'the best allround athlete in the colonies, a champion swimmer, a champion with the gloves, a splendid gymnast and a prize winner in all the exercises such as the sabre, the sword, and the lance, pertaining to military work. He is a tactful, affable young fellow, well educated and a great favourite "down under" with all the classes. Snowy made armies of friends when he was in England four years ago, and he will, I am sure, have the best wishes for success in his new line of all old friends at "home".'

Coinciding with that gushing praise was the release of Gordon Inglis's *Sport and Pastime in Australia*, which over 308 pages explained extensively to those at 'home' where Australia stood in its various sporting pursuits. Snowy received a special mention, being described as 'probably the finest allround athlete Australia has ever produced'.

Inglis wrote: 'I read some little time ago an article by a fervent admirer in which Baker was treated in his capacities of boxer, wrestler, swimmer, acrobatic and fancy diver, waterpolo player, footballer, rower, expert in military sports including wrestling on horseback, tent-pegging, bayonet v bayonet, sword v sword, lemon-cutting, rescue races and alarm and rush. It is added by the precise chronicler of these virtues that Baker, when at school shone in jumping, hurdling, running and walking, but, comes the grave comment, "He necessarily had to give up some of these forms of athletics." It will not be accounted to him for lassitude or a desire for a life of ease that Snowy patiently abandoned these last-mentioned recreations.'

Snowy put his copy of *Sport and Pastime in Australia* pride of place on his Stadium office bookshelf, producing it any time someone wondered where he stood in the world. But he wasn't often in the office, instead constantly wandering around the Stadium, looking for ways to improve the facilities. It wasn't hard.

His first innovation at the Stadium was to get the women involved. In his first advertisement as Stadium director, Snowy announced that at Thursday afternoon matinees, free afternoon tea would be provided for any lady who attended. As well, there would be a 'first class musical programme', with a string band playing the hits of the era.

Ethel helped out with the cooking, while her two daughters, who had both just started school, appeared as able waitresses, working the room and trying to woo anyone with the Baker family charm. They were gone well before the fights, Ethel explaining to her daughters that it wasn't good etiquette being seen enjoying the sight of two men belting into each other.

Women, apart from the few who snuck into the Johnson–Burns fight, had generally been discouraged about going anywhere near a boxing stadium. But Snowy was shrewd enough to realise that if women became interested, they would lure more men to the Stadium. He also realised that if ladies were going to be a willing part of the crowd, the Stadium would have to rid itself of its ramshackle look.

He knocked down the old, primitive toilet blocks, even providing seating in the men's lavatory, while perfume bottles were strategically placed in the women's. Fire hoses were installed, air ventilators fitted around the Stadium, and those at ringside were given far more leg room. He tried to convince everyone that the spectator was his number one priority.

Just as importantly, Snowy decided to update the time clock above the ring, allowing spectators to know exactly what was going on. The clock took four minutes to do one lap, ringing after three minutes to indicate the end of the round and again a minute later to start a fresh round.

Snowy was making strong headway, but was still extremely edgy about being seen as a puppet for Wren and Huge Deal. In May 1913, five months after taking over, he wrote an extraordinary letter to *The Referee*, where he tried to convince everyone who exactly was in charge. A short time before Snowy wrote the letter Huge Deal had appeared in a court case, where he was asked if he was still a large shareholder in the Sydney Stadium. Obviously for Snowy, the answer wasn't satisfactory, prompting him to write: 'As a matter of fact, both counsel in his question, and Mr McIntosh in his reply, were referring to Stadiums Ltd, a company which formerly controlled the Stadium business at Rushcutters Bay, and which is still in existence. As a matter of fact, Mr McIntosh at the present time has no interest of any kind whatever in the Stadium, as I have purchased the whole concern – lock, stock and barrel – from him, and the cash represented in the transaction has been paid over.

'I would be obliged if you will publish this explanation, as the circumstances referred to, which has become pretty well known, has created an entirely erroneous impression regarding the control of the Stadium.'

Stadiums Ltd. Stadium. A bit of clever semantics. But hardly anyone was convinced by that argument, with the insinuation remaining that Huge Deal still had his grubby hands involved in the Stadium, Baker being the mere public face. As Ruth Park and Rafe Champion indicated in their outstanding biography on Les Darcy, *Home Before Dark*, no-one in the boxing world was convinced that Baker was the Stadium boss. Maurice O'Sullivan, a close friend of Darcy's, is quoted as saying: 'Snowy was a capable businessman, hard as nails. But how he jumped when McIntosh whistled. The story was that when the Baker brothers bought the Stadium from H.D., the latter funded them. So Snowy was obligated, and when you were obligated to McIntosh he whistled real loud.'

Wren also whistled real loud in Snowy's ear.

Not surprisingly, to avoid all the confusion, Snowy opted for a Stadium name change. And for someone known as 'The Great I Am' there was only one alternative. He needed no convincing what the new name should be.

Suddenly the Sydney Stadium was 'Snowy Baker's Stadium'. Now no-one could be under any misapprehension over who exactly was in control. Photographs of the interior of the Stadium at that time showed that it had turned into a cozy venue. The ring now looked like an oversized four poster bed, showered with flags of the leading nations, including England and the United States. On top of the ring were wooden advertisements, with the most noticeable being one which said: 'Snowy Baker. Why not learn boxing.'

Those near ringside sat on collapsible chairs. Up in the bleachers, they sat on wooden tiers in front of signs advertising Gilbey's Dry Gin, King George IV Whisky, Penfold's Wines, Hansa Cigars and Sanderson Scotch. Obviously a thirsty crowd.

In the ring, Snowy continued to bring them the best.

To froth up the crowd even further, Snowy publicly began the search for the 'great white hope', believing that Australia would at last develop someone who could be of world standard. He knew a local hero would whip up the crowd and be far cheaper than an international star, as he didn't have to pay his freight to and from a faraway land. But he didn't make it known that, as with Huge Deal, he was determined to rip-off the boxer wherever possible. For years, local boxers had been distressed that Huge Deal had given them only 25% of the takings from major bouts. Despite calls for it to be increased to 30%, Snowy showed no willingness to give the boxers a better deal.

Snowy also immediately showed an aversion to any boxer who turned up with a manager by his side to haggle a deal.

'The boxers were always reasonable chaps to deal with, but when a man had a so-called manager hanging on to him, it was a different proposition. The manager thought it was his duty to dictate ridiculous terms and generally held up the management over small clauses in the agreements. The clauses meant really nothing,' Snowy said.

'The boxer works on the road over long distances, goes through hard gruelling times in his gymnasium, and has to take the punches in the ring. It is then only reasonable to suppose that he should be the man who should receive all his end of the profits, and that a percentage such as 50 per cent, should not, under any circumstances be handed to a manager. If things like this are allowed to go on, the boxing business will suffer.'

Snowy was laying down the ground rules very early on. He made it quite obvious that he was not going to be stood over, and that he was always going to be boss. Not surprisingly it wasn't long before Snowy had a dubious reputation for being a hard, and often brutal, promoter. He was not always the boxer's friend.

Every few weeks in *The Referee*, Snowy would make a plea that he knew Australia had 'so much undiscovered boxing material', and he was willing 'to give a good trial to any aspirant in any class'.

The item was always strategically placed, usually just above or beside a large advertisement promoting Snowy's gymnasium, which explained how you could become 'A Stronger, Sturdier, Healthier, Happier Man'.

Why be a wimp? As Snowy said in the ad: 'There's a bully in every town – blustering, ill-tempered fellow, ever ready to humiliate the inoffensive. Usually his knowledge of self-defence is very crude – his principal asset is a loud mouth and a bad temper. When he bumps a man who knows how to "use" his hands his downfall is quick and certain. Why don't you equip yourself so as to be sure you can keep your end up against a bully? Boxing is no load to carry, but mighty handy when you're in a scrape. Boxing is a great pastime. It's easy to learn by my system. And most convenient for you, because you can learn in your own home.'

How could anyone resist? Soon Snowy had the scrawny and the strong, either writing to him hoping he could save their miserable lives, or fronting at his Stadium office, explaining that he had just met the next champion of the world.

Snowy was just as eager to get some uniformity in the laws of boxing, which differed from state to state, country to country, and over the years caused enormous friction between different bodies. He wasted no time in organising a national conference, attended by boxing authorities from all over the Commonwealth and sporting journalists, to formalise a boxing code. Even though it was partly a public relations exercise, it was still a master stroke by Snowy. The meeting, held at the Hotel Australia in Sydney, succeeded in its task of determining hard and fast boxing rules, and in a world first, properly setting the weights for all divisions.

The conference determined that the referee should be in the ring, and not observing from outside as was the case in many countries; the maximum points per round be five not three; kidney blows and the 'rabbit killer' – a blow which lands on the back of the neck – be barred; boxers had to wear protective groin shields; ringside weigh-ins at major bouts were compulsory; to avoid rigged fights a boxer would be disqualified as soon as his second entered the ring during the course of a round; a second would be thrown out if he made offensive remarks during a bout (Snowy had obviously not forgotten the Clabby incident); blows not struck with the knuckle part of the hand would not count; and when a boxer is knocked down, the other man must retire to the farthest corner.

The conference also gave guidance to judges by determining that 'aggressive without effect be not considered, and the same applied to defence without motive'.

'That means the boxer that is trying to make a fight of it, while the other fellow, by far the better boxer, indulges in nothing but defence, the aggressive one should be determined the winner,' the conference notes said. Such was Snowy's authority that the new rules were accepted throughout the Commonwealth and boxing was no longer a hazy, crazy affair.

Throughout 1913, Snowy made numerous trips to Brisbane, Melbourne and Adelaide in search of stadiums, realising that a string of new venues in the main cities would enable him to farm out fighters and use them as lead-ups to the big events in Sydney. By May, Snowy was telling *The Referee* that he had organised temporary stadiums in Melbourne and Brisbane.

Snowy knew that because of Wren's influence, breaking into Melbourne would be difficult, while getting a foothold in the hick town to the north should be a breeze. Brisbane still had that OK Corral feel about it and Snowy thought a switched-on Sydney entrepreneur like himself would have no problem winning over the locals. However, reality proved a little trickier. In the end, he had to grease a few palms.

'It occurred to me that there was a great necessity in Australia for a circuit like that in vaudeville,' Snowy reminisced. 'If a boxer was not the type to suit the Sydney public, or after enthusiasts had grown tired of seeing him perform in one city he could then be moved to another. I first gave my attention to Brisbane.'

At the time, George Lawrence was the chief Brisbane boxing promoter, working out of a ramshackle open-air city venue called the Olympic Club. When Snowy asked what it would take to move Lawrence out of the equation, a colleague of Lawrence told him: 'Money will not buy him out.'

So instead, Snowy spent the week ingratiating himself with local members of parliament and aldermen, and visiting every land and estate agent and builder in a bid to find a spot to build a stadium.

By the end of the week, Snowy was granted a licence to promote a fight in South Brisbane at Cremorne Gardens — an unused open-air amusement park. He also leased a large block of land in Stanley Street, contracted the timber and had 100 workmen ready to start the erection of a large 6,000 seat stadium. But it was never built.

The first fight at the temporary stadium at Cremorne Gardens was between Harry Stone and Johnny Summers. But Snowy was hit with a bomb the following morning when the two local daily newspapers declared it a 'crying shame' and an 'outrage' that such a fight was held at a spot with two private hospitals in close proximity. The 'yelling of the crowd' apparently disturbed the patients.

The place was condemned. Then the next morning, the Chief Secretary's Office, obviously under pressure from the locals who didn't want a Sydney spiv breaking into their territory, declared that only one boxing licence would be permitted in Brisbane — the one already held by Lawrence.

Snowy had no alternative but to convince Lawrence it was in his best interest that he was bought out. After three days of 'intense discussions', Lawrence agreed on 15,000 pounds for Snowy to take over the licence at the Olympic Club.

Within a few hours, a new stadium on the corner of Albert and Charlotte Streets was being erected. Named Baker's Olympic Stadium, Snowy boasted that it was the largest building of its kind in Queensland, seating 6,000 and with six shops built in.

Getting started in Melbourne was simpler. Wren, through Huge Deal, gave his blessing and Snowy headed south. For his arrival in Melbourne, Snowy had opted to travel in style. Snowy again made the trip by train, but was met by his chauffeur who had loaded his boss' Rolls Royce onto the SS *Katoomba* and shipped it to Melbourne, so that Snowy could use it while negotiating in the southern capital. Appearances, appearances, appearances.

Even though Wren was heavily involved in the boxing scene, the chief public fight promoter in Melbourne at the time was the former Australian heavyweight champion Bill Lang. Lang ran the Melbourne Pavilion, a city hall long identified as a prominent boxing venue.

Snowy didn't have to work too hard to buy out the lease from Lang. For a measly 500 pounds he bought the lease, which also included a licence to conduct boxing.

Worried about the small size of the Pavilion, Snowy looked far and wide for a suitable plot of land to build a bigger stadium. The most appealing spot was in West Melbourne, a large block owned by the Bank of Victoria. Within three months, the stadium was built, hosted fights and boasted the largest steel spans in any building in Australia.

Next, Snowy headed to Adelaide, where he again took over an open-air venue, ensuring that by September 1913 he was in charge of four venues from Brisbane to Adelaide. In less than a year he had become the undisputed czar of Australian boxing. Working with him from his Sydney base was his brother Harold, who had the official title of Publicity Manager, four stenographers, an office manager, charity carnival officer and advertising manager. Still, Snowy wanted to control all areas – including refereeing.

Although not appearing in the ring as often as before – especially since he kept flitting from state to state to make certain no-one was trying to dud him at any of his venues – Snowy still wanted to be in charge of the big fights. His ego always got the better of him and usually placed him into further predicaments.

Yet again he earnt the ire of the 14,000 plus crowd during the first meeting of the bronzed Melburnian Hughie Mehegan, and the pale Englishman, Matt Wells, at Snowy Baker's Stadium in August 1913. Mehegan was hugely popular to the Stadium crowd, and knowing that he didn't want to let them down, approached Snowy at the start of the lightweight bout to say: 'Now, remember, referee, the towel from my corner don't count with me. I'm the only bloke to stop this fight outside the other fellow, you, or the police – while I'm on my feet it's a go.' Snowy just grinned.

Snowy looked resplendent in an immaculate tuxedo, but the bulk of the crowd wanted to bury him in that suit when after 20 rounds he awarded Wells the fight on points. Mehegan was still on his feet and couldn't believe he had been overcome by an opponent who spent most of the competition running away from him.

When Wells, after hearing the decision, threw his arms around Mehegan and kissed him on the cheek, the hooting over Snowy's decision was, in the referee's words, 'full and hearty'.

Snowy, following the Huge Deal line, showed footage of the fight at special screenings in Sydney and Melbourne, and grew accustomed to being loudly booed for his dubious officiating of the fight. During screenings, Snowy was constantly asked if the ropes had been placed around the ring to stop the elusive London rabbit from getting away from Mehegan. Snowy didn't care. He had already enjoyed the last laugh, taking the punter's money, yet again, through admission to the film.

It was still obviously a dud decision. Even *Famous Fights at the Stadium* by C.A. Jeffries, which was bankrolled by Huge Deal and Snowy, had a big dig at the boss. 'Baker's decision received the endorsement of the bulk of the press, but was hotly disputed by a large number of regular ringsiders,' Jeffries wrote.

'One thing was certain judging from the remarks heard afterwards in trams, trains and boats – and that was, that if Baker was wise he would referee no more fights in his own Stadium.'

Upsetting the fans wasn't Snowy's only specialty. He was soon also alienating most of the key stadium fighters, especially those who dared to have a manager.

Snowy, a man who revelled in his own power, quickly earnt a poor reputation for being an incorrigible dictator. If boxers wanted to fight under the large Baker Stadium umbrella, they basically had to do what Snowy told them to do. He was the match-maker, deciding when, where and who a boxer would fight. And they had to fight when he told them, including at short notice, even if injured or unfit – especially if he needed them to bolster the undercard for a big fight night, or wanted them to impress the locals in Melbourne, Adelaide or Brisbane.

As the local boxers, and even many of the imports, were often down to their last feed, they invariably agreed to Snowy's demands, even when the pay was poor. Any money was good money.

The usual deal was that in the preliminary bouts, the fighters would box for a set fee, while those in the main bout usually agreed upon a percentage of the gate. Even with the big names, Snowy always held the upper hand.

Snowy immediately took 50% of the gate receipts, but on top of that would hand the boxer a bill for the use of doctors, incidental travel expenses and promotion. The two boxers would share what was left in the pool, which was now hovering around the 40% mark.

The boxers were never able to properly gauge what the gate receipts were, or the exact size of the crowd. That was completely up to Snowy's discretion, and most times he would publicly announce a smaller crowd figure so that he didn't have to hand over the proper amount of funds. The official gate takings were also cleverly manipulated to ensure that Snowy received way over the actual 50%. Devious shaving of figures was occurring all over the place.

Some fighters employed official spotters, who tried to count the crowd as they entered the Stadium, before confronting Snowy with what they believed was the proper attendance figure. Snowy would laugh them off, claiming that if they persisted with the practice, their boxer would be barred from competing in his venues. That practice immediately dropped off.

From what was left, the boxers also had to pay a commission ranging from 25% to 50% to their trainer or manager, fees to their sparring partners and seconds, and all other major costs, including training facilities and masseur. In the end, the boxer had suffered a bashing for little more than pocket money. It was the ultimate mug's game, as all the hangers-on and go-betweens, and not the actual combatants, made the money.

One small consolation for boxers at Snowy Baker's Stadium was that at least the boss had erected two electric fans above the ring to make life a little more comfortable for the combatants. However, the cynics countered that it was as much to do with making it easier for the cameramen and photographers perched above and around the ring, who were shooting the action, from which Snowy got his royalty cut.

Snowy also worked on the boxers' paranoia, repeatedly telling them if they demanded too much, they would be pricing themselves out of the market. He constantly told boxers and their managers that they were 'a dime a dozen'. Consequently, in most cases, boxers dropped their fee. Again Snowy had won by KO.

Nonetheless, the boxers kept queueing up outside Snowy's Stadium office, pleading for their big chance. And so the bizarre and ridiculous bouts continued.

Mugs like 'Nutty' Curran hopped into the Stadium ring, where according to C.A. Jeffries he 'suffered from a sub-acute form of sleeping sickness, or that he was the most indolent and bedridden circumstance that ever got into a boxing ring'. Throughout the bout against another has-been Bill Lang, Curran kept falling over. Not even drinking flat beer from a bottle at the end of each round could revive Curran, who would amble back out and fall over once again. The crowd apparently loved it.

Then out came a New York Hebrew called Harry Stone who smashed Johnny Summers to oblivion. 'When referee Arthur Scott [who had replaced Snowy in the ring] placed his hand on Stone's head,' Jeffries wrote, 'that youth bounded three times into the air, leaped wildly from the ring, kissed 14 fat, hysterical Jews, and left Summer's blood and his own chewing gum over their faces.'

Stone was a big favourite with the Stadium crowd because 'all the while he chewed gum . . . He chewed while he smote. He chewed while he was smitten. He chewed while he was in the air, on his feet and betwixt and between.'

Summers, then the welterweight champion of England, got it together a few weeks later when, against Arthur Evernden, he decided to take swigs from a colourless medicine bottle, which he claimed contained holy water. Evernden succumbed to the special powers.

But more importantly for Snowy, from up north was emerging a special power who didn't need holy water or chewing gum to humiliate his opponents. The Australian boxer Snowy had been waiting for was about to come into Snowy's range of vision. His meal ticket was about to arrive.

Chapter 13

The Czar of Australian Boxing

SNOWY'S INVOLVEMENT WITH HUGE DEAL AND WREN, HIS RAMPANT EGO and the need to stay on top in a corrupt boxing industry had turned him into a hard, uncompromising, sometimes devious character. He'd now learnt all the tricks of the trade and become the master of saying one thing, and doing the exact opposite. He was no longer the innocent athlete, but a mischievous, often manipulative promoter. Gone was the Mr Clean, Mr Innocent tag. He'd hung around with too many dodgy types for too long.

By now, Snowy's consistent cry that he wanted to push the talents of local boxers was starting to sound really hollow. Particularly since Snowy remained totally infatuated with overseas talent, his Stadium cards dominated by fighters from either the United States, England or Europe. This had already led to letters being sent to *The Referee* arguing that the practice of Snowy ingratiating himself with overseas boxers was to the detriment of those closer to home, who were often ignored or warded away.

That included a young Irish Catholic blacksmith's apprentice from Maitland called Les Darcy.

Since 1912, Darcy, a highly popular and personable teenager who was family orientated and community minded, had been freely acknowledged as Australia's great boxing hope.

Although just 17, Darcy had beaten all and sundry in a series of bouts in Maitland and Newcastle throughout 1912 and 1913. He won his first 17 fights – three by knockout and seven by a technical knockout where the opponent was unwilling or unable to continue.

Around the Hunter, Darcy was the undisputed local hero. He was also the ideal product to promote. He was handsome, boasting trademark Australian features – an innocent, sometimes cheeky demeanour, an endearing smile and an impressive physique. He had proud working-class values. He was adored by all. The ultimate boy next door, who wanted to improve the lot of his large, impoverished family by repeatedly putting his body on the line. Adding to the immense charm was that he was sometimes embarrassingly shy and always so modest.

But Snowy wasn't interested.

Will Lawless, the respected boxing journalist and as good a judge on a fighter in Australia, repeatedly approached Snowy at the Stadium, singing Darcy's praises. Lawless had regularly travelled to Newcastle to watch Darcy in action. He immediately recognised Darcy's star quality and privately told his seconds that with proper nurturing he could be Australia's first high-profile world champion.

However Snowy would repeatedly ward 'Solar Plexus' off with the remark: 'No, mate, he's only 17. He's too young for the Stadium, and he's only beating has-beens from the bush. Too early, Solar. Too early.'

Others tried, including respected fighter Les O'Donnell and an entourage from Maitland. Darcy's close confidant, Father Coady, sought meetings with both Snowy and Huge Deal, but struggled to get past first base.

Frustrated in not getting a start at the Stadium, Darcy had instead agreed to fight at a rival venue, the Olympia Athletic Club in Newtown, where in front of a small crowd he defeated Englishman Jack Clarke in nine rounds. In a small filler item, *The Referee* recorded the fact that 'D'Arcy' [sic] had 'made good at his first Sydney appearance. After being many times sent to the canvas, Clarke was compelled to quit in the ninth round'.

A fair effort considering Darcy worked that morning in the local blacksmith's shop, made the four-hour trip to Sydney that afternoon and then after the fight caught the 11.15 pm ferry to Newcastle. Arriving at 6 am, Darcy walked to Newcastle Station, caught the first train to Maitland and by 7.30 am was back in front of the forge.

Snowy was still not impressed.

After the Olympia triumph, Father Coady demanded another meeting with Snowy. In Raymond Swanwick's biography of Darcy, *Les Darcy: Australia's Golden Boy of Boxing* he notes that Father Coady was 'fobbed off with vague promises of an engagement for Les "later on", when he was a little older and had more experience'.

'"But how can he gain experience if you don't give him a chance to gain it?" Father Coady asked.

'"That's his worry," said Baker. "He's an apprentice blacksmith and an apprentice fighter too."

'"You wouldn't care to put on the gloves with him yourself, would you?" Father Coady asked with a smile.

'"Not me!" Baker admitted. "I'm told he hits like a sledgehammer, and has muscles like iron!"'

In the end, Baker offered Father Coady a half-promise. If Darcy continued winning several important bouts, Snowy would consider giving him a chance against an overseas boxer at the Stadium later that year.

But Snowy had more pressing business.

The next day he was off on a world tour, with the main aim of luring talent from America, England and Europe, in particular Georges Carpentier. Darcy and the rest of Australia would have to wait.

Snowy's farewell was treated as if royalty was departing. First there was a farewell dinner which involved all the Stadium staff. There, Snowy had to deny allegations he was a 'wowser', because of his aversion towards alcohol. 'I am told that a wowser is a person with a vinegary face,' Snowy told his staff, 'who never touches a whisky bottle, yet drinks that refreshing beverage out of a lemonade bottle. If that is the true definition, I am certainly not a wowser, because I have never touched strong drink.'

Snowy had obviously forgotten his European adventures.

Then he was the special guest at a black tie function, hosted by the Lord Mayor, at the plush Australia Hotel in the centre of the city. Attending was a who's who of the Sydney sporting, political and social world, headed by Lord Mayor R.W. Richards, and the Speaker of the House, R.D. Meagher. Seated around a large table, where the rich and famous were entertained by The Primrose Five from the Tivoli, were Huge Deal, E.S. Marks, Harold Baker, Cecil Healy, Ted Larkin, Frank Underwood, Arthur Scott, and writers J.C. Davis and Will Lawless. Boxer Dave Smith was a late arrival and received a rousing round of applause, even if a few nights earlier he had been knocked out at the Stadium by the American boxer Eddie McGoorty, just two minutes into the first round.

In January 1914, Snowy headed for the United States, but was hampered in his negotiations when his wife suffered a fever during the early part of the voyage. She was bedridden for several days, the fever recurring when they arrived in the US. At least they didn't have the extra burden of looking after the children as they had stayed behind in Sydney in the care of a nanny.

Also not helping Snowy's situation was the endless allegations that Wren had bought the Sydney Stadium. *The Referee* tried to quash the rumour in late January, but the small item was hardly convincing. In answering the rumour about Wren being in charge of the Stadium, *The Referee* said: 'I am assured it is not so. Mr Wren, I understand, has purchased shares from two of those who held them. But the Stadium business is going on just as usual.'

This wasn't exactly the truth, as shown when the Stadium success-fully made a takeover bid for the Olympia Athletic Club to ensure that there was no opposition in Sydney. A new company was registered, called Stadiums Ltd, the nominees being Wren, Snowy and solicitor, William Drew. The company directors included another of Snowy's brothers, Fred Baker.

This was more than just purchasing a few shares; Wren and Snowy were now publicly connected. Huge Deal's name was missing from Stadiums Ltd's company records, but no-one disputed that he remained the silent partner.

Another problem Snowy struck while overseas was that he was being pursued by countless boxing nobodies who believed they could make it rich in Australia. In March 1914, Snowy wrote home: 'As you might guess, great numbers of second and third raters are applying for trips down to our sunny land, but my experience is that our sportsmen and followers of the game only want the best.'

But Snowy did find the occasional gem in between visits to White Sox baseball games, attending a banquet in his honour at the Biltmore Hotel in New York which attracted more than '1,000 prominent people of the United States', attending major title fights in various states, signing up his old agitator, Jimmy Clabby, being made a special member of the New York Athletic Club and visiting Young Griffo.

Young Griffo, otherwise known as Albert Griffiths, rose from being a newspaper boy in the Rocks to Australian featherweight champion, before heading to the United States in search of a world title fight. In his fighting days, he would often hop into the ring totally drunk and still knock out his opponent. After retiring with a proud record of 166 fights with just a handful of defeats, Young Griffo became a hopeless alcoholic, a derelict who spent most of his days being a pest in New York saloons. He ended up in an asylum.

Snowy tracked him down in a Manhattan back alley. He wrote in April 1914: 'I saw Griffo the other day, and did everything I could to help him along, but am afraid it will not be of much use. He is in a bad way.'

He also had time to conduct some weird, wildly racist interviews in the local press. Robert Edgren of the *New York Evening World* dragged some tasty morsels out of Snowy, in particular that he expected to find among the Australian Aboriginals a world heavyweight champion.

'They're absolutely game,' Snowy explained. 'They don't know what it is to quit. Before boxing came in the Aboriginal way of settling disputes over a gin was rather curious.

'Two Aboriginals would sit facing each other on a log. One would take a heavy club and bring it down with all his might on the other's head. Then he'd pass the club over and the other fellow would have his turn. They'd keep this up until one or the other fell off the log. The fellow who stayed on won the gin.'

The revelations continued.

'The Australian Aboriginals have the thickest skulls in the world. The African negro's skull is an egg-shell in comparison. It's almost impossible to hurt an Aboriginal with a blow. When they're fighting or being clubbed they laugh all the time. They think it's a joke.'

Not surprisingly, before long Snowy was referring to Jerry Jerome, the boxer who became the first Aboriginal to win an Australian title. Jerome didn't take up boxing until he was 34, winning the Australian middleweight title in 1912 when he was well into his forties.

'Jerry Jerome is 47, and I've seen him go out without any training and run 100 yards in 10.4 seconds. Once Jerry Jerome fought another Aboriginal – a fellow with a great round body like a barrel, and a big round head set on his body without any neck, and the thinnest legs I ever saw. Jerry gave him an awful beating.

'Every round Jerry would say: "You'd better quit right now; I'm going to kill you."

'And the big fellow would laugh and say: "I'll be killing you, Jerry."

'He never showed a sign of being willing to quit. His name is "Black Paddy", and he is known as the "Smoked Irishman". Black Paddy is a good many years older than Jerry Jerome.'

Along with the article were several cartoons of Aboriginals banging each other over the head with a club.

In another article in the *New York Globe*, Snowy was described as 'the Jim Thorpe of Australia', comparing him to the legendary all-rounder American athlete.

And more big statements from the effusive Snowy. 'Pardon me for the statement, but I believe that Australians are the best athletes in the world,' Snowy told a stunned *New York Globe* journalist.

'True, you Americans hold most all the world's records, but that is because you specialise. Australians do not. They are all-round athletes, and it is not unusual for a champion of one sport to be a champion at several others. Then, too, I would say that you have too few athletes in proportion to your population.

'There are too many spectators and too few athletes. The proportion in Australia is five times as great as here. I also believe that in years to come Australia's status in athletics will be recognised as superior. We live a simpler, plainer life than other countries do — that will be the reason.'

Before Snowy made any more ludicrous statements, he headed off to France that same year to attempt to lure Carpentier southwards. As Carpentier continued to evade him, Snowy moved on to England where the wining and dining continued, including a lunch in London in honour of the newly appointed Australian Governor-General, Sir Ronald Munro Ferguson. Snowy used the moment wisely, offering Sir Ronald free entry to the Stadium when he arrived in Australia and a promise of the best ringside seat any time he ventured down the road from Government House to Rushcutters Bay. Snowy knew this was a way of keeping the many boxing detractors at bay.

Snowy also excitedly wrote home to Solar Plexus, who relayed it to all his *Referee* readers, that the Sydney promoter had just bought a state-of-the-art Sheffield Simplex in England, had driven the automobile from London to Brighton in just over an hour, and was 'having it packed and labelled, Sydney, to arrive there before it is my pleasure'.

Snowy eventually returned home on June 1, 1914, and was accorded 'welcome home hero' status — another dinner at the Hotel Australia, countless more speeches from state and federal politicians, and a eulogy from R.D. Meagher that Snowy 'on his trip abroad had done more to boom Australia than men who were paid to do so'.

This time the 'Vaude and Verne' vaudeville act and Mr Talleur Andrews of the Tivoli 'delighted the gathering with their vocal contributions'. Providing some of his prime acts from the Tiv was the least Huge Deal could do for his old mate. W.C. Fields almost did the honours, but the dates didn't quite suit. In a master coup, Huge Deal had lured Fields back to Australia for a successful season at the Tivoli as 'The Silent Humorist'. He was just as successful off the stage, travelling around Australia with someone he purported to be Mrs Fields. The real Mrs Fields was back at home in the United States. The dinner frivolities over, Snowy was off to the Stadium to sort out a few dilemmas.

Harold Baker was as much an opportunist as his elder brother and while Snowy was overseas had used the period to improve his power base with Stadiums Ltd. Through the funds he had received in public dontations for his involvment in the Coogee surf rescue, Harold had bought a considerable stake in Stadiums Ltd. But he wanted more.

Arthur Scott was gone as the chief Stadium referee, and Harold, with hardly any experience in controlling boxers, was the new head honcho. In March 1914, an odd item appeared in *The Referee*. In an official statement, the manager of Stadiums Ltd, Harry Keesing, said that he was very dissatisfied with Scott's decision to award Eddie McGoorty the fight over American boxer, Jeff Smith. 'Unfortunately the referee's decision cannot be upset and will go on record against Jeff Smith as a defeat,' the statement said.

'Furthermore we have undertaken to take all possible steps to make our action and opinion known in other countries, where Smith is even better known than in Australia. In future, Mr Harold Baker will occupy the position of referee. He is a brother of the proprietor; a well known sportsman, has a great name among amateurs, and is a good boxer himself with considerable experience.'

Underneath the item was an anonymous comment, probably from Solar Plexus. It inferred that Scott had been unfairly shafted. 'He [Baker] may do better, but it seems too big an experiment for him to jump from the small contests to those of world-wide significance, with the consequent nervous tension to the man who is sole arbiter.

'Work of this nature calls for the cool nerve of an old campaigner, so that experience of the game over years is essential.'

Like Snowy, Harold could be a nasty piece and was a notorious thin-skin. He wasn't going to let that criticism ride and immediately contacted *The Referee* for his right of reply.

Harold moaned that his inexperience was immaterial, especially as his brother, Snowy, was one year younger than him when he was appointed the official referee.

'Also, I would like it known that Reg, unlike myself, up to that time had not even refereed a ten-round bout, such as I have been doing of late. In fact he had done no refereeing whatsoever,' said Harold, showing that a family which fights together can whine together.

'He was young, but had a very varied knowledge of boxing craft. He was gifted with a normal amount of human intelligence, which enabled him, although so young, to render some of the best decisions that we have ever seen awarded in any contest here.'

To prove he was Mr Innocent, Harold said that 'in taking up the position vacated by Mr Scott, I do so merely as part of my duties as one of the Stadium staff. I was selected by the management merely because they thought I was thoroughly competent to carry out the duties. This, I have unbounded confidence in myself in doing.'

But *The Referee*, while allowing Harold his right of reply, was not going to let him get away with totally rewriting history. At the end of the item, *The Referee* corrected Harold about his brother, arguing that he'd 'evidently forgotten' that Snowy had refereeing experience well before Huge Deal made him the official head referee at the Stadium.

Harold soon earnt a reputation for being cold, lugubrious and unapproachable. Some years later, boxing writer Jim Donald in describing Harold, who was now for some inexplicable reason demanding that people call him Harald, wrote that while being an impressive figure, immaculately dressed as a referee in evening dress where 'dignity clothed him like a well garment', he was still a 'remote, detached personality'.

'In the ring and on the job he was a man with a marnie mouth and a jaw of steel – a man of ice with frozen eyes and a frozen voice.' When he said 'Break', 'don't nod', 'Step back', 'Box on' – it 'had the snap and crackle of a stock whip', Donald wrote. 'Naturally his aloofness bred a hostile feeling in the boxing camps . . . but he had a difficult part to play and he donned a frozen mask to play it.'

Even when Snowy was away, the name Harold Baker evoked trouble. Throughout the United States, Snowy discovered that a con man had been impersonating his brother and had borrowed large sums from different sporting centres. They were soon chasing Snowy in the hope of recouping funds. Snowy played dumb, even denying he had a brother called Harold or Harald, and fled town as quickly as he had evaded testy opponents during his boxing career.

Snowy's first act on returning was to give his approval to Harold being his chief in the ring. Snowy was delighted with the arrangement, knowing that it meant he could also control exactly what was going on in the middle. Like Huge Deal at the Johnson–Burns fight, Harold knew that Snowy would be his eyes outside the ring, proferring the necessary hand signals to ensure that the younger brother gave the decisions Stadiums Limited wanted to see. Snowy also knew that Harold's stitch up of Scott would improve his base. Boss, proprietor, promoter, and now pseudo head referee, except someone else would face the heat. Within days, Harold was handed his first important task – refereeing Les Darcy's first fight at the Stadium.

Snowy and Huge Deal had eventually succumbed. While Snowy was away, Darcy kept winning bouts, establishing himself as Australia's most promising boxer from any division. Once again the Darcy entourage headed to Sydney to try to talk sense into Snowy. He continued to play hard ball until Darcy's backers from Maitland told him that they would guarantee gate takings of 500 pounds if Darcy was matched at the Stadium. Now Snowy had absolutely nothing to lose. He had no option but to agree to a bout on July 18, 1914, where Darcy would fight the Dutch–American, Fritz Holland.

Chapter 14

Riot at the Stadium

TODAY ELITE SPORTSMEN GET TESTY IF THEY HAVE TO ENDURE TWO training sessions in the same day, are asked one too many questions by a pesky sports writer, or pestered into being involved in just one more sponsorship endorsement.

How different it was in Snowy and Harold's time.

While Les Darcy's first appearance at the Stadium has been extensively chronicled, what has never been mentioned is what Harold Baker actually got up to that day. Even Darcy would have struggled to top what Harold Baker did on July 18, 1914.

At 3.00 that afternoon, Harold ran out on the Sydney Sportsground as part of the Australian rugby forward pack to play the New Zealand All Blacks in the first of three Tests. Six hours later Harold refereed one of Australia's most notorious fights, which ended up in a riot.

Apart from his overwhelming lifesaving skills, swimming prowess, wrestling capabilities, the honour of captaining the Australian water polo team, excelling as an oarsman and weighlifting, plus his heavy involvement at the Sydney Stadium, Harold had also established himself as one of New South Wales and Australian rugby's most formidable forwards.

A tall, rangy, swift back-rower, Harold was a notable player for Sydney, Eastern Suburbs and Randwick, from 1911 becoming a New South Wales forward representative. Harold picked a fascinating day to follow his brother and become an elite member of the Australian rugby representative club.

Just half an hour before Harold played his first Test, the 10,000 crowd were overwhelmed by a touch of history when French aviator Maurice Guillaux completed the first successful flight from Melbourne to Sydney, flew over the ground and landed on a specially made airstrip in Moore Park, just 250 yards from the playing field.

After flying nine-and-a-quarter hours, Guillaux was carried by spectators to the Sportsground where he was presented to the Governor-General. Monsieur Guillaux was soon ushered off as the Australian team, with Harold at the front of the line, charged out of their dressing room, hungry for a rare victory over the dreaded All Blacks. If Guillaux thought flying from Melbourne was tricky, that was nothing compared to bobbing and weaving past 15 exuberant Australians who were after blood.

It wasn't to be though, with New Zealand winning 5–0. But the home side was still accorded hero status after a marvellous performance described by *The Town and Country Journal* as the 'finest game ever played by an Australian team'.

The Australian pack, where Harold was surrounded by such notables as Harald George, Doss Wallach and Fred Thompson, totally dominated their opposites on a wet, miserable day. Unfortunately their back line were unable to take advantage of a glut of possession to score the necessary try.

The *Sydney Morning Herald* was as effuse in its praise of the Australian forwards, explaining: 'Never did eight better trained men bow their heads in a scrummage, never did eight players go from first to last with greater determination. They pushed their opponents off the ball, and when it got into the loose, they were simply immense.'

In contrast, the All Blacks were castigated in the local press for their rough-house tactics, following a first half that was a succession of fist fights – Harold Baker usually right in the middle of it, hitting whoever he could. When the All Blacks' manager walked into the Australian dressing rooms, he was heard to say: 'Whew! But your forwards did give us a shock.'

As darkness descended, a gloomy Harold, who had been cheered from the field for a stoic Test debut, headed for the dressing rooms and checked his body for damage. His back and stomach were a stinging mosaic of criss-crossed deep red lines, caused by straying New Zealand boots at the bottom of rucks. One of his eyes was weeping from a well-directed right hook from his opposite, and his left hand was thudding with pain – the result of him retaliating after a king hit.

But there was no time to moan. Harold had to conduct hasty farewells to his team-mates, knock back an invitation to the Test match dinner, make a quick visit to the victorious dressing rooms and then start walking the 4 kilometres from the Sportsground to the Stadium for his next athletic pursuit.

He had to walk fast, even running at times, knowing that he had to beat the crowd into the Stadium, or he would struggle to get in on time to referee the main bout.

As Harold, wincing with pain with every step, arrived at the Stadium, he couldn't believe the chaos. Every street around the Stadium was crammed with fight fans, all of whom had been enticed by the first major sighting of the great Australian hope.

A healthy proportion of the swarming crowd had travelled from up north, where special trains had brought thousands of excitable Darcy fans from Maitland and Newcastle. One train had waited until the last horse race at Maitland, filled itself with inebriated and broke punters, and arrived at Central Station in time for the first tram to Rushcutters Bay.

To ensure that all the Novacastrians were at the Stadium in time, Snowy decided to hold back the fight an hour until 8.45 pm. This didn't perturb Darcy. He simply sat in a corner of the dressing room, nonchalantly playing a harmonica.

Nonetheless thousands missed out on getting into the Stadium in time and angrily milled around the entrances, demanding any news of what was happening inside.

It was soon obvious who the favourite was among a swirling crowd, which had pushed past the 17,000 mark. All those from his district had crowded the bleachers section of the Stadium and were hooting and screaming wildly, especially when their man had a quiet peek at the surroundings from his dressing room, which was noticed by all and sundry.

Then when Darcy made his grand appearance wearing green trunks and a faded gown, and headed to his corner where an Australian flag was draped, there was general pandemonium. The crowd banged their feet and bashed the galvanised iron, all the while screaming 'Darcy, Darcy, Darcy'.

At that moment, Snowy knew his search for the ideal home-grown was over. 'His extraordinary personality was evidenced as he stepped into the "square",' Snowy wrote. 'Practically the entire audience stood and cheered. He smiled and they all smiled with him and cheered again. The boy had the most contagious smile of any athlete I ever saw.'

The arrival of Fritz Holland a few moments later was practically ignored. Holland was hardly a high-profile boxer, but was no mug, having lost just four of his 49 fights, which included bouts against most of the leading United States welter and middleweights. He was more a scientist than a slugger.

Eventually Harold Baker, who had showered and spruced himself up by wearing brown boxing boots, long cream flannels and a cream polo neck jumper, beckoned the two fighters in and gave his instructions. The lights were dimmed and the first round began. All Darcy could see apart from Holland's darting eyes, was the flicker of thousands of glowing cigarettes and a thickening cloud of smoke billowing towards the ceiling.

Darcy began well, as usual taking the initiative. But Holland continued to fight back when least expected. It was very much the case of the enthusiasm of youth being countered by the experience of someone who had been there, done that. All of the early rounds were extremely tight, with Holland earning a rare applause from the crowd when he helped Darcy up to his feet in the fifth round after the Australian had slipped.

Darcy hadn't encountered anyone like this, Holland far more clever and craftier than the rough and tough bushies he had tussled with in Maitland, Newcastle and at the Olympia. In the final two rounds of the 20-round bout, Darcy appeared to be getting on top, but once more Holland knew how to evade trouble and usually came back with the impressive retaliatory blow. Holland had also accumulated a sizeable points lead from the earlier rounds.

In the end, it came down to Harold Baker's decision. After looking towards Snowy, sitting ringside next to the police inspector, who gave the nod in Holland's direction, Harold placed his hand on Fritz's head to indicate victory by points. There was a split second of silence before the crowd, intoxicated by Darcy's relentless enthusiasm and passion to win, went ballistic. Disgusted by the decision, and believing Darcy had been dudded by the Sydney spivs, his supporters decided to try to burn the place down.

'Bedlam broke out,' Snowy recalled. 'I have seen many hostile demonstrations at a boxing contest, but the worst was a Sunday school picnic to that at the Stadium that night.

'The crowd screamed in derision at Harold's decision, until it could hoot and scream no longer. Then hell broke loose as the miners from Newcastle and Maitland stormed the ring threatening my brother with all kinds of violence.

'I was standing at the ringside. "Baker, the robber." "Oh, you . . . , . . . , . . . , robber . . . , and Baker, the . . . . " are only a small example of the lurid compliments that angry, wild-eyed audience handed me that night.

'They also picked up every movable article in the Stadium from bottles to boards and heaved 'em at Harold. Bottles flew through the air. I stopped a full one between the shoulder blades. A well fluid-laden beer bottle whizzed past my ear, and smashed into smithereens a foot behind me. By agile sidestepping, I dodged another one – a dead marine this time. Then from another angle a piece of masonry about two pounds weight caught me on the heel. They wanted my blood – why me in preference to the referee, goodness only knows. I was a couple of steps up the bleachers when a half-dozen hefty angry boys picked up a Stadium usher standing close by and hurled him at me. All parts of him it seemed, landed flat on my face, and down the seats we rolled.

'Ringsiders scrambled from trouble. Then some crazy loon yelled: "Let's set the joint on fire." So they set the joint on fire in several different places at once.

'Hotheads began gathering up newspapers and breaking up the seats, with fires breaking out in a dozen different places.'

Luckily for Snowy, his brother Fred, who had refereed one of the preliminary bouts, had remained at the Stadium. Fred doubled as a fireman and immediately called for reinforcements. Within seconds, Fred had the firehoses working, aiming directly at those causing the trouble. Fred didn't first shoot at the flames, but at the culprits, drowning them with high volumes of water. They eventually dispersed.

The police had also called for reinforcements, somehow getting Harold and Snowy to safety by pushing through the wild mob back to the main Stadium office. In the middle of all the mayhem, two revolver shots rang out, reverberating around the venue.

When the brothers entered their office, they saw that every window had been smashed – the demonstrators outside still lobbing missiles through the openings.

Crouched beneath a desk in one corner of the room were three men. Snowy stepped closer and recognised that one of the figures was rather important. It was the Governor-General, Sir Ronald Munro Ferguson, who had accepted Snowy's offer in London of a free Stadium pass. Cowering under the desk, either side of the Governor-General, were his two aides.

'Hope you don't mind us taking refuge in your office until the situation quietens down a bit,' the Governor-General said. 'That was quite a fight, Baker. Quite a fight.'

Harold, still dodging the stones and bottles which were showering the office, nodded. 'Yes, your Excellency,' he agreed. 'And so is this.'

Eventually peace was restored, helped by the fact that Darcy's loyal supporters had to rush to the Sussex Street wharf to catch the 11.30 pm night steamer to Newcastle. The Governor-General's car was 'brought around to a distant dark street' so he could leave the Stadium unscathed, but apparently 'very excited'. The Governor-General was definitely coming back.

The *Sydney Morning Herald*, under the headline 'Riot at Stadium', described it as 'a disgraceful episode', explaining that 'the trouble came from the crowd in the cheaper seats'. Prices for tickets ranged from 10 shillings reserved, to two shillings in the bleachers.

The *Daily Telegraph* blamed the police for not controlling a 'frenzied crowd'. The newspaper complained that the police were not eager to restore order in the Stadium, only intervening in street disturbances.

This, according to the *Telegraph*, forced Snowy to become his own policeman. 'Most of the crowd had departed when Mr R.L. Baker saw three men loitering on the premises and making use of violent language. There was not a policeman handy, so Snowy put the three of them out himself.'

Adding to the drama was that 'heavy wagering went on, despite the management's notices: "Betting prohibited." Wagers were made openly, and big sums were freely talked of. The decision apparently hit the Newcastle and Maitland element hard, and they found many whose actions demonstrated that they had been carried away by the wildest and most unreasonable bias for the Australian novice, to support them. Blasts of hoots and howls, shouts of "robbery" and "burn the place down" swept the building.'

The newspapers also agreed that Baker's decision to award the fight to Holland was 'quite fair'. The Maitland *Daily Mercury* approached Snowy the following Monday and he made it blatantly clear who was to blame.

'There was a pretty rowdy element, and it is a strange thing that the trouble ended about half an hour before the steamer was timed to leave for Newcastle,' Snowy said. 'It was evident early in the night that the majority of the onlookers had only eyes for Darcy. This sort of thing is likely to jeopardise the young Maitland boxer's chances, instead of assisting him.'

Snowy was immediately putting Darcy in his place. However the promoter also knew that through the mayhem and headlines Darcy's first fight in Sydney had caused, he had at last found the local boxer he wanted to whip up local sentiment and guarantee capacity Stadium crowds.

But Snowy had to suffer a lot of flak. 'For a week after that fight, Harold and I were hooted as we walked the streets, so there were others besides the Maitland and Newcastle fans who thought they were robbed.'

After being so reticent about giving him his first Sydney fight, Snowy didn't hesitate in immediately organising a return bout involving Darcy and Holland in early September.

Still there was a proviso. Snowy was eager for Darcy to get some proper boxing tuition, and be taken away from what he termed 'a group of country bumpkins' whom he believed would thwart his progress in Maitland. On the advice of Will Lawless, Snowy recommended a long-time colleague, Dave Smith who had just won the Australian light heavyweight title by beating Jimmy Clabby in Brisbane.

Snowy believed if Smith took control of Darcy, an unrefined source would turn into fine wine. Smith, despite holding serious doubts about Snowy, knew that he had to stay sweet with the Stadium management to ensure that he kept getting good, lucrative bouts. Smith accepted and was soon travelling to Maitland, giving Darcy necessary tuition before the Holland fight. Apart from in the ring hints, Smith also had to teach Les how to eat properly at the dinner table, how to speak correctly and how to be the country gentleman.

So that Darcy could train properly, Snowy claimed that he paid three pounds a week for a fully qualified blacksmith to take over from Les at Billy Ford's East Maitland forge shop. This agreement has been disputed by other sources, which claimed that Darcy had been granted leave.

Until the return bout, both Snowy and Harold found themselves distracted by expected and unexpected international events. Harold took a break from refereeing to represent Australia in the Second and Third Tests against the All Blacks. Unfortunately Australia's enthusiasm in the First Test died out in the next two, and they suffered two serious losses – 17–0 in Brisbane and 22–7 in Sydney.

In between the two Tests, the most serious of announcements was made. On August 5, 1914, the Governor-General notified all State Premiers that war had broken out with Germany. This sad news was posted within minutes on the scoreboard at the Sydney Sportsground where the All Blacks were playing a Metropolitan XV. The lie of the land immediately changed, and Snowy, as expected, was quick to adapt.

As thousands immediately volunteered to join the Australian Imperial Force, Snowy knew that he could improve his standing within the local community by showing that he and the Stadium were right behind the war effort. Obviously paranoid about his Germanic–Dutch background, Snowy was among the first to put his hand up and say that he would do everything to back the Australian war cause. Within a week of the declaration of war, Snowy was in *The Referee* explaining that he was organising a 'patriotic carnival' at the Stadium where the ring would be removed to permit 'an assault-at-arms, wrestling on horseback, tent-pegging and other military exercises' to be carried out.

The final arrangements were far more grandiose. It began with a long, tiring three-mile procession through the city to the Showgrounds, where the crowd were entertained by trick and bareback riding; a fire brigade display, where a canvas structure marked 'Berlin, To Let' was burnt to the ground; boxing by Snowy's schoolboy classes; bayonet exercise; tug-o-war; chariot racing; buckjumping; boomerang throwing by the Aboriginal Wandy; and a succession of piped bands. The only mishap was in the motor cycle trick display, where a rider crashed into the boundary fence after his front wheel fell off. He apparently escaped unscathed.

Then onto the Stadium for more boxing exhibitions, with Fritz Holland agreeing to belt his fellow American, Gus Christie, around the ring; Fred Baker performing 'boxing acrobatics'; jujitsu demonstration; and then big laughs during the blindfold boxing bout. Still the highlight of the night was a hot pie-eating competition for newsboys.

All in all, Snowy raised 1,800 pounds for the War Fund, while he made a few bob on the side from selling off the leftover pies as the crowd dispersed. To further ingratiate himself with the armed forces, and the state and federal politicians, Snowy pledged that he would donate sets of boxing gloves, punching balls, skipping ropes, medicine balls and body developers to each troopship leaving Sydney for the European theatres of war. Snowy also began preparations for a similar 'patriotic carnival' in Brisbane.

Five days later, everyone was back at the Stadium for the eagerly awaited Holland–Darcy return stoush. And again there was high drama.

Smith's tuition had worked, Darcy out-manoeuvreing Holland in the early rounds and repeatedly hitting his more fancied opponent with clean punches. But there was something whiffy in the air, as indicated by *The Truth*'s report of the fight, which said that the break after the sixth round 'was as interesting to the crowd as the fight had been, for a couple of bookmakers who had been attempting to do a little business were emptied out by the police'.

Despite Snowy's public call that betting was forbidden within the Stadium, the majority of those around the ring had either secured a bet with an illegal bookie, or were involved in side bets with other spectators. Gambling on boxing was rife, and nothing Snowy said or did would stop that. Consequently punters, and bookies, repeatedly put pressure on boxers and their seconds to convince them to either play dead, or fight out of their skin, to ensure that the betting market worked in the favour of those offering the sling. A few refused, but many boxers took the bait to become the puppet of the bookies and the big punters.

Darcy led on points until the 15th round, when he started delivering regular, illegal low blows on Holland, often hitting him in the groin and even on the top of the thigh. Why Darcy was doing this was bewildering, considering that at the time he was so far ahead on points.

Many of them were missed by referee Harold Baker, and Holland often didn't complain about the illegal punches. However in the 16th round, Holland was floored by another questionable punch from Darcy.

While Baker applied the count to Holland who was squirming on the floor in pain and holding his groin, those in the American boxer's corner kept screaming out that he had been fouled.

Darcy again fouled him in the 17th round and, for the first time, Baker cautioned him, explaining that if it occurred again he would be disqualified.

To everyone's astonishment, in the 18th round, Darcy did it again, slamming Holland in the groin. Baker had no alternative but to disqualify him and give the fight to Holland.

Baker had made the right decision, and even though it prompted a few isolated boos, there was nowhere near the general derision which occurred after his decision in the first Darcy–Holland fight. After such unnecessary behaviour, only Blind Freddie could support Darcy.

Almost immediately Darcy was accused of throwing the fight, especially after he had been in such a commanding position, only to squander it with unnecessary tactics. The sudden eviction of bookmakers from the fight added to the mystery, while the way in which the two boxers conducted themselves in the final rounds suggested collusion.

The Bakers were even accused of being deeply involved in the 'rigged fight'. Many sceptics argued that Darcy had been promised further Stadium fights by Snowy if he allowed Holland to beat him, as it would make the American a better drawcard. This would explain Darcy's bewilderment that Harold Baker did not stop the fight after his first foul blow.

Even Snowy publicly admitted to feeling more edgy about Darcy. But a visit to the dressing room, where Darcy was in tears and inconsolable, had Snowy in two minds, wondering whether he was either a great actor, or still honest and innocent, and probably the victim of some clever tactics by the old fox. After all, Holland later admitted that he was involved in certain 'strategies' to keep Darcy at bay in the final rounds.

The ever cautious Snowy knew he had to keep a closer eye on his Maitland meal ticket. He and his Stadium lackeys kept the pressure on Darcy, making repeated trips to Maitland to convince Les and his family that it would be in his best interest to head to Sydney and train with Dave Smith.

The family, which was dominated by his mother as his father was often distracted by a healthy passion for the drink that ensured money was always a scarcity, was reticent. And Darcy's boss, the manipulative

Billy Ford, opted to use the moment to bleed as much money as he could out of Snowy.

When Stadiums Ltd offered to pay for a blacksmith to take over from Darcy, Ford demanded a replacement had to be organised through the Farriers Union in Sydney. He argued that there was no better blacksmith in New South Wales than Darcy, and so he would lose out with whoever came as his replacement. To compensate for that inconvenience, Ford demanded renumeration of 300 pounds, and that Stadiums Ltd pay for the replacement blacksmith's return second–class fare from Sydney.

Snowy was seething. Ford's demands were ridiculous. So Snowy brought in the 'big guns' – namely his solicitor, William Drew, who was also Wren's right-hand man, to convince Ford that his indentures with his apprentice were flawed and could easily be disputed in a court of law. In desperation, Ford dramatically dropped his price, agreeing to compensation well below the 300 pound price. Drew laughed Ford off, telling him that Darcy would never work for him as an apprentice again, because the agreement was 'not worth the paper it was written on'. Ford, through his own stupidity, was squeezed out.

Even though Snowy knew he was being duped by a bunch of ill-educated bushies, he realised it was just a small investment in his campaign to take over control of Darcy.

The squeeze worked. On September 20, 1914, *The Sunday Times* reported that 'arrangements have been completed with Darcy's employer in Maitland by which Mr Baker has been able to substitute a tradesman in Darcy's place immediately to have a fortnight's training before his contest with K.O. Marchand on Eight-Hour Night, October 5'. The article added that Dave Smith would be in control of Darcy's preparation.

Three days later, in *The Referee* column 'Among the Boxers of the World', written by Solar Plexus, appeared the most interesting snippet. Amidst items that Snowy was on his way to Adelaide to 'have his boxing circuit extended to the City of Churches' was a paragraph, which read: 'Les Darcy was very keen on going to the front, but being under age, his application was declined by the military authorities.'

When, where and how wasn't explained, and the statement was virtually overlooked. Nonetheless it was the first inkling of an increasingly tense situation that would deeply affect both Darcy's and Snowy's life.

Freed of his Maitland duties, Darcy headed for Sydney and began his transformation into a quality international class boxer. Basing himself at the Spit, Darcy spent hours with Smith, where they worked away at improving his fitness, physique and technique.

The improvements were on show when Darcy at last won at the Stadium on October 5 by knocking Marchand out. Harold Baker declared Darcy the winner after the French boxer strangely somersaulted in the ring before collapsing on his stomach. A month later, Baker was again raising Darcy's arm, proclaiming him the winner on points after 20 rounds with the American middleweight Gus Christie. A trip north to Brisbane also proved fruitful for Darcy, defeating the 'Welsh Wizard' Fred Dyer on points.

As the winning streak continued, Snowy could at last plan what he had been dreaming about for so long – promoting, staging and taking the cream from a world middleweight title fight involving an Australian.

Chapter 15

The Real Les Darcy

SNOWY WAS QUICK TO BLUFF THE SYDNEY BOXING COMMUNITY INTO believing they were about to witness the great world title fight between Darcy and the American champion Jeff Smith. Reality was somewhat different.

Boxing has never really changed. Fighters get bashed to oblivion. They get ripped off by managers and promoters. And no-one can confidently claim who exactly is the world champion in what division. Almost a century on from the Darcy days, it is even more confusing, with endless boxing bodies fighting over who exactly is king in certain weight divisions.

In Snowy's time, it was more a simple case of telling blatant lies. As soon as he organised Darcy to fight Jeff Smith, tagged 'The Wonderful American', Snowy began advertising in the Sydney press that the Stadium fight on January 23, 1915, was for the world middleweight title.

His argument was that Smith, a cunning New Yorker who boasted an impressive overseas record, was the American champion and justified titleholder after defeating Jimmy Clabby in Sydney the previous year. Snowy's claim was disputed by United States authorities, who instead argued that Al McCoy was world champion.

So what, Snowy thought. The United States is a long way away, not too many who frequent the Stadium read the Yankee papers, and there's not much difference between saying someone is a contender or a champion.

It also wasn't too hard to hoodwink the local press, in particular *The Sunday Times* and *The Referee*, especially after the ever-expanding Huge Deal empire took over both newspapers. In 1915, Huge Deal bought a controlling interest in The Sunday Times Newspaper Company, which had *The Referee* and *Arrow* in its stable and had a paid up capital of 40,000 pounds.

Even more than before, both papers, in particular *The Referee*, became publicity rags for both Snowy and Huge Deal who religiously pushed their boxing and business interests. Snowy used the link wisely, advertising extensively in both newspapers, and often giving them news leads, snippets and anything and everything about himself. They invariably ran it under large headlines, or placed his ads in highly prominent positions. No-one wanted to upset the boss, or his golden snowy-haired boy, and so everything they said had to be run, did.

Snowy promoted the Darcy–Smith bout with gusto, flooding the newspapers with gossip and ensuring that anyone who came near the Stadium received their free Snowy Baker boxing postcard. For some time, Snowy had been producing a series of impressive postcards, which on one side boasted a stunning photograph of a fighter, and on the other was a brief history of the boxer and his record. There were even postcards that doubled as guessing competitions, where punters could predict who would win the fight, in what round, and how. Five pounds went to the winner.

For this fight Snowy brought back the pre-fight matinee on Thursday afternoon where, after an orchestra rendition and tea and scones for the ladies, they could watch Smith and Darcy work out in the ring. The ladies flocked, especially as they were allowed in free if accompanied by a gentleman who had to fork out two shillings. It became the meeting place in Sydney.

But this genteel atmosphere was totally different to fight night, where Darcy and Harold Baker again found themselves embroiled in controversy. The Stadium had to erect a 'House Full' sign as the Darcyites filled the sweat box. They were easy to pick, all wearing Les Darcy badges on their lapels – ensuring that one lucky badge-maker was able to take an early holiday. And the bookies were hovering, sneaking into strategic corners and offering Darcy fans lucrative odds to back their own man. Those in the know around the ring were nodding and winking, suggesting that another fix was on and to get onto Smith while you could. The bookies were swamped.

What occurred in the ring did little to quell anyone's suspicions. Yet another Darcy fight was dodgy and claims continue to this day that not one, but both fighters, tried to throw the bout. One persistent suggestion has been that Smith had backed Darcy to win the fight and would do all in his power to somehow get fouled out of the fight. Another was that Dave Smith had the money on the American fighter. One fact is for certain – the bout was not on the level.

The first four rounds were relatively even. Then in the fifth round, everything went awry. Darcy took the initiative, swinging a powerful right which hit Smith in the left ear, before the American ducked under another. From there, Smith swung his right, connecting Darcy suspiciously low.

Darcy immediately dropped his left hand low and despondently walked towards his corner where he complained to his seconds, in particular Dave Smith, that he had been hit low. Smith, who for some time had been in dispute with the Bakers over trying to improve the boxer's payments percentages at the Stadium, started screaming at Harold and Snowy that his boxer had been fouled. But both ignored him, with Harold pursuing Darcy to the corner, touching him on the arm and saying: 'Fight on! Fight on!'

Smith then showed great sportsmanship, according to *The Referee,* by refraining from 'taking advantage of the Australian's apparent desire not to continue'.

As Darcy regained his composure, Dave Smith continued yelling at Snowy that if his fighter complained when he returned to his corner, he would throw in the towel.

'Don't do that, Dave,' Snowy yelled over the crowd. 'See, he is not hurt. Otherwise how on earth could he be fighting as he is?'

However as the gong sounded, and 'as Darcy hobbled to his angle', Dave Smith threw the towel into the ring. As Smith's actions indicated that Darcy had quit, Harold Baker, who had not witnessed the earlier foul blow, announced Jeff Smith the winner.

Yet another Baker decision incensed the crowd, with the *Daily Telegraph* reporting: 'Not since the night that Mr R.L. Baker as referee had a forcible argument with Jimmy Clabby as second for Cyclone Johnny Thompson has a contest ended in such an extraordinary fashion . . .'

When Harold announced Smith the winner, 'for many minutes a section of the crowd raved and hooted. But there was no resort to violence.' The *Sydney Morning Herald* said that 'some in the highest-priced seats excitedly demanded their money back. The crowd was in an ugly temper.'

The crowd anger emanated from the fact that they believed Darcy had been blatantly fouled. This was amplified when Darcy tore down his trunks to show Harold Baker the damage that had been done to the aluminium shield, which protected his groin. It was substantially dented.

However both Bakers claimed they didn't see the foul blow, and even insinuated that Darcy may have been up to a bit of gamesmanship. Maybe it was meant to camouflage the fact that he wanted to end the fight early.

The scribes around the ring were divided in what they believed occurred. *The Truth* correspondent was adamant Smith's punch was 'low', and 'the foul was deliberate'. However one of Darcy's biggest supporters, Will Lawless, was far more cautious. He couldn't believe that one punch would dent a protector. He wrote in *The Referee*: 'It surprises me very much that a blow that would break an aluminium protector, built in such fashion as to resist ordinary human force, did not put our man down and out, tough and all as Darcy undoubtedly is.'

That didn't help Darcy's case at all. If there was one person who would defend him, it would be Solar Plexus. Instead even Solar Plexus had his doubts over what Darcy was up to, amplifying the mystery surrounding this fight. The suggestion was that Darcy had thrown the fight.

As Harold Baker was telling boxing scribes 'I did not see any foul', Darcy was showing off his dented protector in the dressing room to anyone who wanted a look. 'Directly the blow landed I felt giddy and sick, and did not know what I did for the moment,' Darcy explained.

Jeff Smith, delighted that, in Baker's eyes at least, he was now the official middleweight champion was as adamant that he was not guilty of a low blow. Smith argued that if he was guilty of such a foul deed, he would have immediately taken the initiative and obviously followed up with a killer blow. Smith and the Bakers snuck out through Darcy's dressing room to avoid the madding crowd.

Despite the zealousness with which many biographers have portrayed Darcy as being holier-than-thou and the undisputed champion of the people, he didn't always have the unstinting support of those in the bleachers. Glossed over by many Darcy chroniclers is the fact that when he and Holland fought for a fourth time in Melbourne, both were resoundingly booed by the crowd.

John Wren had for some time been pestering both Huge Deal and Snowy about getting their biggest card to Melbourne, but after the bout, which followed Darcy beating Holland on points in Sydney in March, he would have second thoughts.

Even the referee Vic Newhouse was disgusted with how both fighters messed around, prompting the 6,000 crowd at the Melbourne Stadium to endlessly hoot both boxers. The crowd had noticed Newhouse between rounds approaching both corners, and threatening to call it a 'no contest'.

'An extremely unsatisfactory contest,' Newhouse complained to 'Bendigo', *The Referee*'s Melbourne boxing correspondent. 'I hardly know what to say of it. They appeared afraid of each other.'

The bout, staged on May 1, 1915, just five days after Australian soldiers had stormed Gallipoli, had lured the Melbourne establishment, eager to see whether all the Sydney spin about Darcy was true. They were left flabbergasted, especially as Holland didn't appear eager to fight, and Darcy spent most of the bout half-heartedly following him around the ring.

The Referee was scathing, headlining its report, 'Worst Big Bout Yet'.

'The men frequently were counted out, and their futile efforts to connect a good punch made a certain section wrath. It hooted vigorously,' Bendigo wrote.

At the end of the round, Newhouse expressed the sentiments of all in the ring when he told Holland: 'Take a risk, for heaven's sake, do liven up.'

Darcy was little better, but because of Holland's lethargy, was well ahead on points. Eventually in the 13th round, Darcy caught Holland with a right to the jaw, toppling the American over for nine seconds.

'Holland struggled up with the aid of the ropes, and the battle was about to proceed when the towel came in from his corner. All this time, instead of the crowd's being excited by the turn of events, it hooted. Darcy immediately left the ring – almost unnoticed. It is safe to say that a more unsatisfactory bout beween two leading boxers has not been witnessed in Australia.'

The crowd left, believing they had been duped by yet another contrived fight. The concern was that Darcy may have been corrupted by bookmakers and was carrying fighters for extra rounds for dirty money. Dave Smith was in Darcy's corner and naturally tried to defend his boxer. He placed the blame on the referee, suggesting he was incompetent. Smith approached Wren, who laughed him off, saying that Newhouse was the best referee in Australia. For Smith, it wasn't exactly a smart career move to tell Mr Manipulator of Australian Boxing that he basically knew nothing.

Snowy was scheduled to be part of the crowd, but had problems of his own. At the time, he was recuperating at home after an horrific car accident where one of his best friends was killed.

Late in March, Snowy had decided to take a group of friends on a drive from the city to Manly in his Sheffield–Simplex, which one Sydney scribe had already tagged 'The Yellow Peril'. In the back seat was George Redmond, news editor of *The Sun*, with Engineer-Commander McKean of HMAS *Brisbane*. In the front seat sitting next to Snowy was McKean's wife.

Snowy was travelling along Sydney Road at around 3.30 pm when, while going down a steep slope about a mile before reaching Manly, one of the front tyres blew out. Snowy tried to wrest control of the Sheffield, which was zig-zagging across the road, but failed. The car overturned three times and came to a stop in a bush near the roadside.

Snowy and Mrs McKean were thrown out on the right side, while Redmond and the Commander were flung to the left. While the McKeans were only slightly injured, Snowy and Redmond were both unconscious on the side of the road.

The first person on the spot, Clyde Sawyers, rushed to Snowy, and revived him. After asking how he was, Snowy replied: 'I think my spine is gone, but go and see to Redmond.'

Redmond had been hurled out of the car onto his head, sustaining a fracture at the base of his skull. He never regained consciousness and died at Ashbourne private hospital two hours after the crash.

Snowy was taken to St Ronan's private hospital by his brother Harold, who had taken the same road as his brother and arrived at the crash scene fifteen minutes later.

Snowy suffered internal bruising and spinal damage, which forced him to remain in hospital for several weeks where he also experienced deep bouts of depression, prompted, naturally, by his friend's death. For the rest of his life, he never forgave himself. Redmond's death always hung heavily on Snowy's shoulders.

Snowy eventually resurfaced for the return Darcy–Smith bout at the Stadium. By this stage, the financial arrangements at the Stadium had also changed. Snowy remained the frontman, but Wren had successfully bought out other partners and had taken control of the company. Snowy was now strictly working for Wren and Huge Deal.

At the time, the financial arrangement had been kept relatively quiet, but many years later Snowy happily revealed Wren's involvement. 'The trio of stoush houses were going well when, through the friendship of Dan Green, I met sports promoter John Wren, with the result that a few weeks later the three stadiums were a private company with John Wren chairman of directors, and I managing director.'

Although Snowy was still shaken by the Manly car crash, he knew he had to be on hand for the Smith fight, as he was concerned that his bout with Darcy could again be not exactly on the level.

Snowy's suspicions were spot on. Smith was immediately up to something. In the first round, after being shaken early, Smith began punching low, prompting Harold Baker to stop the fight and give him a warning. It persisted in the second round, with a rattled Smith swinging a heavy left into Darcy's groin. Everyone in the crowd saw the despicable blow. Baker stopped the fight, disqualified Smith and named Darcy the world middleweight champion.

The crowd booed Smith all the way to his dressing room, while Snowy decided it was time for drastic action. Believing Smith had deliberately fouled Darcy to avoid defeat, he immediately announced that the American would be barred from any further bouts at the Stadium and his fight payment withheld. The insinuation was that Smith had backed Darcy to win. Smith's percentage of 464 pounds, which was 25% of the actual gate, would now be handed over to the Australian Patriotic Fund.

Snowy said he had the backing of all Stadium directors, including Wren, who all believed that, 'We have had far too many fouls at our Stadiums lately, and we must protect the boxing game in Australia.'

'There is no doubt about Smith's foul. We had four angles on it. Something had to be done.'

Smith, who screamed that he was innocent, and manager, Al Lippe, were naturally infuriated by Snowy's decision and instigated court action in a bid to get their share of the prize money. The case was eventually heard in August 1915, in front of Justice Ferguson and a four-man jury.

The transcripts of the four days of evidence reveal much about how Snowy and the Stadium worked, and show that the claim that Harold Baker was in the ring acting solely as a puppet for his elder brother was angrily debated.

Snowy, dressed in a smart London-cut jacket and matching hat, arrived at Sydney's No 2 jury court surrounded by silks, described by the plaintiff's representative, Mr Fred Gannon, as 'a regular Baltic Fleet of barristers'.

The plaintiff began its case by arguing that Smith was always going to be unfairly treated because of a pre-fight argument he had with the referee, Harold Baker. It was further alleged that Snowy Baker was at odds with Lippe over a previous fight contract. Smith told the court that Harold Baker was biased, and had stated that 'Americans were swines'.

However during cross-examination, glaring holes were immediately picked up in Smith's story. When asked by Snowy's defence lawyer, Mr Broomfield, whether he had actually heard Harold Baker use the words 'Americans were swines', Smith replied: 'No, but I was told . . . '

Broomfield turned to Smith's lawyer, Mr Gannon, and said: 'You can't have that. You're a King's Counsel – you ought to know the rules of evidence.'

Gannon immediately chipped his client with: 'I thought it was said to you. I'm getting into trouble through trying to keep you straight.'

That retort hardly convinced Justice Ferguson or the jury that the jumpy boxer was a reliable witness.

Smith's manager Lippe was next in the box and said that Baker had not seen Smith deliver a foul blow, but had reacted to the crowd. 'A man in the crowd jumped up, waved his cane and called out: "Foul." When Baker disqualified him, Smith told him that he had not fouled Darcy. When they went into the office afterwards, Harold Baker said: "I'm sorry this occurred."'

According to the transcript, Lippe said to Baker: 'He didn't foul. Darcy did not complain.'

Baker replied: 'If I see a foul, I warn a man once, and if he fouls again, I disqualify him.'

Gannon then asked Lippe: 'Does he do that?'

'No, I have seen him warn a man half a dozen times. One night he leaned over and asked Mr R.L. Baker what he should do.'

Broomfield pursued the same subject, asking Lippe if Snowy Baker was at the fight.

'Yes Harold Baker was always looking at him, and I'm of the opinion that R.L. Baker was really the referee.'

'Why do you think that?'

'Because Harold Baker does what he is told.'

'Why do you say that?'

'Well, on the night of the McCoy–Kay match, Harold Baker leaned over the ropes, and said to R.L. Baker "What shall I do?" R.L. Baker walks round the ring all the time.'

'Is the track kept clear for him?'

'Yes.'

'What is that for?'

'To give his brother the office.'

'Then, according to your view, it is Reg Baker who gives the decision, not his brother?'

'I should say it is.'

'Do you suggest that Harold Baker had not sufficient experience to referee?'

'Yes.'

'You swear that Harold Baker deliberately disqualified Smith for no cause?'

'Yes.'

'Why?'

'Because I would not renew the contract with Reg Baker.'

'Do you suggest Reg Baker was in the swindle too?'

'I don't say that.'

'It was only Harold Baker.'

'He disqualified the boy for nothing.'

Lippe reiterated that Baker was antagonistic towards his boxer by calling him a swine. Lippe fronted Snowy about the slur, to which the promoter replied: 'Oh swine is a favourite word of Harold's. Don't take any notice of him.'

On the third day, Dave Smith took the stand, revealing that he had been a shareholder at the Sydney Stadium, but had 'dropped out of the business'.

Darcy was next, and his animosity towards Smith was obvious. He couldn't remember shaking hands with his opponent after their first bout, and when asked if he claimed a foul in the second bout, Darcy replied: 'No, but I was hit foul just the same.'

When asked if he had ever been hit low before, Darcy said: 'I was never hit that way before.'

'Do you think Smith's fouling of you was accidental?'

'No.'

Darcy was then allowed to leave the court, with Broomfield explaining as the boxer headed towards the exit: 'To communicate with the punching ball.'

One Darcy biographer has stated categorically that Harold Baker did not testify. However, Harold did follow Darcy into the box, having gained leave from the Expeditionary Force which he had recently joined. A Lieutenant in the Light Horse, he was allowed to leave their Liverpool camp for a day to attend court. As always, Harold was his sour, strict self. He was not going to stand for any nonsense, not even from a high-flying, big sounding silk. His low, moaning voice reverberated around the courtroom.

Harold Baker reiterated that in the second round 'I considered the foul blow was deliberately struck and immediately disqualified Smith. Smith said he had not fouled his opponent. Later on I told my brother I thought it was a most deliberate foul.'

Baker said that he later walked into his brother's office, where there was an animated conversation involving Snowy, Smith and Lippe. Harold heard Snowy say: 'I am sorry for this; it is a bad thing for the business.' Snowy Baker said he couldn't keep the sport on the plane to which he had brought it if he didn't take notice of the deliberate foul.

'Smith had very little to say. I told him he had been warned once (he assented to that) and that there was nothing for me to do after the second but to disqualify him.'

Broomfield asked Harold Baker if he was in the habit of referring to Americans as swines.

'I did call Lippe a swine,' Baker replied. 'On every occasion four or five times, when I had given a verdict against his man, he was very offensive, and on one occasion I called Lippe, himself, a swine – under great provocation.'

Broomfield continued: 'In support of part of the replication it was suggested that both Bakers were crooks – Harold says Americans are swine, and Reg Baker walks about outside the ring and tells his brother what decision to give. That is what the plaintiff says.'

Baker replied: 'Lippe would say "You ought to referee; you ought. I'll take my men back to America. You'll never referee a fight for me" and things like that, highly insulting and offensive.'

'Were you honestly of the opinion that Smith committed a deliberate foul?'

'I was.'

'Did you come to that decision on collusion with your brother to defraud Smith?'

'Emphatically no.'

'You have no interest in the contest.'

'None whatsoever.'

Harold also denied that he had asked Snowy during the Kay–McCoy fight, what he should do. He had instead asked Snowy if Dr Bullock was in the Stadium, because one of the fighters had claimed he had been fouled.

Gannon tried to probe Harold about who exactly were his masters.

'In the ring, no-one is your master. The contest is in my hands solely. Once when I gave a decision against Darcy, there was an attempt to burn the place down.'

'And sometimes they have kicked up a row about you?'

'Yes.'

'It wouldn't be too safe to give a decision against Darcy?'

'I don't think that. The public usually like a fair go and a square deal.'

Gannon decided to put the personal squeeze on. Those who were and weren't fighting in the war had gradually become an emotional issue.

'You haven't gone to the front yet.'

'No one regrets that more than I. I'm in the hands of the authorities, and want to go. Perhaps Mr Gannon will enlist and come with me?'

'Unfortunately I'm barred,' Gannon replied. 'I couldn't get my running shoes finished in time.'

Gannon then claimed there was huge betting on the fight, that Wren had demanded that the Stadium directors investigate whether there was any 'swindle', and that there had been an attempt to declare 'bets off' to save the public who had backed the loser, Smith. Harold Baker denied any knowledge, stating defiantly: 'Betting is not allowed in the Stadium.'

Snowy was next to give evidence, and predictably denied he had any influence on a referee's decision, in particular his brother. Snowy knew the best way to convince the jury that he was on the level was to be buoyant, confident and sure of himself. He bounded into the box, bowed to the judge, smiled at the jury and looked deeply intent on ensuring the truth came out.

Snowy gave his recollection of the post-match meeting, which started with Harold stating: '"That was the worst foul I have seen." I replied: "I did not see it." Jeff Smith and Lippe came to the office, and I said it was bad business, and a very unfortunate affair. Lippe said: "It didn't hurt him." I replied: "It's not a matter of hurting, but of deliberate fouling." Lippe said he'd seen men trodden on the ring in America. I said: "Well, we don't do it here. We do business on a higher level."' Snowy added that five minute after the contest, he had decided that Smith shouldn't be paid.

Broomfield asked Snowy if it was true Smith was disqualified because he would not renew a contract.

'I asked him before the Darcy contest to renew his contract.'

'Is there any truth in the statement that you communicated with your brother as to what he was to do in that match – to disqualify Smith?'

'No.'

'Is it true that you fraudulently procured your brother to defraud Smith by deciding the contest in favour of Darcy?'

'It is not.'

Snowy confirmed to Gannon that the disqualification of Smith was endorsed by the Stadium directors, following a telegram from Wren. 'I took no notice of the telegram, beyond acknowledging it.'

'But Wren owns 58,000 shares in the Stadium?'

'He is a director only.'

'With 58,000 of the best in it.'

'I do not allow betting in the Stadium, and have had men ejected for betting.'

Wren's telegrams to Baker were then presented. They read: 'Think it advisable not to pay till matter thoroughly investigated.' 'If after investigation you think contest a swindle, the matter should be investigated immediately as settling takes place today.'

Baker replied to Wren: 'Best that can be done is to hold the money pending investigation, as the law of NSW prohibits betting.'

In his address to the jury, Broomfield said that the case rested entirely on Lippe and that he was basically telling a string of lies to get his share of Smith's percentage of the gate.

Gannon meanwhile lampooned both Harold and Snowy to the jury. 'You have heard the childlike, bland innocence that Mr Reg Baker never made a bet in his life. It was never mentioned that Jeff Smith offered to box Darcy and give the profits to the War Fund. Does that cast a reflection on Jeff Smith's character? It is well that Jack Johnson is not here, for he would surely be tried for murder, or something.

'Reg Baker saved the money for Stadiums Limited, under the guidance and at the instigation of John Wren.'

Gannon said he was not alleging criminal conspiracy between the Bakers, but that the disqualification was an afterthought of the Stadium, and the Bakers, both officials of the Stadium, did not act independently within the four corners of the contract.

The jury adjourned for 90 minutes and sided with the defendants. Yet another technical knockout for the Baker boys.

There was still an unseemly aftermath. While the Bakers may have won the case, the hearing opened up many festering sores, bringing into the public arena allegations of collusion between the two brothers and the deepening shadow of Wren and the bookies over Stadiums Limited's head treated as fact by sections of the boxing community. Whispers had turned into informed opinion. Mud always sticks.

As well, Smith and Lippe, who immediately returned to America, made certain everyone on their side of the world knew that the Bakers could not be trusted and that under their control Australian boxing was shonky. Lippe long and loudly said it to anyone in the United States who wanted to listen.

As Lippe was an influential boxing figure in the United States, his successful smear campaign had serious ramifications on Snowy and Darcy a year or so down the track. Darcy also never forgave Smith. He said some months later: 'I do not like Jeff Smith. He fouled me five times in our last fight and was not paid for his work.'

Another ominous sign was what those at ringside were screaming at Harold in the ring, and Snowy as he did laps.

The cry was persistent. 'Hey, you two, why aren't you at the war?'

The embarrassed pair would just look away.

Chapter 16

Keeping Control

SNOWY AND HAROLD CHARGED DOWN THE TUNNEL FROM THE MAIN Stadium ring and barged their way into Les Darcy's dressing room. Both were extremely agitated, perspiring, edgy.

It was only minutes before the first round of a world middleweight title fight and the pair had just been told a fix was on. The challenger, Eddie McGoorty, the 'Oshkosk Terror', a formidable American pug who loved girls and gambling, had apparently backed Darcy to win. At ringside they were saying 'the fight's schlenter ... fake ... dodgy'.

The brothers had been out at the Randwick races where, during the afternoon, the betting odds of Darcy winning among the rails bookmakers had suspiciously and quickly drifted away from him being a rank outsider to virtual favourite. There was suddenly a big plunge of money on Darcy. Also adding to their suspicions was that McGoorty had sold his share of the film rights for the fight for just 50 pounds. As he was scheduled to get at least twice that amount, it was taken as a sign that he wasn't going to try.

Snowy and Harold found Darcy in his customary corner of the room, dressing gown on, head down, playing his harmonica. They pushed their way through the hangers-on, before an irritated Snowy bellowed: 'Les, I'm just telling you, if either you or McGoorty attempt to throw this fight, I'll declare it a no-contest, and there'll be no prize money. I'm warning you ... I'll be watching you very closely.'

Dave Smith pushed in between the two and tried to put Snowy in his place by suggesting if there was any doubt, he should pay the boxers their share of the prize money before they hopped into the ring.

'That's not necessary,' Snowy snarled.

Darcy tried to appease Snowy. 'Mr Baker, there's nothing in that story. I don't fake fights. I'll be doing my best to make sure it's a good scrap.'

McGoorty, a proud fighter who boasted just three losses from 90 fights, was not so conciliatory about being stood over by the referee and promoter just before a title fight. He came close to telling both of them to get out of his dressing room. McGoorty was disgusted that Snowy was reading him the riot act.

'If that's what you think Mr Baker, this is the time to act. Get into the ring before we start and declare all bets off.'

McGoorty knew Baker wouldn't do that, considering he was so eager to hoodwink all into believing that betting didn't happen within his sanctimonious Stadium. Then McGoorty, who had been told by his fellow American, Jeff Smith, not to trust Baker, added: 'If you hold out on my money, I'll make certain your name's mud in the States.'

Snowy retreated, dishevelled and deeply concerned that his control of proceedings was slipping. First Smith, and now this. It was all falling apart and he was bracing himself for yet another riot.

He knew it was partly his own fault. He had promoted this fight vigorously. Even in the fight programme he had gone for the hyperbole, stating that this fight would be the greatest boxing match of 1915.

As for McGoorty, Baker was frothing in his praise. 'McGoorty is the most distinguished and most dangerous boxer of his weight in America. I think he is the most brilliant white-man fighter whom the United States have ever sent here – I do not exclude Tommy Burns.'

With such a build-up, it was no wonder that the Stadium was once more struggling to hold an overflowing crowd. Even the pieman and hot sausage sellers were struggling to get to their main customers in the bleachers. And on the iron roof, torrential rain pounded and reverberated.

Down the corridor, Snowy could hear the crowd who were already jeering and laughing. He placed his head in his hands for a second and composed himself before confronting the punters.

Another Baker had already upset the Darcy fan club that night. Fred Baker refereed a preliminary bout involving Darcy's younger brother, Jack, who struggled against Arthur Corbett over six rounds. Baker had no alternative but to award the fight to the far superior Corbett. But the one-eyed Darcyites didn't like it, hooting Baker as he left the ring.

Heading back towards ringside, Snowy discovered another of his suggestions had proven to be a disaster – not just to the Darcy followers, but everyone in the Stadium.

Forever ingratiating himself to politicians and the military, Snowy, through the prompting of Huge Deal, had invited his old mate the Premier, W.A. Holman, and the Leader of the Opposition, C.G. Wade, to address the crowd about war recruitment. As soon as the pair were sighted in the ring, dressed in dinner suits, they were booed by the workers. They were here to see a fight, not two stiff, toffee-nosed political grandstanders.

Holman put up his hands, and started with, 'All good sports here . . .' The rest of his speech was drowned out.

A wounded soldier in khaki attempted to make the peace by joining them in the ring and explaining: 'Boys, be sports. This is not the spirit of the men who are fighting for you in the Dardanelles.'

But it was to no avail. The din continued and after a few minutes, Holman and Wade gave up and retreated. State Parliament later heard that their speeches had been interrupted by 'some of the lowest scum that would disgrace the worst city in the world'. Snowy instead blamed it on the Germans in the crowd. Strange statement, considering his own background. But as usual, Snowy was determined to rewrite history.

Eventually order was restored when the two fighters came to the ring to receive their pre-match instructions from Harold. The wait was worth it, the fight exceeding everyone's expectations. At last Darcy showed his true worth against a world-class opponent. Darcy seemed obsessed, and driven by Snowy's pre-fight warning was determined to show that he wanted to win. McGoorty likewise, prompting a feverish, brave battle, where each boxer kept thrashing away at the other. The second round was as good as anything seen at the Stadium, where each appeared about to deliver the knockout blow. Somehow both were still standing at the end, despite being hit with every punch imaginable.

Darcy continued to chase McGoorty, who between rounds seemed astounded by the ferocity of his opponent. McGoorty had heard a lot about Darcy, but didn't realise he was that good. With the large, ghoulish Harold Baker, dressed in dinner suit, hovering over both fighters, McGoorty had to change tactics. He tried to block and counter Darcy's blows, but too many were getting through.

By the 14th round, McGoorty was gone. As he had never been knocked out in his career, McGoorty was determined to remain on his feet, but the rest of his body looked terrible. His face and lips were swollen and bloody. In the 15th McGoorty's knees suddenly sagged. Darcy's uppercut had hit the required target, an exposed chin, and down went McGoorty. But McGoorty was determined to get up. At the count of seven, McGoorty was back on his feet, only to walk into another Darcy punch and down he went again.

Harold Baker had seen enough. This fight was legitimate. No-one would suffer such pain to ensure a fix was on. As the police superintendant rushed to ringside, demanding a stop to the fight, Baker pushed Darcy away from his delirious opponent and announced the home boy the winner.

This time there was no dispute. Darcy was something special. McGoorty, still dazed and confused an hour after the fight, was overwhelmed by whom he had just been attacked by. 'That boy's the best fighter I ever fought,' McGoorty declared. 'He's the greatest fighter in the world.' Darcy still had his doubts about his opponent, some months later saying that he 'found out that he [McGoorty] lay down in our first fight'.

Also at ringside was a very important international figure. Jack 'Doc' Kearns, later described as 'the greatest fight manager of them all' because of his intense involvement with Jack Dempsey, had travelled from the United States accompanying his boxer, 'Fighting' Billy Murray.

Kearns, a devious, shifty character and another mad gambler, loved what he saw. He immediately wanted to take Darcy back to the United States with him. There were greenbacks dripping out of this boxer. He telegraphed a US business colleague after the McGoorty fight: 'Got my eye on a big one.'

The next morning Kearns broached the subject with Snowy. Snowy was aghast. Snowy knew all about Kearns, his shifty ways, his ability to suck every last dollar out of a boxer before leaving him dry, and his genius at self-promotion.

As one Kearns biographer put it, the one time cardsharp and gold prospector had the combination of 'the swashbuckling D'Artagnan, the rollicking Robin Hood, the daring Jimmy Valentine, the wily Richelieu and, withal, one possessing the charm, wit, impishness and savoir faire of a larcenous leprechaun. He was a poised rapier of a man with quicksilver tongue, puckish grin and powder-blue eyes that hinted alternately of Arctic ice and Killarney mischief.' And as one of Kearns's colleagues explained: 'When you first meet Jack you are inclined to dislike him, but when you know him for awhile, you really get to hate him.'

Kearns, delighted that he was described as a con man, a grifter, knew them all – Al Capone, Wyatt Earp, Klondike Kate and Damon Runyon – and so thought Snowy, a mere colonial, was easy meat. As Runyon put it, Kearns would be the only person in the world who could successfully promote a snakeburger.

Kearns started the hard sell, explaining what he could do for this boxer. Make him an international star. But Snowy stopped him in his tracks. Huge Deal and Wren had been in contact. The instructions were implicit. Darcy can't go to the United States. He was a minor. He was under 21. He couldn't get a passport without his parent's consent. And besides, the government wouldn't let him go. Unlike the United States, Australia is at war. They will not allow potential soldiers to leave Australia for anything other than fighting on a larger battle scene.

Snowy was all bluff and bluster. It had nothing to do with being an innocent minder. His prime concern was that Darcy, who'd become his number one ticket seller as he was the only fighter who could guarantee a sell-out Stadium, was about to be snaffled from under him. His licence to print money couldn't be allowed to disappear so easily.

Kearns saw through Snowy, bid him farewell and decided to apply the drip treatment. Stay in Australia for a few months and beaver away in the background. Kearns knew he had to work on his feet as, unbenown to anyone else, he was broke. The horses had cleaned him out yet again.

Kearns later boasted that he bided his time, waiting for the opportunity to sign up Darcy, by learning Australian rhyming slang. He claimed to be the first to take it back to the United States. 'It sounded like jive talk and Damon Runyon, for one, got a great kick out of it,' Kearns later wrote in his flashy autobiography *The Million Dollar Gate*. 'Just to give you an idea, here's a sample. "The twist and twirl had the neatest mumbley pegs you ever saw till the day she went to her haircut and shave." All of which means: the woman had pretty legs until the day she went to her grave. Crazy man!'

Snowy, naturally fearful of Kearns, changed his tact, believing the best way to convince Darcy not to follow the American promoter to New York was not via the boxer, but through his mother. Darcy idolised his mother, relying on her for advice and guidance. He wouldn't want to earn the ire of Mrs Margaret Darcy.

Snowy had heard that in some United States newspapers Kearns was quoted as saying he already had Darcy in his stable. Snowy organised a meeting with Mrs Darcy and pleaded with her to convince her son that his future was far brighter in Australia, because the United States was full of corrupt fighters, managers and promoters.

'I can guarantee you I will look after him,' Snowy said with the saddest of eyes. All for effect of course.

In desperation, Snowy even said the Stadium would close down if Darcy headed overseas. Mrs Darcy was sceptical about that last remark, but promised Snowy she would talk to Les. Her major concern was not that he would head for the United States with a sneak. It was instead that he would try to enlist. She was determined to do everything in her power to stop him becoming part of the carnage in Europe.

To ward off Kearns, Snowy kept organising bouts for Darcy, even though the boxer desperately needed a rest, evidenced by his hands being badly swollen. Snowy even gladly matched Darcy against Kearns's man, Murray. In the end it was a non-event, with Darcy hardly extending himself to beat Murray on points over 20 rounds.

But Snowy's ploy to keep Kearns at a distance didn't work. After the Murray fight, Kearns fronted Darcy and explained his plan, saying that Darcy was basically wasting his time in Australia. He could make far bigger amounts of money in the United States, in front of bigger audiences. He could guarantee him the top fights. None of this second-rate stuff at the Stadium, but real bouts against real fighters like George Chip, Al McCoy and Mike Gibbons. Kearns said he would be mad if he didn't return with him to the States later in the year.

Darcy, an uncomplicated man, was impressed. He told Kearns he would seriously think about it, even though he was contracted to Snowy for a return bout against McGoorty and another title defence the following month.

Kearns replied that Snowy was unfairly working him like a dog. If he joined the Kearns stable, he would look after him, treat him like a world champion, rather than a slave to the masters of Australian big business. Darcy was swaying, but repeated: 'I'll seriously think about this.'

As if keeping Darcy roped in wasn't hard enough, Snowy also had to deal with another problem when he suddenly lost his other Sydney boxing venue. In late August 1915, the Olympia Stadium in Newtown was burnt down, causing more than 20,000 pounds damage. The fire was suspicious, the anti-boxing brigade, which had intensified in numbers since the start of the war, the wowsers being joined by members of the clergy and parliament, immediately being blamed for the fire.

Snowy wasn't so sure, believing that he had been successful in appeasing the anti-boxing contingent in the community by using both Stadiums for patriotic shows. Instead he blamed someone who had a vendetta against either himself, or another member of Stadiums Ltd. However, if you sat down and listed those who were anti-Baker or anti-Stadium, the list would have gone over several pages.

At least Snowy's physical culture premises was flourishing, with more than 7,000 students passing through the doors and receiving tuition from either the former Olympic medallist or his brothers. Another 13,000 students, from as far as Fiji, India and California, had also embarked on Snowy's boxing by correspondence course. However, in the past 12 months, Snowy's correspondence listing had dropped slightly, with many pupils writing to him calling an end to the lessons because, 'I am off to the war.'

Still, the professional boxers had nothing to distract them, with a vast queue lining up to fight Darcy for the middleweight title. The next was Jimmy Clabby; the same Jimmy Clabby who five years earlier had been decked by Snowy after disputing his refereeing skills.

Solar Plexus hyperventilated over it all, writing in *The Referee* on the morning of the fight that it was 'undoubtedly the most important middleweight contest that has ever been decided in this country, if not the world' for more than 25 years.

Old Will Lawless was pushing it a bit, but the fight certainly rose to expectations, being a clever, and sometimes wild, bout. As Harold Baker was on his way to the Front with the Light Horse, Arthur Scott took over the refereeing for a fight where Darcy's intensity grew from round to round.

In the end, both fighters were totally exhausted, and almost out on their feet. But Darcy had built up such a comfortable points lead by the time of the 15th round that Scott had no hesitation in naming him the winner.

With Doc Kearns still hovering around Darcy, promising him the world, Snowy decided to get as much out of him while he could, organising another fight just nine days later in Melbourne. But ridiculously it was against Kearns's pupil, Murray. This gave Kearns more time to work away at Darcy. For the Melbourne crowd, it gave them the opportunity to boo yet another Darcy opponent.

The Melbourne Stadium audience were dismayed by the farce Holland and Darcy got away with six months ago, and again blew the raspberry at Murray when he blundered away on Melbourne Cup eve.

Darcy was rated as 10-1 on to beat Murray, and within a few rounds it was obvious that the American opponent, a very average conveyance, wouldn't last the distance. Darcy ended the embarrassment in the sixth round when he jolted Murray's jaw, prompting the eight count, before the towel was thrown into the ring. The crowd were unimpressed, howling at Murray as he left the ring.

The least concerned about Murray was his manager, because Doc Kearns, planning to leave Sydney for San Francisco on December 18, was chasing a bigger prize. And the sweet-talking had worked. Darcy was coming his way.

While in Melbourne, Kearns again cornered Darcy and told him that the boxing game was dying in Australia, the war authorities were about to close down the Stadiums, Snowy Baker could not be trusted, and the only place where he would be properly treated was in the USA. All this coincided with Darcy deciding against renewing his contract with Dave Smith.

Darcy hid himself away for a few days, but revealed all in a letter to Will Lawless, explaining that he had decided to go to America with Kearns 'and try my luck on that side'.

'No doubt some will be right up against me for doing this, but some, I hope, will be with me. And if I fail, Mr Lawless, it will be my own misfortune. There is not much left for me here now.'

Lawless was not impressed, writing in *The Referee* that he did not look upon a United States tour involving Darcy 'with the happiest of feelings'.

Snowy was more than unimpressed. He was deeply distressed that Darcy was about to leave him. To counter the letter to Solar Plexus, Snowy again tried to convince Darcy to stay in Australia through his mother. He again travelled to the Maitland household, explaining to Mrs Darcy the pitfalls of his son going overseas. More importantly, Snowy had just organised a return bout for Darcy with McGoorty on

December 27, 1915, and he promised that her son would receive more than 1,000 pounds from his share of the fight. When Mrs Darcy heard the 1,000 pound figure, and knew that it would pay off a new house which at the time was being built for the family, she told Snowy: 'Don't worry, I'll talk sense to him.'

The upshot was a seething Kearns left for America without Darcy, Les remained in Sydney to prepare for the McGoorty fight, and the family house was built. It was named 'Lesleigh'. Mrs Darcy was a formidable figure.

In the background though the mood in Australia was changing. The Dardanelles campaign had been a fruitless disaster, prompting an embarrassing retreat by the ANZAC troops. What was thought to be a friendly frolic on the other side of the world had turned into a deathly experience, which would only get worse if Australia didn't mobilise its forces.

Recruitment had dropped off and at the same time the belligerent Billy Hughes replaced Andrew Fisher as Prime Minister. Hughes was adamant that the war effort had to be intensified, which made Snowy jittery because of the threat that the government would close down virtually all entertainment venues, including the Stadium. As Snowy put it, the Melbourne Stadium had already closed down 'for the simple reason that practically all our young Melbourne boxers are now serving their country'.

Snowy continued to crawl to the military authorities, making public, through *The Referee*, his plans to send a cluster of wattle trees to Egypt to be placed on the graves of Australian soldiers. He had already sent more than 500 pairs of boxing gloves to the front, and called on Australia's best-known swimmer, Fanny Durack, to give a special diving exhibition at the Stadium, with all proceeds going to the War Fund. Snowy also envisaged erecting tablets at each of his Stadiums, listing the names 'of all boxers who have fallen in battle'. He even went through the charade of enlisting himself, but according to Snowy was knocked back because of the bad back he suffered in the Manly car crash.

Countless families around Australia had received official notices that their loved ones had died, and the pressure on those eligible for military service but who hadn't volunteered intensified. Suddenly the nation found itself divided, between those who had, and hadn't served. Those who hadn't served were targeted and described as slackers. At the same time that the Department of Home Affairs ruled that no military-age male could leave Australia without a passport, the pro-war lobby began focusing on Darcy – the ideal target, considering he was the country's premier fighter, and ideal antagonist to lead the way from out of the French trenches. Darcy began receiving white feathers – a symbol of cowardice – in the mail. The argument that he was still not of military age to fight didn't stand with some. All Mrs Darcy was praying for was that the war would be over before Les turned 21 on October 31, 1916.

Yet Darcy was still intensely popular with the khaki brigade, who attempted to storm the ring to touch their hero after he sent McGoorty to the floor with a right uppercut in the eighth round of the return bout. Their enthusiasm was justified, as they had just witnessed a special performance by Darcy, who showed that he warranted world-class status following a bout described by Solar Plexus as the 'greatest fight of 20 years'.

In the dressing room, Darcy tried to convince himself that he had made the right move, telling reporters: 'I'm pleased I didn't go to America, let them come to me, and I'll accommodate them one after the one.'

They were hollow sentiments, because despite what Snowy was babbling on about, Darcy knew not many quality boxers would be coming his way. To keep himself entertained, while Snowy tried to find anyone of quality to fight him, Darcy joined the vaudeville circuit, making guest appearances at the Tivoli. Huge Deal, the chief honcho of the Tivoli circuit, organised the deal, but like Snowy, Doc Kearns and the rest, he had ulterior motives.

Darcy had basically been invited to the Tivoli so that Huge Deal could badger him about his get-rich scheme. Huge Deal also wanted to take Darcy to America, offering him a series of fights, as well as a bonus of 6,000 pounds for a six-month vaudeville tour of the country where all he had to do was show up, prance around the stage for a few minutes, and pick up the cash.

Darcy was now even more confused. In one ear he had Snowy pleading 'stay here'. In the other his long-time associate, Huge Deal, was muttering: 'You wanna see New York. Stick with me, lad.'

It was getting more bewildering by the minute, especially as Snowy was playing both sides. Unbenown to both Darcy and Huge Deal, Snowy had also been talking to various American contacts about the possibility of a Darcy tour through the United States. As the plan was only in its formative stages, Snowy kept quiet about it and instead kept looking for boxers at home to keep Darcy entertained.

Eventually Snowy convinced one of his old swimming and football comrades, Harold Hardwick, to have a go against Darcy.

Hardwick, another to learn all his tricks by frolicking at the Domain pool, had also learnt to box from Arthur Scott and George Seale and was in many respects a mini Snowy. A reasonable footballer and competent surfer, Hardwick excelled at both swimming and boxing, gaining prominence at the 1911 Festival of the Empire, held in London to celebrate the coronation of King George V.

After winning the 100 yard swimming event in an ornamental pool thick with reeds, a few nights later Hardwick jumped into the boxing ring to confront the English and Scottish heavyweight champion, William Hazell. Conceding almost two stones, Hardwick thrashed Hazell. Likewise an hour later, when he belted another policeman, Canadian Julius Thompson, to win the title.

Although dejected that boxing was not part of the 1912 Olympic programme in Stockholm, Hardwick focused his efforts on the swimming pool. Not surprisingly, he excelled in the pool and apart from earning bronze medals in the 400 metre and 1500 metre freestyle events, Hardwick won gold in the 4×200 metre freestyle relay. Returning to Australia, Hardwick was later persuaded by Snowy that he could overcome his virtual penniless state resulting from his amateur sporting pursuits by making some money in the professional boxing ranks.

As the competition had thinned out because of the war, Hardwick had little trouble winning the Australian heavyweight title, but still struggled against an assortment of top line boxers.

Darcy wasn't overly impressed about facing Hardwick, believing him to be easy pickings, nor was he excited about moving up to the heavyweight ranks. But as there was nothing else around, Darcy relented and agreed to the bout on February 19, 1916.

As expected, Darcy toyed with the much heavier Hardwick, who was well out of his class and was planning to retire after this fight anyway. Hardwick never believed he would defeat Darcy, and for most of the fight hung on for grim death. But he was instrumental in an incident that in the end contributed to the death of another.

In the third round, one of Hardwick's punches hit the intended mark. While Darcy was working away at Hardwick's ribs, Hardwick threw a straight left that hit Les square in the mouth. Two of Darcy's front teeth were spat out – one landing in the lap of a prominent politician sitting ringside. Darcy was so angry that at the end of the round he asked his seconds, 'Are my teeth gone?' They nodded, prompting Darcy to utter, 'Well, he'll go now.'

Four rounds later, the referee, yet another member of the Baker clan – elder brother Fred – stopped the fight after Darcy had repeatedly knocked Hardwick to the canvas. Darcy's missing teeth were found. When Darcy later asked Hardwick if he was sorry for knocking his teeth out, the loser replied, 'Yes, Les, I am, but it's the fortune of war.'

The next day, Darcy went to a Sydney dentist, who haphazardly pivoted the front teeth back into his mouth, securing them to their stumps with the application of a gold pin. It was a messy job.

Next followed a succession of second-rate bouts, Darcy becoming more and more convinced that he should have left with Kearns all those months ago. Darcy even ended up fighting his old mentor, Dave Smith, in two shambolic fights in Sydney and Brisbane. Surviving footage of these fights show they were little more than a push and shove, D-grade wrestling affair, where Darcy was noticeably worried about hurting his long-time friend. The boxing crowds at those two events were blatantly robbed by Snowy, as shown by Darcy rushing to Smith's aid after he had been floored in Brisbane. Throughout the fight, Darcy could be heard saying to Smith, 'Sorry Dave.'

Another fight was against a Romanian, Alexander Costica, which lasted just four rounds. The next day, Costica told Snowy that he couldn't remember anything about the fight.

'What! You don't recollect being beaten by Les Darcy in the ring here last night?' Snowy asked.

'No. All I remember was coming late to the Stadium and sitting in your office.'

All this was part of a deal Snowy had signed Darcy up to, where he was contracted for six fights in six months, after which the understanding was that he was supposedly going to appease the war mongerers by enlisting.

To build up excitement and keep Darcy under his wing, Snowy even wrote to the *New York Police Gazette*, explaining that despite the titled

Australian boxer not being rated in the United States, there was no doubt he was the undisputed world middleweight champion. The letter was as much a dare for any American boxer to come to Australia and have Darcy on, as a desperate measure, Snowy was realising that quality opponents for Darcy were quickly drying up. He needed someone from somewhere in the United States to stop the Darcy phenomena from collapsing.

'According to some of the American sporting papers, the critics are not unanimous in recognising Darcy as the champion,' Snowy wrote. 'Well you may take it from me that this boy Darcy is the real middleweight champion of the world, if there is such a being.

'I am not trying to boost the boy from any selfish motive, but have reached that conclusion, after watching him closely and critically in all his contests in Australia since the day he first started.

'Can you point anyone out to me who ever gave Eddie McGoorty a thrashing in every round that he stood before him, and then knocked him out as Darcy did? Will you name any middleweight who has made Jimmy Clabby look cheap through a 20-round contest?

'Clabby has fought practically all of the good men in that division, and you must admit that he is clever and game, still Clabby was beaten decisively in every round by Darcy. Jeff Smith is a clever boxer, but he never had a chance to stay with Darcy, even at defensive work, which was his long suit . . .

'I wish you would get in touch with the best class of middleweights in America to come over here and meet Darcy. I will guarantee that they will get good money for their trouble.'

Then on August 25, 1916, a most revealing article was printed in the *Newcastle Morning Herald*. Just a few days after an item was published which indicated that Darcy was about to enlist, the article read: 'Mr R.L. Baker stated today that Les Darcy will not be given any more contests with Stadiums Ltd, after his present contract expires, unless he enlists.

' "Darcy was stated to have enlisted when I was in Brisbane last week," said Mr Baker, "and I was interviewed. I understood that he had offered himself, and said so, and I also congratulated Darcy on the step he had taken. Later I saw in the newspapers that Mrs Darcy had refused to give her sanction to his enlistment. I understand that since then Mrs Darcy has refused to agree to Les going to the front before he is 21 years old. He will not be of age until October, and realising that there might be a misunderstanding as far as my position is concerned, I went to him this morning.

'"His mother was there, and there is no doubt that her health is bad. A glance satisfied me of that score. During the conversation I had with Darcy it was pointed that he had wished to enlist and that his mother had refused point blank to allow him to do so. I then explained to him that he was under a contract for three more contests, one of which will be with George Chip – and I would mention here than I have guaranteed Chip 2,000 pounds to come to Australia to box Darcy – and that it has been decided the moment that contract has been carried out he shall have no further contests under Stadiums Ltd unless he enlists.

'"As a matter of fact, Darcy was not only agreeable, but anxious that this condition should be made. Darcy explained, however, that he is the sole support of his family, and that it was quite necessary for him to leave his people in fitting circumstances before going to the front."

'Mr Baker added that he thought that it was practically certain that Darcy would enlist when he attained his majority. "It wasn't my place," said the promoter, "to ask him if he is going to enlist, but during the conversation I had with him I got the impression that he will offer his services. He was satisfied with the stipulation I made – in fact, he wanted it."'

The article appeased Baker's political mates, including the NSW Premier and shadow of Huge Deal, W.A. Holman, and Billy Hughes.

To further convince them that he was serious, Snowy once more submitted himself for enlistment on September 6, 1916, and again his sore back saw him overlooked. Snowy was in a difficult position. He was repeatedly criticised by the Stadium crowd for allegedly being a shirker and was desperate not to let slip his family background, which involved Germanic links. The only way to overcome that was to appear to do everything for the war effort, except actually join. Waving a military reject badge, which Snowy received after his second unsuccessful attempt at enlistment, eased the pressure momentarily.

Snowy was also involved in a precarious balancing act with Darcy. Financially, it was suicide for Snowy if Darcy enlisted and left the boxing game. Without Darcy, Snowy basically had nothing, and he could see the Stadium goldmine become a ghost town. However he knew he couldn't dissuade anyone, in particular Darcy, from enlisting because such action could see him gaoled under the *War Precautions Act*.

Snowy was just as mindful of the horrors Harold had encountered since he left for the front. Harold Baker's war records reveal that his time as Lieutenant with the 12th Light Horse regiment was short and sour. Having left for Egypt in late 1915, within a month he was in the Government Hospital in Suez suffering from a serious back injury.

A story repeated to this day was that Harold, still believing he was the master of the ring at the Stadium, was an over-officious officer on the *Moldavia*, unfairly bullying his underlings and whenever possible asserting his authority. As ever, he was an unpopular, solitary figure, who turned so many people off with his pompous voice and high and mighty attitude.

One day Harold fell, or was pushed by other soldiers, down a man-hole, seriously damaging his back. The official line was that he suffered a spinal injury in a riding accident in Palestine. By March 1916, Harold was returning to Sydney on the *Kanowna*, suffering from paraplegia.

Harold gradually improved and was eventually able to walk again. But he spent the next few years in a variety of Sydney hospitals, immobilised and in agony. How he damaged himself was a family secret, as was a certain misunderstanding involving his wife, Nellie.

The war diaries of Tom Richards, the famous Australian rugby representative, revealed that just before he left for the front almost two years earlier, Harold came down to the Army camp in Queen's Park, Sydney, 'on a lovely horse and took me away to his home in Randwick for dinner'.

'His wife is nice and very young. They were married when she was only seventeen years of age,' Richards wrote. 'It appears that Harald, as well as the girl's mother thought she was nineteen, but when her mother's lawyers in England started to fix up her estate they discovered their mistake.'

War was messing everyone up.

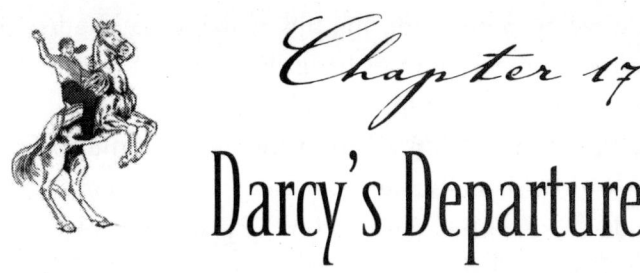

Chapter 17

Darcy's Departure

SNOWY WAS IN A RIGHT TIZZ. LES DARCY HAD SUDDENLY DISAPPEARED, and Snowy couldn't find him anywhere. In desperation, he telephoned the new chief boxing writer at *The Referee*, W.F. Corbett.

'Is Mr Corbett there?'

'Yes, Mr Corbett is speaking.'

'Get out, you're kidding me. Well, what do you think of that? A man just assured me that he saw Les Darcy off by a boat from Newcastle on Friday morning, and you had gone with him as his manager.'

'If that be true,' Corbett replied. 'I am dreaming very real, because I think I am in my den at *The Referee* office.'

'Darcy is not in Melbourne, Sydney, Maitland or Newcastle just now, as we have been able to learn. We have scoured those places, and we scoured The Spit at Middle Harbour without result.'

'Did you scour the Harbour?'

'Surely, you don't suspect he committed suicide,' Snowy gurgled. 'A young man so well placed financially, chockful of ambition concerning his vocation, and yet only on the threshold of life. Perish the thought!'

Snowy's mail was fairly close to the mark. Darcy was gone. He had stowed himself away in a boat which left from Newcastle. No, Corbett wasn't with him, but someone far dodgier was.

A lot had happened in the past few weeks and Snowy, for a rare change, was completely out of the loop.

It all revolved around a meeting on the Brisbane to Sydney train. Darcy was on his way back home after the Dave Smith debacle, and bumped into a shady figure, known by a variety of names, including Ed, Tim and Tom, but was best known as Sully – E.T. O'Sullivan. He was a track tout, an urger who hung around the periphery of boxing and racing venues offering tips, managing nobodies and being a spy for certain bookies. He was basically a pest, a big talker, and had the knack of sucking in the impressionable.

He got into Darcy's ear at the perfect time. O'Sullivan had hovered around Brisbane Station for some time, waiting for the arrival of Darcy, and as soon as he appeared on the platform, tailed him.

Within a half-hour of the train leaving Brisbane, O'Sullivan was by his side, weaving his magic. Darcy explained how frustrated he was with the local scene, how he thought the money would soon dry up and that eventually he would have to enlist. Darcy kept mentioning how much he wanted to prove himself in the United States, and that he had been trying for six months to leave for the US, but he couldn't get the required passport and his mother was always on his back.

O'Sullivan sensed an opening. He explained that the Australian Government, so eager to use Darcy as an example in their conscription campaign, wouldn't let him leave through official channels.

But O'Sullivan could help out. He had the plan and the Government contact to organise a fool-proof alternate way of leaving Australia. O'Sullivan said he would accompany Darcy and act as his manager, but at this stage it had to be top-secret.

Darcy agreed to get back to O'Sullivan in a few weeks' time, after he had fought Jimmy Clabby once more, and George Chip. That Darcy was eager to leave Australia as a fugitive, and with someone who was just a passing acquaintance, showed that he was desperate, and not exactly the sugar-sweet, squeaky-clean figure portrayed by so many. It also indicated he was motivated by money. Being surrounded by so many unreliable characters for so long had seen a few less endearing traits rub off.

Nor was Darcy an innocent bystander, knowing full well what the ramifications would be if he stowed away. Realising how the war issue had divided Australia, he knew he would be ostracised for running away and cast as a traitor. But he took that gamble and on October 27, 1916, almost a month after knocking out Chip at the Stadium – just four days before his 21st birthday and on the eve of the first national referendum on conscription – he and O'Sullivan hid themselves under tarpaulins on the cargo steamer *Hattie Luckenbach*, which was leaving from Newcastle Harbour heading for Chile. From there, they would hop onto another ship for New York.

By the middle of the following week, with Darcy and O'Sullivan well on their way to Antofagasta, their departure was common knowledge and was reported in numerous newspapers.

Snowy, Wren and Huge Deal immediately went on the attack, condemning Darcy for his rash actions. All three realised their meal ticket had dudded them. Snowy and Wren were furious that Darcy had left before his planned return bout against Chip, while Huge Deal felt duped by the fact that a boxer he wanted to take to America, had done exactly that with someone who was probably even more of a dubious character than himself. He felt doublecrossed by an upstart pug.

Snowy was playing both sides well, as there were serious accusations that he too had been eager for Darcy to travel to America, only as long as he managed the trip. A *San Francisco Bulletin* writer, Marion T. Salazar, claimed that Snowy had written to him stating that if Darcy wanted to go to America, he would do all that he could to help.

Still, when Darcy left without saying anything, for all three it was the ultimate public face slap, and each was determined Darcy would pay heavily for humiliating them. Their acts of revenge were vindictive and, in some instances, shameful. Never before, or since, has an Australian sporting hero been so publicly castigated.

Wren, who after reading of Darcy's departure in the Melbourne *Age* threw the paper out of his office window in disgust, immediately telegrammed Baker stating he would make certain Darcy was black-banned in America. He would contact Billy Hughes and tell him to put pressure on the American Government so as not to allow him to land. And if they couldn't stop him from landing, then make certain his life in the United States was hell.

Snowy, who felt that he had been betrayed by someone he called a friend, immediately cranked out the anti-Darcy line. In a press release that was sent to American as well as Australian newspapers, Baker said: 'Owing to Les Darcy's unpatriotic action in clearing out from his country, at a time when he should be doing his bit with his Australian comrades, it has been decided to strip him of his middleweight and heavyweight championship titles.

'Australia no longer considers him the middle and heavyweight champion as he was before his "covered" departure. Should America join the allies in this desperate struggle, Australia wants to know whether Darcy will enlist in the US or slip across the border to Canada.'

Snowy was as acidic when approached by a journalist. 'I know no more about Les Darcy's movements than the ordinary members of the public,' Snowy explained. 'I believe that Darcy has got away – as far as the Stadium is concerned we have forgotten him.'

He even tried to bluff everyone into believing that Darcy's departure would be good for the local boxing scene. Snowy told *The Referee* he couldn't give away complimentary tickets if Darcy wasn't appearing.

'"Is Darcy fighting?" would be asked. Darcy completely overshadowed, even absolutely obliterated his contemporaries as an attraction. Things may right themselves now that there is no Darcy to so nearly fill the public mind.'

Snowy was having himself on. That statement was one ridiculous smokescreen. Snowy was instead bleeding internally. However, he knew if he took a strong stance, he would get the support of an influential power group within Australia.

Darcy's departure was treated by those of a Protestant persuasion as the latest example of how negative some sections of the Catholic community were to the war effort. For those in the middle and upper classes it was a further indication that the working class were not doing their bit. Snowy always made certain he ingratiated himself with the proper mix. He had also never forgotten what had happened to the Palatines, all those centuries ago.

Huge Deal, who used the *Sunday Times* to push the 'YES' vote for conscription and was then disgusted that the first national vote had been lost to what he termed the 'traitor brigade', now ordered his newspaper lackeys to back Snowy and put the boot right in. In a *Sunday Times* editorial, Darcy was viciously attacked. Huge Deal was showing who exactly was boss.

Under the headline 'Cold-Footed Les Darcy Bolts from Australia to Escape Home Defence', the editorial called for the Australian Government to seize his property.

'He is fit for military service and he has made all this money out of the people of Australia. Australia has put him into a position of advantage that few young Australian men at this crisis enjoy; he is independent for life, if need be, and in case of his death his parents are abundantly well provided for.

'All this Australia has done for Les Darcy. What has Les Darcy done for Australia? He has turned tail and made a bolt of it the moment when it seemed that he could no longer dodge his plain duty to the country that has fed and pampered him.

'There need be no magnifying of this man Darcy's importance. He is not important in the least. In the scale of civilisation he counts for very little. The point is that he is a young Australian, and all he can find to do with the large sums of money Australia has poured into his pockets is to pay some other mean fellow to help him to bolt from his natural obligations.

'Australia can surely have no use for that sort of young Australian, and Australia at this moment is not in the least disposed to make excuses for him. Nor are we.

'What is to be done? The Commonwealth Government surely cannot sit down meekly and submit to the indignity of this man's lawlessness and breach of common faith. Is there not some way in which the Government can seize his property?'

The editorial had no name on it, but it was common knowledge in the *Sunday Times* office that McIntosh's number one crawler, W.F. Corbett, had written the piece. Understandably Corbett, who agreed to do his dirty work, had begged McIntosh to leave his name off this vitriolic piece. Still Corbett couldn't demand too much as he knew what happened to those who earnt the ire of either Huge Deal or Snowy. He had more or less taken over as *The Referee*'s boxing scribe, because the pair weren't happy that Solar Plexus had been questioning certain Stadium procedures, including their persistance in overtaxing their boxers, in particular Darcy, with a succession of 20-round bouts. Solar Plexus had also made the fatal error of writing a letter of encouragement to Darcy after he had fled Australia. He was fined and shown the door at *The Referee*.

When Darcy eventually arrived in New York, after almost two draining months at sea, he immediately placed the blame on Huge Deal for leading the vendetta campaign. Darcy said that Huge Deal had early in 1916 arranged 'to take me out of the country. When he thought others were going to do it, he set about preventing me going away'.

Darcy, who was snaffled up by another big-time gambler and shyster, Tex Rickard, on arrival in the United States told the flashy promoter: 'Hugh McIntosh offered to send me here, and get me five thousand pounds sterling for three fights. I would have taken that offer, if he'd posted the money beforehand in a bank. But he refused.'

At least one newspaper sided with Darcy, the Sydney *Sportsman* ridiculing the stance of the *Sunday Times*, arguing it was just Huge Deal being vindictive. The *Sportsman* said Darcy 'must have hit some local folk either on the solar plexus or in the pocket, judging by the way they continue yelping and snarling at him. While these denouncers of Darcy continue affirming that they are solely disgusted because Darcy did not enlist, it appears to us they are more concerned because he did not stay in Sydney and continue to be a meal ticket for the squealers and their friends. This snarling and slandering of an absent man is quite dingo-like in its methods.'

Huge Deal was getting very edgy, even instituting legal action against the *Mirror* newspaper group for having the temerity to run a piece from the *New York Police Gazette* that Darcy, a few months earlier, was to go to America under his management. Even though Huge Deal wanted that to happen, it didn't, and he didn't want the public to know that he had missed out on the golden egg. He also didn't want to be seen criticising Darcy for heading to the United States when he was pursuing exactly the same course only a few months earlier. Instead, like so many devious and hypocritical businessmen, he lived a lie, sued, and won, forcing the *Mirror* to run a grovelling apology.

Snowy was also persistent. He wrote a piece for the *New York World*, where he threw a few hard lefts at Darcy, but softened several of the blows. It was published four days after Darcy arrived in the United States. 'Sporting Australia is seething with excitement at this moment,' Snowy wrote. 'Our great pug, Les Darcy is missing. There are rumors that an unknown pirate ship, with all lights out, stole through the Newcastle, NSW Heads and kidnapped Darcy from his home some few miles from the harbor front, and that that pirate ship now lies some few miles from shore in neutral waters, awaiting the sporting public's response to a demand for a huge ransom.

'That's only one of a thousand rumors. Perhaps I should know the champion's whereabouts – but I don't! I do know, however, that Darcy five days ago sat in my Stadium office discussing the details of his return match with George Chip. Darcy was to call on me the following day for his Melbourne transportations. He did not call, and after two days' wait I got busy and had a search made. His mother, his sweetheart and his close personal friends know nothing of his whereabouts.

'According to military regulations, Darcy or any other military eligible young man are prohibited from leaving the country. Darcy had applied for a passport from Australia to America, and had been refused, so that the only conclusion to come is that the champion has defied the law and his national duty as an Australian, and has been smuggled or smuggled himself out of the country.

'Darcy was born in Australia, but his country, taking its honorable part in the European struggle, was no place for Les. The gold for fighting Dillon, Gibbons or some lesser light affected his heart more than the honor of fighting for his country. The sight of bulging bags of dollars just carried him away so to speak, at least that is the present public view of his quick change act.

'There is talk, supposedly to be in high authoritative circles, that something official will be done regarding a special order to have him returned to Australia, as they desire to make an example of a deserter who is so prominently before the public.

'People who pass over the questionableness of Darcy's action in "jumping out" preferring to leave these matters to those in authority, are at the moment concerned with him as a boxer, and are inclined to think that the long sea voyage on a 9-knot ship with comparative enforced idleness will settle Darcy as the fighting wonder we saw him last. Darcy in Australia had a sincere and sweet regard for his money, so here is much speculation as to whether he will take unto himself a manager or prefer to do his own business.

'Despite his aims I doubt not every Australian sportsman, be he soldier or otherwise, would watch with the keenest interest the clashing in America of Darcy and Dillon or Gibbons. The betting on such a match would be easily odds on Darcy being returned victor.'

In New York, having been told that he'd been slagged by several of his supposed friends, in particular Snowy, Darcy used a first-person piece in the *New York World* to state his case.

Under the headline, 'Les Darcy insists that he is not a shirker', he wrote: 'There is nothing of the shirker in my heart.'

Darcy said he still had every intention of going to the front, explaining that he went to the military authorities himself and 'offered $5,000 of my own money as a bond that I would return in six months if they gave me permission to come to America in order to earn enough to keep my mother and father, brothers and sisters in comfort before enlisting.

'You know, some of our boys who went to the trenches are never coming back. I wanted to be sure that five brothers, four sisters and my mother and father would not want if I was not alive at the end of the war. They are not rich and the brother older than myself is a cripple. Is it unreasonable that I should want to protect them?

'Hugh McIntosh was arranging to take me out of the country. When he thought others were going to do it, he set about preventing my going away.

'I want to make three or four good fights here, and then O'Sullivan and myself will go to Canada or England and enlist. I will join the Aviation Corps. I've never been up in the air, but they've promised me my first flight tomorrow. I'll be flying over the trenches before most of them even leave Australia, but my folks will have been provided for in the meantime.'

In another letter home, Darcy soon made it known he was associating with undesirable characters. He described one vaudeville manager who was pursuing him as 'a loud-mouthed Jew', while some of the other promoters who were hovering around him were described as 'a gang of pickpockets, gunmen, burglars, etc'.

Within a few days, Darcy was given enough clues that his time in the United States was heading towards being a debacle.

The smear campaign was working. Huge Deal and Wren had used their contacts well, put pressure to bear on Australian Government officials and told enough American contacts, including boxing authorities, of Darcy's dubious background, that suddenly the publicity trail turned sour.

Snowy also kept sending his newsletters which repeatedly provided an anti-Darcy slant, to American newspapers. Many of them ignored the Baker newsletters, which were written either by Snowy or a hired journalist, Phillip Arber, an American scribe who had joined Stadiums Ltd to take charge of the publicity department. Arber knew exactly which American newspapers to target to ensure Stadiums Ltd's slant was published. Some newspapers did use the material, either directly or as background to their own writer's piece. It didn't help Darcy's case for a fair go in a new country.

It wasn't long before several of America's leading sports writers were questioning Darcy's motives. W.O. McGeehan in the *New York Tribune* said it was 'hard to see how one can make a hero out of Darcy'. The highly popular Damon Runyon, who met Snowy on his US tour and became a close friend, added that: 'We like to believe that if left to his own devices, Darcy would have joined the colours . . . but the commercial eye of the fight promoters recognised his money making possibilities and they caused him to forget his duty.'

It was obvious McGeehan in particular was being fed from a reliable source from Australia – more than likely Snowy. In numerous other slanderous articles, McGeehan called Darcy 'Les Slacker'. American newspapers suddenly began printing the exact amounts Darcy had earnt from his last seven fights. That information could only have come from one source – the man organising the cheques, Snowy. For the record, the overall amount was 12,683 pounds – the highest 2,845 pounds against George Chip and the lowest 646 pounds for beating Les O'Donnell.

Suddenly Darcy was running out of friends, discovering that despite all the promises, actually getting a fight in the United States was going to be excruciatingly hard. Too many people were turning against him.

Darcy arrived in the United States at a time where boxing was illegal in many states and attempts were being made to rub it out in major cities, including New York. He quickly discovered that the boxing game was not as healthy in the United States as the spin doctors tried to make him believe. Fights kept falling through, he had a bitter split with his so-called manager, O'Sullivan, and a short vaudeville tour was laughed at.

The killer blow though was when shortly before Darcy was to face Jack Dillon at Madison Square Garden, New York Governor, Charles Whitman, stopped the fight. Following the death of a local boxer in the ring, Whitman had been attempting to institute legislation that would prohibit the sport in his State.

Australian authorities were aware of Whitman's opposition to boxing and through either the Federal Government, or from Huge Deal and Snowy's extensive list of American colleagues, the Governor was fed crucial information about Darcy's seamier side.

Whitman had the soap box he had been waiting so long to stand on. He explained his decision to stop the fight, saying: 'Darcy, so I am informed, is a runaway from his own country. In disguise and under an alias, he left his native land because he was afraid to fight in the cause for which his fellow-countrymen are sacrificing their lives. He prefers to give a brutal exhibition at some personal risk for a purse of $30,000.

I believe that the citizens of this State will support the Governor in his insistence that this thing shall not be permitted in New York.'

Darcy approached the Governor to get his proper explanation and according to his closest colleague, Mick Hawkins, who eventually joined his friend in America, was told: 'I haven't got anything against you, Darcy . . . but there's a guy named McIntosh who must have a big pull back in Australia. I just can't allow you to fight.'

Hawkins elaborated, explaining that Huge Deal had worked on the Governor as a way of punishing Darcy for not signing with him several months earlier, when he offered him 6,000 pounds for a six-month vaudeville tour and three fights.

'One "gander" at the contract was enough for me,' Hawkins said. 'It was chicken feed in my book. I wanted 6,000 pound for one title fight, and would have got it. Yes, I scrubbed the contract as soon as I read it.

'H.D. was as mad as a hornet. Very few people bucked H.D. in those days, and he was sore. He threatened us there and then. Said he'd move heaven and earth to stop Les getting fights if he went to America under his own steam.

'But Les had made up his mind to go. Les was as stubborn as a mule once he had made up his mind on anything. His first definite offer was in New York, where he was lined up with the winner of Al McCoy and Jack Dillon, who fought for the world title.

'I saw the fight advertised as a non-decision affair at Madison Square Garden, and as sure as I'm talking to you, Les would have beaten either of them. This was when the poison started to pour into America about Les from Australia. H.D. McIntosh told us when we turned down his contract that he would stop us ever fighting in America. And he made good that boast.'

Hawkins said as Huge Deal controlled a section of the Sydney press, and was a 'toady' to many politicians, he had the power base to launch a powerful campaign against Darcy.

Governor Whitman's decision was backed up by the State Athletic Commission, who announced that Darcy would be barred 'for all time from boxing in New York State'.

Darcy was running out of avenues.

Tex Rickard was considering dropping Darcy, and even Doc Kearns was mouthing off, complaining that he believed he had a contract to manage the boxer in the United States, but had been duped both by the fighter and O'Sullivan, a seedy character who could not be trusted.

When eventually dumped by Rickard, Darcy decided to act as his own manager and to his relief suddenly received offers to fight elsewhere, including Cleveland and New Orleans. This coincided with the United States joining the war in April 1917, prompting Darcy to enlist as a reservist in the American Flying Corps, where he was elevated to the rank of Sergeant. In Chicago, Darcy took the oath of allegiance, signifying his intention of becoming a US citizen.

Still his thoughts were much attuned to home. The previous month, Darcy wrote to Snowy, seeking forgiveness and the opportunity of another start in Australia.

'You will no doubt be anxious to know of my whereabouts and doings, despite the mean way in which I left you,' Darcy wrote. 'I am very sorry indeed to have left the way I did, but I thought I was doing the best.

'I thought if I told you I was going you would have me stopped for sure. I tried to do the right thing. I offered the authorities 1,000 pounds before I left to let me come over here for six months, and then go home and enlist, but they turned me down.

'To tell you the truth, Mr Baker, I did not want to go to the war just then, and I don't think anybody else in my position would want to go either. I have, as you know, right now a chance of setting my family on their feet for the rest of their lives, and can do it in a short time: then I don't care what becomes of me.

'I'll go to the front, but I think I would be a bigger cur if I went to the front and left a starving family at home. The British Army wouldn't miss me for a few months.'

Darcy said he still intended to enlist after a few fights in America. 'If the authorities over in Australia will overlook my wrongdoings, I will return and enlist in the Australian Army. If they are going to grab me and gaol me, I'll stay where I am or go to Canada and enlist.

'If you thought it worthwhile, and the military authorities are not going to do anything, I would be glad to have an offer from you. I could box for you and give a percentage of my earnings to the different funds for the war while I was in Australia. This would be worth a good deal to them and the Stadium too.

'. . . Now Mr Baker, I won't do anything until I hear from you. If the military authorities will forgive me for running away without a passport, I will return in a few months, and perhaps, make yourself and them a lot of money before I go to the front.'

It never happened, because suddenly Darcy took ill in Memphis. After a meeting about a prospective fight, Darcy told friends his joints were aching and he suddenly felt very stiff. He was taken to hospital, where it was discovered that his teeth were badly infected and that his tonsils had to be removed.

Within days, Darcy was fighting for his life against septicaemia and peritonitis. In hospital, he contracted pneumonia. On May 24, 1917, surrounded by several close friends and girlfriend Winnie O'Sullivan who had travelled from Sydney, Les Darcy died.

The common consensus was that Darcy had died 'of a broken heart', but in reality it was the Hardwick blow at the Stadium which had knocked out Les's two front teeth, and the shoddy dentistry work afterwards, that led to his sad demise. Nothing could stop the toxins going through his body and poisoning the bloodstream.

At the same time of Darcy's death, the latest Snowy Baker newsletter arrived in America and yet again the Australian boxer was being mercilessly sledged either by his former colleague, or someone, most probably Arber writing under Snowy's name.

Most newspaper sporting editors threw Snowy's latest sledge in the bin, but a few did run it, despite its appalling timing. The newsletter said the general feeling among Australians was that Darcy had enlisted as an aviator because it required extensive and long stretches of training. By the time Darcy became a proficient flyer, the war would probably be over and he would miss the chance of actually fighting for the Allies. Another smart mouthed line that came a few weeks later was that possibly Darcy had suffered his illness from pilot training, getting a chill at high altitude.

All this did was ferment even more acidic division between the pro-Darcy and pro-Stadium factions. Even with Darcy dead, the squabbling was far from over.

Chapter 18
Keeping Face

ON SUNDAY MORNING OF JULY 1, 1917, SNOWY BAKER HEADED TO Redfern Station to catch the Maitland train. The destination was Les Darcy's funeral.

As he walked along the platform in one of Sydney's toughest areas, Snowy found it surprising that most people were either turning their back on him, or ignoring his presence. It happened again as he took his seat in one of the front carriages. Those around him moved away, going to other compartments. Several rubbed their noses with their fingers, as if to indicate something stunk.

Snowy knew they were referring to him.

On arrival at Maitland, the reception was even chillier. As his head appeared through the train door, the locals began to jeer him, calling him names and screaming out: 'You're the one who killed our Les.'

Snowy didn't exactly get to the funeral. As he later explained, 'I was warned off.

'At Redfern Station I was met by a friend who asked me if I had seen the story in the morning paper in which I was held partly responsible for Les Darcy's death. I had not read or seen the newspaper article, but it was quite noticeable that most people on the station and train shunned me as though I were a plague-carrier. As I walked down the platform at Maitland, I was openly hissed by several who evidently had read the story and believed it.

'On my arrival at the cemetery, boxer Dave Smith drew me aside and asked me not to go to the graveside as feeling was running so high against me that some of the unruly ones were threatening to dig a grave and bury me alive. I thought discretion the better part of valour and quietly withdrew.'

Snowy took the next train back to Sydney. His wreath, passed onto Darcy's mother, was also returned. Snowy was not wanted. The biggest surprise surrounding the funeral altercation was that Snowy was sincerely taken aback that the general public had turned on him. Such is the problem of having a thick hide. It can obscure your senses.

The anti-Snowy feeling was understandable, considering the vicious campaign he, Wren and Huge Deal conducted on Darcy after he fled the country. This sad situation was hardly helped by the fact that in the month between Darcy's death and his body arriving in Sydney, the local press had taken sides over who was right and wrong. Snowy was often cast among the baddies.

Even after Darcy's death, Huge Deal kept slagging him off in several wild editorials in *The Sunday Times*, where good taste and manners were totally disregarded. At the time, Huge Deal was involved in an enormous grab for power, after his political mate, W.A. Holman, had secured him a cushy position in the NSW Parliamentary Upper House. The initials MLC were now proudly added to his name.

The Sunday Times editorial of July 8, 1917, was the most inexcusable. The headline read: 'Canonising Les Darcy. How calm we are when the VCs come home! Morbidity and false ideals.'

The editorial raged that when an Australian winner of the Victoria Cross returned to Sydney, he was basically ignored. In contrast, a shirker like Darcy had received the most outrageous and overwhelming of public receptions.

'It is irritating, and it is pathetic. There is something radically wrong with a community that celebrates its sporting men and leaves its heroes largely unacclaimed. The nation that does that sort of thing has not yet fully found itself. With the splendid heroism of our stalwarts shining as a constant glory at the front, it is somehow sadly ludicrous to make heroes of professional boxers who prefer to evade the risks of war.'

The Sunday Times thought it was disgraceful that the state railways had provided extra trains 'to enable a curious huddle of outsiders to follow a body to Maitland ... There is reason in all things, and reason goes with decency.'

Everyone knew Huge Deal was behind this slur, and everyone knew Huge Deal was still thick with Snowy. So Snowy was also blamed. At the Stadium on the night the news was announced that Darcy had died, Snowy found himself booed, while scribes from *The Referee* and *The*

Sunday Times were openly hooted and abused. Those from other papers more sympathetic towards Darcy were 'cheered and congratulated'.

With it came a newspaper war. *The Truth* and the Sydney *Sportsman* decided to put Huge Deal and Snowy in their place.

The Truth ran a series of articles over a number of weeks under the headline, 'Only a pug and only an Australian', where Snowy received a regular boot to the rear. They also ran an article from Bert Lowry, of the *San Francisco Call*, who had no hesitation in describing Snowy as Darcy's arch foe. 'And Snowy Baker,' Lowry wrote, 'by what right does he condemn his fellow man? Les Darcy brought thousands upon thousands of dollars into his coffers, and did more than hundreds of those at home to make Baker what he is today.

'Of all men, Snowy Baker should have been the last to condemn, or even hint at condemning, Les Darcy. But Baker forgot, and, with a vitriolic pen, he branded Darcy a slacker; and while Darcy was dying in Memphis, the mailman brought letters from Snowy Baker, in which he abused the deceased. The writer threw those writings in the waste-basket, and will continue to throw all that Snowy Baker may write into the waste-basket.

'Sporting editors are human, and have much to contend with. You who reads these pages do not know the calibre of men they must deal with, nor how hard it is sometimes to write. Yet, to the credit of the profession, let it be said that more of Snowy Baker's mouthings were torn up and scoffed at than were credited and printed.'

The Truth printed numerous anti-Snowy letters. They included J.H.L. from Cowra, who said: 'Baker ought to be the last man to condemn anybody else. The fans used to call out to the Baker crowd: "Why don't you go to the war, Baker?" Why didn't he condemn poor Les when he was bringing him in dollars, and not wait until the lad had decided to go away and earn money to keep his mother and father?

'Perhaps if he had condemned Les before, it might have made a difference to Baker's pocket, Baker was like a rooster cackling: "I will not match him again unless he enlists."'

Fairplay of Bulli asked: 'Why doesn't Mr Baker, with the patriotic spirit he possesses, make a little sacrifice, as others have been asked to do, and ask the boxers of military age under his management to enlist? If not, to refuse to allow them to fight.'

V. Cox, an ex-soldier from Mortdale, complained: 'Who is the slacker – Darcy or those who boycotted him? I say it is them. Let Baker try to enlist, and if he passes I will go again, but I will not go away again, while he is here.'

J.P. Lawson of Paddington said that if Baker's condemnations deprived Darcy of a living, 'why not deprive Snowy Baker, and other interested persons in the Stadium, from accumulating the wealth to be accrued by the control of the same by closing the place up, and so render unnecessary such alleged condemnatory correspondence'.

J.J. Gooley from the City said he and countless others were contemplating boycotting the Stadium in protest to how Darcy was badly treated by Snowy.

True Australian Native from Redfern extended the net, asking what Snowy and Huge Deal were 'doing to help the unfortunate returned soldiers who are fighting their cause? I don't see them giving benefit shows.'

Former soldier 'Had Some' was bewildered that Snowy would not match Darcy again until he enlisted. 'Don't you think that Baker would have been more of a man and more encouraging to one younger than himself, to say: "Let us both enlist." '

Still the nastiest letter was directed at Huge Deal. Salt Spray from North Sydney had been disgusted by *The Sunday Times* smear campaign. 'Fancy Magnificent McInstoush, the head serang of the Sunday Slimes, also ex-caterer, alleged bicycle starter, pug referee, company (ahem!) promoter, theatrical expert, millionaire (in his mind and mostly on paper) and finally MLC (mainly loyal cringer) howling and crying because our late champion Darcy was accorded a decent and truly fitting funeral. One thing is certain, and it's this, McInstoush is never likely to be canonised.'

The *Sportsman* also went on the long run over *The Sunday Times* vendetta. Under the headline, '*Sunday Times* tripe . . . Still gnashing over Darcy', the editorial lampooned Huge Deal for complaining about special trains being provided for Darcy's funeral.

'What the *Times* conveniently forgot was that the "outsiders" who travelled by these trains paid full fares for the journey. They were not dead-head MLC spongers on train transit, or bum actors or actorines flitting at reduced fares, or even newspapers being carried at a loss to the State.

'When H.D. McIntosh, now director of the *Times*, was a promoter of pugilistic contests at the Stadium, and special trams were run to carry his meal tickets, the public, to see niggers and foreigners bruise and batter each other there, the *Times* raised no protest, nor shrieked for the scalps of the Railway and Tramway Commissioners, as it does in the Darcy case.'

So overwhelmed by the public backlash, Snowy and Huge Deal decided to lay low for a short period, especially as they were treated like lepers every time they made a public appearance.

Snowy, ever thinking, decided to change tack. Ridiculed for not enlisting, he decided to make his third attempt at a public appearance. He organised a recruiting rally at the Stadium, calling on anyone to join, to climb into the ring, where they would be officially examined to determine whether they were fit enough to join. About 25 wrestled their way between the ropes to the cheers of the crowd, who were waiting for a succession of fights to follow. Then as the enlistees formed themselves in a line, a spotlight was directed on Snowy, standing ringside, as he made the brave decision to 'offer his services for recruitment'.

On cue, the crowd cheered, as Snowy stood at the end of the line. But all to no avail. Snowy was examined, and a certain Dr Howes turned him down. The spinal and abdominal injuries sustained in the car crash had according to Dr Howes 'rendered him incapable of service'.

The crowd groaned; Snowy waited until he was in his office before letting out a huge sigh of relief, and the fights began.

Wherever possible, usually in *The Referee*, Snowy kept pushing how he was helping the war effort. One week Snowy would be explaining how he wanted to erect a roll of honour at the Stadium, the next how anyone who was accepted at a recruiting rally would be placed on the Stadium's free list for life, and the following week how he wanted to start up a Sportsmen's Unit.

Snowy had also been involved in building a house at Frenchs Forest, which would be used by returned soldiers. Before Darcy left for America, he even spent one afternoon on the shovel helping with the construction. In tribute, Snowy had decided to call the house 'Darcyville'. That was until Darcy dudded him. In yet another backhander to Darcy, suddenly, without any fanfare, the house was renamed 'Cestus'.

Despite his attempts to distract the public, Snowy couldn't overcome the Darcy stigma. Even Darcy's mother, deeply disturbed by the many articles where Snowy was blamed for her son's death, contacted the Stadium promoter wanting to know what he had to say for himself.

Snowy decided there was only one way to end what he termed a 'nonsense'. He had to be given the chance of standing up in front of his detractors and state his case. Until then, Snowy thought, rumours and lies would be allowed to turn into truths.

Snowy told Mrs Darcy that he was willing to travel to Maitland and explain his case in front of the Les Darcy Memorial Committee, where he would answer claims that Darcy had been hounded to his death by one man – him.

In October 1917, Snowy went to Maitland, taking a train rather than his usual chauffeur-driven car, for the meeting at the town hall. With Snowy was his lawyer, W.H. Drew, and Solar Plexus.

When Snowy walked into the room, his progress was followed by hundreds of angry eyes, in particular Mrs Darcy, who believed this was the occasion to at last put a horrible upstart in his place.

But she didn't properly understand Snowy's cunning. He hadn't come here to be ridiculed. He, as usual, was going to fight it out. Surrounded by his chief enemies, Snowy was not going to back down.

The chairman of the committee, D.J. Ryan, started by explaining that the meeting had been convened following a letter sent to Snowy written by Mrs Darcy and a reply sent from him to her denying 'certain things charged against him in connection with the late Les Darcy'.

Ryan said that the general feeling in the Maitland area was that Snowy had been instrumental in Darcy's demise, being a prime mover in him being banned in Australia, and 'what they wanted from Mr Baker was an explanation'.

Snowy immediately rose to his feet, explaining that the 'trouble began' after the Darcy–Dave Smith bout in Brisbane in August the previous year.

An article had appeared in a Brisbane newspaper stating that Darcy was going to enlist. Consequently Darcy did not enlist when told he had to get his parents' permission. When Darcy and Snowy returned to Sydney a few days later, they were both severely attacked in the newspapers, with the reported enlistment being regarded as a cheap publicity stunt.

Snowy said he told Darcy that the boxing business had been placed in a bad position because he had not enlisted, after saying he would.

He asked Darcy what could be done to make matters right, and Darcy replied: 'Well, if I don't enlist after three more fights you need not give me any more fights.'

Snowy asked Mrs Darcy if she recalled this matter being discussed. She replied that she could not remember whether Snowy or Darcy made the suggestion of three more fights. He said the newspapers stated that he would not give Darcy more than three fights if he did not enlist, but instead was adamant that it was Darcy's request. Snowy quoted extensively from letters he had written to various sporting writers in America, before admitting that he 'felt angry about the way that Darcy had left Australia, but that was forgotten, and I endeavoured to assist him in every way possible in regard to getting matches in America'.

The Referee reported that Snowy said 'he was in no way responsible for the embargo that had been placed upon Darcy, but his idea was that Governor Whitman had his own reasons, and was not prompted by any person in Australia'.

Snowy then said he was willing to furnish copies of any of his letters sent to America, or answer questions from the floor. Not surprisingly Snowy was immediately asked about the offensive Snowy Baker newsletter, which appeared shortly after Darcy's death and accused the boxer of having joined the Aviation Corps because it would take so long to become proficient as a pilot. He cleverly diverted the blame, explaining that he did not write that newsletter, but a Sydney journalist had been paid to write them under his name. The crowd were not convinced by that feeble argument, prompting Snowy to add that he would supply all copies of the newsletter to the Darcy Committee.

Replying to the Chairman, Snowy said he had not, directly or indirectly, done anything to militate against Darcy's success in America, and had written nothing as to his having lost cast among his friends. He had not stated that he knew Darcy's idea in enlisting in the Aviation Corps was that it would take several months training, and give him the opportunity for fights in the meantime. He thought Governor Whitman was the only one to call Darcy a slacker, and he did not know of anyone who did so here in Australia.

Snowy then asked if in writing to his mother or anyone else, had Darcy made any reference to him. There was no response. He sat down, relieved that he had appeased the angry mob. The Maitland crowd were not exactly overwhelmed, knowing that Snowy had successfully slipped himself out from the danger zone, but at least gave him credit for having the courage to front his detractors.

The Committee also agreed to not make a final decision until Snowy had supplied copies of letters and printed material sent from Stadiums Ltd to the United States from the time Darcy left until his body was brought back. Snowy later claimed victory, as nothing further was ever said by the Committee about the issue.

A few months later, shifty O'Sullivan, the man who helped Darcy flee Australia, wrote to *The Referee*'s W.F. Corbett, after reading about Snowy's appearance at the Maitland Committee meeting. O'Sullivan said that 'neither Mr Baker nor anyone else connected with the Sydney Stadium, did anything towards stopping Darcy from boxing over here.

'I will also make an affidavit stating that anything Mr Baker wrote about Darcy was always in the boy's favor. To my way of thinking the persons who were responsible for all Les Darcy's troubles in America were nobody else but his so-called friends, who succeeded in poisoning the boy's mind against me.'

O'Sullivan's word didn't really mean much, because on endless occasions he had shown that he could not be trusted. He could have easily been trying to stay on the good side of Baker, Huge Deal and Wren, in the hope of one day getting a job from them.

Bat Masterson, one time gunfighter, marshal and Wyatt Earp's sidekick in the Wild Wild West, who later became sporting editor of the *New York Morning Telegraph*, also came to Snowy's defence. He wrote to *The Referee* that 'so far as we are concerned, Mr Baker never wrote us anything against Les Darcy, and we received quite a number of letters from him about that time.

'All Mr Baker ever wrote us about Mr Darcy that we now remember was of extremely laudatory character. Mr Baker thought Darcy had been ill-advised by certain persons who seemed to exercise a most pernicious influence over him ... We know Mr Baker wrote to Tom Andrews, the Milwaukee newspaper man and promoter, asking him to assist Darcy in every way possible to get matches in this country.'

Masterton's words must also be treated carefully. He was one of Huge Deal's American agents and representatives, while Andrews recruited for Baker. The brethren were trying to protect each other.

Holding greater weight was an article Solar Plexus, one of the more level-headed boxing scribes, wrote many years later in *The Sporting*

Globe. He had attended the Maitland inquiry and argued that Snowy had been badly treated.

After explaining that Snowy 'is still being blamed by fellows who do not know', Solar Plexus said: 'The man who pulled the strings for those on this side was said to be a certain Member of Parliament, who happened to be in America at the time.

'Harkening to his master's voice, he did the dirty work. But as the parliamentarian had been gathered to his father's doing since, I need not mention names.

'At the inquiry at West Maitland, Baker cleared himself of every charge but that of not giving Darcy another fight unless he enlisted. There he was cornered, and his tale that the published paragraph about the affair was not as he wished it to appear, but merely that it was Darcy's own suggestion, was not accepted.

'Having every letter Darcy ever sent to me, I brought to light one communication which bore Mr Baker's statement out to the very letter. Seeing the turn affairs had taken I begged to be allowed to say a few words (at the Maitland committee meeting). They were to the effect that though I was present to get first-hand information for my own little paper and did not wish to take sides, I would never forgive myself if I sat tight and saw an innocent man judged wrongly.

'I not only assured them that Darcy had told me it was he who made the suggestion that he not be engaged unless he enlisted but showed the lad's letter to the effect. But never after was I able to sell a single copy of my paper in either East or West Maitland.'

Not surprisingly Snowy's name in Maitland remained mud for decades afterwards.

Back to Sydney to other pressing problems, including the first fatality at the Stadium. A little-known 19-year-old Sydney boxer, Gilbert Alexander, died after being knocked out in a minor bantamweight fight by another of the rank-and-file, Tom Rolston. In the seventh round Alexander was felled by an uppercut to the chin.

In the dressing rooms, the Stadium doctor, Howard Bullock, examined him, pronounced Alexander as having slight concussion and as a precaution should be taken to Wootten private hospital in Darlinghurst for observation. Several hours later Alexander died of a brain haemorrhage. This was not the type of publicity Snowy wanted. The jackals who wanted to close the Stadium had been hovering for some time, and the death of a boxer in his ring was exactly what they wanted to hear.

Just as alarming were the crowd figures at the Stadium which had dramatically dropped off. With Darcy gone, there were no good boxers around and the Stadium punters were getting sick of watching B-grade bouts. Boxers were fighting in front of a handful of people.

In desperation, Snowy tried all forms of new competitions and side acts to suck in the public, including physical and facial competitions for the ladies, and the introduction of vaudeville acts from the Tivoli – from Burt Wilson, the 'double-voiced tramp', to 'sharp-shooters' Bosie Rifle and Co, and those remarkable hand balancers, Haig and Haig. W.C. Fields and his juggling balls were otherwise detained.

It didn't work. The attendances continued to drop off. First the Brisbane Stadium closed its doors in December 1917, and two months later the Stadiums Limited directors decided that the Sydney Stadium's days were also over.

The Referee reported that for some time Snowy had 'been at his wit's end' endeavouring to stage attractive contests, 'but the best proved poor as a rule compared to what used to be.

'The poor matches staged at the Stadium were not by any means his desire, they were his necessity. Endeavouring to carry on under such conditions was suicidal. It meant boxing too, in a sense, stank in the nostrils of the public. No businessman would think of allowing the situation to continue longer. It had gone on long enough.'

On February 9, 1918, the final Stadium bouts under Snowy's control were held. Newspapers were all sentimental about the last night, excited that with Fred Baker as chief referee, all but one fight lasted the distance. But when the Stadium was no more it wasn't missed by too many.

Suddenly Snowy was out of a serious job. Worried that the numbers training in his Sydney gymnasium had also slumped dramatically, Snowy looked around for other money-making ventures. As usual, it didn't take long for him to pick the ideal vehicle to make money, rewrite history, and again become a star. But this time on the big international screen.

Chapter 19

Hollywood Bound

FOR SOME TIME, SNOWY HAD BEEN SURROUNDED BY MOVIE CAMERAS, movie directors and show-offs who wanted to be movie stars.

As 'Snowy Baker's Stadium' was one of the largest entertainment venues in Sydney, it had often been used for showing the latest films from both Australia and overseas. It was the ideal spot for a flickering light to draw in the moths, all astounded at an extraordinary new form of entertainment. And Snowy, forever curious, was immediately tantalised by the unexpected and the exciting.

The Stadium had also been a haven for some of the first Australian film experiments. Raymond Longford was among the pioneers involved in the making of the feature-length documentary in 1908, *The Burns–Johnson Fight*, and at the time Baker had made himself known to the crew, in particular the man who would become one of Australia's most influential film directors.

The Stadium was also used by a variety of film directors as a backdrop for crowd shots, or whenever a boxing scene was required. Snowy would volunteer himself to be either the referee, or a boxer. He knew how to work an opening.

As the Australian fight game began to fade from 1917 onwards, and Snowy now had to look for other ventures, he soon realised that the movie industry, even if in its infancy in Australia, was a healthy financial alternative. He had been impressed by the large crowds which attended Stadium flicks nights, intrigued by the get-up-and-go of those involved, and it all seemed so magical, mysterious and marvellous.

For an egomaniac, it appeared the ideal vehicle to gain wider recognition, and maybe even regain some respect.

By 1914, motion pictures were by far the most popular form of entertainment in the world, especially in Australia, where it was assessed that each Saturday night, one in eight were 'at the flicks'.

Moving pictures had become a national obsession since they were first shown in Australia in 1896 at Harry Rickard's Melbourne Opera House. Hundreds of movie houses were built across the country, even in the most remote country towns, which for some time had been relying on the travelling picture show man to entertain a crowd that sat in awe. By the 1920s, it was estimated that every man, woman and child went to the cinema at least 23 times a year. There they were treated to an assortment of films, ranging from *Living Sydney – the London of the South*, newsreels, primitive action movies, crude comedies and more sophisticated slapstick involving Charlie Chaplin, epics like D.W. Griffith's *The Birth of a Nation*, which Nellie Melba claimed she saw six times, to the latest footage of either local or overseas fights.

One mischievous picture show man showed the first seven rounds of an American title fight three times, and no-one noticed, as they were totally captivated by a new phenomena that captured time and movement, and mirrored life. Footages of Melbourne Cups and Victorian Football League matches were highly popular, while the film of the Burns–Johnson fight, as Huge Deal found, made money wherever it was shown, especially after one Sydney newspaper described it as 'a veritable triumph in the art of motion picture photography'.

Adding to the charm for Snowy was that Australian film-makers were immediately trying to appeal to the country's growing sense of nationalism. Australia's earliest movies had a common theme of showing off the country's special qualities. With it came a proliferation of outback stories, bushranger tales, the excitement of the gold rush and the difficulties of country life. The wide-open spaces and a sense of freedom were repeatedly expressed, and 'bush' flicks reminded a country becoming more and more urbanised of its roots.

As there was always so much action, films were the ultimate escape from the drudgery of day-to-day life. And with them came titles like *The Story of the Kelly Gang*; *Robbery Under Arms*; *For the Term of His Natural Life*; *The Squatter's Daughter*; *Thunderbolt*; *Moonlite*; *Ben Hall and His Gang*; *The Golden West*; *Keane of Kalgoorlie*; *The Sundowner*; *Gamblers Gold*; *Cooee and the Echo*; *Call of the Bush*; and *The Waybacks*.

Many were extraordinary successes, in particular the Kelly Gang film, which at its first Melbourne screening in 1906 ran for almost six weeks to full houses, recouping its production cost of 400 pounds in the first week. Most Australian films made a reasonable profit.

These movies relied on an assortment of Australian actors, but no-one really stood out as a matinee idol, or consistent star. The films were too diverse to allow one person to dominate. But mindful of how already in the United States, certain swashbuckling actors had become stars, Australian directors and movie makers began looking around for someone who could be the bronzed Australian hero, a down south version of Tom Mix, Douglas Fairbanks and the likes.

Snowy was an obvious choice. Even though now in his 30s, and not having been involved in proper competition for almost a decade, Snowy was still one of Australia's most recognised sportsmen – and he had the physique to match.

Despite his hectic life as a diverse businessman, Snowy had kept aside several hours each day to either swim, run, dive, box and ride, usually combining two or three activities. He knew that if he was to remain the head of a physical culture school, he couldn't be excused for any form of flab. His best advertisement was himself. He proudly boasted that his weight was exactly the same as when he hopped into the ring against Douglas in London. He may have aged slightly, but the body was still powerful and imposing. If someone was looking for a fearless stuntman, Snowy was still your man, and he made that known.

Snowy was mindful that several of his sporting colleagues had dabbled with the flicks with varying success. Dave Smith had impressed Snowy in appearing in two Australian sporting movies, the first in 1913 in *An Australian Hero and the Red Spider* where he showed off his cricketing prowess by hitting a six to win the game, upset his family by secretly marrying his girlfriend, became a boxer to support the family, and then disappeared to run a farm.

Three years later, Smith appeared in *In the Last Stride*, where he was a swagman, a fugitive from justice, a successful first-grade rugby league player, a renowned boxer who fights Les O'Donnell in the ring, and then trains a horse, Sunlocks, to win the Sydney Cup 'in the last stride'. Throw in opium smuggling and a wild speedboat chase around Sydney Harbour and you have the ultimate escape movie.

Smith was followed on the screen by the fighter he trained, Les Darcy, who appeared in a two-reel semi-documentary called *The Heart of a Champion*. Snowy thought if Smith and Darcy could do it, then someone with an even bigger front would be a natural. He began to enquire whether there was any opening for him in the movie industry, adding that he was also interested in becoming a financial partner in what he assumed was a burgeoning business. His links with Huge Deal and Wren helped as well, as both had their tentacles in the entertainment business. The word was out. Snowy was available if someone was looking for an Australian he-man. It didn't take long for the first nibble.

The opening came in late 1917 when a J.C. Williamson stage producer, Roland Stavely, came up with the idea for a film, which he stressed was not propaganda but instead appealed to those who were angered by different cliques that had vehemently opposed Australia's involvement in the war. In other words, it was war propaganda and had received Government backing.

A nationwide general strike, involving more than 95,000 workers, in July and August 1917 had divided Australia, especially as one of the prime reasons for the walkout was the growing opposition to the war. It had also fermented near hysteria among the conservative classes that Bolshevism, Communism and general unrest was on the rise. It was a ripe time for a spy movie that would entertain, while giving a less than subtle message that Australia had better watch its own back door. It was aimed at pricking the masses.

Snowy's first movie – *The Enemy Within* – centred on German infiltration in all areas of Australian life, from the social set to the working masses. Snowy obviously didn't tell Stavely about his own family background, as instead of being the man designated to break the spy ring, he could have so easily been one of the infiltrators having more obvious Germanic links than any of the so-called agents in the film.

The story was based loosely around a true event when the German raider *Wolff*, which had laid a series of mines, was blamed for a trading steamship, *Cumberland*, sinking off the New South Wales coast near Gabo Island. *The Enemy Within* revolves around Snowy's character, Jack Airlie, described as a Special Agent for the Secret Service, who has the task of stopping a group of foreign agents from causing civil unrest within Sydney.

In an obvious dig at the International Workers of the World, known as 'the Wobblies', who were criticised for both the general strike and pro-German feelings within Australia, the film portrays the baddies as working-class subversives, spreading their poison in the Sydney Domain with a series of inflammatory speeches.

The leaders of the spy ring are identified as members of Sydney high society, whose headquarters, a stately mansion at Palm Beach, are used for plush parties and recruitment purposes. The focus of the film is on action, the drama intensifying when Jack's sweetheart, Myee, is kidnapped by the spies, prompting a merry chase all over Sydney where Snowy performs crazy stunt after crazy stunt, gets involved in a shoot out, and eventually rescues the damsel in distress, played by American actress Lily Molloy, for the happy ending.

Who approached who can't exactly be confirmed, but Stavely immediately had a willing star in Snowy who would do anything required of him, including the most daredevil stunts. What was most astounding was that just three months after being knocked back for enlistment because of a bad back, Snowy had no qualms about diving 25 metres into a bay to rescue a heroine, leaping from horse to horse, hurling himself from one car to another, or catapulting himself from a rooftop to a passing wagon, and with his bare fists knocking out anyone who got in his way. All this made a mockery of his repeated public stunt with the Army Enlistment Officers.

Snowy was hoping that everyone would have a short memory. That wasn't the case, as those who remembered sometimes jeered when he appeared on the screen. Most of the audience laughed it off saying it was just another case of Snowy being Snowy.

His acting abilities were minimal, with his younger brother Frank saying he 'was something cut out of wood'. But Snowy tantalised the masses with his outrageous deeds, which were often straight off the pages of *Boy's Own Annual*.

The film was set throughout Sydney, the dramatic diving shot filmed at Bronte Beach on a public holiday. This naturally attracted hundreds of confused spectators, all wondering why Snowy was repeatedly clambering over the rocks before hurling himself into the swirling sea.

A spectator became a little too inquisitive and stole one of the props – a phial of chloroform which was used by a German spy, played by John Faulkner, to knock out the heroine. When the scene was about to be shot, Faulkner, ever the old pro, improvised, instead grabbing a stick of greasepaint, dabbed it onto a hankerchief and placed it over Lily Molloy's nose. Lily feigned unconsciousness.

After the movie was shown, a well-known Macquarie Street doctor approached the actor and asked: 'I say, Faulkner, I wish you would tell me what anaesthetic you used on the girl in that kidnapping scene. I've been looking for one like it for years. It's the quickest and most effective one I've ever seen used.'

Faulkner replied that being a German spy the anaesthetic was a German chemical secret, known only to Kaiser Bill and himself. The doctor turned on his heel in a huff.

Other scenes were shot at the old Spencer studio in Rushcutters Bay, where the temperature on the glass-walled stage hit well over the 45°C mark, and in the roof garden of Farmers Department Store in Pitt Street. To broaden the cast, Snowy's friends and relatives were used to fill the scenes. This included Snowy belting his older brother Fred in one shot, their father smoking and playing a game of chess in another, Harold and Frank Baker scuffling in the background, and even old Solar Plexus, Will Lawless, makes an appearance standing between Snowy and a waitress. Snowy's chief sidekick in the movie was Aboriginal boxer Sandy McVea, who had made his share of appearances in the Baker Stadium ring, while J.C. Williamson's long-time property master, Mrs Rock Phillips, appeared in several of the cafe scenes.

Frank Baker recalled many decades later that the making of the movie was haphazard and 'wasn't by any means a good job'. But the film, which according to Frank was made 'for the government', had its moments. For one particular scene, Stavely told Frank that he thought his features were 'too immature for a hardened crook' and advised him to grow some stubble. He couldn't do it overnight, so he asked a well-known character actor, Jerry Harcourt, who was assisting with make-up, to apply some finely chopped horse hair to his face. At the end of the day, when Frank needed Harcourt to 'remove the goo', he had disappeared. 'Fearing, no doubt, that I may commit mayhem on him when I learned that he had forgotten his spirit gum that morning, and had used instead some shellac obtained from the set painter, I used every known potion and salve to remove the stuff. But of no avail. And it was at least a week; by the aid of broken glass and sandpaper that I rid myself of Jerry's makeshift shellac spirit gum.'

Frank also found Faulkner, the chief German spy, a slippery character. 'The dignified and austere Mr Faulkner was endowed with a prevailing habit of forgetting his pocket book, and touched me for a few bob to see the day through. Another prevailing habit appeared to be his forgetfulness of the transaction.'

The film was first shown in March 1918 at the Strand Theatre in Sydney, with advertisements assuring the public that this was 'not a war drama'. Instead they were about to see 'a magnificent story of a brave man's fight against the Kaiser's spies in Australia'. Snowy 'will perform stunts which other actors can only fake. See his terrific fight against four men, his 80-foot dive into the harbor, his leap from the flying cars.

'The piracy of the Raider "Wolf" ... The wrecking of the "Cumberland" and the mine setting at Gabo — you'll see a fight against the men who caused these things.'

The movie was a success, despite mixed reviews. *The Sun* said it was a 'presentable' movie, which 'under more experienced and critical directionship might have been an excellent one'.

'The strength of "The Enemy Within" lies in action rather than characterisation and intrigue. There is evidence that the author himself has no very definite knowledge about conspirators or the way in which they work. His conception too, of a secret service officer is not wholly flattering to a corps that is supposed to be very wide-awake. Jack Airlee [sic] is too easily trapped and deprived of his revolver.'

Also of concern was that Airlee [sic] loses all interest in his girlfriend after the first scene, and though he rescues her, 'the act is prompted by neither sentiment nor passion, nor revenge. One suspects that the author makes him do it merely to give Airlee [sic] a chance of enacting a sensational rescue. Snowy Baker's work in the role of Airlee [sic] is capitally done. There is no pretence at acting. He is just his plain, natural, everyday self.'

Another reviewer was concerned about the film's long length, and some strange settings, including one sealed room. 'Its hidden entrances, and walls with mysterious trapdoors, are as out of place, at least in Australia, as the slinking walk of the conspirators.' Even the actor Faulkner conceded that the movie was 'crude in many ways'.

Despite these barbs, Snowy was inspired by the success of *The Enemy Within*, and by early 1918 had formed his own film company. It was named, simply, Snowy Baker Films.

Snowy was determined to take advantage of the positive publicity from his first film and immediately started organising, writing and filming his second. So fast was the turnaround that yet another Snowy Baker film was appearing in Sydney cinemas by September 1918.

There was no mucking around in the making of *The Lure of the Bush*, the latest swashbuckling Snowy Baker adventure. While several of the cast members remained the same, including Faulkner, Snowy again relied on family members, including his step-daughters Joan and Margaret, now aged 11 and 10, who appeared as either horse riders or passers-by, while his wife Ethel helped in feeding the cast.

Ethel was an important ally during this period, relishing the chance to be involved in an exciting new venture. The supposed glamour of the entertainment world appealed to Ethel and her willingness to entertain, and ability to mix it with anyone, was crucial especially when Snowy needed to woo prospective financial backers. Having two extroverted daughters hovering around also helped in the public relations stakes. Ethel also had a strong work ethic and while hanging around on set didn't hesitate when it came to doing various menial jobs, including making certain that no-one was complaining about a lack of food.

Snowy had decided to give the film a professional touch and enlisted a proficient screenwriter, director and cameraman. This added a touch of slickness. The screenplay was written by Sydney journalist, Percy Reay, under the pseudonym Jack North, from a story which had won first prize in a *Bulletin* magazine competition. It was a typical city meets bush tale, revolving around a young boy from an outback station who is sent to England to complete his education.

Some years later, the boy returns home as the English 'dandy', wearing a monocle, dressed to the hilt and carrying a riding cane. Not surprisingly he is ridiculed by everyone on the station. To play a trick on him, several of the station hands stage a fake hold-up involving bushrangers. But it all backfires when the hero Hugh Mostyn, played by Snowy, believes it is all serious and attacks the bushrangers, otherwise known as the station hands, knocking them all unconscious.

Then to prove his prowess, the one time 'dandy' turns into a fighting machine, successfully duelling the chief shearer in the boxing ring, breaking in the craziest brumby on the station, and yet again shows off his swimming, diving and riding skills. Naturally, through his heroic exploits, he wins the hand of the manager's daughter, played by well-known Sydney society girl, Rita Tress.

Who actually directed this film remains in dispute. Claude Flemming, a much travelled actor who had hit the boards of the British and American stages, has often been credited with being the director. But the film's chief cameraman, Franklyn Barrett — one of Australian cinema's most innovative early photographers and a close friend of Huge Deal's, who would lend him Tivoli actresses to fill background scenes — repeatedly argued he was the director. No clues can be found from the movie, as unlike *The Enemy Within*, all copies of *The Lure of the Bush* have long disappeared.

One fact is for certain though. Snowy decided that this movie required authentic bush settings, prompting the film company to leave Sydney and head for his friend Eric Mackellar's stud Merino station — Kurrumbede — near Gunnedah for the outdoor action shots. The move to Gunnedah worked, Barrett's photography being so vivid that according to Faulkner 'one can almost smell the gums and the whistleblossom'.

'A man must love the country and fully understand its influence and charm to get this atmosphere over on the screen. This Mr Barrett has succeeded in doing.'

Along with filming came some wild times. Eric and his brother Malcolm, who were related to poet Dorothea Mackellar of 'My Country' fame, were larger than life farmers. As Frank Baker recalled: 'Eric was basically harem scarem, and the wildest thing that ever lived. Snowy convinced his brother Malcolm to get involved in one of his films . . . yet Eric wouldn't have anything to do with it, primarily because he loved the bottle. But he could carry it too. Eric was most renowned for giving people on the station the wildest rides in his automobiles, driving them through creek beds, and even barbed wire fences.'

The Bakers and co survived the experience, the shots taken on Kurrumbede giving the film a special edge.

When the film opened at the Globe Theatre in Sydney in September 1918, the bush theme was pushed to the limit, a display containing clumps of foliage and an assortment of animals and birds, including caged kookaburras, dominating the lobby. The film advertisements pushed the action line, with the most graphic showing Snowy smashing his fist through a door so that he can rescue Rita Tress 'from the man she loathed'.

The ad for the film screamed the words:

'Can't Ride, eh!

Can't Fight, eh!

A Fool, is he?

The wild bunch out back thought he was—

—they took him for a greenhorn—

—until—

—he licked their bully—

—broke the wildest outlaw—

—stole their girl—

—became boss of the whole outfit!

That's—

Snowy Baker

in his newest drama that is full of typical Australian recklessness'.

The reviews were also far more positive. *The Referee*, as one would expect from a Huge Deal production, gave Snowy their seal of approval, saying that the film: 'Is a capital representation of Australian station life in all its most interesting phases.

'There are brushes with bushrangers, encounters with wild Aboriginals, a kangaroo drive, musterings of cattle and sheep, a shearers' shed in action, a shearers' ball, some attractive little scenes of farmyard life, also possums and native bears are seen moving in trees. The production is certainly an eye-opener as evidencing what can be done in that way in Australia.'

Theatre Magazine was just as impressed with Barrett's photography, explaining that 'there are some great views of mobs of cattle and horses and flocks of sheep and the many birds and animals snapped include a mob of some hundreds of kangaroos'.

The magazine said that one scene involving a punch-up was outstanding, and that 'no imported film has shown anything surpassing in realism and skill what is witnessed in this thrilling mix-up. Six reels in a truly Australian bush setting, with plenty of thrills and not a dull moment, must be the verdict of all who see the picture.'

It was also a major box-office hit. According to Andrew Pike and Ross Cooper's book, *Australian Film 1900–1977*, 'the film reportedly grossed 20,000 pound for an outlay of 1,500 pound on the production'.

Snowy contacted a Queensland entrepreneur, E.J. Carroll, who was involved in skating rinks in Townsville before specialising in film and vaudeville production, to distribute the movie. This proved a masterstroke, the movie gaining wide exposure along the eastern seaboard where the strong Australian scenes made the film a favourite for thousands of movie goers.

Snowy was now convinced this movie game was a goer. There was only one avenue for him to take. Go to where it was really happening. Head to Hollywood. Learn the business. Meet the stars. Discover the tricks. Find out the short cuts. Unearth the right talent. Brainwash them into believing they should come back with you, and return to Australia bigger and brighter to basically pillage the market.

The Man From Kangaroo

SNOWY, ACCOMPANIED BY HIS WIFE ETHEL, USED HIS TIME IN HOLLYWOOD wisely. Within days of arriving in Los Angeles in late 1918, he was writing letters home boasting about how he had met with Charlie Chaplin, Douglas Fairbanks, Cecil B. De Mille, D.W. Griffith and the likes.

It was a perfect time to be living and learning the international motion picture business. Chaplin had just built his own studio, having finished his war film, *Shoulder Arms*, and Griffith, the industry's first major producer–director, and De Mille, king of the epic, were turning Hollywood into the world's movie mecca.

Not surprisingly they had heard of Baker and his involvement in a movie business offshoot in a faraway outpost. They were intrigued by the import, particularly his eagerness to send money their way to reshoot scenes from *The Lure of the Bush*, with the view of selling the movie to the American market.

Carroll's success in distributing the film in Australia had convinced him to join forces with Snowy, sharing finances so that the new movie star could spend several months in Hollywood studying American production methods. On his return to Australia they could then confidently start up a Carroll–Baker film production programme.

Snowy was the spy, spending weeks on the various Hollywood blocks watching film directors, including Chaplin, work, and talking to those at all levels of production.

At the Lasky film lot, in conjunction with directors Walter Edwards and Mrs Crawford Ides, Snowy reshot many scenes from *The Lure of the Bush* using American actors, explaining that it was all part of his apprenticeship 'in the study of the new art'.

He also worked the network, seeking out every major director and star to introduce himself, show his film and warn there was more to come. According to Snowy, De Mille was overwhelmed by the cattle and kangaroo shots in *The Lure of the Bush*, telling him that 'they could not be done any better in America'.

Snowy even had dinner with Chaplin shortly after Chaplin had secretly married Mildred Harris, a starlet who had fallen pregnant to the silent screen star. The pair had a short and strained marriage.

Chaplin and Snowy got on well, but he didn't tell the inquisitive Australian everything. 'I had no idea when I had dinner with Mr Chaplin and Miss Harris that they were married,' Snowy told *The Green Room* magazine. 'Later he told me that the public always expected him to put something over them – so he kept his marriage a secret.'

Snowy returned to Sydney in the New Year, with grand ideas and big dreams, while Ethel and her daughters stayed behind. What he saw in Hollywood he believed he could reproduce down-under, convinced that there was an international market for Australian subjects. He could see no reason why another Hollywood could not be developed in Australia, even if he would be relying on Australian themes.

'We could weave a romance about the bush, that would make Australian bush films sought after just as eagerly as the pictures dealing with Western life in America. We can stamp our type the same as the Western type. There is a wonderful field. Even our Aboriginals have not yet been exploited as they should.

'The field is vast. Thursday Island, Queensland, New Zealand and the Northern Territory, with its wild buffaloes, is practically virgin soil for motion pictures. Films taken in these parts would sell all over the world.

'I am fully convinced that Australia can and will yet rank with America as a producing field for motion pictures, provided that the foundations are laid in the right way.

'We are going out after the essentially Australian. Australia abounds with so much that is different to any other country that it should not be difficult to find plenty of suitable subjects for pictures that will stand out for their originality, and Australian atmosphere, thereby suiting the requirements of both the Australian and foreign markets.'

His dream was to 'see the words "Made in Australia" flashed on every screen where the motion picture is shown'.

The first bricks were provided when Carroll–Baker Australian Productions was formed in early 1919 with capital of 25,000 pounds. The subscribers were Snowy, an Adelaide company, Southern Cross Feature Films, and brothers E.J. and Dan Carroll.

The Carrolls, apart from impressing Snowy with their successful marketing of *The Lure of the Bush*, knew the local trade, having been involved in film screenings in Queensland for well over a decade. They knew all the pitfalls of distribution, who to trust and not to trust. They had as much faith as Snowy that Australian films, with distinctly Australian themes, would work.

But they were as mindful as Snowy, and his wife, that overseas expertise would also be required. While in Hollywood, Snowy had sought out many high-ranking American directors, writers and cameramen, asking whether they were interested in an adventure, lucrative money, the chance of seeing a faraway land and be part of a new, exciting industry. To Snowy's surprise, several notable names, with vast movie knowledge, showed more than passing enthusiasm.

He told them to be patient, he would organise the capital when he returned to Australia, and 'get back to them'.

Despite Snowy's big statements, he'd decided not to devote all his forces to movie making. He knew he still needed a base income to pay the basic bills, especially as his Sydney gymnasium was, at the time, a moderate, rather than major success.

Snowy decided to use his name in another area – journalism. In May 1919, *The Evening News*, otherwise known in Sydney as 'The Snooze', announced that Snowy was their new sporting editor. This staid afternoon newspaper suited Snowy perfectly. All he had to do was provide a short piece daily, usually on boxing, and the rest of the afternoon was his to organise his numerous other business ventures.

For well over a year, Snowy used his column to reminisce about past boxing battles, interesting characters, altercations that he had as a promoter, and even cover the occasional fight at the Stadium, which had re-opened several months earlier under the control of Jack Munro.

Occasionally his column contained fascinating anecdotes, insights and revealing quotes. They included the difficulties he'd had in getting several boxers into the ring, including English lightweight, Johnny Summers, and the Aboriginal fighter, Jerry Jerome. Summers often disappeared just before a fight and was once found wandering lost in the bush in the Blue Mountains, while Jerome, who would also repeatedly wander off on fight night, was often found in Maroubra 'playing cards, or smoking his pipe around the fire, and quite oblivious to the fact that he was that night contesting a championship'.

There were tales of boxers throwing fights, tricks of how one fighter would upset the other by applying raw alcohol to their hair and rubbing it into the other's eyes to try to blind them, and old Snowy prejudices, including that Jews 'would rather sell you a watch than fight you'.

His position of power was also important in promoting yet another good. Snowy was now in the miracle cure business. Suddenly the largest ad in *The Evening News* sports pages was for 'Snowy Baker's Unfailing Liniment'.

Each day, some sporting superstar was explaining how a few smears of Snowy's liniment on the body had worked wonders. From the American six-day cycling team, to Australian Imperial Force bantamweight boxing champion, Digger Evans, to eminent English comedian, Dan Agar – they owed all their success to Snowy and that magic bottle sold by all chemists for two shillings and nine.

How could one resist, as according to Snowy's snake-oil pitch the liniment was 'invaluable for sprains, aches, lumbago, rheumatism, athletes' exhaustion, stiff muscles, or for training of pupils in athletics'.

Snowy revealed that the magic formula in his liniment was originally discovered by Sioux Red Indian Braves – 'the human panthers of the American continent'. Naturally he'd modified it for Australian use, believing that the athlete's motto should be: 'Mind the muscle and keep this liniment in mind.' Who made it and what was actually in the liniment was unknown, probably just snake oil under another wrapper.

According to Dan Agar, appearing in Australia in *Bing Boys on Broadway*, Snowy had even found the cure for the common cold.

'I got a very severe cold on the chest just before our opening night,' Agar wrote. 'Some friends at the theatre recommended your Liniment, and I used it for two or three days with the greatest success. So efficient was your preparation that on my first night the cold had competely disappeared. I am convinced that you know how to fight a cold.'

Movie production had to be in the mini-league to eradicating the common cold. And by the middle of 1919, Snowy had made important inroads there as well.

Snowy's plan to import American talent had worked, with three of Hollywood's leading movie identities agreeing to travel to Sydney to work on his next film. Before then Australian films had been dominated by local talent, prompting a certain amateurish feel, which had diminished its appeal.

As E.J. Carroll put it, bringing in overseas talent would ensure that the pictures were no longer one dimensional, and instead 'be entirely cosmopolitan in their appeal'. The Carroll brothers and Baker assumed that this would make their movies far easier to sell overseas, especially in the lucrative and large American market.

Carroll–Baker Productions aimed high, and succeeded, the husband and wife team of Wilfred Lucas and Bess Meredyth, cinematographer Robert Doerrer and actress Brownie Vernon, arriving in Sydney in September 1919, together with Snowy's wife and two step-daughters.

Ethel Baker, who had stayed behind in Hollywood to stitch up the deals, found herself caught up in the social whirl of partying and big noting, including further meetings with Chaplin, 'who was awfully kind to me and I may mention that he has never missed a mail in writing to "Snowy" since he first met me'.

Ethel was an important ally for Snowy. Although eager to stay in the background and be a doting wife, she also had an acute business mind and had been one of the major spurs behind Snowy trying his luck in the movie game. Ethel loved the glamour and glitz, and made certain that she and her two daughters, now 12 and 11, were on the set of his early movies, helping wherever possible in the background. Joan and Margaret soon found themselves in front of the cameras, while Ethel, still an enthusiastic equestrian rider, made sure that the horses involved in the shoots were properly groomed and in good physical shape.

Privately Ethel was delighted that Snowy had moved away from boxing promotions, believing movie making was far more respectable. Hobnobbing with the stars in Hollywood was far more appealing than having some broken down pug banging on their front door, pleading with Snowy to give him a break. Snowy was always the showman, Ethel the backbone and the voice of reason. She also remained his biggest fan.

Ethel even encouraged Snowy to dabble in another form of entertainment. Snowy told *The Picture Show*, the movie trade magazine which was owned by film advertising agencies, that since returning from

Los Angeles he had been practising for the stage. The song which Snowy hoped to make a big hit was 'The Hours I Spent With You, Dear Heart'. It went nowhere and Snowy never mentioned singing again. Instead, he was singing other people's praises.

All those signed by Carroll–Baker Productions were notable Hollywood names. The Canadian-born Lucas had acted in many movies, being one of the stock company of actors at American Biograph, before appearing in several D.W. Griffith films, including the title character in a two-reel adaptation of *Enoch Arden*. From 1914, Lucas had directed at Universal Studios and also produced *The Romance of Tarzan*.

His partner Meredyth, a small, vivacious blonde, was a respected screenwriter, having written the scenario for Australian actress Louise Lovely's first Hollywood movie, *Stronger than Death*, as well as working on Lucas's productions, including his Tarzan production and *The Trey O'Hearts*.

Doerrer was chief cameraman with a variety of companies, having filmed 12 of William S. Hart's silent western movies, as well as being involved in Chaplin's *The Immigrant*. Snowy boasted that he had lured 'one of the very finest cameramen in the film world'.

Doerrer had worked with Snowy on the remaking of scenes for *The Lure of the Bush*, and Lucas was introduced to Snowy through a mutual contact – veteran American director, Allan Dwan.

Brownie Vernon was not quite on the same level, being contracted to Universal for a number of minor movies, but had still appeared in films opposite many major stars, including Tom Mix. Just before leaving Hollywood, Brownie had appeared in *Bare Fist Gallagher*.

The stars didn't come cheap. Lucas, according to the press, commanded an exorbitant wage of 100 pounds per week. In reality, the figure was far more incredible, with Lucas receiving a weekly cheque of 500 pounds. The rest weren't getting quite so much. But the pressure was immediately on Snowy and the Carrolls for the radical adventure to work, or their foray in the film business would be short, and hardly sweet.

At least they had the backing of the business press, *The Picture Show* editorialising that they took their hats off to Snowy and E.J. Carroll 'for the action they have taken to put Australian motion pictures on the map.

'They consider the field is limitless, and are prepared to back their judgment with good, hard cash. More than that – they have actually backed it. We have no hesitation in saying that the pictures the Baker–Carroll–Lucas combination achieve will be the greatest advertisement for Australia we have ever known.'

The mutual appreciation society worked overtime when the Americans jumped off the *Ventura*. Doerrer couldn't believe the quality of the Australian light. 'The light and atmospheric conditions here are very good, and almost equal to those in Los Angeles; and as to locations, well, your country is just unique in its advantages. Why, within half an hour of the city we have seen locations that we would have to travel days to find in my country.'

Lucas's vision was broad. 'We want to make films in Australia, which can compete in the world's market,' the big talking Lucas told *The Picture Show*. 'We have been in the moving picture business since the old Biograph days, and hope to build up the industry here just as it has been built up in America.'

Meredyth meanwhile headed to the NSW State Library in search of story ideas from local newspapers, literature and historical books. After spending several days going through documents and a mountain of books, which revealed little that could be turned into a screen potboiler, Meredyth opted for an easier formula – basic melodramas set in natural Australian settings, such as on sheep or cattle stations, where the camera could camouflage the frailty of the story with impressive sweeping rural shots. She soon came to the realisation that the only film-worthy Australian stories were those involving station and bush life.

Meredyth then remembered a story idea Snowy's wife had told her on the ship voyage to Australia and took it as her own. It was a simple, silly tale, but if filmed properly would work. Meredyth, Lucas and the Bakers agreed on the title – *The Man from Kangaroo*.

The story revolves around a former middleweight champion boxer, John Harland, who becomes a parson and is posted to a country town called Kalmaroo. There he teaches the local youngsters how to fight, and demonstrates his diving skills with a series of death-defying stunts at the local swimming hole. Watching the display is a local beauty and rich property owner, Muriel Hammond, played by Brownie Vernon, who playfully ties knots in his clothes.

While Harland may be king of the kids, he is ostracised by the locals, who frown on him teaching children how to box, and are less than impressed with his interest in Muriel. A group of disbelievers are also trying to drive the church out of the area.

Hammond's devious guardian, Martin Giles, has the disgraced Harland sent to the city, where his fighting skills are put to the test when rescuing an elderly gentleman who has been robbed by a group of thugs. More skits, more fights, more chasing scenes through Paddington and Darlinghurst. And more stunts, including one where Snowy, just behind his actual family home, leaps from a road bridge, near St Vincents Hospital, landing on a van below, as part of the chase for the bad guys.

For his good deeds in Sydney, Harland is somehow rewarded with a posting to an outback town, which has been taken over by a group of outlaws. A touch of the Wild West hits Australia, until Harland attempts to start a church group in the town. Another chance meeting with his sweetheart, and Harland discovers that she has been kidnapped by the ultimate baddy – station overseer, Red Jack Braggan.

Depressed that he is a failed pastor, Harland becomes a station hand, has endless fight and chase scenes, but as expected rescues the damsel once again, the pair leaping to safety out of a stagecoach into a raging river below. A story full of holes, but alluring nonetheless because of its pure escapism.

All the planning for the movie coincided with yet another Snowy business venture. Suddenly Snowy was an expert in the theatrical arts and started using his gymnasium as an acting school. For ten lessons, at the meagre cost of three pounds and three shillings, Snowy was willing to show anyone how to be a movie star. The lessons included deportment, make-up, Grecian body culture, and possibly even the chance to appear in one of Snowy's blockbusters.

The advertisements for the course pushed truth to the limit. Snowy claimed that during several months in the United States he had worked with such celebrated stars as Charlie Chaplin and William S. Hart, where he 'acquired a very comprehensive knowledge of motion picture work in all its branches, which, combined with my experience in locally-made pictures, places me in a position to control every phase of the work'.

The sucker punch came when Snowy announced that opportunities were bound to appear for those 'who are ambitious to win fame on the screen', because he and Carroll were planning to make a series of films locally. With it came some ifs and buts though: 'I do not guarantee any pupil any position in these pictures, but if opportunity arises will endeavour to use their services.'

Snowy also called in the big guns to impress the students, with Lucas and Vernon attending one of the first lessons. Lucas's word of advice would have totally confused the aspirants. 'Let me impress upon you the following words: "Learn not to act." That may sound strange to you, but it is the secret of the art of screen-craft as far as acting is concerned. Perfect naturalness is one of the absolute essentials for the picture artist, and extravagant gesture has no use upon the screen.'

Lucas didn't have that problem with Snowy. The only extravagant gesture Snowy knew was whether to opt for the double somersault or pike when diving into the rockpool. All Lucas wanted Snowy to do was box, jump, dive and run from scene to scene. Snowy was always sprinting around too much to slow down to act, or even attempt to act. And in those few melancholy moments, where Snowy had to attempt some character acting, everything was forced or fake. Romantic scenes revolved around acting by numbers. If in doubt, Snowy, with his face caked in make-up, would throw a cheesy, near Vampirish, smile. When hovering around children, he appeared more like an uncomfortable predator, rather than a friendly guardian. So more running, more horse chases and another flashy uppercut to the jaw – his brother Fred again getting belted by his brother in a scene where one smack to the face was definitely not faked.

Lucas realised that he had to bring some acting expertise to the film and so slotted himself in the picture as the chief bad guy, where he could get rid of a lot of aggression and show that his skills existed on both sides of the camera.

Interior shots were staged at the Theatre Royal in the centre of Sydney, while the outdoor locations switched between Kangaroo Valley – where the Hampden Bridge was used for the final Snowy stunt when he jumps with Brownie Vernon from the coach into the river – and Gunnedah, the film crew returning to Eric Mackellar's property. This time the softener was that Eric's younger brother, Malcolm, was given a screen role as the station foreman, inevitably helping Snowy rescue the damsel.

While Lucas worked quickly and demanded high standards from his staff, he soon discovered that he and Snowy had to overcome several unexpected problems. During their time in Gunnedah, the area was in drought, forcing the crew to bring in fodder for 150 horses because of a shortage of grass. That added 225 pounds to the bill.

Snowy was also a casualty during one scene where he had to ride a wild buckjumper. He had successfully stayed on for half a minute, before the horse swerved and crashed into a tree. Snowy was hurled into the trunk, while the horse fell into a heap a metre away. Lucas rushed to the scene to find Snowy unconscious, his nose badly broken, shoulder dislocated and two ribs fractured. A splash of water revived Snowy. He painfully rose to his feet, insisting on finishing the scene before heading to the doctor. He was back on set, strapped up and ready to go, a few hours later.

Just as dangerous were Snowy's sequence of dives, where he flung himself from a cliff top more than 20 metres above a rockpool, which was little more than a metre deep. Several times Snowy crashed into the bottom, but waited until the cameras were off before screaming in anguish.

There were also dramas on the other side of the camera. In a radical manoeuvre, each scene was simultaneously shot by three different cameras, which had the desired effect of dramatically improving the quality of the action scenes and adding drama to Snowy's stunts. And for the first time on an Australian film, light reflectors were used, while three different light screens – silver, gold and blue – were involved in reflecting the sun. All helped to improve the lighting effects.

Assisting Doerrer were several Australian cameramen, including the exceptional Alfred Burne. 'The American cameraman was supposed to supply his own camera,' Burne said in an interview in 1966 conducted by the National Film Archives, 'but all he brought out was a small wooden box. He did no good with it. He then hired a Pathe similar to mine and filmed about 3,000 feet at Kangaroo Valley which was all fogged.

'When I came along with another Pathe he wouldn't have anything to do with it. They eventually got hold of a Bell and Howell camera, the only one in Australia, at 10 pound a week. They also paid the salary of Tas Higgins to look after it at 10 pound a week.'

Burne's most vivid memory was of Snowy's stunts.

'Snowy was a great stuntman. He never had a fill-in,' Burne said.

'One of his stunts was diving off the top of a coach off the Kangaroo Valley bridge with a dummy on his back. The other one was where I was involved in a bit of a stunt, when he built a platform on the front of his car.

'I had to rig up the camera and with my back to wherever we were going, he would be doing about 60 mph, and I'd just be hoping that he'd pull up steady, otherwise I would go clean off the car with everything. Another of his stunts was that he dived overboard from the wharf at Balmoral. He also jumped off a horse onto a train and then into a river.

'For that scene we hired a train from Campbelltown to Camden, where Snowy raced the horse along the tracks, jumped off the horse and onto the train. He was excellent, and never worried about what happened.'

Snowy's performance soon earnt the praise of Lucas.

'I have worked with Fairbanks and Walsh in the movies in America,' said Lucas, 'but I can say without fear of contradiction that Snowy Baker can enact stunts which beats even the best they can put over. I have never known Mr Baker to lie down on even the most hazardous risk. And, as a matter of fact, he had me jumping because of his anxiety to do what looked to me the impossible.

'He did it, but I tell you I held my breath while he was on the job, and gave a mighty sigh of relief when the stunt was finished. You know there are some risks which even the hardest picture director won't allow his stars to make.'

Snowy also had an important prop by his side during the filming of *The Man from Kangaroo*. Involved in several of his stunts was his favoured horse 'Boomerang', which had been bred by one of Snowy's Irish uncles on the family estate in Limerick. As a three-year-old, Boomerang had performed with credit in Irish steeplechase events, before being presented to Snowy by the family as a gift. Snowy immediately shipped Boomerang to Australia, knowing that he could make him a star.

Predictably, in a bid to be perceived as the biggest star of all, Snowy couldn't help himself. In a full page advertisement in *The Picture Show*, in an obvious pitch for financial backing and broader film distribution, Snowy Baker gave 'an account of himself'.

Snowy explained that 'we are in the throes of producing the greatest Motion Picture that has yet been credited to Australian brains and effort . . . Can't stay long, as I am wanted back at Kangaroo Valley, where Mr Wilfred Lucas is waiting to "shoot up" some more scenes.

'Mr Lucas says I am a better stunt actor than anyone living. He ought to know. Anyway, he has had me leaping from crag to crag, diving hundreds of feet into roaring chasms, saving heroines – by the hundreds it seems to me – fighting for my life – and these toughs Wilfred picks out are the real thing. They come at me with murder in their eyes. I have got to beat 'em up. I do! Because I know that the crank of the camera is relentlessly grinding on and on, and every punch I "get home" will be recorded on the screen for you.'

It was all part of Snowy and Lucas's pitch that 'Australia shall be a great motion picture centre'.

Even E.J. Carroll got in on the act, also taking out a full page advertisement in *The Picture Show* to express his intentions. These included opening the 'doors of opportunity to Australian talent' and 'to Australianise motion pictures as against the avowed Americanisation of the industry'. Carroll stressed that Australia had to realise 'that we, too, have sufficient romance in this country to entertain ourselves and the world'.

However the more independent critics were not entirely convinced. While *The Man from Kangaroo* was a local commercial success, others had their doubts about the quality of the finished product. Some believed it wasn't Australian enough.

The *Sydney Mail* complained: 'It seems a pity that so much Americanism should be injected into films that are advertised as purely Australian. In "The Man from Kangaroo", for instance, apart from the fact that the scenes have been taken on Australian soil, and that the leading man, Snowy Baker, is an Australian, there is nothing in it that is not steeped in Americanism.'

The Bulletin found that 'the frequency of his [Snowy's] marvels tends to make him monotonous'. In another article, the passionately pro-Australian *Bulletin* added: 'Uncle Sam gets in his dirty work, and the Australian story becomes starred and striped.' *The Bulletin*'s critic, who used the pen name 'Norbell', said that a group of stockhands storming a church meeting 'simply couldn't happen in Australia. In our backblocks the parson is as inevitable as the drought. Then the explanatory stuff thrown on the screen makes the rouseabouts talk like cowboys in a Bill Hart eruption. Also the heroine goes for a stroll in "the woods". But what else could you expect, Brownie Vernon was imported from the Fillum's Own Country to impart the correct Deadwood Gulch atmosphere to this Australian picture. When will we get an Australian film? Barring the "Bloke" pictures, they all have the flavour of chewing gum.'

Smith's Weekly thought the movie 'shows that picture-production in this country is making giant strides' adding that they hoped to see Brownie Vernon 'in a better part'. 'The picture is quite well played, and the interest is sustained until Mr Baker starts to ride, which he does ad nauseum, and with an unnecessary amount of violence.'

The Sun thought Snowy 'as an actor, pure and simple, has considerable headway yet to make'. However the outdoor scenes were 'well photographed and save for such Americanisms as the parson drive and the cattle rustling are typical of Australian country life.

'Here and there are traces of the director's want of knowledge of Australian conditions. On the other hand his anxiety to conform as far as possible to local conditions is none the less obvious.

'There is none of that lassoing and gunplay which makes Western drama of America so picturesque and snappy. If Australia is to develop a Western drama of its own some substitute may have to be found for those handy adjuncts to picturemaking. Athletic stunts are of transitory interest. But a strong and appealing story, brightly acted and pictured, is an abiding delight.'

Eighty years on, *The Man from Kangaroo*, the only Baker movie available on video, holds up well. Snowy cannot act, but his stunts are impressive. The storyline is good enough to hold your attention for well over 70 minutes. But it is the calibre of the camerawork, using brightness and shadows to great effect, which gives the movie a special quality and makes it one of the most important early Australian films. Several scenes, including the lovers' moon-lit encounter atop a brick wall, are as well shot as anything from the silent film era. Snowy's chase through the back alleys of inner Sydney, including his dramatic leap from a bridge, is also cleverly filmed, using inter-cutting of shots to great effect. The gamble to bring in American talent worked, giving the movie a certain class and style. And as effective in that area was the use of Syd Nicholls, the cartoon creator of Fatty Finn, who designed the titles.

The Man from Kangaroo justifies being called an early Australian cinema classic. Yet the Carroll–Baker team, with Lucas and Meredyth tagging along, had no time to ponder past efforts. As soon as *The Man from Kangaroo* was in the can, they were off to make another movie. Time was tight.

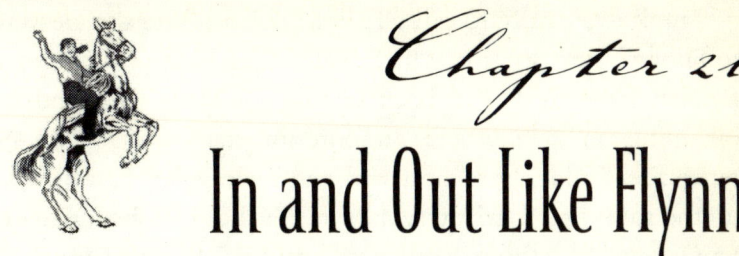

Chapter 21

In and Out Like Flynn

SNOWY'S GYMNASIUM ATTRACTED ALL TYPES. THERE WERE THOSE AFTER THE body beautiful, and others out to stimulate the mind through a physical diversion. So many were attracted by Snowy's motto, which hung in a frame over the main door – 'A clean mind in a clean body.'

The gymnasium was not just confined to the athletic, the physically minded, or the he-men. Amongst the heaving, perspiring bodies were numerous literary figures, familiar names from the stage, and even the odd aspiring movie star hoping to be spotted by the latest matinee idol – Snowy.

It was an eclectic mix, one early regular being Ion Idriess, well before he became a respected and admired writer boasting more than 40 books. About to head off for a stint prospecting for opals in Lightning Ridge, and then on to do a bit of rabbit-exterminating and boundary riding, Idriess wanted to make sure his body was ready for the grind.

There was also a small Queenslander who became a daily visitor, usually demanding that Frank Baker, who was acting as one of the chief instructors, face him in the ring for a vigorous three rounder. He was Charles Chauvel.

Before, during and after the fights, the lad, known only as 'Charlie' in the gymnasium, would prod Frank about introducing him to his brother, explaining how fascinated he was with the film industry, and asking if there was any chance of getting him a job with the Carroll–Baker Company.

As Snowy was here, there and everywhere except at his gymnasium, Frank, to keep this little pest at bay, kept replying, 'Sure, sure, sure, I'll talk to Snowy. I'll get back to you.'

Frank eventually forgot all about it, until one day he was beckoned to Snowy's new studios, which were being built at Waverley, in Sydney's Eastern Suburbs. It had been raining for three days, and the grounds, including an area where an outdoor stage was to be built, was a quagmire. Suddenly a 'drenched and bedraggled figure' was staggering up the submerged driveway, carrying 'a shoulder-borne load of timber'. Frank saw something familiar in the half-drowned figure. It was that inquisitive little Queenslander from the gym.

'For the love of Pete,' Frank called out. 'What the hell are you doing out there? Drop that damn wood and get in here out of the rain.'

The dripping figure joined him under a half broken piece of awning. 'What the devil do you think you're doing out in that rain and mud?'

'My job,' he exclaimed with a broad grin.

'What do you mean, your job?'

'Well . . . you didn't do anything about getting me a job in the company, so this morning I noticed an ad in the *Herald* asking for labourers to apply at the Carroll–Baker Studio. So I gave it a go, and made it.'

'Righto, you win,' Frank grunted with resignation. 'I'll take you in to see the Production Manager. But first let us get you in some dry clobber from the wardrobe.'

A few minutes later, the labourer was dressed in a flaming red Crimean shirt, a mounted trooper's jacket, moleskin breeches and high-topped boots. He followed Frank into the Production Manager's office.

'This is an old pal of mine, Charlie Chauvel. I'd appreciate it if you can find him a job with the company.'

The Production Manager scratched his chin as he stared at this strange array in front of his desk.

'Can you ride a horse?'

'Strewth,' Frank started, 'He was born with a saddle under his backside, and reins in his hands.'

'Well that's good. We need someone to help Jim Warwick take that Cobb and Co coach up to the Kangaroo Valley location. So I guess you're hired Mister Chauvel. And I hope you'll enjoy being in the movies.'

Thus began the illustrious career of one of Australia's most important cinema figures who directed some of this country's best-known films including *In the Wake of the Bounty*, where Chauvel discovered Errol Flynn, *Forty Thousand Horseman*, *Jedda* and *The Rats of Tobruk*.

Frank Baker was reticent to originally help Chauvel because of his relationship with his uncle, General Sir Harry Chauvel, the Commander of the Desert Mounted Corps, whom he had served under during World War I.

Frank Baker knew that Chauvel was from strong colonial pioneer stock and didn't think he should be devoting himself to the movie business, which he considered at the time to be 'a hazardous gamble'.

'So I gave him no encouragement, and helped him not one iota.

'But I failed to understand Charles Chauvel's grim determination, and the almost fanatical desire to learn the why's and wherefores of the film medium. I would later learn that Charles was governed by two mistresses. One the cinema. The other his beloved great land of Australia.'

Then still very much a dogsbody, Chauvel drove the coach to Kangaroo Valley, introducing himself to Snowy.

'Where in the world could you fit in, young man?' Snowy asked.

'Horses,' said the ever determined Chauvel. 'You will be using horses, and I know all about them and can ride.'

Snowy thought the best way to discourage the overzealous Queenslander was to offer him a miserable job – that of horse and stable hand. But Chauvel immediately accepted, knowing that his foot was at last through the door. He worked on the final stages of *The Man from Kangaroo* as a general assistant and horse handler, before getting an on-screen role for Carroll–Baker's next movie extravaganza – *The Shadow of Lightning Ridge*.

Snowy worked Chauvel hard, especially in ensuring that the Cobb and Co coaches were at the right location at the right time. This often meant driving at night and every now and then sleeping under the coach. If the following day was overcast, making filming impossible, while the actors trooped home Chauvel would have to find backyard accommodation for the horses, coach and himself.

But as his wife Elsa Chauvel wrote in *My Life with Charles Chauvel*: 'Nothing that he did for Snowy was a task. Snowy was his idol, and remained a strong factor and influence throughout his life.'

Chauvel was the most fascinated of the on-the-set watchers, learning so many of the tricks and pitfalls from Snowy and Lucas. As well, he was overwhelmed by Snowy's obsession with wanting to turn the Australian movie industry into a world phenomena.

The first stage was movies aimed at an international market. The second was to build a studio in Sydney to fulfil the company's dreams.

The trio of Baker, Carroll and Lucas, who had convinced themselves that they should produce a quota of eight films per year, had been looking around for vacant property, close to Sydney, which could be turned into a venue where they could shoot both indoor and outdoor scenes, thus alleviating the costs involved in constantly searching for ideal locations outside the city.

They eventually found what they wanted on a hill above Waverley Oval. There stood a 28-room mansion, known as 'Palmerston', situated in the middle of five acres that included 'picturesque gardens, artificial lakes, rustic bridges, natural fernery and stately timber'. There were even waterfalls in the deeply wooded part of the property.

By the time shooting began on *The Shadow of Lightning Ridge*, parts of the mansion had been turned into interior studios, an outdoor stage was being constructed, and Boomerang even had his own paddock to graze in. Snowy boasted that every room had been fitted with 'special electric lights for picture-making', and that in time the facilities would be 'equal to anything of its kind in any part of the world'.

He was also just as proud that at last Sydney had its own little pocket of Hollywood. Still, travelling was required if *The Shadow of Lightning Ridge* was to have any sense of authenticity.

Bess Meredyth attempted to give their next film script a more worldly touch, even if the base was intensely Australian. The story revolves around a young Australian who is sent to England for his education and while there discovers that he is the illegitimate son of Sir Edward Marriott, whom he believes to have forsaken his mother.

After many adventures, including big game shooting in India and 'bronco busting' in America, he sails up Sydney Harbour on the trail of his supposed father. Seeking revenge, he becomes a bushranger, a mysterious outlaw known as 'The Shadow'. The Shadow trails Sir Edward everywhere, repeatedly robbing him, and even attempts to kidnap the famous thoroughbred horse, Warrigal, which is being sent by train to compete in the Melbourne Cup.

Then comes the romantic interest. Sir Edward's young fiancée, Dorothy, is kidnapped by another group of outlaws, and The Shadow comes to the rescue. Naturally The Shadow and Dorothy fall in love.

During all these escapades, Sir Edward recognises the familiar Marriott ring on The Shadow's finger, and realises that the bushranger is actually the heir to the family property. The Shadow is welcomed back into the fold, where Sir Edward convinces him that he is not The Shadow's father, but actually his uncle.

Realising that he has no hope of standing in between The Shadow and Dorothy, Sir Edward instead refocuses his love interest towards an old sweetheart, and everyone lives happily ever after.

The main reason for the over-the-top story was to give Snowy enough of an excuse to be even more outlandish with his stunt work. This time, insured for well over 5,000 pounds, Snowy exceeds himself, leaping from a galloping Boomerang onto a train, jumping Boomerang through the roof of a hut up on a mountain, riding him along a narrow log, negotiating tight ledges around a waterfall, and even fighting a guard in a horse's box. What made that last scene more tantalising was that the pair were rolling around on the floor of the box underneath the feet of the nervous horses, before The Shadow was able to escape with the Melbourne Cup favourite. There was even a scene where Snowy jumped Boomerang seven metres from the luggage van of the train into the Nepean River.

Snowy doted on Boomerang, explaining: 'The horse was the real star, anyway. He was a better actor than me, and it was he the public paid to see. He was amazing. He could, and would do anything you asked of him.'

While the interior shots were conducted at Palmerston, Chauvel and co found themselves transporting horses all over the Bulli Pass for the next Snowy stunt. Chauvel was in charge of 30 blood-horses, including four well-known racers, jumpers or show prize winners. Even though Chauvel had a special knack with horses, unlike his boss he couldn't admit that he was a 'horse whisperer'.

In one interview for *The Picture Show*, Snowy explained that he'd discovered from a family friend in Ireland what was involved in becoming a 'whisperer' – so that with the 'use of a few whispered words in a horse's ear and gentle handling they will quietly mount and ride an "outlaw" that would buck the saddle off with an ordinary rider on board'.

While in Ireland in 1907, Snowy had spent time with a member of the Brady family – a well-known 'whisperer'. *The Picture Show* gushed:

'Brady assured him that he [Snowy] had this "way wid" horses, and subsequent experiments proved the truth of his contention. Snowy had found this "way" of great assistance when persuading ordinary untrained animals to take headlong dives into water, or off moving trains.'

The gift apparently had its drawbacks. As Snowy was such a calming influence, well-known 'buckers' refused to play up when he was in the saddle. This forced Snowy to place a 'burr' under the saddle to irritate the horse into bucking and pigrooting.

Yet again the Australian crowds loved the action, and Snowy's eagerness to kill himself. In Perth, on opening night, film goers queued for nine hours outside The Palladium in the hope of getting a ticket. Audiences were as enthusiastic on the eastern seaboard.

However, the critics hated it.

Smith's Weekly led the charge by declaring that despite Shadow being marked with 'the Made in Australia sign ... the film is almost pure Yankee ... The entire population of the country town "tote guns" and wear cowboy hats. A foreigner, seeing this film, would picture Australia as a sort of Bill Hart's backyard.'

One reader wrote to *Smith's Weekly*: 'Snowy Baker's six-shooters make me laugh. I don't suggest arming him with boomerangs. But haven't I seen advertisements of his suggesting that he can use his fists.'

The Bulletin complained that the 'only Australian thing' in the movie 'is the setting'. 'The scenery is dinkum, but the story iself is a mixture of old melodrama and Wild West movie. Australia wants Australian films, and in spite of Snowy Baker's great athletic business, she will refuse to swallow "The Shadow" as the thing her soul cries for. Leading woman Brownie Vernon, also being American, adds nothing Australian to the picture. But the photography is excellent.'

Another *Bulletin* critic was as angered that 'the frantically Australian firm of Carroll's has given a boost to native girl actors by importing an Amurkan movie leading-lady to play Australian roles written for her by the firm's just-imported dyed-in-the-wool Amurkan scenario writer, Bess Meredith [sic]. One of these days the Australians will get annoyed enough to cut out of his visiting list the theatre that might and doesn't give Australia a lift.'

Even Raymond Longford fronted Lucas during this period, to get an explanation as to why he was so keen about Americanising Australian films. Lucas gave it all away by replying: 'If I want to get one of your

Aboriginals or natives in a picture, I am going to get him; and if I care to stick a few feathers on him, this is my business. I am looking after my home market, and am not worrying about the Australian end of it.'

Undeterred by the lack of critical or industry acclaim, Snowy and Lucas pushed on. Lucas, who apart from his hefty salary was wasting exorbitant amounts of the company's money on his own lavish lifestyle, even convinced Carroll–Baker that he should return home for several months, with the express purpose of buying 'up-to-date' equipment, and making 'arrangements with several other experienced film people to come to Australia'. The aim was to bring back another leading lady, as the Australian audiences were tiring of the limited talents of Brownie Vernon, who had been upstaged in *The Shadow of Lightning Ridge* by the young local J.C. Williamson actress Bernice Vere.

While the Carrolls were getting more and more concerned with how Lucas was bleeding the company, the American director gave himself a bit of breathing space when he returned to Sydney in June 1920.

He first made excuses for thinking and spending big. 'Of course we have to make pictures that will appeal to the outside world,' Lucas said. 'Australia represents only three per cent of the English speaking motion picture audience, so it would not pay in the long run to turn out films of local interest alone.

'Every year thousands of pounds of Australian money goes to America in payment for films. Well, I think it's up to all you Australians to see that some of that wealth is kept in your own land. The trouble is when you have to produce a picture cheaply, that audiences can't help contrasting it in their minds with some big imported film which has cost close on 100,000 pounds to make. Then, of course, they go away with a prejudice against the local product, not realising that the producer of the inferior film could have done better if he also had had unlimited money.

'I am expecting great things here though.

'I say without hesitation that we have at Waverley the most compact studio in the world, and we are going to show other countries what can be done in Australia.'

What could be done is that Lucas could rehash an old idea and bleed another movie out of it. Thus appeared his third Snowy Baker extravaganza entitled *The Jackeroo of Coolabong*.

While the Carrolls awaited news on whether *The Man from Kangaroo* and *The Shadow of Lightning Ridge* would be distributed throughout

America, they gave Bess Meredyth open rein to rewrite one of Snowy's previous movies – *The Lure of the Bush*.

Lucas and Meredyth probably knew their time with the Carrolls was up because the film was completed in just over a month. Not surprisingly, considering the speed involved, the storyline lacked complication.

This time, Snowy played an English toff who takes a job as a jackeroo on a cattle station. The station hands, including Chauvel, treats this supposedly effeminate character, who wanders around the property wearing a monocle and spats, with contempt. He is called 'dearie' and as *The Picture Show* explained: 'His clothing bespeaks Piccadilly, his vocabulary includes the newest words; his accent is decidedly polished.'

The toff eventually earns their respect when he is able to tame the station's most notorious buckjumper. The station manager beckons Snowy to travel with him to the city in the hope of convincing his daughter, who is working among the destitute in the slum areas, to return home with him.

However, by the time they arrive in the big smoke, the maiden has fallen into the hands of a gang of thieves. Yet again Snowy comes to the rescue, knocks over every member of the gang with his bare hands and 'romantic bliss is assured'.

In between are some madcap adventures, which include an extravagantly filmed kangaroo hunt and an encounter with 'wild' Aboriginals, where Snowy escapes underwater.

There was also one fatality. The film crew had returned to Gunnedah and during the shooting of the kangaroo hunt, Nellie Park, the daughter of a Narrabri doctor, was killed when she was thrown from her horse and dragged some distance.

Shooting was stopped for the day out of respect for a 'gallant horsewoman', but the next morning everything was back on schedule, with the Carrolls worried that an extra day's filming would bust the budget. *Everyone's* magazine even heartlessly suggested a dramatic moment was lost because 'the cameraman did not, as stated in an evening paper catch the full details of the incident' as he had forgotten to turn the camera on.

The film was obviously rushed, because even Snowy's biggest supporters were unimpressed when it was released. *The Picture Show*, which never said a harsh word about anyone, admitted that the Jackeroo was 'a worthwhile picture – not a great one, certainly'.

Snowy (hugging the donkey) with other members of the Uplifters club before a game of donkey polo.

Snowy *(left)* with Frank Garbutt, Hal Roach, Winslow Felix and Big Boy Williams at a Riviera polo match.

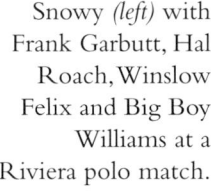

The Las Amigas polo quartet which won the US Championship in 1939. Joan Baker is second from left and Spencer Tracy's wife is at far right.

Charles Chauvel *(far left)* with Snowy, his step-daughter, Joan, and an Austrian fencing instructor in Hollywood.

Snowy fencing with his Los Angeles Athletic Club colleague, Professor Uyttenhove.

Snowy, in his Los Angeles Athletic Club garb, messing around with Duke Kahanamoku *(centre)* and Frank Beaurepaire.

(Photo: Author's collection)

A typical gathering of riders outside Snowy's bungalow, 'Gunyah', after solving a mock murder mystery devised by Snowy.

Snowy, with Ethel, at the Uplifters club in Los Angeles.
(Photo: Author's collection)

Movie poster for
The Sword of Valor
featuring Boomerang
the wonder horse.

Spencer Tracy and Snowy. (Photo: Author's collection)

The Riviera Country Club.

Snowy, official attaché to the Australian Olympic team in Los Angeles in 1932, was persuaded to be part of a riding exhibition on the polo ground during the Games. (Photo: Author's collection)

Snowy, on his final trip to Sydney in 1952, at a civic reception at the Sydney Town Hall with Deputy Premier R.J. Heffron *(left)* and Lord Mayor Ernie O'Dea.

Others didn't soften their blows about a movie which was extravagantly advertised under the tag – 'Kangaroo hunts! High dives! Wild blacks! and a bit of Sydney's underworld.'

The Picture Magazine said that while the film involved good photography and scenery, it was flawed by a 'weak and improbable story written around stunts for Snowy Baker, who as the dashing young hero looks old enough to be the heroine's father. Come off, Snowy!'

The Bulletin reviewer said he was tiring of Snowy's films because 'there is nothing so American as the Australian movie play.

'Instead of seeking to depict Australian life, the local producers in nine cases out of ten strain all the points to give a thing that is the living picture of Yankee Doodle. In the Baker film there was an unmistakable struggle after a Douglas Fairbanks effect, even to the overworked smile on the hero's face, and Snowy is not one who smiles easily and happily.

'Until Australian producers have one eye put out we shall not get good Australian film plays. The eye, to be sacrificed is the one they keep fixedly on "The Texas Steer" when trying to depict "the Australian merino".'

The movie also failed to attract the public, who were obviously tiring of yet another Snowy Baker stunt movie. Released in Sydney in October 1920, it failed to get an interstate release until well into the next year. The dream was starting to turn into a nightmare.

After all the grand dreams, reality hit when *The Picture Show* revealed in September 1920, before *The Jackeroo of Coolabong* was released, that the eight film a year scheme was over, and Lucas and Meredyth were on their way home to Los Angeles. The Carrolls had abruptly terminated their contracts.

Adding to the confusion was that at the time of the announcement E.J. Carroll was overseas as part of a 14-month venture through South Africa, England and America where he was the tour director for Scottish music hall entertainer, Harry Lauder. On his return to Sydney, Carroll said that he had arranged the English release of all three Carroll–Baker films, and also secured a contract for Snowy in America with the major American producer, William Selig. According to Carroll, Selig 'considers Snowy the finest athlete on the screen'.

The reasons for Lucas and Meredyth being sacked are manyfold, but the most glaring was that for some time the Carrolls and Snowy had been worried about the husband and wife's expensive habits, and not just on the film set. They lived the high life, and spent money, not always their own, extravagantly.

The Picture Show said euphemistically that 'the Australian firm found American methods of production too expensive, considering the result'.

They were simply taking too much money out of the company, for too small a return. As Chauvel caustically admitted many years later, the only thing he had learnt from the American visitors 'was how to spend money when you had it'.

Suddenly the Carrolls cut back their involvement in local films. Palmerston was handed over to Raymond Longford for local productions, and a short time later the Carrolls, after several more movies including one which lost more than 25,000 pounds, severed their ties with movie making. The Carroll–Baker Film venture disappeared as quickly as it had appeared.

But behind the scenes were several other major hurdles, some of which weren't revealed until the 1927 Royal Commission into the Australian Film Industry. Another important factor wasn't brought to light until many decades later.

Outside forces were trying to squeeze the Carrolls out, which included threats by Australasian Films that if they didn't leave the production field, they would terminate their overseas film supplies.

Australasian Films, a production and distribution company, were part of the dreaded 'combine', being in partnership with the exhibitor Union Theatres. The 'combine' were feared by many film-makers because of its pursuit to dominate the local industry.

Longford, who at that time had directed *The Sentimental Bloke* and *On Our Selection*, told the Royal Commission how he had talked to E.J. Carroll during a period when Snowy's partner was in hospital.

'He [Carroll] informed me that the outlook for local production was very dark,' Longford said. 'Their dealings, as owners of a chain of Queensland theatres [Birch Carroll Circuit], with the combine was unsatisfactory. He depended upon the "combine" for his supply of film, and if they were opposed to local production it would be quite impossible for him to continue as they were the source of his supplies. This blow was a very serious one to the industry.'

Dan Carroll also appeared before the Royal Commission, explaining the reasoning behind bringing Lucas and Meredyth to Australia, an expensive experiment which failed to make the company an international success. The Carrolls doubted the overseas value of movies like *The Sentimental Bloke*, *Ginger Mick* and the *Steele Rudd* movies, prompting them to bring in an American producer and scenario writer to make 'pictures which would be entirely cosmopolitan in their appeal'.

However Bess Meredyth, after spending days in the Mitchell Library, told the Carrolls that she was unable to get any great inspiration for local stories, because 'Australians had as yet not developed any really outstanding national trait or character'.

The only truly national subject around which a romantic theme could be worked was horse racing, but that was a waste of time because of a glut of English movies with that exact subject. The only remaining stories revolved around 'station and bush life'.

While believing *The Shadow of Lightning Ridge* was 'a very fine picture', comparing 'favourably with the American product of that time', they struck unexpected difficulties, both in Australia and abroad, in marketing their pictures.

Their initial success brought 'into the field in Australia, a flock of mushroom producers, numerous small syndicates with capital from 1,000 to 2,000 pound, who started out to make films. These films were released, but were of very poor quality and generally exceedingly low grade.'

Carroll argued that these movies saw Australian films regularly ridiculed, eventually affecting the earning power of their far superior product.

'Consequently, when we went to market our films in other countries, we found such an abnormal glut of pictures that the earnings of our films, although they compared favourably with other products, were infinitesimal.'

Carroll said in the end they abandoned picture production in Australia for several reasons, in particular a lack of local stories. Australian film also appeared out of date, because they were so behind in women's fashion, while the light in Australia could not compare with that in Lower California because there was a lack of variety of colour in Australia's natural foliage.

But it appears Carroll was not telling the entire truth.

While researching her landmark documentary on early Australian cinema, *The Passionate Industry*, historian and film-maker Joan Long dug up some dirt. Carroll–Baker had apparently been swindled out of thousands from a corporation, based in Chicago, which had been contracted to distribute Snowy's films in America and Europe. It was assumed that the films would net more than 25,000 pounds from America alone. However the Carrolls and Baker received virtually nothing.

The information was passed onto Joan Long from Snowy's brother, Frank, in a series of letters and a recorded interview in the early 1970s.

In his letters, Frank Baker revealed: 'E.J. Carroll and my brother put up considerable sums to finance the company. It is my view that the venture would have been more than assured as a financial success had it not been for the malfeasance of the American release company which had been contracted to handle the overseas release and exhibition of the pictures.

'The organisation and production costs necessary for the making of those films had been quite substantial. And, as you, no doubt, realize, could hardly be covered by the box-office receipts from local and Australian exhibitors. It was considered that these may barely cover the individual production costs of each picture.

'But it would depend on the success of the films in the world market to produce the necessary profit to continue the hoped for policy of long-range and continuous production of films, as was the original plan of the Baker-Carroll organization.

'However, the receipts from overseas bookings were disappointing and insufficient to carry out the original plan. As it would not be known for a further couple of years, "swindling" operations of the release company, had bled a very considerable share of the, known only to them, quite large and successful overseas profits into their own pockets from the pictures.

'But by the time that this was disclosed by the United States Federal authorities, it was too late.'

Baker said in the mid-1920s, the United States Federal authorities discovered, while instituting criminal proceedings against the Chicago agency, that they operated three books. One to show the Federal Income Tax Department. Another to show their trusting clients, complete with juggled figures. And the final set of books 'for their own eyes only, to show the true nature of things, and their own bloated and illegal profits.

'If they had been successful in the United States, the company would have continued,' Frank Baker said. 'But they thought "why throw money down the drain?" '

The Carrolls eventually gave in, instead devoting themselves to the development of a chain of theatres throughout Queensland. Palmerston was sold, redeveloped and turned into several nondescript blocks of units.

But Snowy hadn't quite thrown up the surrender flag just yet. He still believed he could recoup some of that lost American money. Within days he was following Lucas and Meredyth to Hollywood.

Chapter 22

Tom Mix Mark Two

SNOWY'S MOVE TO HOLLYWOOD IN AUGUST 1920 WAS NO HALF-HEARTED measure. He packed up the family, Ethel, Joan and Margaret all highly excited about their move to Tinseltown. Ethel, Joan and Margaret had all been tantalised by their brush with the film-making industry, and the thought of their father making good in Hollywood was the stuff of dreams.

Snowy organised his brother Harold to replace him as boxing scribe for *The Evening News*, convinced Fred and Frank to take a larger role in the running of the gymnasium, and was off. He never lived in Australia again. The stigma of being blamed for Les Darcy's death had hurt immensely. He had grown tired of being abused by strangers on Sydney streets, believing he was an innocent victim of the pro-Darcy brigade. Even if the evidence was weighted heavily against him, Snowy still thought he was wrongly maligned. He honestly thought he helped rather than hindered Darcy. Ridiculously though, he refused to accept any guilt over the issue.

Snowy treated his inability to keep the Stadium's doors open while he was in charge as a personal failing. And he knew that lucrative money-making opportunities in Australia were starting to dry up. He had exhausted every avenue and realised the only way out of the quagmire was to think even bigger. Go to a larger territory and start afresh.

The lure was the contract E.J. Carroll had secured with William Selig, which involved Snowy performing his stunts in a string of American movies, as well as acting in a similar vein to that in his Australian movies – the hero who always rescues the damsel in distress. The contract was for 12 months, with a five-year option if he decided not to return to Australia.

The seriousness of the Snowy venture was shown in a snippet in *The Picture Show* in December 1920, which said that the production of a 30,000 pound Selig and Fork movie was being delayed until the arrival of his faithful grey, Boomerang, who was being shipped across under the care of a groom.

Hollywood looked upon Snowy as an alternative to Tom Mix and Douglas Fairbanks. But not without some required changes. The first was a change of name. Reg Baker was a bit like Archie Leach. Reg and Archie weren't exactly powerful names. Snowy quickly became known around the Hollywood backblocks as Rex Baker, and was billed in the local press as 'the millionaire sportsman'. The second requirement was finetuning and improving on several of his acts. To be a competent cowboy, he had to be proficient at rope-spinning and stockwhip cracking, prompting the studio to call in Will Rogers, the renowned American rustic humorist and Oklahoma cowboy, to teach him the tricks. Snowy and Rogers were soon inseparable friends.

Apart from working in local productions, Snowy involved himself in preparing several of his Australian films for American release. With the aid of the Selig production team, the pictures were re-cut, re-constructed and given new subtitles. They were also given new titles. *The Man from Kangaroo* appeared on Broadway as *The Better Man* and *The Jackeroo of Coolabong* became known as *The Fighting Breed*.

With the changes came favourable reviews, *The American Motion Picture News* describing *The Better Man* as 'a picture which is far above the average of the ordinary Western . . . Baker will not need to take a back seat for any American star. Blessed with magnetism, possessing a million dollar smile, and an adaptability for any kind of hazardous work, he is the kind of stuff from which stars – real stars are made.'

But back at home, *The Bulletin* kept it all in perspective by caustically commenting that Baker had 'an unscrupulous enemy – the man who told him he could act'.

Despite his obvious inabilities in front of the camera, Snowy was soon making inroads. No-one could underestimate his drive and commitment, and his refusal to give up. He was receiving minor parts in B-grade movies, but more importantly was ingratiating himself with the Hollywood high rollers. From his boxing promotion days, he knew that networking was imperative, and if that meant spending exorbitant amounts of money to make sure you got photographed next to someone important, so be it.

Snowy was writing back to Australia about incredible dinner parties he and his wife had organised, under the theme 'Hail, Australia, land of beauty, sovereign of the Southern Seas'. He must have immediately been a curiosity item, because among those seen at his 'happy parties at the famous Sunset Inn' were Tom Mix, leading lady Pauline Frederick and Hal Roach, the director who was heavily involved with Laurel and Hardy, and comedian Harold Lloyd. To emphasise the Australian theme, Snowy would drive around Hollywood in the latest shiny automobile with a garish silver kangaroo mascot on the hood. Snowy wasn't the only Australian in Hollywood, as there were a smattering of 'Colonials' working in the studios including Snub Pollard, Sylvia Braemer, Louise Lovely, Enid Bennett and Clyde Cook plus directors Rupert Julian and Alfred Goulding. But Snowy was eager to turn himself into a one-off. He knew that to be recognised among the thousands of aspirants you had to have some sort of gimmick.

Snowy knew the right clubs to join and was immediately at the front door of the Los Angeles Athletic Club (LAAC) seeking membership. Anyone who was anyone in Los Angeles was involved with the city's first private club, its membership including Mary Pickford, Harold Lloyd and Johnny Weismuller. By the early 1920s, the LAAC was regarded as the 'quintessential sports club in America', boasting the country's most extensive sporting facilities and a membership list that incorporated the best-known names in American sport and business.

Al Jolson always stayed at the LAAC when in town. Charlie Chaplin, delighted by its fastidiousness in protecting the privacy of its members, lived at the club for long periods in one of the 134 'sunlit guest rooms' of the grand 12-storey building, noted for its elegant decor and rich furnishings. Chaplin explained: 'There was a camaraderie about the club which even the declaration of the First World War did not disturb. The LAAC was a centre where the elite of local society and business gathered at the cocktail hour. It was like a foreign settlement. A young man, a bit player, used to sit around the lounge – a lonely fellow named Valentino who had come to Hollywood to try his luck but was not doing very well. I did not see Valentino again for a year or so, in the interim he jumped to stardom.'

With a guest list that included William Randolph Hearst, Jack London, George S. Patton and World War I flying ace Eddy Rickenbacker, it was definitely the place to go if you wanted to get to know the who's who of Hollywood. At one banquet, aviation pioneer Glenn Martin was stunned to find his early biplane being used as a dining table in one of the banquet rooms.

The Athletic Club boasted state-of-the-art gymnasium facilities, immaculate Turkish baths, top-quality sporting facilities and an intensive fitness programme. It was also the first building in Southern California to have a swimming pool on an upper floor. Among its first lifeguards was famed Hawaiian swimmer Duke Kahanamoku, who was instrumental in introducing surfing to Australia. On the roof was a 'Sky-High Nine Hole Golf Course' where members could play on an 'undulating putting green of billiard cloth' between hills and hollows made out of modelling clay, alongside driving nets. The gymnasium also had an electronic baseball scoreboard, so that members could train and be right up to date with the major league games around the country.

Snowy's athletic prowess quickly became known, especially as he showed off his Olympic silver medal at the interview, and he was immediately made a member. He was soon telling all how he had ensured Australia won the LAAC 'international' handball championship, beating Harold Lloyd and Buster Keaton along the way.

And as one Australian visitor, Jack O'Brien, wrote to *The Picture Show* after a sojourn in Tinseltown: 'Snowy Baker is certainly making his presence known here. While I am writing this letter in the Los Angeles Athletic Club, Snowy is up in the gymnasium, cracking good old Australian stock-whips, and the sound from them echoes right through the club. Snowy is very popular over here, and is connected with various kinds of functions.'

Whenever he could Snowy would stay at the Athletic Club, constantly fascinated by who he bumped into. 'Early every morning during one visit, I noticed a small, unobtrusive young fellow with a script or two tucked under his arm,' Snowy said. 'The office clerk told me he was trying to break into the movies with his scenarios.'

It was Darryl Zanuck, who went on to head 20th Century Fox.

While awaiting Boomerang's arrival, so he could work on his first major American release *Sleeping Acres*, Snowy joined a local polo club, heading a team that comprised Tom Mix, Douglas Fairbanks and George Walsh, and for a year they were unbeatable.

He was wasting no time in palling around with the Hollywood heavyweights. But even the ever-confident Snowy had to admit in his quieter moments that breaking into the Hollywood market was an onerous chore. He hinted at it in a letter printed by *Everyone's* magazine in September 1921. 'Many letters reach me, by every Australian mail, from boys and girls who wish to come to Los Angeles and get into the movie business.

'Many of the writers have no practical experience at all. My answer to the lot of them is – Don't. Stay away from here unless you can afford to make the trip a holiday one. Then if you are fortunate in breaking into the movies, so much the better. There are thousands, aye, many thousands, just like those who write to me; they come from all parts of the world, including the USA, and their letters are all couched in similar terms.

'The disappointments, heartaches and ultimate stranding of a majority of these misguided people are appalling. You have no idea of the great numbers of aspirants in this city who are starving, or next door to it!'

Snowy wasn't exactly starving, but he soon discovered that he had to diversify while waiting for the movie roles to come. He joined the Orpheum vaudeville circuit and found able allies to help him in his hair-raising act – two Australians who had also arrived in Hollywood with the highest of hopes, Charlie Chauvel and Snowy's younger brother Frank.

After getting a taste of movie making while working on several of Snowy's films, Chauvel was convinced that the movie business was for him. And like Snowy, he knew the only way he was going to learn was to head to movie mecca. In early 1922, Chauvel made a snap decision to follow Snowy to the States. For months Chauvel survived on odd jobs, including helping Snowy in his vaudeville act. Snowy's performance involved whip cracking, stunt horse riding, demonstrating the punches with which various champions had won their world heavyweight titles, and fencing against his step-daughter Joan. Snowy and Joan had become very close, mainly because of their similarly strong sporting interests. Joan was as avid about horses as Snowy, while her keenness to try out fencing soon gave her step-father a willing and more than competent competitor. He didn't hold back on Joan. And Joan didn't hold back on her step-father. Many of their fencing duels were tense, unforgiving encounters.

The highlight of the vaudeville show was Snowy's feats of skill with the stockwhip. Most importantly for the act Snowy needed to find someone with absolute faith in him to be his prop for the famous 'Sydney Flash' trick. Chauvel responded, gladly putting a glowing cigarette in his mouth and standing to attention before Snowy whipped it from his mouth. It always drew the biggest cheer of the night.

Renowned American boxing writer, Nat Fleischer, was in the audience one evening and recalled: 'It was back in 1922 when I was sports editor of the *New York Telegram* that I first met Snowy. I was in California with several newspaper men, Tom Sharkey and James J. Jeffries, and had been invited to the Golden Gate Theatre, where Snowy's act was booked.

'I had visions that Snowy had come to America to promote fights in opposition to Coffroth, Carey and Rickard, but I learned he had no such intentions. Watching his act, I was particularly struck with the fencing and boxing of Snowy's 15-year-old niece [sic] Joan.

'Sharkey, beaming with delight at her skill, remarked: "I'd hate to be the young fellow who tries to give her any Blarney. Nor would I like to have Snowy get after me with one of his fourteen foot long whips."

'Tom was referring to the skill with which Baker cut a cigarette out of a fellow's mouth with a whip that long, a stage performance that drew rounds of applause.'

Another time, at the Artists' Ball held at the plush Ambassador Hotel, where Tom Mix was master of ceremonies, Snowy convinced Chauvel to hold a lighted candle on his head and a cigarette in his mouth. Then he cracked them both out. 'Charlie was much braver than I would be under the same circumstances, and he did not have any life insurance policy, either,' Snowy wrote home.

Chauvel eventually found casual work in the movies, including acting as an extra in western horse operas, forcing Snowy to find a replacement. Frank Baker arrived at the right time.

However, Frank didn't find the 'Sydney Flash' trick so appealing. One night, Snowy was extremely nervous as there were many notable cowboys and Hollywood agents in the crowd watching his act to see whether it could be incorporated into any future films.

With a hand unusually unsteady, Snowy ended the act with the usual cigarette trick, but was slightly off-line. He instead collected the tip of Frank's nose. Blood spurted everywhere. Frank collapsed onto the stage. The curtains were drawn. But the crowd thought it was all part of the act, cheering uproariously.

When he'd recovered a little, behind the curtain a screeching Frank chased his brother out the stage door exit, bellowing that he would get his revenge.

Frank had taken a more unusual route than either Snowy or Chauvel to get to Hollywood. After the collapse of Carroll–Baker Films, Frank said to himself: 'To heck with it, I have to get out of civilisation.' He bought himself an old schooner, a camera, film, books, artists' materials, and for the next two and a half years 'wandered around the South Pacific' writing and filming.

Eventually Frank found himself in Samoa, where one night as special guest of the American Naval Governor, the subject of film making was brought up. The Governor asked Frank if he knew of the silent movie director Francis Ford. Frank replied that he hadn't met him, but that he knew and admired his work. The Governor told him that Ford was 'just down the coast, looking for locations for a movie, and had taken ill with rheumatic fever'. Frank went to see him and immediately struck up a close friendship, which saw him accompany Ford back to America. On the long trip the pair decided to join forces, agreeing to make movies and serials as part of a small collective. Moving into the Los Angeles Athletic Club when he arrived in the United States, Frank was told by Francis there was someone he wanted him to meet.

Frank's first meal in the United States was at the home of Francis's younger brother, John Ford, another film man, who at the time was taking his first steps towards becoming one of the world's most influential movie directors.

'In those days he'd bleed you dry,' Frank recalled of his first meeting with John Ford. 'He'd talk to you and talk to you, and suddenly you'd find half of what you've said appear in the picture that he's making.'

Frank treaded warily around John Ford, and in between getting cigarettes whipped out of his mouth, stuck closer to Francis, whipping out five feature films and three 12-episode serials over the next three years. The movies and serials included such ripsnorters as *The Diamond Bandit* and *Lash of the Whip*.

'We did the whole damn lot, everything, right from writing the stories, all the advance work, shooting them, acting in them, cutting the picture, doing the titles, and shipping it to the release company. Francis and I took turns in writing the stories. The only thing that we had done outside was processing the pictures. The cameraman would be in as an actor, and I'd grind the camera. Francis would be the character leads, and one or two of us would be capable of handling the direction. The whole damn thing. The leading lady and everybody did at least five jobs.'

Snowy's movie moments also began to happen. The roles didn't vary much, Snowy usually required to be the hero on the white horse rescuing anyone who was in trouble. One of his most interesting movies was *His Last Race*, which was reputed to be the first 'all-star' production where every member of a large cast, which included Gladys Brockwell, William Scott, Pauline Starke and Harry Depp, had star billing. That included Boomerang, who received as much publicity as the rest.

'Whoever was production manager of that film pulled a very fast one,' said Frank, who played a minor role in *His Last Race*. 'In those days actors between pictures were offered so much for a day's work. As a lot of the stars did not have definite contracts with any company, those making "His Last Race" were able to get all these names, so that every role was played by a major star. Nonetheless to keep costs down, they only got one day's work, where the directors worked the skin off them. But it still a picture of all stars.'

The 57-minute film is yet another love-struck melodrama. Snowy, played a character called Richard Carleton who is in love with Mary (Gladys Brockwell). However Mary is lured away by a romantic rival. To overcome the hurt of losing Mary, Carleton retreats to the mountains, where he runs a health resort. One day, Mary, now a widow, arrives at the resort, hoping to restore her young son's health. While Snowy and Mary renew their relationship, a group of crooks plan to steal Carleton's horse, Mankiller, who has just been entered in a thoroughbred race. Somehow in the one breath, Carleton is able to win Mary's hand and get Mankiller to the track on time to win the big race.

In *Sleeping Acre*, Snowy was involved in a cowboy quickie, where he and Boomerang were decked out in beaded suiting, allegedly made by the chief of the Sioux Indians, 'Sitting Bull'. The suiting was insured for 1,000 pounds – Snowy and Boomerang were insured at a lower rate.

Boomerang was used heavily in promotion, in particular for *The Sword of Valor*. In movie halls and advertising hoardings, this 1924 Phil Goldstone production was promoted through an impressive, large, classical poster, which had an artist's impression of Snowy atop a leaping Boomerang. The poster states that Snowy heads a 'stellar cast including Boomerang the wonder horse'.

The poster was far simpler than the movie, where Snowy was cast as Captain Grant Lee Brooks of the American legation in Madrid, who was on his way to the French Riviera 'for a well earned holiday'. At the same time, a Spanish don takes his daughter to the same area in the hope of finding a husband for her. The captain and the daughter meet at a party, disappear to a nearby beach and naturally fall in love, but not before he saves her from drowning.

The Spanish don is distressed, because he has suddenly promised his daughter to a wealthy cad. Adding to the confusion is a third man, Roderigo the gypsy, who is also in love with the daughter. Undeterred Snowy pursues the woman he loves, arriving at the family home, only to be met by the angry father, a distressed gypsy, and an esctatic daughter, who exclaims: 'There are those here who will not be over-cordial, but your coming brings to me only great happiness.'

A short time later, Snowy is duelling a Frenchman in a sword fight, while the gypsy appears on the scene wanting to 'rid himself of the hated American'. While trying to shoot Snowy, he instead kills his opponent. Understandably the gypsy flees. Along the way to his hide-out, the gypsy kidnaps the daughter, taking her up into the mountains.

Snowy is on the chase, finds the gypsy, who produces a knife and starts to attack him. Not for long though, because during the scuffle the gypsy falls off the cliff. Now the Spanish don is esctatic that Snowy has saved his daughter.

'For a second time,' the Spanish don says, 'you have done me a service that I, myself, cannot repay.'

On the screen appears: 'The Sword of Valor was ever the right hand of romance. Yet who will say that bright eyes have not pierced more hearts.'

Snowy and the daughter look into each other's eyes.

They embrace.

They kiss.

The End.

It was hard to follow that one up, but as ever Snowy did with another Phil Goldstone extravaganza, *The Empire Builders*. This time Snowy is in Africa as Captain William Ballard of the Territorials who is sent to make a treaty with the natives. Not surprisingly he meets resistance from the Boers. After the usual fights, horse chases and rescues, Snowy 'wins the natives over to the British way of life, and gets the girl'.

Snowy was even able to show off some of his in-the-ring prowess in *Fighter's Paradise* where he plays a small town jerk who resembles the famous fighter, Cyclone Carter. Constantly ridiculed, he is eventually forced into a fight where he is knocked about badly. However a blow to the head turns Snowy into a fighting machine. You know the rest . . . he becomes the hero and the darling of the girl he has always loved, but had been snubbed by until now.

From there Snowy moved straight onto military melodrama in *The White Panther* where as Major Bruce Wainright, he rescues the daughter of a British governor who rules over an Indian province. With the help of his horse, now called 'White Panther', he risks his life to save the damsel in distress.

Snowy even worked with Frank in one film. While Frank had a starring role in *The Bushranger*, Snowy was the technical director for a film described as 'a romance of Australia'. The slang ran wild, with New Zealanders described as 'Pig Islanders'. They retaliated by calling Australians 'Cornstalkers' or 'Banana Sliders'. An Englishman in Australia was called a 'pomegranate' and was usually referred to as a 'Blinking Pommie'.

The American audiences were astounded to see a tramp called a 'sundowner', his blanket roll a 'Matilda', while carrying it on the road was described as 'Waltzing Matilda'. Add some boomerang throwing and bullwhip fighting and the locals were impressed.

Not so *The Bulletin* when the film appeared for a brief period in Australia. 'Nothing as farcical in the way of films has been produced in Australia as "The Bushranger". Hollywood's attempt to put Australia in the pitchers.'

The Bulletin said that Snowy had 'forgotten all about Australia, and his "ranger" is merely a Wild West bad man. There is a general prevalence of unconceiled revolvers, but the stockwhip replaces the lasso, and as a bit of local color the boomerang soars through the picture, landing, amongst other places, in a stately ballroom, which has apparently wandered into the bush for an experience of the simple life.'

Snowy couldn't win. Some Australian authorities weren't prepared to forgive Snowy for selling out. And to add to the despair, the movie roles in Hollywood began to dry up.

Just as Snowy had discovered in Australia, there are only so many stories you can base around a person who can't act, but can ride horses, crack a whip and perform wild stunts. Slowly, but surely, the movie studios stopped contacting the Baker household.

For a short period Snowy contemplated returning to Sydney and resigning himself to running the gymnasium. However a trip home in 1925 convinced him that while he could make money in Australia, there was a greater fortune to be had in the United States. This was despite his return being an unmitigated success. But that had more to do with whom he was accompanying.

Pauline Frederick, who in the early 1920s was among America's most popular actresses on stage and screen, was in San Francisco performing in a play *Spring Cleaning*. In the audience one night was Snowy's old film partner, E.J. Carroll, who at the end of the performance sent his card back to her, stating that he wanted to see her about 'a very important matter'.

Carroll met her in the dressing room that night, with the offer of taking her to Australia for a tour of *Spring Cleaning*. Frederick readily agreed, particularly after Carroll said he would approach Snowy to be the tour manager as he knew the lie of the land, still had impressive contacts in Australia and was a whizz at self-promotion. This immediately put the actress at ease, as Snowy was already on her favourite's list after coming to her aid a few years earlier when she put on a special charity function for the local hospital for crippled children. Frederick had turned part of her large Los Angeles estate into a rodeo ring, and Snowy followed acts from Buster Keaton, Roscoe Arbuckle and Will Rogers, with a trick riding display on Boomerang.

After a wild trip on the *Ventura*, which saw one woman swept overboard during a typhoon, Frederick and the Bakers arrived in Sydney in March 1925 to rapturous scenes.

A banner stretched across the wharf announced 'Australia welcomes Pauline Frederick', and thousands of people swarmed to get a look at the movie idol of the time. As Frederick walked down the gangway she was mobbed, hundreds of women rushing to greet her. Frederick was terrified, a group of policemen coming to her rescue before she fell and was trampled on. She was eventually able to scramble into the waiting car, but the bouquet of flowers which had been presented to her were now just shredded stems. Mr and Mrs Baker were also pushed along in the middle of a swirling typhoon of screaming fans, until they also found themselves shoved into the same car as Frederick, who by this time was laughing, but shaking noticeably.

They were then involved in a slow procession to the Sydney Town Hall, with the travel slowed appreciably by hundreds of spectators jumping off the footpath, standing in front of the cars, in their bid to touch the actress.

'Never in Sydney's history had an actress been so tumultuously welcomed,' reported the *Sydney Morning Herald*.

The following few weeks were just as crazy, Frederick requiring a police escort from the theatre each night. Even the theatre audiences, which were filled with movie goers who wanted to see their favourite film star in the flesh, would regularly interrupt the play by rising to their feet and giving long, rousing cheers of applause whenever she appeared on stage.

While Snowy didn't receive as big a hero's welcome as Frederick, he was guest of honour at several dinners, including one conducted by the Millions Club in Sydney. Snowy told the members exactly what they wanted to hear, including that there was no country in the world with a better future than Australia. Baker claimed that 'the relative prosperity of Australia would be even higher than that of the United States'.

His other pearls of wisdom included that despite being a teetotaller, he couldn't see the value of Prohibition because it only promoted 'bootleggers' whom he described as parasites. He also warned the lunchtime audience to be wary of those pushing for oil exploration. He thought many of them were just as parasitic.

Snowy also provided what he believed to be the sure-fire cure to stop smoking. Although proud that he only had the very occasional Scotch, he'd succumbed to nicotine during his days in Hollywood after being told by one studio head that smoking makes an actor look more masculine. As Snowy would do anything to get another movie role, he immediately took up the smokes. 'I thought it was manly and rugged to smoke,' Snowy told one Sydney dinner. 'That is until one night on the ship coming across, I was teaching Pauline how to play euchre. She suddenly turned to me and said: "Oh Snowy, how unpleasant your breath is!"

'I immediately walked to the side of the ship, and threw my cigarettes into the Pacific Ocean. I haven't smoked since. It just shows what a man's hurt vanity will do to him.'

The hurt pride did work. Snowy never smoked again.

Although it was just a short stay in Australia, there was time for a quick visit to see the family before heading back to America with a delighted Frederick.

Back in Los Angeles, Snowy found that his intense networking with the right people enabled him to be offered a lucrative position at exactly the right time.

Snowy was invited to become a member of the exclusive club within the LAAC, known as the Uplifters, whose motto was 'brotherhood, fun and the sharing of artistic talent'.

The Uplifters club had its own orchestra, held weekly lunches and even had its own hideaway in a canyon near Santa Monica, where on a 40-acre property with a running stream, springs and a rustic clubhouse, the members would have regular get-togethers. The highlight was the annual Uplifters Outing, a week of wild revelry which included performing circus parades, games of donkey polo, skits, antics, much drinking and debauchery.

As those involved with the Uplifters had money, its members including many rich movie moguls and Los Angeles millionaires, had the resources to build an indoor auditorium, which included a pipe organ, a swimming pool, tennis courts, baseball diamond, bungalows, and they also had high-quality kitchen equipment in the clubhouse. More land was bought which then allowed the Uplifters to build a racetrack and polo field.

One of the most important people Snowy met at the club, and at Uplifter functions, was a man totally obsessed with the success of the LAAC – Frank A. Garbutt. Garbutt had a touch of Snowy about him as he was passionate about sports, including boxing, yachting, rowing and handball, and was also a pioneer racing car driver. Unlike Snowy, Garbutt never had any money concerns as he was one of the first men to successfully drill for oil in Los Angeles. Snowy never had the gall to call him a parasite.

Everything Garbutt dabbled in was a success, including making millions out of being an oil tool inventor. He was also vice president of Famous Players Studio, which he later sold to Paramount Pictures, and was a prominent writer, renowned for his columns in the *Los Angeles Times* which covered a vast range of subjects.

But his passion was the LAAC and an overwhelming drive to make it, without question, the best sporting club in the world. He demanded nothing but the best. Before long, Garbutt was a LAAC director and then the club's president. He was totally hands-on in both roles, for which he never accepted a fee or salary, and was the 'driving force' of the LAAC. His involvement in the LAAC was essentially his big hobby – his pride and joy.

And soon as Garbutt met Snowy he wanted him to be involved in the club on a basis far more lofty than just being a member. Aware of both his sporting and business successes in Australia, including his ability to run a gym, Garbutt offered him the job of co-ordinating the LAAC's athletic pursuits.

For some years, the LAAC had adopted a system of physical fitness where, according to the club's history, *Our First Century* written by Betty Lou Young, those willing to put in the hard work were promised that 'the proper application of thought, desire, and will, leading to concentration, guaranteed a life expectancy of 100 years, with middle age beginning at 70. The regimen included regular exercise, daily baths, correct living, two meals a day, and a proper mental attitude.'

The club needed a public figure to push this system and according to Garbutt, Snowy fitted the bill, because his vast sporting record couldn't be disputed. Snowy was put in charge of co-ordinating an inspired public relations campaign. He became one of the club's frontmen, promoting its many athletic pursuits in the hope of luring new members. Not surprisingly, the ever industrious Baker mixed up his public relations work, which included getting nice write-ups in the local newspapers, with, whenever possible, being a club instructor for various, and in the end varied, sporting pursuits. If an LAAC member wanted tuition on any sport, no matter how minor, Snowy was the man to approach.

As Young observed: 'Baker had the romance, the charm, and the dedication to spread the gospel of sports: "Get out of doors and get into some kind of game ... don't watch games, play them ... play for the fun and the joy of it . . . play hard but clean and fair. Be a good sport on the field, in business and at home."

'While his first love was horsemanship, he envisioned a veritable army of children and adults, who could not only ride and play polo, but who could swim, dive, fence and enjoy every kind of outdoor game – a goal that movitated him during his years of affiliation with the LAAC.'

Snowy's role was soon known to all LAAC members. The club's newspaper, *Mercury*, announced the appointment alongside a photograph of Snowy wearing a bowler hat, coat and tie, and driving a jalopy. Beside him was a mysterious looking man, wearing a cloth cap, holding a camera, and showing off a finely tuned moustache. Under the photograph is an intriguing caption which reads: 'Snowy's distinguished colleague is a gentleman who was later arrested as a German spy.'

Snowy immediately began getting positive publicity as the LAAC fencing commissioner, working in tandem with a Belgian master, Professor Henri J. Uyttenhove, who had taught at the Antwerp School of Gymnastics and also boasted numerous international titles.

Through his movie work since arriving in Hollywood and his high profile at the LAAC, in the movie circles Snowy quickly became known for his dubious acting and far more solid sporting skills. The film studios knew that if one of their stars needed tuition in certain sports, Snowy was the man to be employed to help out. As Douglas Fairbanks was the swashbuckling hero of the time, it was important that his stunt work was authentic. The movie studio immediately beckoned Snowy and the Professor and Fairbanks was given a crash course on fencing. Together the pair taught Fairbanks how to fence for his roles in *The Mark of Zorro*, Snowy in particular involved in some vigorous bouts with Fairbanks, the Hollywood star quickly grasping the fundamentals. From this association, the pair became firm friends.

Rudolph Valentino was another avid student. Valentino and Snowy had met at the LAAC, the young, impressionable actor, eager to learn everything about the movie industry, latching onto anyone who'd had any movie experience – like Snowy. Valentino, like Fairbanks, was keen to become a proficient fencer and became another of Snowy's students. After fencing lessons, Snowy would offer Valentino all kinds of tips. One day Valentino explained that he was moving towards romantic roles so Snowy asked him to show him how he kissed. Using a nearby mirror, Valentino puckered up. Snowy thought it looked forced and clumsy and gave his version of how it should be done, telling Valentino that he'd actually been involved in several romantic roles during his movie days in Australia and this was the way he had charmed the audiences. According to Snowy, the key was confidence, the man necessarily being the aggressor when kissing the woman. Snowy attacked the mirror with relish and Valentino liked what he saw. How much of Snowy's lesson was taken up by Valentino and used in his many later romantic roles is unknown. But Snowy repeatedly told his friends that he was the man who taught Valentino how to kiss.

Snowy, eager to network with the more elite, and rich LAAC members, was also spending more time at the Uplifters ranch, where he was eventually appointed riding instructor, and for a short time club manager. He was now deeply entrenched in the LA way of life. Snowy, ever the opportunist, had successfully ingratiated himself with those with the money at the LAAC, enabling him to earn a good income flitting between his job at the LAAC and the 'club within the club', the Uplifters.

However Garbutt, the real powerbroker, had bigger plans for Snowy.

Chapter 23

Riviera Country Club

ONE AFTERNOON, FRANK GARBUTT, THE PROUD, RICH, EVER IMAGINATIVE
LAAC director, drove along an unpaved road, which would later become
Sunset Boulevard, stopped the car near a canyon, peered out over a large
unclaimed stretch of Santa Monica land and exclaimed: 'This is it! This
is it!'

Garbutt, who was always looking for ways to expand the LAAC,
had found the exact spot for the missing jigsaw piece. The Los
Angeles Athletic Club had every sporting facility except one. It didn't
boast a championship golf course. Garbutt wanted the LAAC to be,
unquestionably, the best sports club in America; and the best way to get
nationwide exposure was to have a world-rated golf course.

Five years later, in 1927, the Riviera Country Club course opened.
Within months it was rated as something special. As golf's most
influential architect Dr Alister Mackenzie remarked when he first visited
the course: 'Riviera ranks among the world's best. Some of its features
are unique in American golf architecture.' According to Mackenzie, the
Riviera site 'was as fine as any he had seen', and the design by George
Thomas 'as nearly perfect as man could make it'.

After just a few years, it was rated the third best golf course in
America, behind Pine Valley and Pinehurst, and even now, Riviera is still
among the most impressive and demanding courses in the United States.
Sports Illustrated magazine in 2001 described Riviera as having 'more
memorable holes than London's Highgate Cemetery'.

Garbutt's grand dream did not just end at a world-class golf course.
He wanted the LAAC to be able to boast the USA's best country club
and be *the* spot in Los Angeles and so he demanded the standout feature
be a state-of-the-art clubhouse.

His wishes were fulfilled. The design of the clubhouse, according to one influential member, was to achieve 'a dream that envisioned on the sunny slopes of these Santa Monica Mountains a principality of pleasure lovelier and even more enchanting than the famous Old World region, from which it derives its name, the French and Italian Rivieras'.

Eventually the clubhouse, built on a plateau giving it spectacular views of the golf course, took an impressive but sprawling Spanish look, costing an extravagant $450,000 to build. The clubhouse soon became known as 'The Grand Hotel of Golf', with 36 guest rooms situated within the 46,000 square feet of imported Italian marble, intimate lounge areas and expensive furniture.

The venture stretched the LAAC financially, but now its members could state with pride that they had the costliest and most exclusive 18-hole layout in the land.

It was immediately the place to be seen. In its opening days, those queueing up at the first tee, just down from the clubhouse, included Hollywood's most influential couple, Douglas Fairbanks and Mary Pickford, who put up the first $1,000 for an open tournament.

Often accompanying them in a foursome was Lillian Gish, obnoxious but brilliant baseballer, Ty Cobb, W.C. Fields and professional golfer, Walter Hagen, who said 'the Riviera greens are without peer in any part of the country'.

Silent screen star Harold Lloyd was often at the course, finetuning his golf game which had already been improved by having a nine-hole course designed by Alister Mackenzie in the backyard of his Beverly Hills home. Other regulars included Mack Sennett, Will Rogers, Reginald Denny, Hal Roach and Walt Disney.

But Garbutt was after more; he wanted the area to provide 'the ideal country club life'. He also wanted the area to be known around the world.

Realising the extraordinary business opportunities that would arise from hosting the Olympic Games, Garbutt had been one of the chief instigators in Los Angeles' winning bid to host the 1932 Olympic Games. Now he wanted his Athletic Club to be the venue for at least one Olympic event. Thus began plans to build the world's best equestrian and polo facilities at Riviera. In January 1928, *Mercury* announced: 'The Los Angeles Athletic Club ever ready to promote and advance a worthy sport, has for some time contemplated the construction of a regulation polo field on a site adjoining the Riviera links. Mr Garbutt met recently with Mr Will Rogers, Mr Hal Roach, Snowy Baker and others to discuss the project. The meeting was full of encouragement for polo players.'

It didn't take long for Garbutt to convince Snowy to leave his position at the Uplifters club, and take charge of the grand Riviera polo project. Snowy was appointed as the Riviera Country Club's equestrian director. While great news for Riviera, Snowy's departure from the Uplifters headquarters caused enormous division between the two bodies, especially as the Uplifters now looked upon Riviera as direct competition. Eventually the LAAC and the Uplifters drifted apart, the 'club within a club' struggling because of intensifying debt, some of it caused by borrowed funds to install a polo field.

But Snowy had no qualms about going to the highest bidder. More importantly, he realised that if he did the job at Riviera properly he could then command both international acclaim, through his facilities which would host the equestrian events at the 1932 Olympic Games, and local prestige by being the man all the Hollywood heroes would have to contact if they wanted to become accomplished horseriders and polo competitors. At last he could be a real identity in Hollywood.

Snowy devoted all his resources in ensuring that the polo complex was at first easily the best in the United States. Within a year of the first meeting, construction had begun and by the early 1930s, with Snowy heavily involved in the planning and layout, five turf polo fields had been built, along with a quarter-mile training track, a practice field, an elaborate steeplechase course almost three kilometres long, stables that could house almost 400 horses, 80 kilometres of bridle paths that wound its way around the golf course and nearby canyons, an international class all-turf showjumping course, and a grandstand that could hold more than 5,000 people.

Visitors who attended the centre for the first time were invariably astounded by its size and the quality of its facilities. Considering that the centre was completed as the Great Depression hit was a testament to the willpower of both Garbutt and Snowy.

Snowy moved into a bungalow close by, which he renamed 'Gunyah', but it soon became known as a little Australian pocket in Los Angeles. With gum trees planted nearby and a fire barbeque set up, Rex, Reg or Snowy would entertain the social set of Hollywood with countless stirrup cup parties and fancy lunches, while 'the billy boiled'. As Betty Lou Young wrote in *Our First Century*, Snowy 'soon built up a devoted following with his Australian Pied Piper charm'.

Frank Baker was also impressed with how easily Snowy fitted in with all the prima-donnas and egomaniacs that made Riviera their second home. 'Snowy did have a terrific personality,' Frank said. 'They used to swear by him over here. He was a great favourite.' Or as Helen Twelvetrees, leading lady of the 1930s, said: 'Everybody in Hollywood knows Snowy Baker.'

Also helping was that Snowy was soon close friends with the Hollywood aristocracy. As with any prestigious club, it helps if you know the important wheelers and dealers inside the doors, and as Snowy could get someone onto both the golf course and polo fields, his bungalow often had familiar movie faces seeking favours, banging on his front-door.

Mr and Mrs Baker, and their two daughters, were always the perfect hosts.

One popular innovation which Snowy devised was using Gunyah as a setting for mock murders. The darling set would then take off for the hills, looking for rhyming clues, hidden by Snowy, so that they could work out who exactly was guilty of the make-believe murder of 'George Shapetric'. Then it was back to Gunyah for a 'jolly' lunch, and more networking. It wasn't long before Snowy was in with all of the Hollywood movers and shakers. It didn't exactly lead to movie roles, but he was soon making a comfortable living teaching the stars and their children how to ride and have a good time at his club.

The most crucial step though was the introduction of polo, which proved an enormous success at Riviera. Snowy convinced Will Rogers and Hal Roach to be founding members of the Riviera polo club, and it wasn't long before Sunday afternoon celebrity matches, involving Walt Disney, Leslie Howard, Gary Cooper, Darryl Zanuck, Spencer Tracy, Big Boy Williams, Frank Borzage and the like, were attracting thousands of spectators to the venue. Snowy also planted a line of fast-growing blue gums around the polo fields which doubled as wind breaks and as a shield from any prying eyes who were wanting to get a free look at the celebrity polo games.

With Snowy presiding, either playing or ensuring that the VIP guests had the best vantage points around the boundary, the Riviera complex became one of the most popular Hollywood haunts. Clark Gable was among the usual Sunday guests, sitting to one end. Gable wanted to play but had been banned from playing by his MGM studio.

'Clark took up riding and became an excellent hand in the saddle. He arranged with me to take a course of polo lessons,' Snowy recalled. 'His film boss got wind of Clark's polo aspirations, and down slammed the axe – "Play polo and your existing contract is cancelled." The film contract won.'

The studio was obviously worried that one of their biggest stars might get injured, possibly delaying whatever picture he was shooting at the time. This forced him to instead become an avid polo watcher, with Snowy or his wife providing a buffer between him and his tribe of adoring female fans. Finally Gable took up golf, traipsing up and down the unforgiving Riviera course.

Snowy even convinced formidable names, including actress Claudette Colbert, to sponsor tournaments, while Gloria Swanson, Marlene Dietrich and Merle Oberon were chaperoned by Snowy to the equestrian centre on various Sundays to present trophies. The day would often end with all the stars returning to Gunyah for an 'Aussie barbeque'.

Amongst the most enthusiastic of polo players was Walt Disney who, in between building America's most comprehensive entertainment empire, was a wild, reckless competitor. However a bad spill during a game, which came just months after two riders were killed during a tournament match, forced a reluctant Disney to retreat to the sidelines. Still, Disney was so passionate about polo that he had a stationwagon with 'Walt Disney Studios – Riviera Country Club' written in huge letters on the side.

Will Rogers, who lived nearby on a ranch and in a huge living room had a stuffed cow to practice his roping on, also saw his life pass by in front of him during another frantic Riviera match. Once, when an opposing player cut in front of him, Rogers flew over the horse's head, causing the nervous creature to crash on top of him. Concerned that Rogers had been crushed, actor Joel McCrea rushed to his side. By the time McCrea had arrived, Rogers was starting to come to. Peering up at McCrea, Rogers grumbled: 'Go away. Don't make an epic out of it.' He hobbled back towards the horse, stumbled his way back on and got on with the game.

Rogers's quick quip wasn't surprising, considering that his wit had turned him into an American folk hero, and one of the most quoted. He would often try the latest lines on Snowy to see whether it would work for a broad audience.

Witty lines such as 'Half our life is spent trying to find something to do with the time we have rushed through life trying to save'; 'If all politicians fished instead of spoke publicly we would be at peace with the world'; and 'the Income Tax has made more liars out of the American people than golf has' were often spouted under a Gunyah gum tree.

As the chukkas were getting more and more vigorous, with various jealous, invariably paranoid actors trying to get one up on someone who may be fighting for the same role, Snowy tried to calm the situation down by acting as referee. And just like at the Sydney Stadium, he found himself the brunt of much abuse.

'The players don't hurl bottles and bits of seating at one like the fans did when I gave the Langford–McVea decision. But their language at times is lurid and expansive – words not available to the student in the dictionary,' Snowy remarked.

Even the shooting of *Casablanca* was delayed for a day after its director, Michael Curtiz, was injured in a Riviera polo match when struck by Snowy. Curtiz eventually arrived on set with his right hand heavily bandaged and a Warner press release in the other hand, which stated that: 'Snowy Baker hit Curtiz with a polo mallet – accidentally.'

But Snowy didn't refine his resources to just presiding over the equestrian centre and Sunday polo tournaments. He also instituted riding lessons, made good money on the side selling clothes and equipment and organised the Saddle Club, where notable stars would be taken on daily rides around the area.

Every morning, Snowy would take charge of a group of riders, who would head to a nearby beach or mountain trails, stopping for a picnic lunch under the sycamores or at someone's plush ranch. The group often included one of Hollywood's most difficult actresses, Greta Garbo. 'Her much publicised "I want to be alone" is no gag, because it held good in her riding,' Snowy said. 'Once she became proficient in the saddle, Miss Garbo always rode alone.'

One day Garbo had been out on her favourite horse, Ned Kelly, one of many horses from the Riviera stable that Snowy had given an

Australian name. Others included Wombat, Possum, Dinkum, Bondi, Wallaby, Wallaroo, Dandenong and Cootamundra.

'This day, Miss Garbo suddenly appeared riding up to the stables at a gallop. She dismounted and rushed up to me breathless and excited. "Oh Mr Baker I've just seen the body of a murdered man back in the hills. I saw it while riding along the rim of the canyon. It looked to me like a dead boy lying on its back with a long dagger buried in its heart."

'She told me she did not wish to be implicated in any publicity in such a horrid crime, and in a hushed voice asked me to keep her out of it and investigate. I had no stomach for such a job, but I hastily mounted and rode off.

'Arriving at the canyon rim trail, I looked down and saw the horrible, blood-stained corpse, with its wide-open eyes and the dagger sticking in its heart. It was all quite noticeable from where I sat on my horse.

'Before notifying the police I decided to ride to the bottom of the canyon and inspect the tragedy more closely. It was an unpleasant job, but nevertheless my duty to check up. Imagine my feelings when, about a half an hour later, I was able to inform Miss Garbo that a motion picture company had been working on location, and the body was a dummy. The company had finished the murder scene, but the property man had failed to collect the "body". Her fears were quickly turned to laughter.'

Snowy also organised a junior group of riders, called the Geebungs, where he would plan paper trails and bandit hunts. Snowy invariably played the role of the bad guy, much to the glee of the youngsters.

If those ever varied duties weren't making his life demanding enough, Snowy continued to stay in touch with Australia, through a regular column in *The Referee*. From 1928, Snowy kept *Referee* readers informed on what exactly was going on in American sport.

In his 'American letter' column, Snowy provided gossip on a vast range of sports, but his passion remained boxing, regularly offering the latest news on the leading fighters, including Gene Tunney and Jack Dempsey.

Not surprisingly, considering that Snowy knew everyone who was anyone in Hollywood, there was plenty of juicy scandal to report, such as when his old rival, boxing manager and promoter, Doc Kearns, was beaten up by actor Charles Delaney. Baker, who could never warm to Kearns after he tried to grab Les Darcy from under him, wrote: 'Kearns is wearing a peach of a pair of black eyes as the result of the fight. Delaney has his nose broken. All of Hollywood is talking of the go. I do not know what the purse was.'

When Australia's most famed racehorse, Phar Lap, arrived in the United States in early 1932 for a series of races, Snowy kept a close eye. In March 1932 he wrote that 'Phar Laps's presence is creating a great stir. In times gone by, Australia held the world's best boxers, tennis players, swimmers and others, but in recent years other lands and the USA have won the blue ribands with their athletes. Let us hope the wonder horse will beat the best and our young Australian men and women will start to retrieve what was once ours.' Within a month, Phar Lap was dead, the insinuation that the gelding had been poisoned lasting to this day.

Polo was another favourite subject, Snowy repeatedly expressing his wish of having an Australian team play in California. The prodding worked, the illustrious Ashton family, the landed gentry of the Australian polo ranks, eventually being lured to play in the United States in the early 1930s.

Snowy was also successful in getting another Australian polo team, the Freebooters, headed by Captain Stuart Pearson and including the formidable Curtis Skene, to Los Angeles where they played a series against the Uplifters. They also teamed up with Snowy, enabling him to represent Australia in yet another sport when in 1929 they competed in the California Challenge Cup. The movie magnate Hal Roach led the California team to international triumph.

Australian visitors were common at Riviera, with Arthur Mailey's troupe of international cricketers, which toured Canada and the United States in 1932, making a special visit to Snowy's house. The group included notable Australian Test cricketers, including Vic Richardson and the latest cricket phenomenon, a young Don Bradman. Bradman had brought his wife Jessie along on the trip and Snowy convinced her to have a riding lesson before the Australian cricketers headed off to MGM studios to meet Jean Harlow, Mary Astor and the Barrymore family.

The team were usually treated as a curiosity item, until they arrived in Hollywood where they were well known by the influx of British actors there and who were trying to establish cricket in California.

Snowy, remembering his Crown Street days and wanderings across to the Sydney Cricket Ground nets in search of a shilling, was lured into playing the occasional game of cricket by the chief cricket buff in Hollywood – well-known English character actor Sir Charles Aubrey Smith. Sir Charles had already enticed many locals to the game, including Boris Karloff.

After making a few appearances for the Hollywood Cricket Club, Snowy soon kept his distance because of the chief's odd behaviour. Once when fielding in the slips, Sir Charles dropped a simple catch. He immediately stopped the match and demanded that his butler appear on the pitch.

'Fetch me my glasses,' Sir Charles demanded.

The game was halted for several minutes until the butler returned with the glasses on a silver tray. A few balls later, the batsman again caught the edge and the ball flew straight to Sir Charles, who fumbled the chance after juggling it. Sir Charles snatched at the ball and bellowed at the butler: 'Damn fool, you brought me my reading glasses!'

The main highlight of 1932 was the staging of the Los Angeles Olympic equestrian events at his course at Riviera. The dressage competition and three-day event were held on the main polo field, while the endurance event was held over a twenty-two and a half mile course, which included 50 obstacles. In the main area, more than 20,000 spectators were accommodated through temporary bleachers and hillside seating.

During the Games, Snowy handed over his baby to the Olympic organisers, because he had other duties to perform. Earlier that year, Snowy had been appointed as official attaché to the Australian Olympic team, his prime role being to ensure that every athlete felt at home in Los Angeles and were able to practice, train and compete without distress or interruption.

Snowy's appointment was a master stroke. As he knew everyone, he was able to cut through a lot of red tape, ensuring that the small Australian team were treated like royalty. Snowy organised visits to the major Hollywood film studios, where the team met with his close friends Pickford, Fairbanks and Joan Crawford, and they were also guests of honour at several lavish dinners at Riviera. As swimmer Frances Bult recalled 60 years later to author Harry Gordon: 'It was like a wonderland, and all of us, particularly the girls, were star-struck.'

Snowy also made certain that the true stars of the team were properly looked after. He was at the wharf with renowned sculler Bobby Pearce when the team arrived and hovered around them for the rest of their stay, explaining to them that he 'was at their beck and call'.

Through *The Referee*, Snowy also provided intimate details and observations of the Australian Olympic campaign, his enthusiasm in again being involved in an Australian Olympic team never far from the surface.

Shortly after the team settled in Los Angeles, Snowy cabled back to *The Referee* that 'meeting these bright young people from Australia made one proud of them and their country ... Australia has every reason to feel proud of the splendid team of athletes she has sent here to represent her at the forthcoming Olympic Games. Never have I been associated with such an earnest band of patriots.'

After one team lunch with 'society horsemen and women', Baker wrote: 'They were all favourably impressed with the Aussies, the athletes' quiet charm of manner and pleasing personalities winning them instant friends. The four women stars under Mrs Chambers' pleasant chaperonage are just about the politest foursome of young ladies one would meet in many a moon ... They are as far removed, both in manners and appearance, from their pert, snappy American flapper rivals as a kangaroo is from a Mississippi mule.'

The size of the Australian team was miniscule – just eight men and four women – their expenses and outfitting just as frugal, the team having to live on seven shillings and sixpence each a week. But percentage wise, it was one of the most successful Ausralian Olympic teams, including three gold medallists – Bobby Pearce, rowing, Dunc Gray, cycling, Clare Dennis, swimming – a silver medallist – swimmer Philomena Mealing – and a bronze recipient – wrestler Eddie Scarf. The other big name was Boy Charlton, appearing at his third Olympics.

Snowy was particularly struck by the determination of Pearce and Gray, reporting that Pearce was 'in fine condition. He rows two hours in the morning and an hour or so in the afternoon' at a lagoon, where conditions were 'even better than at our own Parramatta River'. 'Pearce looks well, in fact the beau ideal of an athlete, beautifully set-up and full of zip. It will take a great sculler to beat him.'

Of Gray, Baker observed that he was 'something of a paragon in this country. He does not drink; he does not smoke; he's a good churchman. He is well spoken. Things intellectual and communal have a deep interest for him, and he is very much a man's man.' Snowy was as impressed that Gray had achieved so much in the depths of a Depression. 'In the meantime a steady job would not come amiss. Gray has had a fairly hard time.'

Even Snowy was coaxed into making a sporting appearance during the Games, one longstanding claim being that he represented Australia in the equestrian endurance event. The real story is that as he was so instrumental in turning Riviera into an Olympic venue, he was persuaded to be part of a riding exhibition on the polo ground during a lull in competition.

On the Sunday of competition, with the Riviera grounds crowded with members of Olympics teams, VIPs and the beautiful people of California, the equestrian master of ceremonies announced: 'Ladies and gentlemen, it is now my pleasure to introduce to you an exhibition of jumping by the very popular equestrian director of the Riviera Country Club and the greatest allround sportsman Australia has ever produced – Snowy Baker.'

To resounding applause, Snowy rode out onto the field, negotiating the first three jumps, then organised his mount for the fourth. 'I made the jump all right. But by myself. I went over the top; the horse didn't.'

Snowy dusted himself off, collected his horse, bowed to the crowd, and hobbled off the field. Thus ended Snowy's Olympic career.

Buoyed by Australia's success at the Olympics, Snowy was asked by the team officials if he was keen to follow the team home. He didn't hesitate in accepting the offer, as he expressly wanted to see his ageing father who was in his late 80s. It proved timely. Shortly after Snowy's return to the Surry Hills family home, the unstoppable, incredible George Baker died.

For Snowy, the loss of his father affected him dramatically – especially as he had been his driving spur, inspiration and mentor for so many decades. For so long his father had been the main person he'd wanted to impress and whenever he wanted advice or guidance, he would go straight to his father. Snowy didn't tell him everything, especially during his dubious days as a boxing promoter, and he didn't always follow his advice, especially when Mr Baker warned him of getting too close to Flash Harries like Huge Deal McIntosh. Snowy would whimper: 'It's a bit different these days,' before trying to change the subject.

But Snowy knew that his father was always there for him, and Snowy made certain that George was introduced to the various boxers, stars and glamorous hangers-on who were always hovering around the Baker Stadium. George took full advantage of his VIP Stadium pass, being in the crowd for all the major bouts. But he veered away from being involved in the actual running of the business. Snowy did ask, but Mr Baker immediately replied: 'That's a young man's business. I would be out of my depth.'

Snowy later wrote that his father 'rode every day until he was 89. Then he feared he might slip from the saddle, so he changed to a strenuous five-mile morning walk.'

One morning Mr Baker came home from his walk and said to his wife: 'Darling, I fear it is all over.' The family was beckoned. He shook hands with those members who arrived in time, stretched himself on his bed, his hands crossed on his chest, and, according to Snowy 'was dead within ten minutes'.

Frank Baker was moved to write about his father that, even in his final year, he remained as 'mentally alert and physically fit as a man in his early sixties.

'Possessing a full head of hair, a perfect set of teeth, exceptionally keen eyesight that needed no glasses to read his evening newspaper in even dim light, he had an extraordinary retentive memory.

'The late Charles H. Bertie, one time president of the Royal Australian Historical Society once informed me that my father knew more about early Sydney than any living individual, stating "His amazing detailed knowledge of our city is almost frightening. His tremendous wealth of memory is beyond me."'

Bertie's praise was of the highest quality, considering that the speaker was the first librarian of the Sydney Municipal Library, and an authority on Australiana, his collection one of the most substantial in the Mitchell Library.

Frank wrote: 'As Mr Bertie confided to me, he had begged my father to write his memoirs. But father detested any publicity whatever, and his reply, according to Bertie was: "I may consider doing so, Charles, when I feel that age is creeping up on me. But let's not discuss the subject for some years to come." He was then in his middle eighties.

'Evidently age never crept up on my father. He continued to retain an extraordinary quality of health and strength. Never once in his long life had he suffered the least illness; not even a single cold; nor any minor blemish to those iron-like teeth of his. No doctor or dentist ever earned one single penny of attention to his needs in almost a hundred years. He was unique.'

Snowy spent several days with his family, but was soon called away for the usual round of social occasions and guest appearances, his business mind ticking over the prospect of securing a number of thoroughbred Australian horses to improve the breeding of polo ponies back in the United States.

Nonetheless the highlight of the trip was a nostalgic visit to where it had all happened – the old Baker Stadium in Rushcutters Bay.

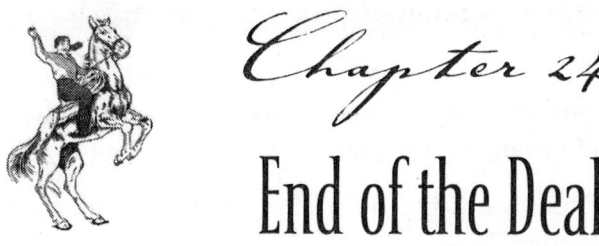

Chapter 24

End of the Deal

THE LOUD, CLEAR VOICE OF RING ANNOUNCER GEORGE DENT BOOMED OUT across the Sydney Stadium. 'Ladies and gentlemen, this is . . .' but before he could finish the sentence, those packed pilchards in the bleachers screamed out: 'Snowy Baker.'

Snowy was back in his home environment, in cahoots with his old partner in crime, Huge Deal. It didn't take much for Huge Deal, back in the boxing promotion game, to lure his buddy Snowy into the ring to referee just one more prize fight involving the latest Australian phenomenon, Ambrose Palmer.

While Snowy's life since leaving Australia had been eventful, it still couldn't compare to the crazy, roller-coaster ride Huge Deal had been negotiating since the last time he had been an integral cog in the Baker story. One day he was enjoying the riches of the world. The next he was overcoming the traumas of bankruptcy. In between, he did everything he could to keep his name in front of the public eye. It wasn't hard, considering that everything Huge Deal touched was colourful, controversial, and often so creative.

Huge Deal continued to be looked after by his political mate W.A. Holman who had organised a cushy seat for him in the Upper House. There he worked as a numbers man for Jack Lang and threw his weight around by being provocative through his newspaper *The Sunday Times*.

Huge Deal was an uncontrollable and totally hands-on newspaper boss, coming up with numerous hair-brain schemes to improve circulation. The most bizarre circulation drive involved a deal he made with a notorious murderer called Simpson, who on the eve of his execution was visited by Huge Deal in his prison cell. Huge Deal promised him 5,000 pounds if he could successfully come back from the dead, and appear in his office before witnesses. Simpson readily accepted, jotted down the address of the newspaper office in Castlereagh Street, so he wouldn't 'get lost on the way', and promised that he would solve 'the age old riddle of whether the dead can return'.

On the night after the hanging, 40 thrill-seekers crowded into Huge Deal's *Sunday Times* office, munching on caviar sandwiches and quaffing champagne, waiting for Simpson's arrival. He never appeared.

Such stunts hardly helped the newspaper, which was rapidly losing readers and revenue. The situation wasn't improved by Huge Deal's extravagant ways, where he was prone to sack an employee he met in the lift, and then buy him a case of champagne, a motor car, or give him an exorbitant cheque to get him out of his way. Not surprisingly, over 10 years the newspaper had a record number of editors.

The Sunday Times boardroom became the place to be seen, especially as Huge Deal ensured that many Tivoli babes were brought along to 'entertain' his special friends, which included Dame Nellie Melba, Sir John Monash and Billy Hughes. From the boardroom came the incessant noise of champagne bottles popping, the rich smell of à la carte food mixed in with the smell of cigars, and Flo Mackenzie singing 'You Called Me Baby Doll'.

On Sunday morning, everyone would head off to the harbour, where they would be guests on Huge Deal's yacht, *Mabel*, which once capsized because he had shifted the ballast to make room for cases of French champagne.

Yet he always craved more of the good life. In 1923, Huge Deal, moved to England after succeeding in leasing Lord Kitchener's 17th century Broome Park mansion in Kent.

To feel at home, Huge Deal's first step after settling in was to import 10 tonnes of the famous Bulli soil, the key ingredient of the Sydney Cricket Ground wicket. After laying down a first-class cricket pitch in a corner of the 600-acre property, Huge Deal went about inviting touring Australian teams to 'come to Broome Park and play on your own soil'. He then built a runway so private planes could land on the property.

Eventually Huge Deal had to return to Australia, as his empire was crumbling around him. While he became a local hero for convincing Lang to fund the Cenotaph in Martin Place, his private life was in a mess, having to transfer his share of *The Sunday Times* to pay off his increasing debts. He even attempted to get back into vaudeville production, but that proved short-lived as the company was soon in liquidation. His big problem was that as usual, as soon as the box-office revenue came in, he seized it, and spent it, often on diamond watches for the latest Tivoli babe he was infatuated by, sometimes for a bit of graft and corruption to keep the Department of Taxation, or his bank manager, at bay. In 1932, a Sydney court declared McIntosh bankrupt.

Huge Deal basically had nothing; his wife had to pawn her clothing and jewellery and they downgraded to living in a small furnished cottage near Centennial Park. As usual, he rallied on, returning to two of his original money streams – fight promotion and the kitchen.

Above the old Tivoli theatre, where he made and lost a fortune, Huge Deal opened The New Sponge Bakery where Sydneysiders could buy the best sponge cakes in the city.

He also convinced Stadiums Ltd to let him have one more go at making the Sydney Stadium the world's boxing mecca. The Stadium was struggling to regain the status it had as a premier fight venue around the time of World War I. There had still been eventful nights, including one when the ring collapsed after a losing boxer knocked out the referee, prompting an invasion of fans, seconds and police, but during the Depression was only occasionally full.

Huge Deal thought he could change all that, believing that bright imports from overseas would again work to lift the standards, crowds and prize money, and more importantly, the gatetakings that would come his way. He convinced the few heavies he didn't owe money to in Sydney, to form a syndicate, known as the National Sporting Club of Australasia, to take control of the Stadium.

To add to the nostalgia, Snowy was beckoned to be part of the proceedings. As a favour, Snowy decided on a momentary return to the ring.

Huge Deal persuaded a list of titled dignatories, who were made directors, to contribute 3,000 pounds to support his latest venture – a fight between Australia's best, Ambrose Palmer, and American heavy-weight title contender, Bill Stribling. It was a lopsided fiasco, with Palmer totally out of his depth and the fight was stopped in the 10th round. Huge Deal's charmed run with the Sydney boxing crowd was over, because they knew they had been duped.

During this period, Huge Deal approached Snowy a second time to see whether he was keen to revive boxing in Australia. But a few old sporting colleagues had given Snowy the hint to tread very warily around Huge Deal. The magic touch had gone, and now Huge Deal was only out to 'touch you'. Snowy said, 'Thanks, but no thanks', and headed back to America.

Snowy never saw Huge Deal again. Huge Deal fled from his Australian creditors, once again heading to London. After several years underground, he reappeared in 1935 for one last bid to resurrect himself, with a grandiose plan to open 500 milk bars throughout London. In the end, only 12 milk bars opened and they soon all went bust. Seven years later, Huge Deal died in London, penniless.

While Snowy could never boast the fortunes Huge Deal had won and lost, he was always fastidious with money and was able to weather the difficult times through his versatility and willingness to try anything as long as it paid right.

He had also worked out Hollywood early, and took advantage of it. His brother Frank was just as successful in that area.

The life and times of Frank Baker has only commanded the occasional, brief line in books devoted to those who have made an impact in the Australian and international film scene. Considering that Frank ended up having one of the most fascinating lives of any Australian who ventured to Hollywood, he has been grossly overlooked.

Frank Baker appeared in more than 60 movies, primarily in minor roles, but most importantly, for many years was the right-hand man to one of motion picture's most influential directors – John Ford.

As Frank wrote near the end of his career: 'I have worked for that extraordinary and very difficult man in more than thirty of his productions in the various capacities of either actor, writer, research director, technical advisor or dialogue coach.' Those productions included several acclaimed features, such as *How Green Was My Valley*, *The Informer*, *Stagecoach* and *The Quiet Man*.

As Ford's biographer, Scott Eyman noted in *Print the Legend*, 'Frank Baker would be the thin, harsh voice of conscience breathing good sense in his ear.' Even though Ford, an incorrigible, difficult and tormented director who produced a string of masterpieces, knew all, in the end he relied most on a straight talking Australian who kept him honest.

Frank Baker never received more praise for his involvement in helping to prop Ford up at times because that is exactly the way he wanted it. Unlike Snowy, who gravitated towards the spotlight, Frank preferred to work diligently behind the scenes.

Through his involvement with Francis Ford, Frank was first offered a small part in John Ford's *Hearts of Oak* in 1924. At the end of one scene, Ford approached Frank and said: 'You're the worst actor I've ever seen in my life.'

Frank wasn't going to stand for that. 'Now may I reciprocate. You are the worst director that I have ever worked for.'

Now John Ford was highly offended, knowing that the only other director Frank had worked for was his elder brother. They argued for several more minutes, until Ford grumbled: 'All right. As long as you work for me, you're not going to get screen credit.'

'I'm very pleased to hear that,' Frank replied. 'I have some very good friends in different parts of the world, and I'd hate to have them see my name on a John Ford production.'

That was the end of it. Frank tussled with Ford for the next four decades, worked on most of his movies, but never received a screen credit and always made the point of ignoring the fact.

In a letter to Australian documentary and film-maker Joan Long, Frank wrote: 'For the following forty years I remained one of the main targets of John Ford's notorious sadistic barbed quips. But I, in most instances, continued to completely ignore them, as I was aware that such treatment of his sarcastic shafts "burned" him considerably.

'Ford was famed for picking on one of his cast or crew on each picture, and thereby making their life miserable for the production run of the show. It could be the star of the picture, or one of the leading actors. But never a woman. At the beginning of each production everybody was wary and tense − waiting to see who was going to be the "goat" of Ford's displeasure.

'This was one of the strange habits of the "Old Man", and a very discomforting one for whoever he picked on. As from thereon the victim couldn't do anything right in the view of "The Boss". He'd ride you to a frazzle with his coldly voiced sadistic sarcasm.'

Frank continued: 'I've seen big Victor McLagan stand there and cry like a child, and I've seen (John) Duke Wayne do exactly the same thing. Blubber like a child, and Ford just sitting there, humiliating the hell out of his star player. He was doing it for a purpose all the while. He was getting the best discipline out of that company, than any company that ever went before the camera.'

Frank and Ford used to argue about everything from movie locations to which way military buttons should be pointing. They even came to fisticuffs over a disagreement about something they had read in the newspaper concerning a murder. Ford tried to make it up to Frank, after Frank had called him a 'shanty Irish sonovabitch', by taking him to a bar for a peace-making drink. Ford approached the barman and shouted: 'I want you to give this stiff-necked Australian bastard a drink on me.'

Frank also worked for other directors, playing a variety of roles, including a police officer, physician, pretzel vendor, judge, Scotland Yard detective, Abraham Lincoln (several times), Major Martling in numerous Tarzan features, an arab and a soldier. He played the part of Robert E. Lee in five different movies, and in *The Sword of Valor*, acted as one of Snowy's allies in several of the sword duelling scenes.

While he was regularly offered acting work, Frank never rated himself. 'I never thought any of the Bakers were actors by any chance. I have been fooling them for years over here. They haven't been wise to me. They've given me work.'

Frank calculated that in the end he had an association with at least 150 movie productions — either as a co-producer, writer, technical adviser, research director or actor — including six Hollywood productions which had an Australian flavour. He even appeared with Snowy's old director, Wilfred Lucas, who on returning to Hollywood had separated from Bess Meredyth. According to Frank, Lucas had gone 'down the drain', relying on work here and there to satisfy his drinking problem.

Meredyth had left Lucas for the director of *Casablanca*, Michael Curtiz. Curtiz, a sadistic character, repeatedly hired Lucas for uncredited bit roles. It was often humiliating work, but Lucas was steadily employed until the 1940s, usually appearing in five or six movies per year. He even had the occasional major role, including at least two Laurel and Hardy movies.

As for his former wife, Meredyth became established as one of Holly-wood's best screenwriters, some of her most famous works including *Don Juan*, *Ben Hur*, *A Woman of Affairs* and *The Mighty Barnum*.

Frank Baker was also showing some flair in the screenwriting game. Charles Chauvel even wanted to use one of his screen stories, called 'For Services Rendered', for a movie he had planned on the Light Horse during the desert campaigns of World War I. However Ford had an option on Frank's script and he was finally forced to turn down the offer from his old Australian friend. However Frank encouraged Chauvel to write his own story about the subject. That then became the celebrated movie *Forty Thousand Horsemen*, which chronicled the Anzacs' heroic work in the Sinai Desert campaign.

Frank also worked with most of the key stars, including a more notorious Australian – Errol Flynn. Frank knew all about Flynn as they had both worked in New Guinea at the same time, well before Flynn became a matinee idol. Frank thought from the first meeting that Flynn was an out and out grub, and that view never changed.

'Flynn was rotten to the core, and was basically run out of New Guinea by a friend of our family, Tom Miller, because he was blackmailing women. Flynn was a complete crook,' Frank said in an interview with Joan Long.

Frank didn't see Flynn again until 1938 when director Michael Curtiz gave him a small part as a jailor in *The Adventures of Robin Hood*. The main star was Flynn. While waiting for a scene to be filmed, Flynn was talking to a group of actors, including Frank, about his New Guinea escapades.

'He was going on with all this rigmarole, and I had a cynical grin. Flynn asked me: "You know where New Guinea is?" '

'He didn't know me from Adam. "Yes I do," I replied, "I have a good knowledge of New Guinea." '

'Who do you know in New Guinea?'

Frank grinned, and said: 'Perhaps you may know Tom Miller. Miller happens to be a close friend of mine.'

'He just stared at me, and walked away, where he spoke to the assistant. Both of them started staring at me.'

A short time later, the assistant walked over to Baker and said: 'Mr Baker, Mr Curtiz decided not to use you for that scene.'

Frank left. About two months later, Frank was at the Riviera Country Club and he bumped into Curtiz, who was an avid polo player and a good friend of Snowy's.

'Curtiz spoke very bad English and got everything back to front,' Frank said, 'He said to me: "You bum you. I get you to play part in my picture. I know you there. We get to scene, and they have someone else. Why you go home?" '

'Mike, why don't you talk to Mr Flynn? Mr Flynn did not want me to be on the set.'

Frank had various other altercations with Flynn, including when raising funds for the Anzac War relief. When Frank approached Flynn for a donation, he waved him away: 'I'm out. I'm not an Australian.'

Frank rose to his full height, and scowled: 'Well you tell that to your father in Devonport. Tell him you're supposedly Irish.'

'No wonder his father detested him. Flynn . . . he was no great honour to Australia; I can assure you.'

Snowy got on better with Flynn, but knew how to handle him, and use him. Flynn refused to pay for anything and was renowned as Hollywood's biggest and most obnoxious freeloader. Snowy would get Flynn to Riviera by offering free golf and polo on the weekends, knowing that if he leaked the information to several Los Angeles newspapers, enough swooning females would head to the club in the hope of seeing their idol and put enough money in his till to make it worthwhile to have the troublemaker on the premises.

Unlike Frank, Snowy's movie appearances were long past, but he was far more comfortable working on the periphery, acting as a stunt adviser for various films, and often called on by the studios when a star or starlet needed to learn how to ride.

Snowy also took delight in the involvement of his wife and step-daughters in his Riviera affairs. Joan and Margaret remained avid equestrian riders and took full advantage of the excellent facilities at Riviera. They were often among the groups of riders heading off down one of the many tracks, and each, in particular Joan, were eager to fill in when there was a late polo game withdrawal.

Now well into their 20s, the two step-daughters didn't leave the Baker cottage, preferring to live at Riviera and commute into Los Angeles where both did secretarial work. Joan was also active around the polo fields, helping Snowy out whenever possible in organising and conducting riding lessons. There was the occasional flirtation, a Hollywood star regularly sniffing around his step-daughters, but Snowy made certain they kept their distance. In 1939, Joan was a member of the Las Amigas quartet from Riviera that won the United States Womens Open polo championship. Another member of the team was Spencer Tracy's wife, Louise.

Ethel remained the ideal host at home, organising the picnics and barbeques when Snowy had to network. It was a busy life.

Five days a week Snowy conducted riding lessons, and the list of notable names in his classes was impressive – Garbo, Celeste Holm, Virginia Bruce, Merle Oberon, Pauline Frederick, Shirley Temple, Robert Montgomery, Valentino and Alla Nazimova. Snowy would also mix in some swimming lessons at the Riviera pool, regulars including Joan Crawford, Betty Grable, Bette Davis, Ginger Rogers and Ava Gardner. He was often called in to give swimming and riding lessons to the sons and daughters of the famous set. More money, more prestige.

Snowy knew them all, but he found the most interesting student was a young, excitable, striking teenage girl.

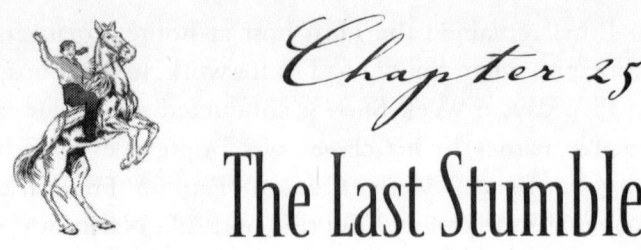

Chapter 25

The Last Stumble

A RECENT SIGHT AROUND RIVIERA WAS SNOWY ON HIS HANDS AND knees with a rope in his mouth for reins, a towel sprawled across his back acting as a saddle. On his back would be a young girl, cracking her crop across his backside, prompting Snowy to whinny and bolt like a racehorse. She was short, had a high-pitched voice and sometimes screeched rather than spoke. But she was beautiful. She was only 12, and she adored Snowy.

The excitable rider was Elizabeth Taylor. And the play-acting was to get her prepared for the riding sequences in the ultimate girl meets horse movie – *National Velvet*.

Snowy was hired by MGM to train their young starlet how to ride, and prepare her properly for the steeplechase scenes, which act as a finale to the film. Snowy took to the task with relish, especially as he was offered the softener of being one of two doubles, with another stuntman Billy Cartlidge, in several scenes, allowing him to fulfil his fantasy of playing a jockey in the movie climax. Watch the final scenes of *National Velvet* frame by frame and there appears to be Snowy, cleverly camouflaged, riding 'The Pi' home to triumph in a rollicking charge down the main straight. But more importantly Snowy had to make certain that in any scene which involved Taylor with a steed, that she looked the complete horsewoman.

Sadly Snowy could no longer use his faithful partner, Boomerang, as the willing prop. His better showbiz half had died in unusual circumstances.

Will Rogers had been pestering Snowy for years to allow him to ride Boomerang in a polo match. Snowy refused. Rogers was an outrageous, aggressive rider, and Boomerang was a too delicate piece of valuable horseflesh to be thrashed about by a sometimes devil-may-care rider.

But eventually Snowy relented. One Saturday afternoon, a team led by Snowy was playing one skippered by Rogers, on Rogers' own perfectly manicured private polo field. When they were heading out for the last chukka, Will turned and asked: 'Snowy, in all these years I've never ridden Boomerang . . . would you let me play one chukka on him?'

Will's team were in an unbeatable position, so Snowy agreed. 'I never saw Will play better and the old horse was in grand form. Then the game ended, we rode off the field and dismounted. As we did, old Boomerang gave a shudder and dropped like a stone. I couldn't imagine a more fitting end for him.

'When I went to arrange for him to be moved Will wouldn't hear of it. That night he and the other chaps who had played in his team buried Boomerang under the goalposts on the field. I couldn't imagine anything more fitting than that either.

'What I couldn't have imagined though was that it was the last time I was to see Will Rogers too. The next day he left to join [aviation pioneer] Wiley Post for their fatal flight.'

Rogers had decided to accompany Post, who was studying the practicality of a trans-Pacific route via Alaska and Russia. The pair were flying around different Alaskan outposts and then, deciding to get out of a storm, landed near a lagoon. After getting their bearings and directions from a group of Eskimos, they took off once more. The plane began to climb, banked to the right, then the engine misfired and went dead. The plane went nose-first into the lagoon.

While a country mourned the loss of one of its wisest of back porch philosophers, wits and entertainers, Snowy described the loss of Boomerang and Rogers in succession as 'one of the saddest periods of my life'.

With Boomerang gone, Snowy tried to initiate Miss Taylor on a far more intimidating horse known as King Charles, a difficult, headstrong grandson of the famous racer Man o' War. King Charles was renowned around the MGM studios for throwing virtually everyone off – including Sir Anthony Eden three times, before he gave up in disgust.

Miss Taylor knew King Charles was 'really a lunatic . . . just for the hell of it, he once jumped over an automobile'. But King Charles took a liking to the young actress, allowing her almost immediately to ride him bareback, eventually following her all over the film lot, and Riviera, like a motherless lamb.

Around the studios, because of her close affinity to the supposedly difficult King Charles, Taylor was treated with reverence. Reporters began to write about her power to cast spells over beasts and birds, and 'hold familiar conversations with them, like the troubadour saint of Assisi'.

Snowy put her on a long, extensive schedule, but MGM intervened because they were worried that with Elizabeth taking riding lessons every available second, she would injure herself. 'I was doing forty jumps a day,' she excitedly told a reporter, 'when the studio grounded me.'

It didn't matter. She kept sneaking out, especially to Riviera, where she discovered that she could eat whatever she liked, as long as no studio heavy found her. Each morning, she would have two helpings of the 'Farm Breakfast', which comprised of four hamburger patties, four fried eggs, two mounds of hash browns, and a large pile of pancakes, which were drowned in maple syrup. For lunch, steaks and salad was her favourite.

The movie was a major success, with Snowy's work invaluable in convincing the public Elizabeth Taylor could, apart from act, actually ride. She later described her involvement in *National Velvet* as one of her two most accomplished performances, the other being *Who's Afraid of Virginia Woolf?*.

In the privileged position of getting to know the stars intimately, and at their most relaxed moments, Snowy was soon the sponge they could tell their secrets to, and use as an ally when in trouble. Many stars discovered that they could successfully hide away at Riviera when the studio, husband, wife, girlfriend, boyfriend, press or Internal Revenue department were after them. Snowy usually knew where to accommodate them on the premises, until the 'coast was clear'.

In this category was Spencer Tracy, who realised that when there was trouble on the set or at home, he could disappear at Riviera where Snowy was a reliable ally. They met through their common love of horses, Snowy teaching him the rudiments of polo, a game Tracy was immediately hooked on after Will Rogers first invited Tracy to Riviera to watch a match.

Snowy described Tracy as 'a real he-man and a grand sport in all respects'. He said that Tracy was one of the most courageous polo players in California, with a penchant for a fast, wild game. 'But his advent on the green sward of the polo field was frowned upon by the big moguls of the film company who had him under contract. The film producers contended that polo was far too dangerous a game for their star. Should he be injured they would suffer a heavy loss.'

On one occasion Tracy showed Snowy a letter he had received from a Hollywood studio heavy. It was an ultimatum – stop playing polo or turn in your contract. Tracy laughed as he read out the letter, before saying: 'Snowy, I get too much happiness from polo. I'm staying in the game.'

Unlike Clark Gable who towed the party line, Tracy told the studio to 'go jump'. As part of the smokescreen, Tracy would play under an assumed name. Often a person who looked remarkably like Tracy would appear on the team sheet as Ivan Catchanozoff.

Snowy saw a lot of Tracy, especially when he decided to move out of the family ranch and into rooms at Riviera. Around the club his drinking bouts were legendary, especially at the Sunday evening polo get-togethers, which also lured Rogers, director Frank Borzage, Fairbanks and Darryl Zanuck for some heavy boozing and womanising. This would often result in Tracy disappearing for several days on a bender. Snowy was grateful that he could disappear early, arguing that he had always been an 'abstainer'. However, Snowy's ability to cover for Tracy saw them becoming close allies, to the extent that the actor convinced Snowy to make a small cameo appearance in one of his movies, *Big City*.

Even when Tracy wasn't on the drink at Riviera, he was often the talk of those who were. Ernest Borgnine was once playing golf at Riviera when he was called away to the clubhouse by his agent. He returned to reveal that the agent had told him Tracy and Ernest Hemingway had just destroyed a bar in Havana. 'The bar owner wants $150,000 to repair the damage, and Jack Warner won't pay it,' Borgnine told his golf partner, newspaper columnist James Bacon. 'So Warner wants me to stand by at a moment's notice to go to Cuba and replace Tracy in "The Old Man and the Sea".'

Eventually Warner paid the damage, and Borgnine stayed put in Hollywood.

Gradually the work at Riviera for Snowy began to dry up. With another world war imminent, polo and horse riding appeared an extravagance, and the numbers at Snowy's lessons began to drop off. Those in charge of Riviera also began to query Snowy's accountancy and costs sheets, as there appeared to be glaring discrepancies.

With the Los Angeles Athletic Club struggling through the Depression, and then suffering dramatically, like all other clubs, following the attack on Pearl Harbor in 1941, the directors looked seriously at ways of raising cash to cut down the debt. They began selling off part of the Riviera land and the LAAC auto park.

They also looked far more closely at what was and what wasn't making money at Riviera. As Betty Lou Young wrote in the LAAC club's history: 'On the surface all had seemed well in Snowy Bakerland, even in wartime. Three games of polo had been played each week, with cavalry drill on weekends, and in 1945 the full entourage of players and riders began to return. The cold fact, however, was that the entire equestrian program had always operated at a substantial loss.'

Young wrote that LAAC director Charles Hathaway Senior, 'who was more interested in balancing the budget than in coddling horses, observed one day that whenever a horse was rented, it belonged to Snowy, and whenever a horse died, it belonged to the Club'.

Snowy started getting the gentle prod and in May 1946 resigned as a Riviera club director ending a rich, fruitful, and always exciting 20-year association. Since 1941, Snowy had also been an LAAC director, but that was also terminated in May 1946.

He left Riviera, moving into town, where he joined up as chief instructor at the Beverly Hills Saddle Club. The equestrian unit at Riviera was leased to a private concern.

Snowy was in the depths of his own depression, especially as the loss of his high-profile Riviera employ, coincided with general sickness in his family. His step-daughter Joan had been critically injured in a steeplechase incident, where she fractured her spine, and had been bed-ridden for several years. After several years of pain, Joan died, causing Snowy enormous grief, as they had been extremely close, especially during the days when she accompanied him on his travels as a struggling vaudeville artist, often being part of the act by duelling him to a sword fight.

His other step-daughter Margaret was hampered with phlebitis, while Mrs Baker was struck with crippling arthritis, that regularly forced her into hospital.

The exasperation came through in several letters Snowy wrote to *Sydney Morning Herald* columnist Leon Gellert, when he explained that he had 'very serious family illnesses. I'm not working, but standing by the family'.

Yet he wanted everyone to know that he was still the Snowy of old. In his letters to Gellert and many other friends, which often were printed in the Sydney papers, Snowy kept explaining he was the ultimate fitness fanatic and was still reaping the benefits. The *Herald* ran an unusual, brief story, which was headlined 'Snowy Baker still active'. It explained that Snowy, now well into his 60s, 'still keeps himself fit by regular exercise'.

'I still swim, take two and a half turns off the springboard, box a little, ride 20 to 25 miles daily, play polo three days each week all the year round, fence and generally keep myself in condition.'

Snowy wrote to Gellert: 'I'm having a birthday today in my 60s and feel as fit as I did at 26, and exactly the same as I did when stepping on the scales for the Australasian Amateur Championship. I'm in the saddle from three to five hours a day. Swim, dive and do my Snowy Baker Physical Culture exercises. Such is life – activity is the law of life, and idleness breeds decay. So let's keep active, Leon.'

Elsewhere Snowy explained that at 59, he had captained a Californian polo team, and five years later, in his first entry, won the annual steeplechase of the San Fernando Valley Steeplechase Club on his New Zealand-bred horse, Tricky.

However it was hard for anyone to be convinced that Snowy was enjoying the elixir of youth when he made his farewell trip to Australia in 1952 – primarily to sound out the possibility of starting up a Riviera-style club in one of Sydney's outer reaches. He didn't exactly bound off the plane, or look anywhere near as chirpy as when he left 30 years earlier in search of fame and fortune. Instead the front page of Sydney's newspapers showed the dramatic shot of Baker being stretchered from the plane after it had landed at Mascot Airport. The headlines weren't exactly encouraging either. The *Daily Telegraph* screamed, 'Snowy Baker comes home a sick man'.

On the final leg between Fiji to Sydney, Snowy, who was travelling by himself, had complained of airsickness, and then was violently ill on the small DC–6 airliner. Not helping the situation was that the plane had to circle Sydney for more than an hour before landing because of heavy, swirling, thundery rain.

While dignatories, relatives, and even former rugby team-mates, including Jimmy Clarken who was Harold Baker's partner in the famous Coogee surf rescue all those decades ago, waited for him in the terminal, Snowy was whisked away in an ambulance.

The next day Snowy passed it all off as his nervousness when flying, but there was more to it. A visit to a Macquarie Street specialist revealed that even the famous, perfect Baker body was starting to wear down. The specialist diagnosed Snowy's condition as being due to arterial sclerosis.

As Snowy was in Australia to spruik the importance of a fitness and sports club, he couldn't afford to be confined to bed. Even though far from fully recovered, he was on his feet the following afternoon, starting off an intensive three weeks of speeches, meetings and receptions.

One morning, he explained to Molly Dye from the *Daily Telegraph* that he still talked with an Australian accent because: 'I'm proud of being an Australian. Why should I speak like an American?' Will Rogers had constantly said that he admired Snowy and Frank because of their refusal to lose their accent, or their Australian ways. Rogers said that he had never met two people more proud of their heritage.

That night, Snowy was at the Tattersall's Club, tugging away at the patriotic strings by explaining that his prime motive now was to return to Australia. 'Sydney has Southern California licked. I'm more determined than ever to go back to America, sell up and come back here with my wife,' Snowy said to a standing ovation.

The rumour remained that Snowy had been able to stay in the United States for so long, without citizenship, by sneaking off to Mexico for a few days every year to gain a visitor's visa for another 12-months residence in America. Snowy had contacts everywhere, including Mexico, where he had promoted rodeo events.

'I have been asked many times to become an American citizen. But I've always replied that I would remain an Australian. The greatest joy of my life will be when my wife is well enough for us to return to Australia to live here for the rest of our lives.'

A few nights later at Sydney Town Hall, there were genuine tears in his eyes when he said: 'I'm coming home. I'm selling up. My wife and I want to come back here among our own people.'

He wasn't going to retire though. After all, as he repeatedly said to so many of his gymnasium students – idleness is decay. In search of a suitable spot for an Australian version of Riviera, Snowy travelled to Bowral, where his brother and former Baker Stadium partner, Harold, was now living. They looked at different sites in the stately, picturesque Southern Highlands, and reminisced about better times. Harold also brought Snowy up to date with what had occurred in his life. Although not on the same scale as Snowy, Harold had also succeeded in making some sort of impact during the 30 years his brother had been 'gallivanting' on the other side of the world.

Harold had kept his interest in boxing, commentating on the big fights for the ABC, and occasionally called in by various promoters to referee bouts at the Stadium. His greatest influence though had been in the local rugby union scene, Harold being instrumental in the Randwick club becoming the great attacking innovators of the Australian game. In the 1920s, Harold coached the Randwick first-grade team with great success, before managing New South Wales and Queensland teams on tour and acting as an Australian selector. Harold, who was still being referred to as Harald, was an outstanding judge of rugby talent and earnt a reputation as being one of Australia's best selectors. But as usual, you didn't cross Harold. He remained a sour, mournful beast.

Harold's love for rugby came through in an article he wrote for the *NSW Rugby News*, where he explained: 'It is the spirit of rugby, the good fellowship, the unselfishness and the teamsmanship in each player that makes him a man worth knowing. He moves in a game that enjoys international significance and is backed by a wealth of tradition – a game in which the right sort of athlete is moulded – and in which some of life's most solid friendships are made.'

Harold had even made a rugby impact in Bowral. Wandering past Chevalier College one day and noticing the first XV training, he asked if he could help. A few months later, under his tutelage, Chevalier defeated their arch rivals, St Patricks, for the first time.

When Snowy left for America, he warned Harold that they could soon be back in partnership again. Harold smiled as he farewelled the ever imaginative, ever opportunistic Snowy at Bowral railway station, but wasn't so sure that the latest scheme would come to fruition. He had observed his brother in decline, and knew he probably wasn't going to see him again.

The joyful return to Australia never occurred. Newsreel footage of Snowy's visit reveals why. At the Sydney Town Hall function, he smiles merrily enough at the movie cameras, but it is obvious he is not a well man. He looked gaunt and very old. He was on his last legs.

On his return to California, Snowy never really had the opportunity to get himself prepared for the triumphant last trip to his city of birth, or creating a Riviera of the South. With his wife still in hospital and Margaret still ill, Snowy struggled to look after himself in their Los Angeles apartment. He was off his food, losing weight rapidly, and lost the will to do much else but saunter around the house. He always felt lethargic, disorientated. Being a riding instructor at the Beverly Hills Saddle Club simply didn't have the same impact as gallivanting with the stars at Riviera.

He eventually had to be admitted into a nursing home. The six days a week intensive training schedules were over. He was now struggling to walk.

At least he didn't suffer long.

On December 2, 1953, Harold Baker contacted various newspaper offices to pass on the news that Snowy had just died of cerebro-vascular disease in his Los Angeles apartment aged 69. As he talked to various hardened scribes, Harold, the most stone-faced of men, struggled to fight back tears.

The eulogies were bright and long, even the London *Times* giving him column inches. He would always be famous in England, simply because he was the opponent which their loyal national cricket captain, J.W.H.T. Douglas, had beaten in the boxing ring to win an Olympic gold medal.

The Bulletin, which had lampooned him during his movie days, was also sympathetic, leading its 'Personal Items' with: 'The last race, the last round, the last lap, the last innings for Snowy Baker, an all-round sport known all round the world. Jack London had his hero of Burning Daylight a giant in strength whose power stemmed from complete coordination of mind and muscle. Snowy was the same; anything he took on – and he excelled in 26 different sports – he mastered with uncanny competence before passing on to the next. Though expatriate in Hollywood for years, he remained staunchly Australian to the end. A colourful ambassador for his country, a sportsman all the way.'

A day later, Frank Baker was among a small group of mourners who attended the service at the Hollywood Memorial Center where Snowy was cremated. Frank, who hated funerals, at least made certain that Snowy's final words were repeated to the crowd: 'I was lucky. The good God was kind to me.'

Snowy made certain his wife and step-daughter Margaret were well looked after, not wasting his savings and leaving an estate of 39,111 pounds. He was described in the legal documents relating to the estate, which were tendered in the NSW Supreme Court, as an 'equestrian director'.

But the Baker family line soon petered out, and his days as an equestrian director quickly forgotten, Ethel and Margaret dying shortly after Snowy. Soon, there was little evidence of Snowy Baker in Hollywoodland, his momentoes, scrapbooks and personal belongings disappearing. Several years later, Frank went looking for anything, but found nothing. An invaluable part of Australian history was lost. They had been snaffled up by someone, or just thrown away. After being larger than life, Snowy and the Baker clan shrivelled away to just fading memories.

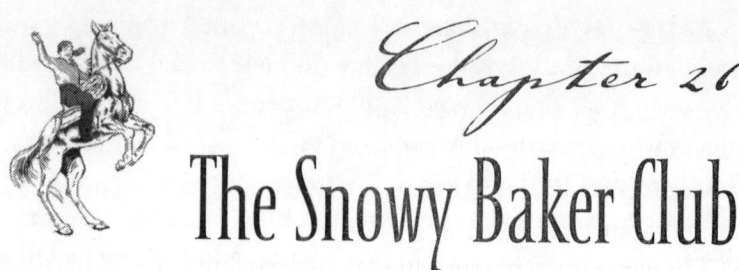

Chapter 26

The Snowy Baker Club

It is half a century since Snowy died. Nonetheless, whenever a bright young athlete shows promise in more than one sport, the name Snowy Baker is mentioned.

'They're doing a Snowy,' is the immediate call. But that cry is becoming less and less common, as the demands of the modern sporting world revolves around the importance of being a specialist. To get to the top of one sport now requires a total focus towards that pursuit.

It is now nigh impossible for anyone to do a Snowy. Anyone who represents a country in more than one sport would in the 21st century be regarded as a human phenomenon.

Australia's greatest sportsman? Probably not, considering that Snowy was a journeyman in several of his national pursuits, and only a standout in two – boxing and rugby. His accomplishments in these two areas were of the highest class, and he probably would have been an even more recognised Australian rugby representative if he hadn't retired early to devote himself to boxing. Of all his sporting pursuits, he was probably best as a horseman, his feats before, during and after his movie days warranting his elevation as one of Australia's most capable equestrian riders.

Snowy Baker undoubtedly deserves the tag of Australia's most versatile sportsman, especially as it involved totally diverse forms of athleticism. To be so competent at so many different sporting endeavours involved genuine skill, but more importantly, incredible willpower and stamina. Snowy never wanted to stop, believing that the only way to enjoy life was to experience it every second. He was hyperactive and totally attuned to success. Having a strong ego helped.

As a sportsman, the Snowy Baker image is glowing. Not so, when other parts of his life are mentioned. The biggest cloud over Snowy's life remains his involvement in the demise of Les Darcy. To this day, there are those who believe that Snowy was instrumental in Darcy being forced to leave Australia, and the man who hounded him to his death in the United States.

There is a trace of truth in that analysis, but it is still harsh. Admittedly, some of Snowy's outbursts were vindictive and inflamed the situation. And despite his vehement denials of the many accusations at the Maitland inquiry, he could not in the end be termed a Darcy ally. It's easy to understand why he was turned away at Darcy's funeral.

However there were greater influences at work. Snowy was very much a puppet to powerbrokers like Huge Deal and John Wren, who were part of the inner sanctum of an excitable and often irrational pro-conscriptionist Prime Minister, Billy Hughes. Snowy should have stood up to them, but didn't because they paid the bills. They gave Snowy the stage he always wanted to strut about on. He also thought they were right, as shown by his anger when discovering that Darcy had bolted. Also, the nervousness over his own European background would have been playing on his mind.

But the accusation that he killed Darcy? Too simplistic. Many more factors were involved.

Darcy was not as streetwise as Snowy, who could mix it with the best and knew when to put in the boot. Like Darcy, Snowy was brought up in a rough area, where any character faults would be immediately seized upon. That's why Snowy was so tough and, always mindful of his small size, obsessed in ensuring no-one stood over him.

Business wise, Snowy was as ruthless. He was hardly the boxer's friend, renowned during his days as boss of the Stadium as squeezing the fighters out of what they thought was rightfully theirs. The money split was always well in Snowy's and the Stadium's favour, and he was never receptive to a boxer or manager who queried their diminishing percentage of the gate. Snowy revelled in the power and loved being a dictator.

Snowy was brash, vain and often incorrigible. He was also sensitive, and aware that his public image had been tarnished badly because of the Darcy affair. He and his brother Harold grew accustomed to being sneered at in the streets, and while they laughed a lot of it off, it still stung. Harold, to his last days a morose character, refused to talk about it. Just before he died, Snowy was reminded of it all when Frank Hardy released his controversial book, *Power Without Glory*.

Snowy was thinly disguised in the book as Snowy Bacon, while Les Darcy is obviously a character called Lou Darby. The argument over whether John West is the warts and all John Wren has been Australian literature's great debate since the book was published in 1950.

Hardy wrote: 'The wrath of Australian sportsmen fell upon the shoulders of Snowy Bacon. Every time he emerged out of doors, people would shout: "There is the man who killed Lou Darby." When a film in which the versatile Bacon figured as the hero was screened in Sydney, audiences booed, jeered and shouted: "He killed Lou Darby." Bacon left for America soon afterwards, never to return to Australia.'

Snowy sincerely wanted to return to Australia permanently, but often was held back because he couldn't avoid the public stigma. The Darcy issue was never going to disappear. It was an issue not to be discussed in the Baker household. His father, who could never see anything wrong in his son, once tried to bring it up in discussion during one Sunday dinner, but from Snowy's tense tone, decided it wasn't worth pursuing.

'Better if I don't know?' Baker Senior once asked.

'Something like that.'

Snowy knew he could get away with a lot more in the city of dreams, and stay put, because they didn't know so much about him. In Hollywood, little was revealed except that he was Australia's best sportsman.

As one LAAC historian explained: 'America termed him "the greatest all-around athlete Australia has ever produced," but that was a provincial view. On evidence, Snowy was the greatest jock in the world.'

Being in Hollywood during a time when hardly any Australians travelled, or had the courage to work in another country, perfectly suited his nature. A showman surrounded by showmen, with a list of illustrious friends, which no-one back in Australia could come anywhere near to matching.

Where Snowy does deserve greater praise is as an Australian film pioneer. His name has generally been lost behind Raymond Longford, Charles Chauvel and Ken G. Hall, but Snowy's commitment to turn local films into an international commodity, by travelling to America and bringing back overseas talent, was a vital step in the history of

Australian movie making. He was no actor, but his business acumen pushed Australian films to another level. It encouraged others, in particular the brilliant Chauvel.

And as a movie stuntman, there were few better.

Someone at Fox Studios in Sydney got it right, by recently naming one of the streets between the production houses after Snowy. Sadly when Snowy died, so did most of his movies. In his garage at Riviera, Snowy had copies of all of his films, but they all went missing when he moved from the club into Los Angeles in 1946. Frank Baker went looking for them, but found no trace. Now only two Australian movies – *The Man from Kangaroo* and *The Enemy Within* – exist, while if you look hard and have the right contacts – you can watch *The Sword of Valor*. But so much other invaluable Australian film history has gone into the ether.

Where Snowy can also be admired is that unlike many other spivs who talk big, act big, are full of their own importance but can only blow disappearing bubbles, Snowy achieved what he set out to do.

He was a trail blazer. He was an innovator. He was so ahead of his time in so many ways. He was someone who thought big and had the rare commitment to trust his instincts. As Snowy would continually tell anyone who listened: 'Don't say it. Do it.'

Snowy was true to his word. He did it.

He was, and is, an important, larger than life Australian, one of the few who really helped to mould this country. Feat wise, not many can surpass him.

Despite his numerous flaws, mysterious corners and carefully manicured background, Snowy Baker deserves accolades . . . a club named in his honour, and much, much more.

Bibliography

The primary sources of material for *The Snowy Baker Story* were the newspapers and magazines of the time, most of which were unearthed at the State Library of New South Wales and the National Library of Australia. My research involved days, weeks, months and years of scrolling through spool after spool of newspaper microfilms, an exasperating, mind sapping, but ultimately rewarding experience. Just as important were a series of letters written by Frank Baker (held in a private collection), which helped to fill in numerous gaps. For those interested in learning more about the life and times of Snowy Baker, important books include:

Corris, Peter. *Lords of the Ring*, North Ryde, NSW: Cassell Australia, 1980.

Eyman, Scott. *Print the Legend: The life and times of John Ford*, New York: Simon & Schuster, 1999.

Fenton, Peter. *Les Darcy: The legend of the fighting man*, Chippendale, NSW: Ironbark, 1994.

Gordon, Harry. *Australia and the Olympic Games*, St Lucia, Qld: University of Queensland Press, 1994.

Hardy, Frank. *Power Without Glory*, Sydney: Random House Australia, 2000 (c1950).

Lindsay, Norman. *My Mask*, Sydney: Angus & Robertson, 1970.

Long, Joan and Long, Martin. *The Pictures that Moved*, Richmond, Vic: Hutchinson of Australia, 1982.

McCaffery, Dan. *Tommy Burns: Canada's unknown world heavyweight champion*, James Lorimer & Co Ltd, 2000.

Park, Ruth and Champion, Rafe. *Home Before Dark*, Ringwood, Vic: Viking, 1995.

Pike, Andrew and Cooper, Ross. *Australian Film 1900–1977*, Melbourne: Oxford University Press, 1980.

Power, Bob. *The Les Darcy American Venture*, New Lambton, NSW: R.G. Power, 1994.

Ritchie, Andrew. *Major Taylor: The extraordinary career of a champion bicycle racer*, Johns Hopkins University Press, 1996.

Roberts, Kenneth. *Captain of the Push*, Melbourne: Lansdowne Press, 1963.

Shackelford, Geoff. *The Riviera Country Club*, Pacific Palisades, California: The Riviera Country Club, 1995.

Shirley, Graham and Adams, Brian. *Australian Cinema: The first eighty years*, Sydney: Angus & Robertson, 1983.

Swanwick, Raymond. *Les Darcy: Australia's golden boy of boxing*, Sydney: Ure Smith, 1965.

Thomas, Arnold. *Heroes of the Fancy: A history of Australian boxing*, Boronia, Vic: A Thomas, 1999.

Tulloch, John. *Legends on the Screen*, Sydney: Currency Press, 1981.

Wells, Jeff. *Boxing Day: The fight that changed the world*. Pymble, NSW: HarperSports, 1998.

Young, Betty Lou. *Our First Century: The Los Angeles Athletic Club, 1880–1980*, Los Angeles, California: LAAC Press, 1980.

An excellent article on Les Darcy, especially of his trials in America, was published in the *Journal of Sport History* (1996: Vol 23, No 2). Written by Katharine Moore and Murray G. Phillips, it is entitled 'From Adulation to Persecution and Back: Australian boxer Les Darcy in America 1916–1917'. A copy of the article can be found on the Web at http://www.aafla.org/SportsLibrary/JSH/JSH1996/JSH2302/jsh2302d.pdf.

Index